Also in the Variorum Collected Studies Series

G.V. SCAMMELL
Ships, Oceans and Empire: Studies in European Maritime and Colonial History, 1400–1750

RONALD G. WITT
Italian Humanism and Medieval Rhetoric

BENJAMIN G. KOHL
Culture and Politics in Early Renaissance Padua

MORIMICHI WATANABE edited by THOMAS M. IZBICKI and GERALD CHRISTIANSON
Concord and Reform: Nicholas of Cusa and Legal and Political Thought in the Fifteenth Century

D.S. CHAMBERS
Renaissance Cardinals and their Worldly Problems

D.S. CHAMBERS
Individuals and Institutions in Renaissance Italy

JOSEPH S. FREEDMAN
Philosophy and the Arts in Central Europe, 1500–1700: Teaching and Texts at Schools and Universities

JOHN GUY
Politics, Law and Counsel in Tudor and Early Stuart England

JOHN M. HEADLEY
Church, Empire and World: The Quest for Universal Order, 1520–1640

SCOTT H. HENDRIX
Tradition and Authority in the Reformation

DAVID B.QUINN
European Approaches to North America, 1450–1640

W.G.L. RANDLES
Geography, Cartography and Nautical Science in the Renaissance: The Impact of the Great Discoveries

MARION LEATHERS KUNTZ
Venice, Myth and Utopian Thought in the Sixteenth Century: Bodin, Postel and the Virgin of Venice

VARIORUM COLLECTED STUDIES SERIES

Seafaring, Sailors and Trade, 1450–1750

G.V. Scammell

Seafaring, Sailors and Trade, 1450–1750

Studies in British and European Maritime and Imperial History

Routledge
Taylor & Francis Group
LONDON AND NEW YORK

First published 2003 by Ashgate Publishing

Published 2016 by Routledge
2 Park Square, Milton Park, Abingdon, Oxon OX14 4RN
52 Vanderbilt Avenue, New York, NY 10017

Routledge is an imprint of the Taylor & Francis Group, an informa business

British Library Cataloguing-in-Publication Data
Scammell, G.V. (Geoffrey Vaughan)
Seafaring, Sailors and Trade, 1450–1750: Studies in British and European Maritime and Imperial History. (Variorum Collected Studies Series: CS755).
1. Shipping – Great Britain – History. 2. Shipping – Europe – History. 3. Great Britain – History, Naval. 4. Europe – History, Naval.
I. Title.
387.5'094

US Library of Congress Control Number: 2003101439

ISBN 13: 978-0-86078-897-3 (hbk)

VARIORUM COLLECTED STUDIES SERIES CS755

CONTENTS

This volume contains x +310 pages

PREFACE

The articles reproduced in this collection were written over the past forty years. Like those in my previous volume *Ships, Oceans and Empire* (Variorum, 1995) they are concerned with the roots of British and European seapower and with how, why and at what human cost this was extended to most of the waters of the world in the centuries after 1400. Nos I–V deal primarily with British shipping and seafaring and with such comparatively neglected topics as the building of merchantmen, the skills of their commanders and the working conditions and behaviour of their crews. Since the first of these essays were written maritime history, like history as a whole, has changed beyond all recognition through the work of scholars, some of whose contributions are noted below. Even so, the study of the sea and its impact on economies, societies and civilizations still commands far less attention in Britain than is devoted to the ever expanding body of other aspects of the country's past.

The rest of the articles in this collection touch on some of the causes and consequences of that global expansion – only recently halted and reversed – of European and particularly British power, whose repercussions are still so plainly evident. It was one of the most fundamental events in history, however renamed as fashion dictates. As the last vestiges of European empires have withered it has generated an overwhelming flow of specialized scholarship, some of whose conclusions I have attempted to draw together in what I trust will be found to be useful syntheses.

I am grateful to the original publishers of the articles in this selection for their kind permission to reproduce them: Professor Richard N. Bailey, of the University of Newcastle upon Tyne, editor of *Archaeologia Aeliana* (I); Dr H. Brasted, of the University of New England, Armidale, Australia, editor of *South Asia* (IX); Professor Lewis R. Fischer of the Memorial University of St John's, Newfoundland, Canada, editor of the *International Journal of Maritime History* (III); Dr Gordon Johnson, President of Wolfson College, Cambridge, editor of *Modern Asian Studies* (X, XII); Professor K.S. Mathew, of the University of Pondicherry, India, editor of the *Pondicherry University Journal of Social Sciences and Humanities* (IV); the President and Council of the Royal Historical Society (II); Presses Universitaires de Bordeaux, publishers of the *Mélanges ... Paul Butel* and Professor Hubert Bonin, of the Institut d'Études Politiques de Bordeaux and Professor Silvia Marzagalli of the Université Michel de Montaigne, Bordeaux 3, editors of the volume (V);

the National Maritime Museum, Greenwich, and its Director (VII); the President and Council of the Hakluyt Society (VIII); Professor Dr João Paulo Salvado and the members of the Comissão Nacional para as Comemorações dos Descobrimentos Portugueses, Lisbon, editors of *Mare Liberum* (XI); Drs Wim van den Doel, Hendrik E. Niemeijer and Peer Vries, of the Centre for the History of European Expansion, Leiden, the Netherlands, editors of *Itinerario* (VI).

I record with gratitude the help and encouragement received over many years from Professor K.R. Andrews, the late Professor Sinnappah Arasaratnam, Dr Geneviève Bouchon, The Rev. Dr John Correia-Afonso SJ, Professor J.S. Cummins, Dr A.R. Disney, Professor Lewis R. Fischer, the late Professor P.E.H. Hair, the late Admiral Avelino Teixeira da Mota, the late Professor Virginia Rau, Professor Teotonio R. de Souza and Professor Luís Filipe F. Reis Thomaz.

I owe an enormous debt to the kindness and friendship of the late Professors Charles Boxer, John Bromley and Denys Hay. I have greatly benefited from the editorial skills of Dr John Smedley. I recall with affection *Ursa* and *Sally* for over fifty years of happy sailing. But my greatest debt is to my wife, companion in travels across or by most of the oceans of the world, and without whose support and stimulus these essays would have neither been begun nor completed.

Cambridge G.V. SCAMMELL
April 2002

PUBLISHER'S NOTE

The articles in this volume, as in all others in the Collected Studies Series, have not been given a new, continuous pagination. In order to avoid confusion, and to facilitate their use where these same studies have been referred to elsewhere, the original pagination has been maintained wherever possible.

Each article has been given a Roman numeral in order of appearance, as listed in the Contents. This number is repeated on each page and quoted in the index entries.

I

WAR AT SEA UNDER THE EARLY TUDORS: SOME NEWCASTLE UPON TYNE EVIDENCE.

The city of Newcastle upon Tyne has a long and distinguished maritime history. It was an active and important trading centre as early as the twelfth century, and a hundred years later, already a considerable wool port, was one of 26 English towns commissioned by Edward I to provide galleys for the royal service.[1] At the end of the Middle Ages, after a series of lengthy and bitter disputes, it had crippled most of its potential rivals, gained effective control of an imposing hinterland, and in large measure defeated the monopolistic commercial claims of such powerful bodies as the Staplers and Merchant Adventurers.[2]

Political accident enhanced local enterprise. The ancient unsolved problems of the North—civil disorder, Border War, French intervention in Scotland—pressed heavily on English government under the Early Tudors, and in any attempt to solve them Newcastle was of capital strategic importance. It was an importance perhaps almost as much naval as military, for there was a general quickening of maritime activity in northern waters, characterized amongst other things by the reappearance of strong French and Scottish fleets—the latter the creation of the vigorous and able James

[1] See my *Hugh du Puiset* (Cambridge, 1956), 215-16; R. J. Whitwell and C. Johnson, "The Newcastle Galley", *Arch(æologia) Ael(iana)*, 4th Series, vol. II (1926), 142-93; J. C. Davies, "Shipping and Trade in Newcastle upon Tyne, 1294-6", *Arch. Ael.*, 4th Series, vol. XXXI (1953), 175-204, and "The Wool Customs Accounts for Newcastle for the reign of Edward I", *ib.*, vol. XXXII (1954), 220-308.

[2] These developments took place roughly in the century after 1450. I hope to discuss them more fully elsewhere.

IV (1488-1513).[3] In a conflict between England and France—and their rivalry was one of the subsidiary themes of European history throughout the period—Scotland was almost invariably allied to France.[4] With the anarchy that followed James' death at Flodden there was a danger, strenuously resisted by Henry VIII, that an even closer association might develop, and so it was that Scotland became the field of a prolonged struggle between France and England to establish their respective power. The easiest route for French supplies and reinforcements was through Edinburgh, just as the surest place to intercept them, as also much of Scotland's most valuable trade, was the mouth of the Forth. But for obvious reasons English naval interests were traditionally in the Channel, and perhaps never more so than under the Early Tudors, who, conservative in this as in so much else, spent large sums on the construction of dockyards at Portsmouth, Woolwich, Deptford and Erith. Thus in the absence of any established base north of the Thames, and with the royal ships generally concentrated in the "Narrow Seas", Newcastle recovered for a brief, and as it transpired final period, that strategic importance it had enjoyed for similar reasons under the first three Edwards.

There were, of course, disadvantages: the North-East coast was notoriously dangerous. The Tyne, with its treacherous estuary, was never an easy river to make, especially in face of a Westerly,[5] and in the early sixteenth century its many hazards were aggravated by heavy silting,

[3] Ch. de La Roncière, *Histoire de La Marine Française*, I, 388; M. Oppenheim, (*History of the*) *Administration* (*of the Royal Navy etc.*), 47; (P.) Hume Brown, (*A History of Scotland to the Present time*, 3 vols., Cambridge, 1911), I, 240-1, 260-1, 276; (H. A. L.) Fisher, (*The History of England from the Accession of Henry VII to the death of Henry VIII*, London, 1906), 171.

[4] Apart from a short-lived alliance between James IV and Henry VII, Hume Brown, I, 244-5, 252-3; Fisher, 93-4.

[5] A chart of the Tyne dating from the reign of Henry VIII bears the note "very nedfolle it is that thare ware at everye pointe of sande or Rockes, a becone or a boye, for at hoye watter bothe sands and Rockes are under watter, Even to the mane Lande", *A History of Northumberland*, vol. VIII, *The Parish of Tynemouth*, ed. Sir Edmund Craster (London, 1907), plate XV. Some of these hazards were moderated shortly after by the work of the Newcastle Trinity House.

due, according to the civic authorities, to fish weirs erected by the churches of Durham and Tynemouth.[6] Many of the larger fighting ships were thus unable to enter and were obliged to use either Tynemouth Haven (already favoured by heavier merchantmen as an outport), the anchorage of Skate Roads at Holy Island, or, if need be, Hull, whilst those of shallower draught had a lengthy passage upstream to the town quays.[7] Nevertheless Newcastle remained, as the Privy Council wrote on one occasion, "the meetest place to mount the sea" against the Scots.[8] It was a walled city conveniently, but not dangerously near the Border, usually tolerably defended and victualled, or at least in a position to command supplies, and with good anchorages within easy reach and material and skilled labour locally available for repairs and refitting.[9] But above all shipping was readily accessible, owned for the most part by a merchant class consistently loyal to the established regime. In 1544 about 50 vessels belonged to the port, of which as many of 25 were fit to be employed as men-of-war—though the figures for the preceding century must have been considerably lower.[10] There was likewise an adequate, though not inexhaustible supply of masters and seamen experienced in what, on the East coast at least, were considered the distant trades—voyages to the Low Countries, Scandinavia, Normandy and Western France—besides men with an intimate knowledge of the seaboard from the Forth to the Thames.[11]

[6] *Select Cases before the King's Council in the Star Chamber*, ed. I. S. Leadam (Selden Society), II (1911), 70.

[7] *Letters and Papers, Foreign and Domestic, of the Reign of Henry VIII*, ed. Brewer, Gairdner and Brodie (London, 1864-1932), (hereafter *LP*), XVII, 836. The importance of Holy Island is noticed in a Venetian report of 1551, *Calendar of State Papers, Venetian, 1534-54*, p. 353.

[8] *LP*, XIX (I), 98.

[9] There is a certain amount of material relating to the early history of shipbuilding in the North-East amongst the muniments of the church of Durham and in *LP*. I hope to examine this evidence more fully in due course.

[10] *LP*, XIX (I), 107, 115, 140 (6); *The Hamilton Letters and Papers*, ed. J. Bain (2 vols., London, 1890-2), II, 185.

[11] These remarks are based on an examination of the Newcastle customs accounts and the records of the High Court of Admiralty, and will be developed elsewhere. For Newcastle's trade with Normandy see M. Mollat, *Le Commerce Maritime Normand à le Fin du Moyen Âge* (Paris, 1952).

I

The purpose of this paper is to examine some of the occasions on which such shipping was used by the crown during that relatively obscure, but none the less significant period of English naval history, from the late fifteenth century to the death of Henry VIII. The general importance of hired or impressed merchantmen serving as transports, victuallers or fighting ships is too well known to require emphasis, but the diversity of their employment merits more attention than it has received.

During the reign of the first Tudor there was little regular naval action of any consequence, and none that concerned the North.[12] But the accession of Henry VIII, whose vanity and ambition were affronted by the growing power of France, led to the return of martial activity on a scale unequalled since the campaigns of Edward III and Henry V. His first French war (1511-14), which was to bring England renown such as she had not enjoyed since Agincourt, opened ignominiously. After some unimportant skirmishings there came the disastrous invasion of Guienne, accompanied by the more creditable performance of a fleet under Edward Howard. Louis XII, beset from all sides, sought the aid of James IV, and in April 1512 his ambassador, La Motte, en route for Leith, gave a timely demonstration of sea-power by capturing several English merchantmen, including a number from the Tyne.[13] Newcastle responded, on orders from the Council, by fitting out the *Elizabeth* and *Trinity*, which may have taken part in the attack on La Motte on his departure from the Forth in July.[14] One of his escorts was captured, another driven to Zealand and the ambassador

[12] A squadron sent north in 1497 in view of James' activities saw no action. Some of its supplies were drawn from Newcastle, *Naval Accounts and Inventories of the Reign of Henry VII*, ed. M. Oppenheim (NRS, VIII, 1896), xlv-xlvi, 102-3; Fisher, 72-3.

[13] *LP*, I (I), 1262; (J. D.) Mackie, *The Earlier Tudors, 1485-1558*, (Oxford, 1952), 274-5; Fisher, 171-8, 185; Hume Brown, 1, 264-5.

[14] P(ublic)R(ecord)O(ffice), Exchequer QR, Accounts Various, E 101/62/63, which may be dated by its references to Sir Richard Cavendish (cf. *LP*, I (I), 1424 (i), to Scottish prisoners apparently taken at Flodden, and to the detachment of the *Elizabeth* to the Thames.

himself "compelled to fly towards Denmark".[15]

Later in the year the *Elizabeth* was ordered south and replaced by the *Edward*, subsequently joined in 1513 by the *Gabriel* and the *George*.[16] The activities of this flotilla are obscure, but appear to be connected with either an attempt to intercept the Scots fleet which left Leith in July 1513 to reinforce the French in the Channel, or with the campaign which resulted in the defeat and death of James IV at Flodden.[17]

Meanwhile the *Elizabeth*, diverted to the Thames, was commissioned into the main royal fleet, first as a victualler to the *Less Carrick* (*c.* December 1512-February 1513) and *Katherine Fortaleza* (*c.* March-April 1513), and eventually (*c.* April) as a fighting ship.[18] Thus it was that under her owner, Lewis Sotheran, she came to take part in Sir Edward Howard's ill-fated expedition to Brest. The story is worth recounting in some detail, not only by reason of her distinguished role therein, but also since there is no adequate description and analysis of this important operation.[19]

Howard, the Lord Admiral, left the Thames in March 1513 with 23 royal, and 5 hired ships, and their victuallers to clear the way for an invasion of France. At almost the same time Prégent de Bidoux, an experienced galley commander of formidable reputation, sailed from Brest on a cross-Channel raid, but was obliged to put into St. Malo through sickness and stress of weather. He was thus already well established in northern waters, and not, as is sometimes

[15] (*Letters and Papers relating to the War with France 1512-13*, ed. A.) Spont (NRS X, 1897), xvi-xvii, 27n. i.

[16] E 101/62/23; *LP*, II (II), p. 1462. *Elizabeth* was in the South by December 1512, *LP*, I, 3591.

[17] Spont, 176 and notes; Fisher, 185-8; Mackie, 279-82; Hume Brown, 1, 267-72. They may have been concerned with French privateers then active on the coast, *LP*, I (I), 1645.

[18] E 101/62/63; PRO, Exchequer TR, Misc. Books (E. 36), vol. 12, 25; *LP*, I (I), 1661, i, iii; Spont, 86-7, 105. Cf. below, note 24.

[19] Cf. the accounts in W. L. Clowes, *The Royal Navy*, I, 455-7; Sir Julian Corbett, *Drake and the Tudor Navy*, I, 21-2; J. A. Williamson, *Maritime Enterprise, 1485-1558* (Oxford, 1913), 353-4, 375-84; Spont, xxx-xl; D. Mathew, *The Naval Heritage* (London, 1944), 7-8; Fisher, 179-80; Mackie, 276-7.

I

suggested, still on passage from the Mediterranean.[20] In the meantime Howard had made contact with some of the heavier French ships (April 11) which, after their encounters with his fleet in the previous year, promptly ran for Brest pursued by the English, who were, however, unable to enter through foul wind and tide. Skirmishing parties were landed, but an attempted attack under sail failed after the grounding of the *Nicholas*, and the French, anticipating further assaults, took elaborate precautions, including the preparation of fire-ships. Howard then established a close blockade, though there were some doubts as to what would happen should the French galleys arrive—the admiral's view being that his own (2, and 2 rowbarges), together with his smaller vessels and ships' boats would "lay them sharply aboard".[21] But on April 22 Prégent, with 6 galleys and 4 foists, broke through the fleet, sinking "the ship that was Mr. Compton's" and badly damaging the *Less Bark* by artillery fire, though at the same time losing one of his foists to Howard's boats and suffering heavy casualties. He anchored in Blancs Sablons Bay, protected by shallows, and with his flanks covered by fortified islets. Howard, short of supplies, but undismayed by the course of events, considered a landing to take him from the rear, but with the arrival of more victuallers (April 24), and on the advice of a Spanish officer, he decided to transfer men to some of his lighter craft and "run upon the galleys".[22]

The assault, it should be stressed, consisted of something more than the 2 galleys, 2 crayers and unspecified number of ships' boats with which it is usually credited.[23] Prégent himself speaks of being attacked by 30 ships and 25 or 30 boats, of which 2 galleys and 3 ships boarded him, and his view is to some extent borne out by Sir Thomas Howard's account. From this there can be identified 2 galleys (probably

[20] Spont, 94-9, 122, 134; but cf. Corbett, *loc. cit.*

[21] Spont, xxxv, 127-8. The French defences were organized before Prégent's arrival at Brest, and were not, as Fisher considers (180), part of a plan to draw the English to a sure destruction.

[22] Spont, 135-6, 143, 146-7.

[23] Corbett, *loc cit.*; Fisher, 180; Mackie, 277.

Swallow, under Sir Edward Howard, and *Sweepstake*, under Ferrer); the *Less Rowbarge*; 2 crayers (Sir William Sidney and Sir Henry Sherburn in one, Thomas Cheney and John Wallop in the other); the *Christopher Davy* (Wiseman); the *Jenet Purwyn* (Guerney); the *Elizabeth* of Newcastle (Sotheran); William Tooley of the *Sweepstake* in some unidentified craft; Sir Wistan Browne in the *Peter*'s boats; a number of other ships' boats, and perhaps the *Lizard*.[24]

Howard, leaving his main fleet to watch Brest, attacked on Monday April 25. He grappled and boarded Prégent's flagship, but his line was either slipped or parted, and he was left on the fo'c's'le to be thrust overboard by pikemen. That this was no accident is perhaps suggested by a letter of 7 May from Thomas Howard to Wolsey, complaining that Cook (*Swallow*'s captain) " did his part very ill that day my brother was lost ". After *Swallow* had drifted clear *Sweepstake* grappled Prégent, but was driven off, to be followed in succession by the *Less Rowbarge* and the crayers. It is not clear where *Christopher Davy*, whose captain " boarded not but had all his men slayne or hurt ", *Jenet Purwyn*, and *Elizabeth* were engaged, but in Thomas Howard's opinion Guerney and " good Lewes (Sotheran) did as well as was possible, as well apperyd by the slaughter (? of their men) and bowging of their ships ".[25] But with Howard's death, and the repulse of five attempts to board, the assault drew off and rejoined the heavier ships. Then, without orders, the whole fleet retired to Plymouth (April 30).[26]

[24] Spont, 136-7, 146-7, 149, 155-6, 160. The vessels may be identified by their officers' names from the tables in Spont, 77-88. I have taken that on 87-8 to represent the fleet in April, since in this *Elizabeth* is a fighting ship and no longer a victualler to *Katherine Fortaleza* (above, n. 18), and it is known that the *Katherine* did in fact sail without a victualler (Spont, 105). It is suggested that Howard was in *Swallow* from the mention of her captain, Cook, which would leave *Sweepstake* as the only other galley present (but on her rating as a galley see C. S. Goldingham, " The Navy under Henry VII ", *English Historical Review*, XXXIII (1918), 481). It is, however, possible that their roles were reversed. It should also be noticed that the crayers of Thomas Howard's account, which lost few men, cannot be identified with the *Jenet* and *Elizabeth*, which had heavy casualties.

[25] The *Jenet*'s master, however, disgraced himself, Spont, 160.

[26] Spont, 136-7, 146-7, 149, 155-6, 160.

Though Dr. Mathew has found a deceptive modernity in this action, it was the very apotheosis of medieval naval war; grappling, boarding, and hand-to-hand fighting. Its most significant features were the indifferent performance of the larger French ships compared with Prégent's assured handling of his squadron, the complete inadequacy of English victualling, and the general and ominous lack of discipline in Howard's command: disputes among the Admiral's advisers; hesitations by the captains of *Swallow* and *Christopher Davy*; failures amongst the rowers in the galleys and rowbarges, all culminating in the final mutinous return to England.[27]

It has often been implied, largely on the evidence of Sabin and Echyngham, two English captains who disapproved of it, that the operation was merely foolhardy and that no such action against galleys could ever have succeeded.[28] Yet Prégent himself felt that he had been in considerable danger, and his squadron was in fact in some measure disabled as a result of the encounter.[29] Moreover Howard, though a young man (he was about 36 at the time), came of a family which had realistic views on seapower, and was by no means inexperienced. He had taken a leading part in the capture of Andrew Barton in 1511, fought a triumphant campaign against the French in 1512, and what is perhaps more relevant, had been at Poyning's successful naval assault on Sluys in 1492.[30] The situation in April 1513 demanded action. He was on a dangerous station—as many subsequent blockading fleets off Brest were to discover—badly supplied, and with undisciplined ships.[31] To have destroyed, or even crippled Prégent's galleys, thus removing the most effective element in French naval power, would have been sound strategy. But the operation was neither well planned nor

[27] Spont, 126, 151, 156, 160, and cf. xl-xli; Clowes, I, 457.

[28] Spont, xxxix, 143, 147; Fisher, 180; Mackie, 277.

[29] Spont, 137, 161.

[30] Spont, viii-x; Clowes, I, 449. It is clear from his correspondence that Howard was a real sailor. A letter in Spont (97) shows him testing the sailing qualities of his ships, carrying a press of canvas so they were gunwale under.

[31] Spont, 126, 154-5.

executed. A diversionary landing might have assisted, but by mid-April there was no longer a chance of surprise. Again, Greek fire (" wyldfier ") might have proved conclusive against closely moored vessels, but the idea was abandoned after some discussion, possibly because of memories of the disastrous burning of the *Regent* and *Cordelière* in 1512.[32] Nevertheless Howard's attack was much more than " a foolhardy venture in 4 small boats ". It was directly into the fire of what was generally regarded as the heaviest naval artillery in the North,[33] but the assault was of a fair size, in which none of the ships were less than 70 tons, and two at least were over 100—incidentally suggesting there was more water available than the contemporary narratives reveal.[34] The opposition to these tactics came from Sabin and Echyngham, neither of whom appear to have had experience with galleys, whilst the admiral was supported and encouraged by a Spanish officer who might be expected to have known something of such things.[35]

Despite her losses and " bowging ", which presumably relates to damage by shot,[36] the *Elizabeth*, whose performance at Brest had clearly been appreciated by the new Lord Admiral, Thomas Howard, continued in service under Sotheran. She was with the fleet throughout the Summer and Autumn of 1513, her casualties apparently having been made good by a draft of Devon men,[37] and though due for discharge at Southampton in September, she was retained with a number of other selected vessels " to keep the sea this winter " in view of Franco-Scottish preparations. Early in 1514 she was in northern waters, probably with Sabin's squadron, ordered to the Forth when Louis XII threatened

[32] Spont, 159.

[33] Spont, 51-2.

[34] Spont, 85-8. It appears that a rowbarge grounded, however, *ib.*, 156.

[35] Spont, 143, 147.

[36] According to Sir Julian Corbett a ship was said to " bulge " herself when she grounded and filled (*Fighting Instructions, 1530-1816*, NRS, XXIX, 1905), 16, n. 1, but this was not the case with the *Elizabeth*.

[37] *LP*, I, 4377; I (II), 2304. The Mr. Crocker who was to supply her retinue was a Devon man, see index to *LP*, I.

I

to despatch the Duke of Albany (cousin and heir of the infant James V, and an ardent protagonist of French influence) to Scotland. She returned south in the Spring, only to be recommissioned into Vice-Admiral Sir Thomas Denys' fleet (9 ships, of which 6 were merchantmen) "appointed to the North Seas", with which she served for some months before England came to terms with France (July 1514) and Scotland (May 1515).[38]

The general European peace of 1518 was soon destroyed by the rivalries of Francis I of France and the Emperor Charles V, and when fighting was resumed in 1522 England, by popular inclination and Wolsey's direction, was allied to the Emperor against Francis, who in turn allowed Albany to reappear in Scotland to occupy Henry's attention.[39] But England, while preparing for action on the Continent, seized the initiative in the North. Before Albany could make any move a flotilla under Sabin, which perhaps included the *George* of Newcastle, attacked Leith and subsequently carried out a significant bombardment of Kinghorn, where they came in "one by one as near as possible and (the commander) made each fire against the town in succession"—which might be taken to indicate broadside firing from line ahead.[40] The damage inflicted on French and Scottish shipping is unknown, though probably slight, and the effectiveness of the whole operation was destroyed by three of Sabin's captains insisting on escorting a prize into Newcastle, thus allowing 3 French men-of-war to enter the Forth "to the great comfort of the Duke and his friends", who were rumoured to be on the point of abandoning Scotland before the timely arrival of this reinforcement (*c.* 20 May).[41]

The following year, after some abortive negotiations for the overthrow of the French interest, the Earl of Surrey

[38] *LP*, I. 4474 (Spont, 185 n. 1); 4682 (i); *LP*, I (II), 2722; 3148 (ii); 3501; Spont, xliv-vi.

[39] Fisher, 205, 227-43; Hume Brown, I, 291-3; Mackie, 305-12.

[40] *LP*, III (II), 2746; *LP*, III (II), App. 33.

[41] *LP*, III (II), 2271.

(formerly Sir Thomas Howard) was appointed Lt. General against the Scots, and Sir Henry Sherburn commissioned (*c.* 18 February 1523) as Admiral or Vice-Admiral (the titles are used indiscriminately) of the North Sea. His flagship was the *William* of York, and his command of 16 (later reduced to 10) merchantmen included the *Jesus*, the *Katherine*, the *Matthew* and the *Mary Katherine* from Newcastle. Operations were under Surrey's general direction, and show a characteristic appreciation of seapower, but what is perhaps most remarkable was the concern—by no means exclusively English—with the disruption of trade and fisheries, foreshadowing in some measure the pattern of later Anglo-Dutch wars in the same waters.[42]

In May 1523 Sherburn in the *William* with his son, Thomas, in the *Katherine*, were detached to seek commerce raiders at Flamborough, whilst Christopher Coo, a distinguished seaman who had already spent some profitable months in the Channel, and four other captains were ordered to lie "two kennyngs in the sea" off Holy Island to cut communications with Scotland. But these dispositions were almost immediately destroyed by storms which drove Sherburn to Holy Island and Coo to the Forth. With his ships so dispersed Surrey was exercised for Coo's safety, and by the danger of a Scots attack on the returning East Anglian Iceland fleet, by which, as he wrote with the pardonable exaggeration of a harassed commander, "the coasts of Norfolk and Suffolk will be undone, and all England destitute of fish next year".[43] But whilst he awaited Wolsey's permission to detail an escort for the fishermen[44]—an ominous anticipation of a situation all too common in certain subsequent periods of naval history—Sherburn, seemingly accompanied by Thwayts in the *Matthew*, fell in with a French

[42] *LP*, III (II), 2836, 3493, 3160; *LP*, IV (I), 691; Fisher, 248-9; Hume Brown, I, 293-5; Mackie, 313.

[43] *LP*, III (II), 3071, 3493. I hope to deal more fully with Sherburn and Coo in due course.

[44] An escort was apparently sent from Yarmouth (*LP*, IV (I), 691). It is possible that Sherburn himself was ordered to support the fishermen, and that the Frenchman he encountered was intended to stiffen the Scots attack.

"great ship" (11 June), with which he fought a brisk, though unsatisfactory action. Some of the *Matthew*'s artillery was disabled, the *William* had 34 men injured, and Sherburn himself was killed, but the Frenchman, despite heavy casualties, held on for Leith.[45]

On Surrey's orders the command passed to the energetic Coo,[46] and there ensued a number of vigorous engagements in the North and in the Channel as the new Vice-Admiral, with a strengthened squadron, attacked commerce, and attempted (and on the whole quite successfully) to sever Franco-Scottish communications. The *Jenet Purwyn*, now a ship "of little value", was recaptured;[47] the *Galere* of Dieppe and the *Marie* of Honfleur were intercepted on passage from the Baltic with cargoes of rye; and at least 5 other vessels were taken, including a Newfoundland banker from Rouen "laden with fish", valued in all at £1,213. Some of Coo's men were wounded—he was allowed £6/18/- "for healing 16 burnt at the taking of the Newfoundland ship"—and several of his command damaged; a small sum was spent on "lead dice and hides" for repairs to artillery; the *John Baptist* of Lynn needed a refit costing £64 after her encounter with the *Paraunt*; and the *William* of York lost her bowsprit, foresail and spritsail in boarding the *Griffin*, before she became a total loss. In view of these activities it is hardly surprising that when in September Albany, who had withdrawn to France late in 1522, sought to return to Scotland, he chose to do so through the Irish Sea and Dumbarton rather than risk the passage to Leith.[48]

With the ignominious failure of Albany's northern campaign (October 1523), and the landing of a large English army on the Continent, Coo's squadron was reduced, though somewhat prematurely in view of the continued presence of French warships on the East coast. The *Jesus*, *Katherine* and

[45] *LP*, III (II), 3116, 3191, 3493; *LP*, IV (I), 691; La Roncière, III, 180-1.
[46] Much to Coo's delight, *LP*, III (II), 3158.
[47] *LP*, III (II), 3158.
[48] *LP*, IV (I), 83, 691; La Roncière, 180-3; Fisher, 249; Hume Brown, I, 294; Mackie, 312-13.

Mary Katherine were paid off late in 1523, but the *Matthew* remained in commission till the following Spring—perhaps, as with the *Elizabeth* before her, on account of her fighting qualities—when there appears to have been a reduction of English armaments as Wolsey tired of the imperial alliance.[49]

The next seventeen years brought a comparative lull in the wars of Charles and Francis, while ecclesiastical and political upheaval left England with little surplus energy for imperial ambitions. But in 1542, with the internal situation somewhat more stable, and France and the Empire again embattled, Henry renewed his attempts to destroy French influence in Scotland, where, through the policies of the Queen, Mary of Lorraine, and James V's chief counsellor, the sinister cardinal Beaton, it had rapidly increased since the late 1530's.[50]

Sir Robert Bowes, Warden of the Marches, was defeated on a Border raid in August, and the king, in retaliation, ordered the Duke of Norfolk (the former Surrey) to attack unless the Scots agreed to humiliating conditions. Operations commenced on land early in October without any formal declaration of war. At the same time a squadron of 8 royal and private ships arrived at Holy Island, with John Cary as Vice-Admiral in *Less Galley*, commissioned to support the invasion and cut communications with France.[51] On about October 3 the Council directed that this somewhat meagre fleet should be reinforced, and nine days later there was talk of sending up 2 ships from Newcastle; James Lawson's *Elizabeth*, and "one of Orwell of which Sabin is owner".[52] But whilst Cary lay at Holy Island, windbound and short of supplies, awaiting his reinforcements, 16 French vessels slipped past into the Forth. The English commanders, undeterred by such setbacks and a series of disastrous mili-

[49] *LP*, III (II), 3493, 3536; *LP*, IV (I), 83, 691; Fisher, 249-52; Hume Brown, I, 294-5; Mackie, 313-15.

[50] Fisher, 453-6; Hume Brown, I, 309-14; Mackie, 404-5.

[51] *LP*, XVII, 895, 946; Fisher, 456; Hume Brown, I, 314; Mackie, 405. I hope to deal more fully with Cary in a subsequent article.

[52] *LP*, XVII, 910, 939; *Hamilton Papers*, I, 206.

I

tary failures, optimistically wrote (October 14) that they would strengthen Cary with 6 or 7 Newcastle ships to aid him "seek the enemies" in the Forth. After some further delay a number of vessels, including, however, only 4 from the Tyne (which may be identified as the *Elizabeth*, *Anthony*, *John Evangelist*, and *Robert*), were said to be joining, and by the end of the month the Vice-Admiral was at last under sail in pursuit of 2 French merchantmen "laden with ordnance".[53] But in the meantime the invasion, pressed with even less urgency, had collapsed. Norfolk was no longer the vigorous and able warrior of his youth, and the campaign, badly planned and worse executed, ended in November with the return of the fleet, which had burned a few villages just north of the Border, and, as the report baldly puts it, "killed certain persons". The irascible Henry expressed a not unreasonable wish that "such a costly and notable enterprise had been more displeasant to the enemies".[54]

Cary paid off some of his ships, and on Norfolk's instructions left the rest "to lie at Holy Island and keep the seas this winter to prevent the Scots from uttering their wool and salmon, which is their only commodity unsold, and put them from their fishing in the seas this winter and in Lent"—a further instance not only of Howard's views on the functions of sea-power, but also of that concern with the disruption of commerce which particularly characterized these early operations in northern waters. The effect of the projected blockade remains obscure, though a number of prizes were apparently taken.[55]

In the meanwhile, on the West coast, another of Henry's armies had won a decisive victory at Solway Moss, news of which killed the unfortunate James. To English politicians it appeared that the Tudor ideal of a

[53] *LP*, XVII, 946, 969, and cf. *LP*, XVII, 996; *LP*, XVIII (I), 765.

[54] *LP*, XVII, 1025; Fisher, 456-7; Hume Brown, I, 314; Mackie, 405.

[55] *LP*, XVII, 1043, 1083; *LP*, XVIII (I), 6. In September 1542 Norfolk had urged that Scots shipping returning from Denmark should be intercepted, *LP*, XVII, 731, 754.

union of the crowns was at last to be realized. To this end, while an Anglophile party was fostered under a suitable puppet, there were renewed efforts to seal off Scotland from French aid and encouragement, and to demonstrate the effects of English hostility by attacks on her valuable trade with the Low Countries.[56] Early in January 1543 the king wrote to Lisle—the future Protector Northumberland—then Warden of the Marches, that the Scots had certain "richly laden ships" in Veere, which it would be both politic and profitable to intercept, the more so since the most powerful Scottish warships were away seeking the English Bordeaux fleet. Six vessels already at sea were to be reinforced by 4 "of the tallest" from Newcastle, and the combined squadron was to lie in wait in the Forth. After some negotiations the "mayor and brethren" of Newcastle were bound by indenture (19 January) to have the *Elizabeth*, *Anthony*, *James*, and *John Evangelist* equipped, victualled, manned and fully prepared to join the Vice-Admiral, Sir Francis Bryan, within six days.[57] But whilst preparations were in progress the Council learned (wrongly, as it transpired), that the Duke of Guise, brother of the Queen Mother of Scotland, was about to leave Le Havre for the North with a Franco-Scottish fleet of 8 men-of-war, 3 or 4 "valuable merchantmen", and 11 English prizes. Since it was essential to Tudor policy that no assistance should reach Beaton and his supporters at this stage, least of all from such a man as Guise, Lisle and Bryan were ordered (19 January) to get as many ships as possible to sea to meet this armada. Powerful reinforcements were promised from the South—including a number of royal ships—and Bryan was given specific instructions that if contact were made he was to take Guise regardless of all else.[58]

By this time, though there were still plenty of "pratie ships" in Newcastle, the town was short of seamen. Nevertheless, despite this and a lack of ordnance, the *Trinity San-*

[56] Fisher, 457-9; Hume Brown, I, 315-17, II, 3-5; Mackie, 405-7.
[57] *LP*, XVIII (I), 17, 19, 43, 59.
[58] *LP*, XVIII (I), 57; *Hamilton Papers*, I, 283.

I

derson and *Mary Grace*, with the *Robert* as a packet, were added to the command. It was originally intended to rendezvous off Holy Island, where the Newcastle contingent, with the Vice-Admiral in the *Elizabeth*, was to meet those from Yarmouth, Hull and London, but by the end of January the Tyne had frozen so hard that there was "great business to get two of the ships loosed out of the ice, which at the quay . . . is 2 fathoms thick".[59] In view of these delays Bryan's final instructions (27 January)—drafted, it should be observed, by Norfolk—were that when the Newcastle squadron was up to strength—which meant a detour to Holy Island to pick up artillery from Berwick for the *Trinity Sanderson* and *Mary Grace*—he was to go south to meet the rest of his fleet, unless Guise had already reached Scottish waters, in which case he was to follow and await further orders. As soon as he had 9 sail he was to lie off Orford Ness and watch for the enemy. Should they put into Zealand they were to be blockaded by "riding between Flushing and the Rumkyns", and cut out if opportunity offered, but if they went into Veere they were not to be attacked—presumably because of the large amount of Scottish shipping already there—but were to be "drawn North".[60]

By now, however, Bryan was so late that when he eventually left the Tyne (2 February) he was informed that 21 "great ships", thought at first to be Guise and his "conserve", but later identified as the powerful Scots, *Mary Willoughby* and *Salamander*, with 19 English prizes, were off Holy Island on a northerly course. Suffolk, then commanding on the Border, rightly feeling that his Admiral was but "slenderly furnished" for an encounter with such a force, advised him to abandon the projected call at Holy Island (and consequently the ordnance for the *Trinity* and *Mary Grace*), and to fall back south for reinforcement. Following this counsel Bryan met the Hull contingent within a day or

[59] *Hamilton Papers*, I, 287; *LP*, XVIII (I), 75, 80.

[60] *Hamilton Papers*, I, 288; *LP*, XVIII (I), 88. Orford Ness to Berwick was a recognized station as early as 1415, Clowes, I, 372.

so, and with his squadron now up to 14 sail he again came north, only to run into heavy weather which scattered his ships, and sent some into the Tyne "with great leaks". By February 7 it was known that the Scots had entered Leith, and the local command despondently wrote that further action was thought to be pointless.[61]

After this fiasco, and in the absence of Guise's threatened descent, there was a short-lived revival of interest in the Scots still at Veere, but plans languished. Part of Bryan's squadron —"the meanest ships"—was ordered to the Downs, and such of the rest as were fit for sea (including the *Elizabeth*) were employed in patrolling between the Humber and the Tyne in conditions such as were later to be only too familiar to British blockading fleets.[62]

But now more than ever, with the English interest apparently on the point of prevailing, Henry's policy demanded that Scotland be isolated, and that Beaton's party (the cardinal himself having been seized by the "English Lords" or "assured Scots", as they were known, on January 27) should receive neither supplies nor reinforcement.[63] Hence on February 28, despite Bryan's failure and an exceptionally severe winter, 4 Newcastle ships (the *Trinity*, *Anthony*, *John Evangelist*, and *Mary Grace*) were appointed "to keep the North Seas between the Humber and Berwick", under the command of William Woodhouse, with his flag in the *Trinity*. The Council gave detailed instructions for the commission. Woodhouse was to be victualled by the Lord Admiral (Lisle) and the governor of Hull, and was not to come inshore unless "upon stress of weather or some chase". All French and Scots vessels were to be taken as prize, and their crews impressed for English service. The ships themselves were to be sent "in Englishmen's charge" into the nearest port, where the local officials were to be ordered to secure their cargoes, and notice was to be given

[61] *LP*, XVIII (I), 108, 123, 127.

[62] *LP*, XVIII (I), 143, 162, 200. The *Elizabeth* was in service till March or even April 1543; *LP*, XVIII (I), 434, 765.

[63] Fisher, 458-9; Hume Brown, II, 4-5; Mackie, 406-7.

to the Council and the Lord Admiral of all such captures. No Flemish, Spanish, Portuguese or Hanseatic ships (a valuable indication of the merchantmen likely to be encountered on the North-East coast) were to be held unless they had committed some hostile act, or were carrying men, victuals or munitions to Scotland, in which case they were to be kept "to the strength and commodity of his majesty's navy" until further instructions. Danish vessels, since the king of Denmark was an ally of Francis I, were to be searched for letters and information, but not otherwise molested, and finally Woodhouse was warned to prevent plundering and acts of violence against neutrals.[64]

These comprehensive instructions for blockade invite comment at a number of points, the more so since a distinguished naval historian has recently overlooked the existence of any such ideas at the time.[65] At the date of Woodhouse's appointment England was nominally at peace with both France and Scotland,[66] and he was thus in fact empowered to treat what in strict law was neutral shipping as lawful prize. But the point must not be pressed too far. Such niceties weighed lightly in Henry's diplomacy, or indeed in the policies of most of his contemporaries, and for all practical purposes the commission relates to a state of hostilities. The machinery of arrest outlined is of a pattern which can be discovered as early as 1426, and there is nothing unusual in the definition of victuals and munitions as contraband.[67] But the power to seize, and even impress neutral shipping found armed or carrying contraband, though again not entirely without precedent, is an example of the increasing severity of prize law in the mid-sixteenth century, and an

[64] *LP*, XVIII (I), 225.

[65] Sir Herbert Richmond, *Statesmen and Sea Power* (Oxford, 1946), 12-13, attributes their origin to the Elizabethans, but cf. F. W. Brooks, "Naval Administration and the raising of Fleets under John and Henry III" (*Mariner's Mirror*, XV, 1929), 378; C. J. Kulsrud, *Maritime Neutrality to 1780* (Boston, Mass., 1936), 204, 214, 242.

[66] War with Scotland commenced December 1543 (Hume Brown, II, 10), and with France in June (Fisher, 460).

[67] Kulsrud, 24, 252-3, 267.

earlier instance of such instructions than those generally cited.[68] The authority to search vessels belonging to the ally of a hostile power for information is likewise an innovation: search itself was long established—it can be found at least as early as the time of John—but it was to ascertain the nature of a cargo rather than to gather intelligence, though doubtless this would have been secured in any period by an enterprising officer.[69]

Woodhouse and his squadron can be traced at sea from March to June, and guided by information from Henry's representative in Edinburgh they appear to have taken a number of prizes.[70] But the English position in Scotland was rapidly deteriorating. By the beginning of April 1543 Beaton was once more at large and speedily had forces at work against which the Tudor puppet, Arran, could make no head. Shortly after, Henry, provoked amongst other things by the intimate connection of France with the frustration of his Scottish plans, declared war on Francis. The ensuing campaigns again reveal strategic ideas of a higher order than the period is usually credited with. The French aimed not only to supply and finance Beaton, but also, in conjunction with the Scots and Danes, to intercept the Flemish Icelandic fishermen and Baltic grain fleets, and so damage the economy of the Low Countries (which belonged to Henry's ally, the Emperor Charles V), whilst the English had plans for a joint Anglo-Imperial operation against the French herring fishery.[71] There was heavy fighting on the North-East coast, in which Woodhouse, now in *Sweepstake*, distinguished himself. A French squadron returning from Scotland in July was so handled as to have to put back for repairs, and in August a number of Dieppe ships were taken

[68] Kulsrud, 18, 116-17.

[69] Kulsrud, 166; F. W. Brooks, "The King's Ships and Galleys" (*MM*, XV, 1929), 44. It should be noticed, however, that in Howard's commission of 1512 he was to examine "monuments, indentures, writings and cokets and none other", i.e. only commercial papers.

[70] *LP*, XVIII (I), 434, 483, 503, 596, 765, 908.

[71] Fisher, 459-61; Hume Brown, II, 5-6; Mackie, 407; La Roncière, III, 396-7.

I

off the Tyne. Not only were Francis's more ambitious designs disrupted, but when in October he attempted to reinforce Beaton it was found expedient to do so through Dumbarton rather than risk any further encounters in the North Sea—a situation comparable to that of 1523.[72]

But despite these admirable indications of sea-power Henry continued to lose ground. In September his one-time creature, Arran, came to terms with Beaton, thus moving the king to characteristic paroxysms of wrath. His first reaction (September 14) was that the pair should be surprised and captured, to which end 5 or 6 ships were to be sent to the Forth from Newcastle and Berwick " lest they should fly by sea ", but a few days later (September 30) he was contemplating large-scale military operations against Edinburgh.[73] No action was possible till the following Spring, when the earl of Hertford was commissioned to destroy Edinburgh and Leith, and sack the surrounding countryside. After Norfolk's failure in 1542, when the army had been exhausted by a long march across difficult Border country, it was decided to put Hertford ashore in the Forth—a further demonstration of Tudor naval power which the Scots were unable to dispute. To convey the expedition merchantmen were arrested all along the East coast—the resultant returns being among the most valuable evidence concerning shipping during the period[74]—whilst the earl of Suffolk was instructed to spread rumours that these preparations were for the invasion of France. A royal fleet was in the Tyne by the end of March 1544 (*Sweepstake* grounding on entering), but though many Newcastle ships were employed in supply, and later, when the disastrous results of Henry's policy became apparent, as privateers, none were used as men-of-war in the operation.[75]

[72] *LP*, XVIII (I), 908; *LP*, XVIII (II), 63, 70; La Roncière, III, 398-9; above, 84.

[73] *LP*, XVIII (II), 184, 234; Fisher, 460; Hume Brown, II, 7; Mackie, 407.

[74] *LP*, XIX (I), 107, 115, 116, 140, 194, 355.

[75] *LP*, XIX (I), 98, 264, 290; Fisher, 461-2; Hume Brown, II, 10-11; Mackie, 407.

The king's "godly purpose" having been accomplished Hertford withdrew, leaving northern commerce exposed to the depredations of Scottish privateers, against which Newcastle, exhausted by incessant royal demands and an epidemic of plague, made little showing. But Henry had now turned all his energies to the South, where Francis, heartened by the Emperor Charles' withdrawal from the war (September 1544) and an English defeat in Scotland (February 1545), had prepared elaborate plans for the destruction of the English fleet and the recapture of Boulogne.[76] To meet this danger the royal ships under Lisle were to be heavily reinforced, chiefly from the West Country, but before the arrival of these auxiliaries there was an indecisive skirmish in the Solent (July 19, 1545).[77] By August 10 the fleet had increased to 104 sail; 24 in the van; 40 in the battle—including the *Mighell* of Newcastle which had served as a privateer in the Spring—and 40 on the wing.[78] Thus strengthened Lisle fought an action off Shoreham which ended in a French withdrawal—strategically at least a fitting conclusion to naval operations under the early Tudors.[79]

There were a number of other duties for armed merchantmen besides fleet service, which have so far attracted little notice. They might, for instance, be employed, under varying degrees of supervision, as privateers in areas for which no royal ships, or what is perhaps more relevant, no royal officers, could be spared, or in routine tasks, such as reconnaissance, convoy escort or guard work. Thus in 1488, when despite generally pacific relations between England and Scotland, civil disorders which resulted in the overthrow of James III produced a resurgence of Scots claims to Berwick, the garrison was strengthened and the *Mary Huberd* (or *Mayr Hayrbred*) of Newcastle sent with an escort to victual

[76] Fisher, 463-6; Mackie, *loc. cit.*
[77] Fisher, 467-8; Mackie, 409.
[78] *LP*, XX (II), 88. This evidence is discussed by Sir Julian Corbett in *Fighting Instructions*, 18-24.
[79] Fisher, 468-9; Mackie, 409-10.

I

the town and remain as a guard during the king's pleasure.[80]

Convoy "wafting" was a more frequent and likewise a more hazardous employment, especially when towards the end of the reign of Henry VIII high policy kept the royal ships fully occupied, and ill-advised Tudor depredations in Scotland had stirred up privateering in the North Sea. In February 1545, when the newly acquired English enclave at Boulogne was in danger, it was planned to supply it with coal from Newcastle and other provisions from elsewhere on the East coast, to which end transports were to assemble off Ravenspur, and from there sail in protected convoy. The coal fleet was to be covered on passage from the Tyne to the Humber by 2 Newcastle vessels which were to wait on the rendezvous till the escort arrived. But the operation was marred by administrative difficulties and a general lack of enthusiasm. The colliers lay in the Tyne for more than a week before one of the masters "revealed" that the escort was already at Hull. There was then some argument as to whether it should be summoned further north, despite the original arrangements, and a marked reluctance to proceed unless this were done. The evidence thereafter is obscure, but it is worth noticing that when in November 1546 another coal fleet was to sail for Boulogne, 2 men-of-war were appointed to join it at Newcastle.[81]

There were also occasional demands for reconnaissance and intelligence. The prominent role of espionage in sixteenth-century war and politics needs no emphasis, though it might be observed that unsuitable agents and impossible delays in communication frequently vitiated its results—as indeed was the case until comparatively recent times.[82] But much information reached the government through less

[80] *Materials for a History of the Reign of Henry VII*, ed. W. Campbell (2 vols., London, 1873-7), II, 297; A. Conway, *Henry VII's Relations with Scotland and Ireland*, 26; Fisher, 49-50; Hume Brown, I, 228-31; Mackie, 76.

[81] *LP*, XX (I), 129, 135, 141; *Acts of the Privy Council of England*, vol. I (ed. J. R. Dasent, London, 1890), 550, 557-8.

[82] A Scottish spy was surveying English ports in 1539 (*Accounts of the Lord High Treasurer of Scotland*, VII, 59). For an English spy in Scotland see *LP*, XVIII (II), 281.

dramatic channels: the mayor of Newcastle for instance—whose services to the crown in this and other respects were very considerable throughout the period—forwarded details of foreign naval operations gathered from masters using the port.[83] At times, however, more active steps were required. Hence, in October 1544, after the Emperor Charles' withdrawal had left Henry to contend alone with France and Scotland, the Council, in order to assess the situation in the North, ordered the royal Lieutenant on the Borders to send out craft "to learn the number of Scots ships on the coast" and their "size and fittment". In due course he accordingly instructed Berwick, Hull and Newcastle to provide 2 vessels each, but Newcastle, stricken by plague and harried by privateers, refused, claiming it had none fit "to view the enemies and yet save themselves".[84]

Such cautious counsels had not always been the case, for the city, like most ports, had a long tradition of piracy and privateering. These activities, much intensified in the mid-fifteenth century, had subsided towards the end of the reign of Edward IV, only to reappear, albeit somewhat less exuberantly, with the resurgence of French and Scottish power in northern waters. Whatever the nominal relations of Tudor, Valois, and Stuart, vigorous fighting continued on the East coast, now perhaps best remembered from accounts of the almost legendary exploits of the Scottish hero, Sir Andrew Wood, and of the no less stirring deeds of the Bartons and Howards. But private war is rarely on such a heroic plane, and far commoner was the profitless plundering of small merchantmen and fishermen,[85] provoking retaliation of varying degrees of effectiveness and legality. In June 1522 Wolsey was informed of a general desire among Newcastle merchants to attack 3 French vessels that were on the coast, and eleven years later, with the Scots out in strength, there

[83] *LP*, XIX (II), 364.

[84] *Hamilton Papers*, II, 330; *LP*, XIX (II), 364.

[85] William Woodhouse himself had been taken prisoner by "wild Scots" while on a fishing voyage "to the out Isles of Scotland" early in his career, HCA, 13/3, 274.

is mention of 2 prizes taken by local ships.[86] Men of enterprise might seek wider fields; in the 1530's a Tynesider, Giles Carr, became master of a vessel from a village near Cromer and subsequently figures in Admiralty records for his assaults on Scottish shipping.[87] But as the century wore on Henry's preoccupation with the continent, denuding the North Sea of men-of-war, and his heavy demands on merchant tonnage combined with enemy action to produce an even more subdued frame of mind.[88] On November 3 1544 Shrewsbury wrote to the Council asking for aid, and pointing out the feats of privateers fitted out by "desperate merchants of Edinburgh and Leith, who having lost almost their whole substance at the army's late being in Scotland, seek adventures either to recover something or lose the rest". They had recently taken the *Anthony* and some smaller craft, whilst earlier in the year the *James*, "loaded with goods valued at 2,000 marks", had been boarded and cut out as she lay within 300 feet of the walls of Veere.[89] The king replied forthwith in a letter of scathing exhortation. Newcastle was urged to emulate the West Country and East Anglia, which sent out their own privateers "and gained much thereby". The "great Navy" in the Channel was declared indivisible—it was at this time, it will be recalled, that England, abandoned by Charles V, was facing France alone—followed by the splenetic pronouncement that "it were over burdensome that the king should set ships to defend all parts of the realm and keep the Narrow Seas withal".[90] These are doubtless the views of a harassed man in a moment of crisis, and as considered indications of strategy they must not be pressed too far. But the resources of the government were badly over-

[86] *LP*, III (II), 2328; *LP*, VI, 606; *LP*, Addenda, I, 835.

[87] HCA, 13/1, 64.

[88] In the year September 1543 to September 1544 only 29 ships used the port of Newcastle, making 38 sailings (PRO, E122/109/9). In a normal year there were often several hundred sailings.

[89] *LP*, XIX (I), 224; XIX (II), 540, and cf. XVIII (II), 281. It is commonly and incorrectly, assumed that Scottish sea power was negligible after Hertford's campaigns in 1544 (e.g. Fisher, 466). For Hertford in Scotland see above, 92-3.

[90] *LP*, XIX (II), 560.

taxed, and despite the much discussed, and often deceptive modernity of Henry's administration, in this matter at least he was forced into a policy of a remarkably antique pattern. It was still a far cry to the omnipotent state that could and would protect all its citizens, and Newcastle was ordered to look to its own defence. But the city was exhausted, and there was little, if any, response.[91]

The following Spring, with Boulogne threatened, the French and Scots active on the East coast, and the fleet, if not decayed, as M. de La Roncière would have us believe, at least heavily committed in the Channel, the merits of self help were once more rehearsed. If Newcastle would emulate the initiative of Hull, which had provided a small flotilla, " the king should be well served on the North Seas ".[92] After some argument the city reluctantly agreed to fit out the *Mighell* and the *George*, but before they were ready for sea the threat of a Franco-Scottish invasion led the local command to seek permission to withdraw its privateers from service. There was some renewal of activity in the Autumn, and a number of unidentified Newcastle ships took a Flemish vessel bound for Scotland.[93]

[91] *LP*, XIX (II), 599.

[92] *LP*, XX (I), 189; La Roncière, III, 411.

[93] *LP*, XX (I), 243, 285, 321, 535; *LP*, XX (II), 332. For a general reluctance to serve at this time, see Oppenheim, *Administration*, 88.

I

Plate XX.

A ROYAL SHIP, 1545.

Plate XXI

A SMALL MERCHANT SHIP, *c*. 1532.

WAR AT SEA UNDER THE EARLY TUDORS—PART II.

The following abbreviations have been used in the notes:

Fisher—H. A. L. Fisher, *The History of England from the Accession of Henry VII to the Death of Henry VIII* (London, 1906).
HCA—High Court of Admiralty.
LP—Calendar of Letters and Papers, Foreign and Domestic. Henry VIII, ed. Brewer, Gairdner and Brodie (London, 1864-1932).
Oppenheim—M. Oppenheim, *A History of the Administration of the Royal Navy etc., 1509-1660* (London, 1896).
PRO—Public Record Office.
Spont—*Letters and Papers relating to the War with France, 1512-13* ed. A. Spont (Navy Records Society, X, 1897).

On a previous occasion the activities of squadrons raised on the East and North-East coasts under the first two Tudors, and more especially during the reign of Henry VIII, were discussed.[1] In this sequel it is proposed to deal with the vessels themselves, and the organization which got, or at least endeavoured to get, them to sea.

Newcastle merchantmen taken up by the crown for fighting service after 1509 were usually those said to be the "prettiest" or "tallest" the port could provide. These were not terms of poetic rapture, but described qualities considered desirable in potential men-of-war. A vessel was "pretty" in the sense that she was well-found and lively, and

[1] *AA*4, xxxviii, 73-97.

"tall" in that, like a warship, she was high-charged, with built-up fore and after castles[2]—vantage points controlling the low-lying waist, and from which, in the prevailing conditions of close fighting, an enemy could be raked with anything from arrows to Greek fire.[3]

In detail we know remarkably little of the appearance of such craft, despite an apparent plethora of sources, but fortunately there has survived, in the *Oyer and Terminer* records of the High Court of Admiralty, a graphic and professional description of an East Anglian pirate or privateer of the late 1540's which had once belonged to Cuthbert Blunt of Newcastle.[4] She was, says a seaman under examination before the court, "a prety black boate of a bowte xxx tonnes or more by his estimacyon, hauyng a Toppe,[5] a Gallyon noose very letyll,[6] a rownde Sterne with letyll Bayles[7] coveryd Withe tarryd Canvas, and a new foremast and nettid before and afte all coveryd over with new tarryd Canvas[8] beyng a very proper snugg boate, With vi peces ordynaunce uppon a syde . . .'. Unfortunately there is nothing more in the same vein, and other features of local craft remain obscure, though doubtless East-Coast sea-going ships had the customary three masts carrying four or five sails—a square foresail, foretop-

[2] See Plate XX.

[3] Many contemporary representations of Early Tudor warships make them look even more unseaworthy than they undoubtedly were, by exaggerating the height of their castles. This may be the result of poor draughtsmanship, or perhaps it is something more subtle—an attempt to impress the spectator with the might and majesty of Henrician sea-power. But Thomas Pettyt's drawings of Calais Harbour (1545), from which Plate XX is reproduced, show much more realistic vessels, which sit well down in the water and look thoroughly practical. The castles in merchantmen were less prominent: an aftercastle perhaps one or two decks high, but a comparatively insignificant forecastle.

[4] PRO, HCA I/34, fol. 201v.

[5] A platform round the head of the lower mast. It was used by look-outs, and in action by archers or bowmen. It also mounted some light guns. A top is clearly shown on the mainmast of the ship in Plate XXI.

[6] *I.e.* with a small beak-head low down like a galleon's at the bow.

[7] Bulwarks.

[8] Netting made of small ropes, and stretched where a modern vessel would have stanchions, was used to prevent boarding. In this case it was also apparently supporting a canvas screen which would act as a spray-dodger and, more important, keep the crew out of sight as the ship closed for action, so enabling her to surprise her prey—she was after all a privateer.

sail (the latter omitted in the smallest vessels), mainsail and maintopsail, and a lateen mizzen—together with a bowsprit, below which there was set a square spritsail. Thus we hear, for instance, that in 1523 the *William* of York lost her bowsprit, foresail and spritsail in an action with the French ship, *Griffin.*[9] The remarkable thing is that this rig was a comparatively recent innovation. Until about 1400 all merchantmen in northern European waters—which included some sizeable vessels—were single-masted, and even as late as 1451 the *Marie* of Newcastle had still apparently just the one mast—it got broken, either by design or accident, and so she escaped impressment.[10] Yet by the 1530's the new, and for the time fairly complex, sail-plan, only introduced *circa* 1450, had spread to quite minute craft—indicating a far higher state of development in the pre-Elizabethan merchantman than is often assumed. Details of this rig, which was much simpler than the technicalities of nautical jargon might suggest, can be seen in Plate XXI, where a small merchant-ship,[11] manned by a convivial crew, is shown running before the wind with her mizzen and spritsail furled, and with canvas set only on her fore and main masts.

Size is more difficult. By their owners' estimation, and by official reckoning, most of the Tyneside craft that saw active service during the reign of Henry VIII were between 70 and 160 tons.[12] But these figures need to be treated with a certain amount of caution. Exact measurement was not one of the strong points of an age still happily familiar with giants and fairies, and a vessel's tonnage—which meant her carrying capacity—was held to be simply something to be settled by observation during the early years of her career: " no owner nor master of a ship . . . being newly made . . .", it was deposed in an Admiralty case, " can warrant the same for her burden ".[13] Hence, in the absence of any accepted

[9] *AA4*, xxxviii, 84.
[10] *Calendar of Patent Rolls, 1446-52*, 411.
[11] Not, unfortunately, from Newcastle.
[12] See below, Appendix.
[13] PRO, HCA 13/4, fol. 284v.

formulae, such as we now have, for calculating tonnage, there were frequently discrepancies—often 20 tons or more—between a vessel's actual and alleged lifting power. Furthermore the size of a ship was peculiarly prone to rise or fall according to whether her owner was being threatened with tonnage dues, or whether he was hoping to extract from the crown some allowance based on capacity. Thus Lewis Sotheran's celebrated *Elizabeth*, which can be traced between 1512 and 1514, is variously described as 120 or 130 ton, and her later namesake, that served with Bryan's squadron, as 140 or 160 ton.[14] Nevertheless it is safe to assume that most of the local vessels with which we are concerned were of approximately 100 tons burthen. By modern standards they were, of course, minute[15]—perhaps roughly equivalent to North Sea drifters. But for the period, though small in comparison with Henry's ostentatious and expensive warships, they were of a good average for merchantmen—indeed the *Elizabeth* at 160 ton was said (1544) to be "over chargeable for Calice (Calais) haven by reason of her great burden".[16]

Another obscure matter is the origin of many of these vessels, since notwithstanding the periodic efforts of publicists and statesmen to discover the volume and distribution of the country's tonnage, there was nothing comparable to a register of shipping until 1572. Some Newcastle craft were doubtless locally built, for Tyne shipbuilding has a history reaching back to at least the reign of Edward I. So in 1544 we hear of a vessel "now in making" on the river, together with three more "in making and reparation".[17] Others were purchased, or acquired by less reputable means, either elsewhere on the Coast, or further afield—the *Mary Grace*, for instance, was formerly the *Bark of Sandwich*, whilst in the

[14] *LP*, I (i), no. 1661 (iv); I (ii), no. 2686; XVIII (i), no. 59; XIX (i), no. 140 (vi); *The Hamilton Papers*, ed. J. Bain (2 vols. Edinburgh, 1890-2), I, no. 206.

[15] The argument is not affected by radical changes in methods of measurement since the sixteenth century. We should still credit most Early-Tudor craft with roughly the same tonnage as their owners did.

[16] *LP*, XIX (i), no. 107.

[17] *LP*, XIX, *loc. cit.*

1520's a local merchant, William Brigham, bought a ship in Scotland, for which he then apparently failed to pay, and a decade later another Tynesider, William Carr, was said to have in his possession the *Mary* of Yarmouth, which her owner, William Woodhouse, had previously lost to "wild Scots" off the Shetlands.[18] In passing it should be noticed that such frequent migrations of tonnage, either through the hazards of war, or by normal commercial processes—and the examples cited could easily be multiplied—explain how knowledge of technical developments in, for example, rig and construction, spread more rapidly than is commonly assumed by historians. But this is a matter which cannot be pursued here, and for the moment it must suffice to note that whatever their origin the majority of Newcastle merchantmen were clearly well-built and well-found; the *Elizabeth* was able to survive heavy punishment in 1513,[19] and working lives of 20 years or more were by no mean uncommon.[20]

With ownership we are on firmer ground. As elsewhere this was generally limited to the whole or partial control of one or two vessels, since the risks of heavier investment were, as a rule, too great in an age when the perils of the deep were so plain and legion, and marine insurance comparatively undeveloped. Hence, in 1544, we find some 39 local ships in the hands of almost as many (28) owners.[21] And so too, as in most of maritime Europe, shareholding rather than outright possession was fairly common: in the 1520's Ralph Duxford and his wife were partners in the *Matthew*;[22] 20 years later Sir Francis Leek (or Leake) and Alexander Holmes of Ipswich were joint owners of a Tynemouth privateer;[23] and

[18] *LP*, XVIII (i), no. 75; *Hamilton Papers*, I, no. 287; *LP*, IV (ii), no. 3613; *AA*4, xxxviii, 95n.

[19] *AA*4, xxxviii, 79, 81.

[20] This was not peculiar to Newcastle, *cf*. Oppenheim, 110; R. Davis, "Earnings of Capital in the English Shipping Industry, 1670-1730", *Journal of Economic History*, XVII (1957), 411.

[21] See below, Appendix.

[22] PRO, HCA, 13/2, fols. 251v-2. The exact date is uncertain.

[23] HCA 13/5, Examination 19 July 1547.

in 1559 a valuation of the goods and chattels of that great and powerful oligarch, Henry Anderson, showed that at his death he held three quarters of the *Michael*, three quarters of the *Anthony*, half the *John*, "two parts" of the *Andrew*, one third of the *Barbara*, half the *Christopher*, and half a lighter, besides some smaller craft.[24] But in Early-Tudor Newcastle the shareholder was perhaps a less familiar figure than in most English seaports—or at least according to a return of 1544 which allocates each vessel to a single owner.[25] We cannot, of course, accept this schedule at its face value, and it is possible that it reflects nothing more significant than a clerk's desire to shorten the day's labours by recording only principal partners. On the other hand, however, there can be little doubt that sole ownership,[26] or something approaching it, was widespread in a port, which, as we know from other sources, was at this date the most important and flourishing shipowning centre on the East Coast.[27]

As in other industries the nature of ownership was an agglomeration of anticipations and survivals, ranging from capitalism, in the Marxian sense of the word, as exemplified by the fleets of merchants like Henry Anderson, to truly feudal expressions of aristocratic power, such as the private navies of the Howards and other magnates. In Newcastle, as elsewhere in Europe—and particularly in the coastal trades, where the practice was to last for centuries[28]—one of the commonest forms was for a master to own either the whole, or some part, of his command. Thus the *Elizabeth*, which

[24] *Wills and Inventories Illustrative of the History etc. of the Northern Counties of England*, ed. J. Raine (Surtees Soc. 1835), I, 167-8.

[25] Summarized below, Appendix.

[26] It will be noticed that Henry Anderson was a sole owner in 1544 and a part owner in 1559—though most of his ships had changed since 1544. This does not invalidate the conclusion reached above. It seems very likely that the disorders on the Coast at the end of the reign of Henry VIII had induced even so wealthy a man as Anderson to lessen the risks to his capital by spreading his investment.

[27] London excluded. See my paper "English Merchant Shipping at the End of the Middle Ages", *Economic History Review*, 2nd ser., Vol. XIII (1961), 327-41, especially 338.

[28] See, for instance, any of the autobiographical writings of the late Lord Runciman.

so distinguished herself at Brest in 1513, was owned and commanded by her former master, Lewis Sotheran,[29] and in 1544 perhaps something like a third of the city's shipowners were either seamen or ex-seamen.[30] But the most important figure, as was almost universally the case, was the merchant who had an interest in shipping—the convenience is obvious—and who, with traditional acquisitive zeal often came to dispose of a substantial portion of the tonnage belonging to a port. So of Sherburn and Coo's squadron in 1523 the *Jesus* (160t) and the *Matthew* (100t) both belonged to Edward Baxter, and the *Mary Katherine* (70t) to Thomas Harbottle.[31] Again, of the ships at sea in the 1540's the *Elizabeth* (140/160t) and the *Robert* (80t) were owned by the ubiquitous James Lawson, the *Anthony* (90/100t) and *Michael* (80t) by the equally wealthy and powerful Henry Anderson, the *James* (100t)—presumably identical with the *John of* the same size—by Robert Brandling, and the *Trinity* (120t) by yet another civic grandee, John Sanderson,[32] whilst in 1544 nearly half Newcastle's tonnage (43 per cent at least) was in the hands of six men—Lawsons, Brandlings, Andersons and Bewicks—who dominated the city and much of its growing coal trade.[33]

II.

The hiring or impressment of a vessel for fighting service generally brought alterations in her manning and armament, and perhaps also in her structure. Changes in the latter, it is true, rarely seem to have been of a radical nature, since there were no fundamental differences between merchantmen and

[29] See below, 193-4.
[30] See below, Appendix.
[31] *LP*, III (ii), no. 3493; IV (i), no. 281; *AA4*, xxxviii, 83.
[32] *LP*, XVIII (i), nos. 59, 434, 765; XX (i), no. 321; XX (ii), no. 27 (2). Some details of the careers of these merchants can be found in vol. II of Welford's *History of Newcastle and Gateshead.*
[33] See below, Appendix, Figures for Newcastle's total tonnage in 1544 are in my paper " English Merchant Shipping ".

I

warships, but occasionally there was need for some minor modification to facilitate the carriage of larger complements and greater quantities of stores and equipment. Thus shortly before the *Elizabeth* left the Thames with Howard's squadron in March 1513,[34] her master was allowed 12/8d. for "bords and naylls for the makyng of byskett Romys and bolke heds within the same schipp".[35] The work, to judge from the materials and charges, was nothing elaborate, and probably of only a temporary nature, but there is an interesting implication—if it be assumed that some of the "bolke heds" were to be used to partition off cabins—that hold and 'tweendeck space was for the most part normally undivided. It would also appear that ship's biscuit, destined to ruin the teeth and digestions of generations of long-suffering seamen, was already sufficiently well-established as a staple item of nautical diet as to merit a special, and presumably official, form of stowage.

But more important, there was usually some increase in the armament of craft destined to relieve or reinforce the Fleet.[36] It should, however, be noticed that even in times of comparative peace, and when not in royal pay, trading vessels were frequently well armed, and that like so much else the merchantman powerful enough to fight off a man-of-war was not an invention of the Elizabethans.[37] A letter from Ralph Sadler to Thomas Cromwell, written in 1537, describing conditions in the North in the closing phases of the Pilgrimage of Grace, relates how he found the gate towers of Newcastle defended by "gret peces of ordenaunces, which wold scowre every way a myle, or 2, and more. All which ordenaunce they told me, that every merchaunte, for his parte, brought out of their shippes".[38] Doubtless

[34] *AA*4, xxxviii, 77.
[35] PRO, E 36/vol. 12, 25.
[36] Most merchantmen were usually armed, if only with a few bows and arrows, even in peacetime.
[37] But *cf.* G. S. Laird Clowes, *Sailing Ships* (Science Museum Collection, HMSO, 1932), Part I, 60.
[38] *State Papers During the Reign of Henry VIII* (Record Commission), I, 532.

the excellence of these weapons, like the sterling qualities of their owners, lost nothing in the telling, but Sadler was a knowledgeable man, and in the technical jargon of the time "great" was only applied to the heaviest pieces of artillery.[39] With such an arsenal under their control—like the classic bourgeois of Marxist orthodoxy—little wonder the city fathers could guard their heritage, subdue the lower orders when "disposed to sedicion and rebellyon", and if need be send out fighting ships which must often have been more heavily armed than many Elizabethan privateers.[40] Indeed the results were at times impressive. When ready to join Sir Francis Bryan's squadron in January 1543 Lawson's *Elizabeth* was said to mount "xxxvi shott in a syde, whereof vi brasen peces, two at poupe and two uppon every borde".[41] From this it would seem that she had been converted to a fairly formidable vessel, mounting the remarkably high total of 72 guns. From their numbers alone it is evident that many of these must have been quite small, probably serpentines—light quick-firers[42] apparently intended to pepper an enemy's topsides and prevent her working her big guns—which earlier in the century had figured so largely in the royal ships. But the "brasen peces" and some others were presumably something heavier, and in professional eyes she was "well ordenaunced". The evidence for the *James* on the same occasion is more specific. She was said to have "foure good port peces and a fawcon of brasse, vi dowble serpentynes uppon wheles, iii single serpentynes and one dozen hakebushes". Her armament—sizeable though not particularly heavy—thus falls into the normal contemporary pattern of "short" guns (heavy-shotted weapons like the port-piece), which, in the expressive phrase, "shook" an opponent, and

[39] L. G. Carr Laughton, "Early Tudor Ship-Guns", *Mariner's Mirror*, XLVI (1960), 242-285, especially 259.

[40] *English Privateering Voyages to the West Indies, 1588-95*, ed. K. R. Andrews, Hakluyt Soc. 2nd ser. CXI (1959), 17, gives some comparative material.

[41] *Hamilton Papers*, I, no. 287.

[42] Relatively speaking.

"long" guns (falcons, serpentines, etc.) whose shot, even if light, "pierced" him. Early naval ordnance is a difficult and obscure subject, but it is known that the port-piece,[43] which first appears towards the beginning of Henry's reign, was a breech-loader of anything from 5½ to 12 inches in calibre—at the latter size it ranked amongst the "greatest" of guns—firing a stone ball which in the less ambitious weapons may have weighed roughly 15 lb. The wheeled serpentine,[44] likewise a breech-loader, could also be a piece of some size, weighing at least 10 cwt. and throwing a 6 lb. lead or 4 lb. iron shot, but the serpentine itself was much smaller, perhaps, like the falcon, only about 2½ cwt. in weight, and firing a 1½ lb. lead shot. The harquebus,[45] an old weapon modified in the early years of Henry's reign, was smaller again, with even the larger pieces merely using lead "pellets" of something like ½ lb. each.

It must not, of course, be assumed that either the *Elizabeth* or the *James* mustered the fire-power of a large man-of-war in full commission.[46] Nevertheless it is particularly worthy of note that at a time of great experiment and development in naval ordnance an area usually regarded as one of the remotest in the kingdom could provide some of its ships with substantial and balanced armaments,[47] including weapons which, if not perhaps of the very latest, were at least of comparatively recent design. Thus the *Elizabeth* was carrying six brass guns. These, we may take it, were

[43] Probably so called since they were mounted in ports on the orlop (*i.e.* the lower deck according to contemporaries).

[44] If this is what we really have here. The double serpentine of *c.* 1515 was perhaps more usually an iron gun weighing at least 5 cwt. and firing a 3 lb. shot, but it was never apparently fitted with wheels. The wheeled serpentine, however, should be a brass gun.

[45] Also a breech-loader, and known in some form as early as 1485.

[46] For details of the size and weight of the armaments of contemporary English warships, and for a discussion of the weapons mentioned above, see Carr Laughton, "Early Tudor Ship-Guns", and Laird Clowes, *Sailing Ships.* The weights of the pieces given above are those known for the early part of Henry's reign from the researches of Carr Laughton. It is possible that some guns had increased in weight and size by the 1540's.

[47] *I.e.* having, as was the tendency of the period, a good percentage of heavy pieces.

I

muzzle-loaders, cast in one piece and then bored—a type which, during the latter part of Henry's reign, was replacing the much feebler "built-up" breech-loading weapons made from wrought-iron bars.[48] True we have no mention of the "very perfect" artillery of the 1540's—cannons, sakers etc. —but these may merely be lost in the generic "brasen peces". Again, though the *James*, like many royal ships of this transitional period, mounted some old-fashioned ordnance—serpentines for instance—the rest of her complement was quite respectable. The port-piece was a cast weapon,[49] introduced about 1515 and developed, it would seem, to replace the old "built-up" stone gun, whilst the smaller harquebus may also have been "new devised" at roughly the same date.

But not all the armament for hired or impressed merchantmen was raised privately. Some came from either the arsenals of Newcastle and Berwick, or even from London —in which case, in view of other and more powerful claims, it was, like Petruchio's sword, not always the best available. Thus in 1543 the *Trinity Sanderson* and *Mary Grace* were to be furnished with guns from Berwick, whilst others of Bryan's squadron were to have bows, arrows, bills and pikes from the keepers of the "kinges ordenaunce" in Newcastle.[50]

The mention of these venerable weapons is indeed a reminder that with guns for the most part severely limited in range and power—effective range at sea in the early sixteenth century was perhaps something like 100 yards—naval war was still, as in the Middle Ages, essentially a matter of close fighting and boarding, with archers sweeping an enemy's decks from the tops and rigging,[51] and boarders repelled at

[48] The bars were welded together longitudinally so as to form a tube, which was further strengthened by having a large number of thick iron hoops shrunk over it.

[49] Apparently of iron. The older falcon and wheeled serpentine were also cast guns, though of brass.

[50] *LP*, XVII, no. 946; *Hamilton Papers*, I, no. 287; *LP*, XVIII (i), no. 88.

[51] Archers were still used at sea in Drake's time.

I

the push of the pike by infantrymen.[52] Hence in 1512, when three Newcastle ships were fitting out, the "Maire and the Comonialte" spent the considerable sum of £35 on 200 sheaves of arrows and 150 bows, and a further £15 on 200 spears and morris pikes, and in 1543 four of Bryan's vessels were issued with 100 bows, 100 sheaves of arrows, 80 bills and 60 morris pikes between them.[53]

III.

Ships commissioned for royal service, particularly during the early years of Henry's reign, were usually, though not invariably, taken out of the hands of their owners and put under the command of captains[54] appointed by the crown. These were frequently gentlemen from the royal entourage with varying degrees of military, diplomatic and administrative experience, many of whom became in effect professional naval officers, almost continually employed in the Service either ashore or afloat. A number, perhaps the ablest—or simply the best connected—rose to command flotillas and fleets, and all moved indiscriminately, and without any apparent loss of status, between royal and hired vessels.[55]

Thus of those who served in, or with, craft from Newcastle William Cook, who commanded the *Jesus* in Sir Henry Sherburn's squadron in 1523, was probably from the household of Katherine of Aragon, and had been in the royal ships *Sweepstake* and *Swallow* in 1512-14.[56] Sherburn himself was

[52] *Cf. AA*4, xxxviii, 79. Complements, or perhaps fighting men alone, were also issued with protective "jackets". 200 of these cost £20 in 1512 (PRO E 101/62/23).

[53] E 101/62/23; *Hamilton Papers*, I, no. 287.

[54] At this date a captain was not necessarily a seaman. He had a general control over his ship, but she was sailed by a professional master. But captains —even aristocratic ones—who were seamen were not unknown.

[55] *Cf.* Oppenheim, 64, 77-8.

[56] *LP*, I (ii), nos. 1852, 2686; *LP*, I, nos. 3591, 4377; see also *AA*4, xxxviii, 83.

of the king's household—a " spear of honour " well endowed with sinecures, and of sufficient standing to be found playing " shoffulborde " in the Queen's chamber in 1519.[57] He was at sea in the *Great Bark* in 1512, held a number of naval commands in 1513-14, and was eventually killed in action in 1523.[58] John Cary, Vice-Admiral in the North in 1542, was another gentleman of the household with nautical experience, commanding the *Katherine Galley* as early as 1522, and later appearing as a captain under Vice-Admiral Sir Rice Maunsell.[59] His successor, Sir Francis Bryan—of somewhat unsavoury reputation—was a major figure of Henrician politics, and a man whose many talents and widely varied employments foreshadow in detail the familiar accomplishments of the Elizabethan courtier. Poet, scholar, soldier and diplomat, he was a gentleman of the Privy Chamber, Master of the Toils, and Chief Butler of England. He was in the *Margaret Bonaventure* in 1513, and again at sea ten years later, whilst in 1543, " experienced in sea matters ", he was one of Henry's ambassadors to the emperor Charles V at a time when a " great enterprise " against the French herring fishery was under discussion.[60]

But not all commanders were courtiers, even before the later years of Henry's reign when demand exceeded supply to the extent that " serving men " (*i.e.* household retainers) and " yeomen " were given ships, and some of the ablest captains and admirals—the real forerunners of Drake, usually forgotten in discussions of the evolution of the sea-officer—were merchants or shipowners (or both) who spent much of their lives in arduous and often distinguished naval service. The energetic and successful Christopher Coo, for instance,

[57] *LP*, II (ii), p. 1460; *LP*, III (i), p. 51; III (ii), no. 2297 (16).

[58] At which time it should be noticed his son was commanding the *Katherine* of Newcastle. For the career of Sherburn himself see *LP*, I, no. 3591; I (ii), nos. 2686, 2842, 2946; Spont, 203-4; *AA4*, xxxviii, 83-4.

[59] *LP*, III (ii), no. 2296; XVII, no. 895; XVIII (i), no. 701; *AA4*, xxxviii, 85.

[60] *LP*, I, no. 3980; II (ii), p. 1480; III (ii), nos. 3237, 3281; XVIII (i), no. 19; XVIII (ii), nos. 253, 305; *Dictionary of National Biography, sub nomine*.

I

who succeeded Sherburn in 1523, was apparently an East Anglian owner and merchant with court and city connections, who had served previous commissions (1513-22) in the *John Baptist*, the *Charity*, the *Lizard* and the *Margaret Bonaventure.* In later life, when clearly a man of wealth and standing, he was employed by Wolsey in some commercial matter, and in 1526 "Cristofer Coo esquyer and oon of the Kynges Capteynes late of the narrow see" was regarded by the Company of the Merchant Adventurers of England as one whose goodwill was well worth having.[61]

Another East Anglian of similar character was William Woodhouse,[62] who replaced Bryan in 1543 with his flag in the *Trinity* of Newcastle. His initial interests appear to have been in shipowning, if he may be identified, as seems highly probable, with that William Woodhouse who, together with his ship, was captured by "wild Scots" in the early 1530's.[63] How and why he transferred to the royal service are unknown, but as a sailor he displayed a dash and zest for hard fighting worthy of the great days of the Elizabethan Navy. When in *Sweepstake* on the East Coast in 1543 he cut away his boat—with seven men in her—for the "more spedye folowing in the chace", and we hear of him in "earnest suit" of his prey. He was commander of the projected attack on the French herring fisheries in the same year, and in 1544 again had charge of a flotilla operating against the Scots. Greater distinctions were to come: he was Clinton's Vice-Admiral in the northern war of 1547, and in 1552 he succeeded another old Henrician sailor, Sir Thomas Clere, as Lieutenant of the Admiralty.[64]

[61] *LP*, I, no. 3980; I (ii), no. 2686; II (i), nos. 68, 287; III (i), no. 575; III (ii), nos. 2480, 2486; IV (ii), nos. 3543, 3744; HCA 13/3, fols. 107v-110v; *Acts of Court of the Mercers' Company, 1453-1527*, ed. L. Lyell and F. D. Watney (Cambridge, 1936), 721-2.

[62] Described in 1543 as "gentleman".

[63] Above, 183. At the time of her capture Woodhouse was owner of half the ship. His partner subsequently gave him the other half and left him to try to recover her.

[64] *Hamilton Papers*, I, no. 456; *LP*, XVIII (ii), nos. 63, 70, 348; XIX (i), no. 432; Oppenheim, 85, 104.

On occasions a shipowner with seagoing experience might sail as captain of one of his own vessels. The point is worth emphasizing since it has recently been argued that under the Early Tudors, as in the Middle Ages, it was particularly difficult for professional seamen to "acquire experience in war-leadership".[65] Yet from Newcastle we have Lewis Sotheran—"good Lewes"—who commanded the *Elizabeth* (his own ship) from 1512-14, and greatly distinguished himself at Brest.[66] The details of his biography are worth examining at some length since they throw a valuable light in that relatively obscure class which owned and controlled merchantmen at the end of the Middle Ages. Apparently of Tyneside yeoman stock—the name was common locally—he was probably apprenticed as a mariner in Newcastle, and in 1489, when perhaps in his mid-thirties, appears in command of the *Mary Harden.*[67] Between 1489 and 1507 he made a number of trips to the Low Countries and Northern France as master of various local ships—the *Mary Harden*, the *James*, the *Trinity* and the *Elizabeth*—whilst at the same time, as was quite common, he was himself trading in wool. hides and wine, both in his own commands and in other vessels. He became a freeman of the Newcastle Boothmen in the 1490's—agreeing with them, as he put it in 1515, "for occupying the craft of selling corn"—and by 1510 he was of sufficient standing to join the select company that supplied the monastery of Durham with wine.[68] His period of naval service coincided with, and was perhaps financially conducive to, the climax of his fortunes. He had probably

[65] Michael Lewis, *The History of the British Navy* (London, 1957), 48-9.

[66] *AA*4, xxxviii, 77-82.

[67] Such details of his career as we have come from depositions in a *cause célèbre* of 1515 published in F. W. Dendy, "The Struggle between the Merchant and Craft Guilds in Newcastle in 1515" (*AA*3, vii (1911), 77-101). In these Sotheran's age is given on one occasion as 62 and in another as 50 in 1515. He describes himself as a freeman of the Mariners Company, and tells how he fined with the Boothmen (98-9). He can be found in command of various local ships in Exch. K. R. Customs Accounts for Newcastle, *passim*.

[68] *Et in ii doliis et i pipa vini Rubei emptis de Lodowico Sotheron* (Dean and Chapter of Durham muniments, Bursar's Account 1510-11), and in the account for 1514-15 we find him supplying Spanish iron.

I

acquired the *Elizabeth* by 1512, and the *Trinity* by 1513—both former commands in which he may have already had shares. He took an apprentice—Thomas Boland—in 1513, and by this time he was clearly able to leave his affairs in competent hands, for the value of his foreign trade made an impressive leap whilst he was with the Fleet, reaching something like £60 in 1512-13, as compared with a mere £15 in 1499-1500.[69]

Some further details of officering may be briefly mentioned. Complements were in general greatly increased for a royal commission. Thus a surgeon was carried in the *Elizabeth* in 1514—perhaps a doubtful asset given the methods of sixteenth-century medicine—and another in the *Matthew* in 1523, in both cases, it may be noticed, some months after the ships had been involved in heavy fighting.[70] And again payments to the *Elizabeth* in 1513 show that she had on board a remarkable weight of what might loosely be termed officers and petty officers; a captain, a master, a master's mate, four quarter masters, two quarter master's mates, a bosun, a bosun's mate, a steward, a cook, a purser, a carpenter, a master gunner and a gunner's mate. Only a cooper, a steward's mate and a chaplain—a suggestive combination—are in fact lacking to bring her up to the strength soon to be found in large English merchantmen sailing on extended voyages of trade or discovery.[71]

Similarly, on a normal commercial run an East-Coast ship of between 80 and 100 ton might employ, as was indeed

[69] Sotheran was associated with the *Trinity* from about 1500, and she appears to have come into his hands early in 1513 when her name changes to *Trinity Lewes*, and Sotheran becomes her principal freighter (PRO, E 122/109/1). He is first described as owner of the *Elizabeth* in naval accounts for 1514 (*LP*, I (ii), no. 2923), but it is very likely that he was already in possession of her when she entered service in 1512. The progression from master to owner was common at the time. For Sotheran's apprentice see *Extracts from the Records of the Merchant Adventurers of Newcastle-upon-Tyne*, ed. F. W. Dendy (Surtees Soc. 1899), II, 186. For his commercial activity see PRO, E 122/108/4 and 109/1 *passim*.

[70] *LP*, I (ii), no. 3501; IV (i), no. 281.

[71] PRO, E 101/61/12, fols. 4v-5; E 315/315, fol. 9, and *cf.* J. A. Williamson, *Maritime Enterprise, 1485-1558* (Oxford, 1913), 363-4. Quarter master's mates are not mentioned as usual in Williamson, *loc. cit.*

quite general, as few as 10 or 12 hands.[72] But with naval service there came the liberal manning standards of privateers and men-of-war. Thus in 1512, whilst working as a victualler, the *Elizabeth* (120/130t) carried only 40 seamen—including, presumably, officers—but when she was rated a fighting ship her total complement was never less than 100, and on one occasion it rose to 74 mariners, six gunners, a "captain's retinue" of 50 (*i.e.* soldiers), a master and a captain.[73] If we assume that the number of her officers and petty officers remained constant at 17 during this commission, this means that she had on board the astonishing figure of anything from 83 to 115 ratings (*i.e.* seamen and soldiers). Other evidence is less rewarding, but we know that in 1512 the *Trinity* (90t) was carrying 84 men, eight boys and four gunners, whilst in January 1543 the *Elizabeth* (140/160t) was to be manned by 50 seamen and carpenters, 40 soldiers and 20 gunners, and the *James* (100t), *Anthony* (90/100t) and *John Evangelist* (90/100t), by 30 seamen and carpenters, 20 soldiers and 10 gunners each[74]—little wonder that with such complements and their paraphernalia and stores crowded into such ships, cruises were so limited in range and duration, and the rate of sickness so appallingly high. It would be tedious to extend this list further, but at least it may be observed that in armed merchantmen, as in warships, gunners came to occupy a more prominent position during the course of Henry's reign, reflecting something of the changing character of war at sea—thus the difference between the *Elizabeth* of 1513 with six, and her namesake of 1543 with 20, and between the *James*, *Anthony* and *John Evangelist* with 10 each in 1543, and the *Trinity* with only four in 1512.[75]

Crews were usually provided from such seamen as were locally available at the place of hiring or impressment, and

[72] PRO, HCA 13/3 fols. 107v-110v.
[73] PRO, E 101/62/15; E 315/315, fol. 9; *LP*, I (ii), no. 3148 (ii).
[74] E 101/62/23; *LP*, XVIII (i), no. 59.
[75] *Cf.* Oppenheim, 54-5.

I

there is some evidence that, as might be expected, men were not invariably willing to serve. A curious entry in the Newcastle Trinity House accounts of "expenses in the chamber when the mariner was prest to go in the *Elizabeth*" seems to indicate some difficulties of an intriguing nature.[76] But there were alternative sources; Woodhouse's instructions of 1543, for instance, empowered him to take hands from enemy ships to be used "as drudges" in his own;[77] and when there was a shortage of mariners landsmen appear to have been pressed to supply the deficiency. This must, indeed, have been a fairly frequent occurrence in times of heavy demand, when not only were there local craft to be manned, but the needs of the Fleet to be met as well—we know, for example, that in 1514 the complement of the royal ship, *Lizard*, was made up of an assortment of contingents from (amongst other places) Beaumaris, Plymouth, Hull and Tynemouth.[78] The use of what might be described as unskilled labour was not perhaps so disadvantageous as might at first appear, since in general crews were apparently required not only to work their ships, but also to assist in fighting them.[79] This at least would seem to be the inference to be drawn from the ratio of armaments to men carried—so from Newcastle in 1543 the *Elizabeth* had only 20 gunners for 72 pieces of ordnance, and the *James* 10 for 26.[80] An able-bodied man, therefore, would clearly be something of an asset to a commander quite irrespective of whether or not he had ever been to sea before.

But the main brunt of any fighting was—or, more accurately, should have been—borne, as had been the case for centuries, by the body of troops embarked in each armed ship.[81] The recruitment of these, variously described in

[76] Welford, *Newcastle and Gateshead*, II, 212. For evidence of local manning see *LP*, XIX (i), no. 107; XX (i), no. 321.

[77] *LP*, XVIII (i), no. 225; *AA*4, xxxviii, 89-90.

[78] *LP*, I (ii), no. 3137 (16).

[79] *Cf. LP*, XX (i), no. 321; Oppenheim, 56-7.

[80] Above, 187, 195.

[81] *Cf.* above, 195. Soldiers were also carried at times in vessels not in royal service.

musters as "soldiers" or "the captain's retinue" is, like so much else, somewhat obscure. Some, possibly even the majority[82]—though this would need further investigation—were raised as bands of indentured retainers, just as for military service, under a system of great antiquity. The captain would enter into a formal agreement (the indenture) with those willing or—a different matter—persuaded to serve, and then petition the Lord Chancellor or Keeper of the Privy Seal for letters of protection in their favour.[83] Thus when a commander joined his ship he was accompanied by a ready-formed fighting force which frequently had no territorial connection with the vessel in which it was to serve. This was equally true of other ways of supplying troops. The retinues of great magnates, such as the Howards for example, would spread into ships with which the family had otherwise no association, whilst vessels in commission might be brought up to strength by drafting into them such companies as were available in the area in which they were operating. Thus it seems that in 1513 the *Elizabeth* of Newcastle was to have been reinforced by a contingent of Devon men, and in 1543 the Warden of the Marches proposed to furnish the royal ships in the North with archers drawn from the garrison of Holy Island.[84]

IV.

Finally some points of naval administration are worth brief notice. At the opening of Henry's reign the methods and machinery for the hiring or impressment of vessels were essentially—in as far as it is safe to generalize on the limited evidence under review—those of the Middle Ages. Letters "plackardes" (*i.e.* documents under seal) would be issued to

[82] This is probably truer of the earlier part of Henry's reign than the 1540's.
[83] *LP* IV (i), no. 293, and *cf. LP* III (ii), no. 2807 (21).
[84] *AA*4, xxxviii, 81; *LP*, XVIII (i), no. 88.

individuals empowering them to take ships—presumably of a specified tonnage and within a given area. These commissioners would then negotiate with, for instance, local authorities, and their labours might result, as at Newcastle in 1513, in indentures between the royal and civic officials on the one hand, and shipowners and shipmasters on the other, stating the financial arrangements for fitting out, and giving a rendezvous for the craft taken up.[85] But it is an interesting reflection on the nature of Tudor government—and hence perhaps some of the persistent popular legends of the *bonhomie* of bluff king Hal—that by the 1540's the whole procedure had in general become much more flexible and informal, with orders frequently given in personal letters—in "state papers" that is—addressed to either the communities concerned, or to important royal officers serving in the area.[86] So, for example, in February 1545, the Privy Council wrote to the Earl of Shrewsbury, the king's Lieutenant in the North, informing him that the citizens of Hull had "set forth" six ships at their own cost, and directing him "to travail earnestly that those of Newcastell may do the semblable".[87] But as difficulties and demands increased in the latter part of Henry's reign, and notwithstanding the presence on the Border of men of the calibre of Hertford or Shrewsbury, there was often much "earnest writing" and "furnishing" before anything was accomplished, and the Newcastle city fathers, after consultations with "owners and masters" and "the most honest inhabitants" were at times quite capable of refusing even the most pressing royal demands.[88]

The supreme government of the Navy was, of course, in the hands of the King and his Council, and where, as with Henry VIII, the sovereign had a real interest in the sea, and his administrators—if this is an adequate word—were as

[85] *LP*, I (ii), no. 1982, i, ii. (This refers to transports.)
[86] Or their deputies. For the change from the formal document under seal to the personal letter, see G. R. Elton, *The Tudor Revolution in Government* (Cambridge, 1953), 276, 298.
[87] *LP*, XX (i), no. 243.
[88] *Cf. AA4*, xxxviii, 95-7.

indefatigable as Wolsey, their concern could extend to minute detail. A list of royal and hired shipping, for instance, of 1512, in which the *Elizabeth* of Newcastle appears as a victualler to the *Less Carrick*, shows correction in the king's own hand, and a similar document of the following year, in which the *Elizabeth* is attached to the *Katherine Fortaleza*, has been closely checked by Wolsey, who has altered the names of the captains and allocated all the gunners.[89]

Operations at sea were handled in similar fashion, and were indeed conducted in an atmosphere of stifling supervision—a situation commonly (and wrongly) assumed to be peculiar to an age in which wireless has put shore-based Admiralties in easy contact with their fleets. As already noticed Vice-Admirals were appointed to squadrons in the North Sea on a number of occasions.[90] The powers enjoyed by these officers are not always easy to define, though they were clearly limited. True they exercised a general, and not always popular, authority over their ships—in October 1542 Cary was obliged to order "all his men to eat and drink but only two times in the day, which hath not been accustomed to mariners"[91]—and they had some responsibility for, and control over, the payment and victualling of their flotillas. They were also apparently answerable for the proper handling of prizes, and there is some evidence that after consultation with their captains they might advise the crown on suitable courses of action within their theatres. But—and as with every other aspect of Henry's reign—there was never any doubt as to the fullness and supremacy of the royal authority, and a commander at sea was left with remarkably little scope for initiative. Thus his fighting instructions, which were fairly comprehensive—indicating his duties and his station, and including perhaps some strategic and tactical directions—were supplemented at frequent intervals by a

[89] *LP*, I, nos. 3591, 3977.
[90] *AA*4, xxxviii, 83, 85, 87, 89.
[91] *LP*, XVII, no. 946.

deluge of detailed orders despatched through a variety of channels ranging from the captains of individual vessels to such magnates as the Warden of the Marches or the King's Lieutenant in the North.[92] And to ensure compliance Admirals were required to report continually—or, in the more pleasing language of the time, to "advertyse the kinges majestie"[93]—and fleets were kept under the closest observation, even to the extent of the Privy Council ordering a search to be made "along the coast" on one occasion to see where a squadron had got to[94]—all of which was quite practicable, of course, in the days before blue-water navies, when almost all operations took place within a few miles of the shore.

V.

In a port which owned at the most something like 50 sea-going ships the hiring or impressment for war service of as few as six or so in a year—as was commonly the case in Newcastle between 1509 and 1547—entailed a disruption of commerce far more serious than these quite modest figures alone would suggest.[95] Vessels taken up were usually, and naturally, the largest and the most powerful available. For these shippers might well have difficulty in finding adequate substitutes. Not all other locally registered craft—if such a term may be used in this loose anachronistic way—worked consistently from their home port, and of those that did some would be away, or refitting, or under repair,[96] whilst foreign bottoms were debarred from certain trades by navigation

[92] *LP*, I, no. 4682 (i); XVII, nos. 851, 1083; XVIII (i), nos. 19, 108, 127; *Hamilton Papers*, I, no. 288.

[93] *Cf. Hamilton Papers*, I, no. 287.

[94] *LP*, XVII, no. 899.

[95] The total number of ships owned in Newcastle seems to have moved from about 30 in 1500 to about 60 in 1550. Details are in my paper "English Merchant Shipping", and see also below, Appendix.

[96] In February 1544 of 11 ships in Newcastle one was building and three others "in making and reparation" (*LP*, XIX (i), no. 107).

laws. Then again, to satisfy the demands of men-of-war and armed merchantmen crews were taken in such numbers, and detained in remote places for such unpredictable periods, as to leave sufficient labour to man only a few of the remaining ships.

But despite these and other hazards—delays, arrests, losses—war was never unmitigated disaster. Many ship-owners were merchants, and as such found lucrative opportunities to victual armies and fleets—and like as not the enemy as well at times[97]—or to supply equipment or timely assistance to hard-pressed commanders. So in 1513 William Brigham was amongst those who furnished Surrey's troops in the North with grain. Almost twenty years later we find "Branlyng of Newcastle"[98] providing large quantities of coal for Calais and Guisnes—with allegations of non-delivery on one occasion when there is reference to an advance of £200, whilst in 1544 Henry Anderson was paid some £28 odd "for money laid out in helping the King's ship *Swepstake*, and in making bridges and slings for the King's horses".[99] And then again if the rates of ship hire were not particularly attractive[100] there was always the chance of prize, or at least of some pleasing bargain in that brisk Tyneside market in the hauls of pirates and privateers. Thus there is mention in 1548 of an East Anglian "adventurer" who knew the North-East well from his more reputable days as a skipper in the coal trade, who "hathe cummen many tymes to New Castell with dyvers pryses", and there disposed of some of their cargoes—grain, meal, saltfish and salmon,[101] whilst on a grander scale it is known that Christopher Coo, for example,

[97] *Cf. LP,* III (ii), no. 3173.

[98] Robert Brandling, surely, and not Henry, as indexed in *LP*.

[99] *LP*, XVI, nos. 286, 918; XVII, no. 1188; XIX (i), no. 476 (2). For the grounding of the *Sweepstake* see *AA*4, xxxviii, 92.

[100] Between 1513 and 1524 the rate was one shilling per ton per month.

[101] PRO, HCA I/34, fols. 164v-6. It was apparently common for seamen who turned to piracy or privateering to dispose of their prizes in areas where they were already known through ordinary commercial contacts—South-coast fishermen, for instance, who in the ordinary course of events often worked in the North Sea, used the Yorkshire coast to sell off the spoils of "venturing" when war brought wider opportunities.

I

took goods and shipping valued at over £1,200 in two years, and according to the King himself even greater sums were easy to come by.[102] But quite apart from this impressive array of windfalls it might be suggested that till at least the late 1540's shipowning, despite the attendant risks, was a more attractive field of investment for Newcastle capital than the coal of Durham and Northumberland.

Some wider implications remain. Against the background of European naval and maritime activity in the greatest age of discovery the campaigns of the Early Tudors, and especially those in northern waters in which Newcastle shipping so largely figured, can easily be overlooked. True the operations with which we have been concerned were a far cry from war at sea as it was to be understood in the next three centuries, but they were by no means without significance. It cannot, of course, be claimed that they were in any sense decisive, though in the general context of Henry VIII's Scottish policy this was scarcely to be expected. It is, moreover, impossible to assess, in the absence of adequate evidence, the effects on Scotland of a blockade which through stress of weather and indifferent intelligence was never more than intermittent. It can scarcely have imposed any widespread hardship on a primitive and largely self-supporting society, but on the other hand, and for the same reasons, even isolated captures of arms and shipping must have affected the prosperity of Scottish merchants and the effectiveness of Stuart armies. Nor should other indications of the value of sea-power be forgotten; that on two occasions at least important reinforcements were deflected from the East Coast, and that in 1544 Hertford's troops were able to land at will in the Forth.[103]

Furthermore there are clear indications that from roughly the beginning of the reign of Henry VIII some English commanders had a broader view of strategy than that preoccupation with the transport and supply of armies, or the

[102] *LP*, IV (i), no. 83; XIX (ii), no. 560.
[103] *AA*4, xxxviii, 84, 92.

interception of enemies already at sea with which the period is usually credited, and that there was a growing appreciation that the Navy had a more continuous purpose than mere attack or defence in fleets.[104] Squadrons—on many occasions formed largely or wholly from hired or impressed merchantmen—were employed in duties ranging from the bombardment of hostile ports to commerce raiding and blockade, and contrary to common assumption, were quite capable of keeping the seas throughout the winter.[105] Insufficient vessels and inadequate communications often destroyed comparatively unambitious plans, and commanders afloat were harassed by minute supervision and crippled by primitive arrangements for supply. Yet even so men such as Coo and Woodhouse were surprisingly successful,[106] and their actions, like those of Sir Edward Howard at Brest, were marked by a boldness and zest for hard fighting which anticipate the great days of the Elizabethan Navy.[107] This was not peculiar to the East Coast, or indeed to any of the other regions which in medieval fashion provided contingents for the Fleet, nor were these the acts of inexperienced amateurs. Rather they were the outcome of a long tradition of war and trade by sea which cannot be omitted from any proper assessment of subsequent maritime achievement.[108]

[104] Thus C. S. Goldingham, "The Development of Tactics in the Tudor Navy" (*United Services Magazine*, LVII (1918)), writes that "in the time of Henry VIII ships were simply a means of bringing two opposing bodies of soldiers into contact" (211), and see also Fisher, 176-7 and Sir Herbert Richmond, *Statesmen and Sea Power* (Oxford, 1946), 2-3, but *cf.* Oppenheim, 68.

[105] John Cary was at sea in October-November 1542 (*AA*4, xxxviii, 85-6); Sir Francis Bryan in February 1543 (*ib.*, 88-9); William Woodhouse in February or early March-June 1543 (*ib.* 89, 91). In April 1544 we hear that Woodhouse kept the seas in the North notwithstanding "the stormes here" (*Hamilton Papers*, II, no. 228). It was the expensive and unseaworthy "great" ships of Henry's Navy that were laid up once the short summer campaigning season was over.

[106] Some contemporaries took a lower view of Coo (*LP*, III (ii), no. 2374) though with little justification it would seem, and *cf.* above, 191-2.

[107] For Howard see *AA*4, xxxviii, 78-9.

[108] The early evidence is overlooked by Professor G. S. Graham in his *Empire of the North Atlantic* (Toronto, 1950), ix, 15.

I

APPENDIX.

Newcastle Ships in 1544.[1]

	Tonnage	Owner
John	100	The Mayor (Robert Brandling)[2]
Elizabeth	160	James Lawson[2]
Robert	80	,, ,,
James	100	Henry Anderson[2]
Anthony	90	,, ,,
John	80	,, ,,
Mary Anne	72	,, ,,
Mary Katherine	60	,, ,,
A new ship on the stocks		,, ,,
Trinity	120	John Sanderson[2]
George	100	Andrew Bewick[2]
Jesus	64	,, ,,
John	52	,, ,,
Martin	80	John Hylton[2]
John	52	,, ,,
Bark	100	,, ,,
Mary	48	Bertram Anderson[2]
Mary Fortune	56	George Davell[2]
Mary Grace	80	William Carr (?)[3]
Jesus	96	Roger Mitford[2]
Martin	72	Bartholomew Bee[2]
Mary Katherine	80	Cuthbert Ellison[2]
John Evangelist	100	Robert Thomson[3]
James	90	Edward Penreth (?)[2]
Anne	80	,, ,,
Cuthbert	72	Thomas Scott (?)[2]
James	88	John Todd[2]
George	72	Robert Hoppen[2]
Christopher	68	James Anderson[3]
Mary Gallant	60	Roger Haton (?)[3]
Christopher	56	Thomas Bell (?)[3]
George	72	William Temple[3]
Little Katherine	48	Thomas Shaldforth (?)[3]
Trinity	48	Richard Harrison (?)[3]
James	44	James Arnold[3]
Nicholas	44	Robert Binks (?)[3]
Hoy Bark	80	Francis Anderson[2]
A ship	60	Robert Lisle[3]

	Tonnage	Owner
Trinity	56	Bertram Orde[2]
*Martin**	65	(?)
*Peter**	30	(?)
*Anne**	40	(?)
*Michael**	70	(?) Henry Anderson[4]
*James**	10	(?)

[1] Names of ships and owners have been modernized. There are two good and fairly complete lists of Newcastle shipping in 1544, only one of which, however, gives owners' names. This is used here, with the original order retained, from PRO SP I/183, fol. 114, with additions (marked *) from the other list which can be found in *LP*, XIX (i), no. 140 (6). This conflation gives 43 ships afloat with a total tonnage of 3,095t. If *LP*, XIX (i), no. 140 (6) is used as a basis and amplified from SP I/183 slight variations in the size of individual craft give us a total of 43 ships of 3,020t. This latter figure I have used in my "English Merchant Shipping". There are also some figures, with slight variants, in *Hamilton Papers*, II, no. 185. None of these statistics are impeccable.

[2] Merchant.

[3] Seaman or ex-seaman.

[4] Probably the *Michael* of Henry Anderson, given elsewhere as 80t, see above, 185. She is also very likely his "new ship" previously said to be "on the stocks".

II

SHIPOWNING IN ENGLAND
c. 1450–1550[1]

IT is a singular paradox that one of the world's leading maritime powers should have virtually ignored the history of its merchant service. Yet such has been the case in England—inevitably, perhaps, in view of the spectacular course of naval and imperial achievement—and this notwithstanding the labours of a host of publicists to demonstrate the importance of the country's shipping as 'a principal means to advance [its] honour, strength, safety and profit'.

Decades of neglect cannot be repaired in an hour, and our purpose here is much less ambitious: to examine the nature and significance of shipowning in England during that heroic century of European maritime endeavour which opened about 1450. True, the initial English contribution to discovery was negligible. Moreover, to set against the feats of Diaz, Columbus, Magellan and a score of less familiar but no less illustrious names, we have early-Tudor complaints as to the decline of native shipping in the face of foreign competition, and the reiterated concern of legislators at its 'marvellous decay' and 'great minishing', whilst the historian of Elizabethan navigation has recently denied its suitability in mid-sixteenth century 'for ocean passages on a commercial scale'.[2]

But this is by no means the whole picture. That early English oceanic enterprise lacked the distinction of that of the Iberian kingdoms is no argument that the country, any more than northern Europe's greatest carriers, the Hanse and the Netherlands, equally insignificant in such ventures, was negligible at sea. On the contrary, the boom in English overseas trade of the

[1] I am much indebted to my wife for her help and criticism in the preparation of this paper. Unless otherwise stated, documents cited are in the Public Record Office, London.

[2] D. W. Waters, *The Art of Navigation in England in Elizabethan and Early Stuart Times* (London, 1958), p. 496.

early sixteenth century brought a substantial rise, though to nothing like Dutch or Hanseatic levels, in the volume and activity of native shipping compared with the bleak years of the 1450's and sixties, and by 1551 a Venetian report could describe the kingdom as 'very powerful at sea'.[1] More than this, the century after 1450 witnessed not only the *panache* of Warwick the king-maker's piracies—to mention merely the most flagrant and familiar—and his bold if irresponsible handling of seapower, but also, and far more important, English penetration of the Mediterranean and the waters of the New World. It saw too the first appearance of names—Gonson, Hawkins, Howard, Raleigh—inseparably associated with the glories of the ensuing age; and, fostered by the opportunities of a generation of disorders, the emergence of that originality and confidence, that dexterous ship-handling and zest for hard fighting, which more than anything ensured the superb achievement of Elizabeth's seamen.[2] Significantly enough it was a Howard, an ex-Lord Admiral, who in 1535, displaying the might and pride of the Tudor Navy to the imperial ambassador, boasted, in striking anticipation of Shakespeare, of his country's ability to 'fight the whole world'.[3]

Nor, indeed, should it be assumed that English merchantmen were inferior to those of other states. That native shipbuilders developed no distinctive types makes them no worse than their contemporaries in Spain, and that some of their craft should prove unseaworthy—and there are indications that East-coast products of the early sixteenth century were at times 'walte' or top-heavy[4]—need not destroy our faith in their competence. After all, South- and West-country ships of the same generation traded successfully to Africa and South America, and the *Minion*, a veteran of the reign of Henry VIII, survived to do valiant service under John

[1] G. V. Scammell, 'English Merchant Shipping at the End of the Middle Ages', *Economic History Review*, 2nd Series, xiii (1961), pp. 327–41. These and other problems will be more fully discussed in my forthcoming book on English Maritime History.

[2] See below, p. 107, n. 1; E. M. Carus-Wilson, *Medieval Merchant Venturers* (London, 1954), pp. 64–73, 96–97; G. J. Marcus, *A Naval History of England* (London, 1961), i, pp. 10, 25, 27–28.

[3] [*Calendar of*] *L*[*etters and*] *P*[*apers, Foreign and Domestic, Henry VIII*], viii, no. 48 (p. 16).

[4] H[igh] C[ourt of] A[dmiralty], 13/4, fos. 218^{r}, 279^{v}, and *cf. L.P.*, xix (i), no. 140 (5).

Hawkins.[1] Then again, in an industry so eclectic and cosmopolitan, knowledge of the great improvements in design, construction and performance that marked the age must have been more or less universal. Seamen, shrewd observers of such things, moved from port to port and from the ships of one country to those of another; agents reported on naval developments;[2] craft changed hands freely; investment in foreign tonnage was common. So in England there were not only considerable purchases of Baltic shipping in the first half of the fifteenth century, but in the 1470's citizens of Newcastle, Southampton and London all bought vessels in the Low Countries,[3] whilst some twenty years later a servant of Sir John Turberville, having acquired, as he thought, the *Seynt Crosse* of Lisbon for his master, found that her owners, with true Latin guile, had meanwhile sold her for 'a more summe of mony' to one 'of gret myght' in Southampton.[4] Again, in the 1500's there was much buying of Dutch and Spanish tonnage—the latter, indeed, so heavy that in 1513 Ferdinand of Aragon instructed his ambassador to raise the matter with Henry VIII.[5] Then in 1536 we hear of an Exeter man with a ship from Aigues-Mortes, and as late as 1545, when Anglo-Spanish relations were at a particularly low ebb, a London grocer was part-owner of the *Salvador* of Cadiz.[6] These, of course, were commercial transactions of varying degrees of regularity, and the list might easily be extended, quite apart from the substantial

[1] J. A. Williamson, *The Ocean in English History* (Oxford, 1941), p. 35, and *Hawkins of Plymouth* (London, 1949), pp. 27–33, 142–45, 150–56. Nor should too great a significance be attached to heavy English buying of foreign tonnage. In a trade boom, or a season propitious for piracy, it was obviously better to buy a vessel which could be put into immediate service rather than to await the efforts of a builder. And foreigners, it should be noted, were willing to purchase English ships.

[2] A. W. Johns, 'The Principal Officers of the Navy', *Mariner's Mirror*, xiv (1928), pp. 32–54, especially p. 37.

[3] *Bronnen* [*tot de Geschiedenis van den Handel met Engeland, Schotland en Ierland, 1150–1485*], ed. H. J. Smit, ii, nos. 1786, 1808, 1853.

[4] E[arly] C[hancery] P[roceedings], 207/1.

[5] *Calendar of Letters, Despatches and State Papers relating to the Negotiations between England and Spain . . . , 1509–25*, p. 144.

[6] *L.P.*, x, no. 538; xx (i), no. 1296. For the building and repair of English ships at Bordeaux, see J. Bernard, 'Les constructions navales à Bordeaux d'après les archives notariales du XVIe siècle', *Le navire et l'économie maritime du XVe au XVIIIe siècle*, ed. M. Mollat (Paris, 1957), pp. 41, 45–46.

royal purchases of Baltic and Iberian shipping. But in addition there were the frequent involuntary migrations of tonnage brought about by the ceaseless activity of pirates, privateers and men-of-war during the disorders of the age: in the 1540's, for instance, that arch-professional, Tompson the Pirate, and some of his *confrères* were operating with ex-Portuguese, Spanish and French craft.[1] In fact so extensive, for one reason or another, were these interchanges, and so cosmopolitan the resultant fleets of many ports, that the quality and performance of much shipping must often have differed only insignificantly from country to country, and the identification of vessels by national or regional peculiarities of rig and construction have been virtually impossible. Hence we have that celebrated occasion on which John Hawkins, in the ex-Hanseatic *Jesus* of Lübeck, boldly leading a squadron of remarkably miscellaneous ancestry—the old Henrician *Minion*, some West-country merchantmen, a French privateer, and three Spanish craft—into San Juan de Ulua, was mistaken at close quarters by local officials for the incoming plate fleet.[2]

But the most eloquent testimony of English maritime vigour, and of a real tradition of the sea, was, as with Holland or modern Norway, the volume of investment in shipping, and the wide diffusion of ownership. Like clothiers in the country's great woollen industry—surely a significant parallel—owners came from every class of society. So we hear, amongst others, of shipowning clergy, both regular and secular (including in 1457 the aptly named David Morgon, parson of Harwich[3]), goldsmiths, butchers, soldiers and aristocrats, and even of a nautically-inclined 'potekary', longbowstringmaker and taverner. As was the case until the revolution in transport of the last century, nearly every creek and haven, today mostly forgotten, could muster some sort of craft fit to engage in trade—much as villages now often have a 'bus, and perhaps for similar reasons—whilst the obscurest testators will vessels or portions of vessels to their heirs.[4] That this was so is not hard to explain, for a ship was a

[1] H.C.A., 1/34, fos. 149^{r}, 295^{r}–296^{v}.
[2] Williamson, *Hawkins of Plymouth*, pp. 104, 115, 135.
[3] C[*alendar of*] P[*atent*] R[*olls*], *1452–61*, p. 348.
[4] *Cf.* J. Heers, 'Types de navires et spécialisation des trafics en Médi-

particularly attractive investment. Despite a superabundance of hazards—poor sailing qualities, inadequately buoyed and charted coasts, the depredations of pirates—many merchantmen had good working lives, and as far as may be gathered, a fairly low rate of depreciation.[1] The *Mary Walsingham* of Dunwich, for example, was active from 1524 to 1548,[2] and the *Sabin* of Ipswich apparently in commission for about 30 years.[3] What return an owner might get on his capital in normal working is unknown, though it has been argued that on the Continent, and somewhat later, the price of a vessel might be recovered in certain great trades in as little as a year or so.[4] This may have been exceptional, but nevertheless, reinforced by higher trading profits—since ownership reduced freight charges, and most owners traded—by the occasional windfalls of piracy, and by other incidental increments, the rate of earnings in England was presumably reasonably good,[5] and certainly good enough to draw in money from an impressive range of sources. Then again, shares were easily transferable, so that, as in perhaps no other field of commerce or industry, surplus capital (by no means rare) could be invested or realized quickly and without difficulty; whilst for the unadventurous, those who simply inherited shares, or those with other and more pressing interests, it was possible to become in fact, if not in law,

terranée à la fin du Moyen-Age', *Le navire [et l'économie maritime du Moyen-Age au XVIIIe siècle, principalement en Méditerranée]*, ed. M. Mollat (Paris, 1958), pp. 107–17, and especially p. 108.

[1] After, it would seem, a sharp initial drop. See also below, p. 112, and *cf.* J. Tadic, 'Le port de Raguse [et sa flotte au XVIe siècle]', *Le navire . . .*, pp. 9–20, and especially p. 13.

[2] E. R. Cooper, 'The Dunwich Iceland Ships', *Mariner's Mirror*, xxv (1939), p. 170.

[3] *Letters and Papers relating to the War with France, 1512–13*, ed. A. Spont (Navy Rec. Soc., x, 1897), p. 9; *L.P.*, xix (i), no. 416; E.C.P., 1175/52.

[4] Tadic, 'Le port de Raguse . . .', pp. 16–17.

[5] This, it might be assumed, was the case in an age dominated by small and comparatively inexpensive craft. In England, where marine insurance was undeveloped, insurance charges must rarely have been borne. Incidental opportunities of profit—piracy, privateering, naval service—were abundant. Nor should it be overlooked that from roughly 1500 to 1550 there was a boom in English overseas trade. But Dr Davis has argued that in the late seventeenth century capital earnings in shipping were unimpressive; see R. Davis, 'Earnings of Capital in the English Shipping Industry, 1670–1730', *Journal of Economic History*, xvii (1957), pp. 409–25.

sleeping partners, freed from the need to manage their investment.[1]

But with many these were doubtless marginal matters. For the magnate, such as Warwick, a private squadron could be a vital instrument of policy, quite apart from its earnings in trade and piracy, or its more mundane function of transporting the ample impedimenta of aristocratic life.[2] Moreover, as such things are wont, large and lavishly equipped vessels brought prestige. Something more modest, on the other hand, might get some useful gleanings, or possibly an occasional plum, by privateering or piracy when commerce failed. So in 1546 a disgruntled owner complained to his master 'that lyffe was not god, willyng the same . . . to goe towards London and if any thyng came in ther way thethurward they wold take it towards ther costs'. Indeed, there can be little doubt that throughout the century, and for years to come, such opportunities—often enough illusory—were for many, in England as in Europe, the most persuasive incentive to invest in shipping. At the lowest level we have that optimist, who, with a 'letyll boate', was to see if he could take a prize 'to make sum money agaynste Christenmas'.[3] But not all enterprise was so pitiful. Much, it is true, was, if not actually disastrous, either fruitless, or limited to the cowardly and pointless plundering of small craft. Yet at times, and allowing for the inflated value usually set on their goods by the victims, the profits must have been considerable, especially as activities were confined to home waters, often in the most literal sense of the word, with little of the expense and natural hazards of later oceanic privateering. In the fifteenth century we hear of captures assessed at several hundred, and even at several thousand pounds,[4] and from Leland there comes (*c.* 1535) a pithy synopsis of Fowey's colourful past: a town 'waxinge riche, partely by feates of warre, partely by pyracie . . .' In the 1540's, according to the Privy Council, there were 'of the west parts . . . 12 or 16 ships of war abroad who have gotten

[1] See below, p. 115. If we accept as relevant the evidence of seventeenth-century conditions, there was the added attraction of limited liability. I owe this suggestion to Professor F. J. Fisher.

[2] See below, p. 120.

[3] H.C.A., 1/34, fos. 8v, 183r.

[4] *C.P.R., 1452–61*, p. 650; *ibid., 1467–77*, pp. 57, 128–29; C. L. Kingsford, *Prejudice and Promise in Fifteenth-Century England* (Oxford, 1925), pp. 94–97, 102, and Appendix, p. 188. And then, of course, there were Warwick's hauls.

among them not so little as £10,000'.[1] That this was not mere political rhetoric may be gathered from a complaint by the Council of Spain to Charles V of the loss to two English ships of a carvel whose lading, including gold and amber, was worth over 5,000 ducats, or the fact that on one occasion that well-known desperado, Cornelius of Calais, disposed of prize goods which fetched over £1,000.[2] And Admiralty records abound with references to the deeds of minute craft—anything from 50 to 5 ton—which, equipped and run at negligible cost, swarmed out into the Channel and its approaches at propitious times, and in that prime artery of European commerce made hauls, if their luck was good, worth two, three, or possibly several hundred pounds.

Of the total wealth invested in shipping—clearly, by contemporary standards, very large—we cannot, in the nature of the evidence, speak with any precision. However, from such figures as are available (Table, on next page),[3] and allowing for vagaries in valuation, and the varying conditions of the vessels and their equipment, we may perhaps assume for the early sixteenth century a pricing of roughly £1/10/- per ton for ships of about 50–200 ton during the first decade or so of their lives.

If, to cover a percentage of more ancient craft, this is reduced to £1/5/- per ton, the shipping owned on the East Coast in 1544,[4] the only region for which we have reasonably complete tonnage figures, was worth something like £13,750, whilst in 1550 that of Newcastle alone very likely stood at over £4,000.[5] Furthermore, and as had probably been the case in most major ports for some time, a fair proportion of such investment was made up of a few large individual holdings. On the most conservative estimate, using if we may the same pricing of £1/5/- per ton, the fleets of Warwick (*c.* 2,300 tons) and William Canynges of Bristol (*c.* 3,000 tons) in the 1460's—the latter including the *Mary*

[1] *L.P.*, xix (ii), no. 560.

[2] *L.P.*, xvi, no. 73; H.C.A., 1/34, fo. 195^{v}. *Cf.* M. J. G. Stanford, 'The Raleghs take to the Sea', *Mariner's Mirror*, xlviii (1962), pp. 22–23.

[3] Some figures for larger craft have been added for the sake of comparison. All relate, as far as is known, to rigged ships. In using this Table allowance must be made for the fall in the value of money after *c.* 1510.

[4] 11,000 tons (round figures) of craft of 50 ton and over.

[5] 3,300 tons of craft of 50 ton and over. Sources for these, and the figures in the preceding note, are in Scammell, 'English Merchant Shipping', pp. 332, 338, and notes.

TABLE

	Ship	Size (tons)	Age	Price	Price per ton (at lowest tonnage)
c. 1460.	*Mary and John* (Bristol)	*c.* 900	new	£2,667	£2/19/–[1]
c. 1466.	Carvel (Dunwich)	*c.* 80	new	£170	*c.* £2[2]
1512.	*Mary James* (Hull)	260/300	3	£260 (sale)	£1
1513.	*Gabriel Royal*	700/800	4	£1,350 (sale)	£1/18/–
	John Baptist	400	new	£1,000 (sale)	£2/10/–[3]
1536.	*Antony Kidman* (London)	100/105	*c.* 8	£160 (sale)	£1/12/–[4]
c. 1538.	*Mary* (Colchester)	40	3	£60 (sale)	£1/10/–[5]
1559.	*Michael* (Newcastle)	80	*c.* 14	£133 (valuation)	£1/13/–[6]
	Antony (Newcastle)	100	*c.* 19	£133 (valuation)	£1/7/–[7]

and John, alone alleged to have cost £2,667—might be put respectively at roughly £2,900 and £3,800.[8] These were no doubt exceptional figures, but in the early sixteenth century ships occasionally changed hands for £500 or £1,000, and other sizeable

[1] Carus-Wilson, *Medieval Venturers*, p. 89.

[2] Calculated from *Manners and Household Expenses of England in the Thirteenth and Fifteenth Centuries* . . . , ed. B. Botfield (Roxburghe Club, 1841), pp. 197 ff. For another carvel, see below, p. 115.

[3] Spont, *Letters and Papers*, pp. 7, n. 1, 61, n. 2, 77, n. 3, 78, 80–82; *L.P.*, ii (ii), p. 1459; *L.P.*, iv (i), no. 1714.

[4] H.C.A., 13/3, fos. 107v, 112r; H.C.A., 13/4, fos. 97v–99r, 109r. With the ship there went 30 weys of bay salt.

[5] H.C.A., 13/4, fos. 161r–62r.

[6] First appears 1545 (*L.P.*, xx (i), no. 321). Valued in 1559 (*Wills and Inventories illustrative of the History . . . of the Northern Counties* . . . ed. J. Raine (Surtees Soc., 1835), p. 167).

[7] Appears 1543 (*L.P.*, xviii (i), nos. 59, 596), and probably 1540 (E. 122/64/15, fo. 2v). Valued 1559 (*Wills and Inventories* . . . , pp. 167–68). This and the preceding valuation may well be too high.

[8] For Warwick, see Warrants for the Great Seal, C. 81/1378/16; E.122/114/3, m. 1; *C*[*alendar of*] *C*[*lose*] *R*[*olls*], *1454–61*, p. 475. For Canynges, see Carus-Wilson, *op. cit.*, p. 89.

holdings were by no means rare. Towards 1540 John Chandeler of London had about £860, and Henry Anderson of Newcastle, like Robert Reneger of Southampton, approximately £500 (a valuation some years later makes it £450[1]) in shipping, whilst three other Tyneside owners had something like £300 apiece.[2] Compared with other investments of a similar nature, with the £100 or £200 which would still suffice to start a coal mine in Elizabethan times, and even with some of the most spectacular—Sir Geoffrey Boleyn with over £2,000 in estates and property in 1463, or the £1,500 spent by that 'exceeding rich clothier', William Stumpe, on the purchase of the site and buildings for a factory—the capital in shipping was clearly of a striking order.[3] And when it is recalled that comparable tonnage figures may have been reached in the fourteenth century not only is the importance of this neglected industry apparent, but also the fact that large-scale investment in fairly complex equipment—one might even say machines—employing many persons has, if not a longer, certainly a richer history than is often assumed.

As has already been suggested, the abundantly assorted opportunities of shipowning drew in money from the widest range of sources, and indeed the only adequate comparison would be with the diversity of that attracted by land. As in Europe, foreign capital appears in a number of ports.[4] Landed wealth was represented on the one hand by a certain Edward Hawte, who sold '100 marks of good land to buy a ship and begin merchandise',[5] and on the other by the extensive maritime interests of aristocrats like the Howards, or of that 'grete tenement man' from the *Childe of Bristowe*, with his cattle, jewels, 'many a shyp' and much else

[1] *Wills and Inventories*, *loc. cit.*

[2] Tonnage figures from *L.P.*, *Addenda*, no. 1430; G. V. Scammell, 'War at Sea under the Early Tudors' (II), *Archaeologia Aeliana*, 4th Series, xxxix (1961), p. 204; G. Connell-Smith, *Forerunners of Drake* (London, 1954), pp. 183–84; *L.P.*, xxi (i), no. 498, all converted at the rate suggested in the text. *Cf.* also Carus-Wilson, *op. cit.*, p. 86.

[3] J. U. Nef, *The Rise of the British Coal Industry* (London, 1932), i, pp. 377–78; Sylvia L. Thrupp, *The Merchant Class of Medieval London* (Chicago, 1948), p. 128; *Victoria County History*, *Wiltshire*, iv, p. 146.

[4] See above, p. 107, below, pp. 118–19, and *cf.* O. Lienau, 'Danziger Schiffahrt und Schiffbau in der zweiten Hälfte des 15. Jahrhunderts', *Zeitschrift des Westpreussischen Geschichtsvereins*, lxx (1930), p. 79.

[5] *L.P.*, xiv (ii), no. 231.

besides.[1] So too, the profits of trade produced owners ranging from merchants of the standing of Canynges to those two obscure Sussex butchers, who, in the 1540's, having disposed of a cargo of beer, put the proceeds into a small bark, which, or so at least it was alleged, hard times soon reduced to piracy.[2] But the precise origin of much capital inevitably defies analysis, and many of the ablest and most adventurous owners—William Gonson of London or Reneger of Southampton, for instance—were prominent as merchants and seamen as well, from all of which roles they doubtless drew their rewards.[3]

Apart, however, from occasional fleets belonging to magnates or wealthy merchants, ownership was usually limited to at most the whole or partial control of one or two vessels (in 1513 there were 20 owners to the 19 craft in Bristol)[4] and as elsewhere in Europe, shareholding rather than outright possession was common.[5] Of this venerable system two features are notable: one that the shares themselves—halves, thirds, quarters, etc.—were, for reasons which do not concern us here, generally of a higher denomination than those current in later centuries; the other the amazing speed and facility with which they were divided, consolidated or transferred. Rapidly and easily formed then, the shipping partnership, one of the most ancient and important kinds of business association, with shares sold and willed like those in later industrial enterprises or joint-stock trading companies, might be anything from a temporary expedient to an alliance enduring for years, and might originate in a variety of ways. The simplest was where an inheritance was divided, as when in the 1530's Elizabeth Johnson of London sold to Humphrey Knight half the share in the *Mary Martin* her husband had left her.[6] But a commoner reason was some form of commercial convenience.

[1] Thrupp, *op. cit.*, p. 243. For the Howards, see *Manners and Household Expenses*, pp. 179 ff.; *The Household Books of John, Duke of Norfolk, and Thomas, Earl of Surrey*, ed. J. P. Collier (Roxburghe Club, 1844), *passim*; G. V. Scammell, 'War at Sea under the Early Tudors' (I), *Archaeologia Aeliana*, 4th Series, xxxviii (1960), p. 80, and below, pp. 119, 120–21.

[2] H.C.A., 1/34, fos. 5ʳ–8ᵛ.

[3] *Cf.* below, p. 117.

[4] State Papers, 1/3, fo. 87ʳ.

[5] *Cf.* Tadic, 'Le port de Raguse', pp. 13–14; M. Mollat, *Le commerce maritime normand à la fin du Moyen-Age* (Paris, 1952), pp. 345, 408–09.

[6] H.C.A., 13/2, fos. 11ʳ–18ᵛ.

A merchant might solve his transport problems by buying a share in a vessel for either the duration of a voyage or for a longer period.[1] Or again, in a world where primitive communications gave such prominence to the initiative and integrity of the local agent, to dispense with factors, cut overheads, increase profits, and ensure that he be 'better and mor deligently . . . sarved', a merchant 'emploienge . . . monye in shippinge' might take a master into partnership—often an alien, presumably knowledgeable about continental conditions—so gaining an associate with the incentive and opportunities to see that their ship be 'kept in better occupienge'.[2] Furthermore, by purchasing only a part holding, and leaving the remainder with a sleeping partner, an astute entrepreneur might economically but effectively control a vessel. Thus about 1460 Richard Felowe of Ipswich secured half the *Gyles* of Hull, the other half being held by Sir William Rider, who some years later was significantly complaining that Felowe, at whose suggestion the arrangement had been made, and to whom he had entrusted 'the hole rule, guydyng and employment' of the ship, 'as yet non profite nor availe of thenployment therof hath giffen nor in nowise will giff'.[3] Another, though unduly emphasized cause of partnership, was the inability of an individual to bear the whole cost of building or operating a vessel. This was doubtless true at the bottom of the scale, of fishing and coasting craft owned in small ports, or in exceptional circumstances, as with John May of Bristol, who, in mid-fifteenth century having to 'hys grete impouerysshement' spent over £500 on a new carvel, was then obliged 'for lak of good' to sell off a quarter share.[4] But for the rest there are no signs of any shortage of capital, and what seems to have been of decisive importance was the widespread and natural unwillingness in so uncertain a world to expose it to undue risk by over-concentration. In 1513, for instance, John Shipman of Bristol, sole owner of the *Matthew* (120 ton), must have had the price of an equivalent vessel in shares in four other craft, just as with similar caution, merchants commonly distributed

[1] A. R. Bridbury, *England and the Salt Trade in the Later Middle Ages* (Oxford, 1955), p. 129.

[2] *Extracts from the Records of the Merchant Adventurers of Newcastle-upon-Tyne*, ed. J. R. Boyle and F. W. Dendy (Surtees Soc., 1895–99), i, pp. 41–42. *Cf.* N. J. M. Kerling, *Commercial Relations of Holland and Zeeland with England from the Late Thirteenth Century to the Close of the Middle Ages* (Leiden, 1954), p. 183.

[3] E.C.P., 27/84.

[4] E.C.P., 32/289.

their cargoes amongst several ships.[1] And then there were subtler problems partnership might solve. In 1539, when two vessels, one French and one English, returned from an expedition to Brazil, their respective owners each took a half share in the other's craft, presumably to confuse the issue of ownership, and to give both adventurers some chance of profit should either ship be arrested.[2]

Like the structure of much contemporary industry, the nature of ownership was an assortment of anticipations and survivals, ranging from the surprising, and by no means specious, appearance of modernity of the fleets of specialist owners like Canynges, to truly feudal expressions of aristocratic power, such as the squadrons of the Howards and other magnates. One of the commonest forms, both in England and on the Continent, and particularly in near-water trades, where the tradition was to last for centuries—witness the writings of the late Lord Runciman—was for a master to own either the whole, or an important share in his command. Thus at Newcastle in 1544 of 28 owners about ten were either seamen or ex-seamen.[3] In part this indicates the profits of a master's private trading—an opportunity of advancement favourably comparable to those open to many other skilled men. In part, too, it reflects the advantages many owners found in partnership with a mariner, whilst at the lowest level there were no doubt then, as later, seamen whose sole hope of command lay in buying or stealing a ship. In fact, the position of the master is a warning to those who like their society neatly classified. On the one hand he might be, like so many other craftsmen, a wage-earner with nothing to sell but his labour and skill. But on the other he could be a shipowner, able (or so it was said of some) to undercut the trade of ordinary merchants through his low costs and sharp practice, and well-advanced on the road to opulence—we hear of one apparently worth over £650 in the early 1500's—and in the common progression to the mercantile bourgeoisie; a skilled man, that is, who, like a weaver or fuller turned clothier, had gained control of his fellow workers and the means of production.[4]

[1] State Papers, 1/3, fo. 87^{r}. [2] H.C.A., 13/4, fos. 274^{v}–275^{r}.

[3] Scammell, 'War at Sea' (II), pp. 204–05.

[4] *Records of the Merchant Adventurers of Newcastle*, i, p. 42; E.C.P., 877/74.

But the most important figure, as had long been the case, was the merchant who moved into shipping—the convenience is obvious—as into so many other fields of enterprise, and indeed the rise of an English merchant fleet was largely the corollary of that emergence of a native merchant class which marked the later Middle Ages. Furthermore, with traditional acquisitive zeal, such entrepreneurs often came to dispose of a substantial portion of the tonnage belonging to a port. In 1544 nearly half of that of Newcastle was in the hands of six men, just as some 80 years earlier 10 of Bristol's 17 or so ships, including most of the biggest, had been owned by William Canynges.[1] Even more striking, and a remarkable indication of a rapidly developing economy, is the appearance of the specialist owner, drawing his profits largely or solely from freights. This would seem to have been the position, perhaps unique, of Canynges himself about 1460.[2] But less than a century later shipowning was a recognized occupation—witness that Nicholas Clercke, 'shipowner, Englishman', lodging in East Smithfield in 1546[3]—and owners[4] were sufficiently common to be known as a class with their own peculiar interests and policies. So in 1540 the omnipresent Cromwell noted 'the shipowners' complaint against the merchants, and the merchants' answers . . .'[5] But on the whole, specialization of this order had, as yet, little to recommend it, and as elsewhere wealthy merchants usually invested in a variety of fields, of which shipping was but one, and not always the most important.[6] William Gonson, a prosperous property-owning London grocer, and founder of a dynasty of seamen and naval administrators which included John Hawkins and Edward Fenton, sold, with his partners, a great ship to Henry VIII; commanded at sea; carried on an extensive foreign trade, including voyages to the Levant; and for much of his life (1524–1544) was profitably employed, in Hakluyt's phrase, as 'pay-master of the King's navee'. So too Henry Anderson of Newcastle, who appears to have owned what might almost be described as an integrated concern—ships, lighters, warehouses—

[1] Scammell, 'War at Sea' (II), pp. 185, 204–05; Carus-Wilson, *Medieval Venturers*, p. 89. Bristol total calculated from Exchequer, K.R., Particulars of Customs.

[2] *Cf.* Marcus, *A Naval History* . . ., i, p. 12.

[3] *L.P.*, xxi (i), no. 147 (p. 65).

[4] Many were, of course, masters.

[5] *L.P.*, xv, no. 322.

[6] *Cf.* Thrupp, *Merchant Class*, p. 12.

had in 1559 only £450 in shipping out of net assets exceeding £2,500.[1]

But by no means all the wealth in the industry was of local origin, and shipowning provides one of the earliest and most valuable instances of the migration of industrial capital, foreshadowing in many ways subsequent developments in coal and other large-scale undertakings. A prosperous provincial merchant might, for instance, hold tonnage in some neighbouring port.[2] More important, by a characteristic expansion of metropolitan enterprise, Londoners, frequently merchants, moved into provincial shipping, just as in Amsterdam their contemporaries established a far greater ascendancy over that of North Holland.[3] So in 1446 the *Trinity* of Sandwich passed to two London drapers and their associates.[4] Six years later a Portuguese master and a London merchant were joint-owners of the *George* of Dartmouth, and in the course of the century under review several other citizens of the capital can be found, for various reasons, in sole or partial possession of an assortment of outport tonnage.[5] Nor was investment necessarily confined to native shipping. By taking shares in alien vessels transport problems might be solved, and difficulties in securing or disposing of freights abroad, obstacles raised by navigation acts, and risks of arrest in wartime, all surmounted, or at least alleviated. Hence we hear of English merchants with holdings in Hanseatic craft in the early fifteenth century;[6] of the purchase by Richard Chilton and William Jenks of half the *Christoffel* of Bergen in 1477;[7] and of Thomas Harrison, part-owner in 1542 of a Spanish ship working to the Americas.[8] Nor, of course, was this merely a one-way flow of capital. The same attractions that drew English money abroad brought foreign money into English ports, and like the ships themselves, or the

[1] Johns, 'The Principal Officers', pp. 35–36; *Wills and Inventories*, ed. Raine, pp. 166–68.

[2] Scammell, 'War at Sea' (II), p. 183; and see above, p. 115.

[3] A. E. Christensen, *Dutch Trade to the Baltic about 1600* (Copenhagen, 1941), pp. 40–41, 47–48.

[4] *C.C.R., 1447–54*, p. 73.

[5] *C.P.R., 1452–61*, pp. 61, 166; *C.C.R., 1461–68*, pp. 287, 405; *C.C.R., 1468–76*, no. 892; *L.P.*, i (i), no. 1262; and *cf. C.C.R., 1447–54*, pp. 41, 138, and Carus-Wilson, *op. cit.*, pp. 10–11, 128.

[6] Bridbury, *Salt Trade*, p. 129.

[7] Smit, *Bronnen*, ii, no. 1810.

[8] Connell-Smith, *Forerunners of Drake*, p. 97. Harrison was resident in Seville.

crews who manned them, the wealth invested in the industry must always have been fairly cosmopolitan. In the 1480's, for instance, three-quarters of a Newcastle-owned craft were sold to two merchants of Goes.[1]

Another powerful and important body of owners, as indeed they remained until the seventeenth century, were the gentry and aristocracy. So we have the carvel of Lord Say (1453), a *Star Rivers* (1475), the *Vincent* of Sir William Trevelyan (1513), Lord Willoughby's *Bark* (1524), Sir Thomas Seymour's ship (1546), and even (1526) an *Anne Boleyn*, with which Lord Rochford payed grateful homage to his justly renowned daughter. On the lowest estimate something like 70 owners of this class held a total of at least 105 vessels in the century after 1450, ranging from the 'lord of Warrewyk . . . his Navey' of some 10 ships, or the six or so of his contemporary, John Howard, to the notoriously piratical balingers, barges and carvels of the provincial gentry.[2] This was not, it should be recognized, something peculiar to England, nor was it anything new: the magnificent Bishop Puiset of Durham had, after all, characteristically owned a 'great ship' in the 1190's, and William de Braose and William de Stuteville supplied vessels to Richard I.[3] No doubt men of good family had for centuries kept ships—the convenience is obvious in a world of primitive transport—much as they subsequently kept carriages. But the later Middle Ages seem to have witnessed a considerable increase in shipowning by such classes. Initially, perhaps, this was occasioned by the frequent Channel crossings entailed by the policies of Edward III. Certainly it was encouraged by the opportunities of the chaotic reign of Henry VI, not least of which were the absence of a royal fleet, and the employment of magnates, such as Exeter and Warwick, in 'sea keeping' with all its attendant profits. Then with the close of the French wars the sea gave some outlet for energies and hopes of gain which under Elizabeth and James were to find expression in colonization, privateering, and exploration in the New World. Furthermore, in such an age a private navy could be as vital as a private army: it was the mobility

[1] Smit, *Bronnen*, ii, no. 1993.

[2] E.C.P., 27/440. See also above, pp. 112, n. 8; 114, n. 1. I am grateful to Mr C. F. Richmond for some references to aristocratic shipowners.

[3] G. V. Scammell, *Hugh du Puiset* (Cambridge, 1956), p. 106; F. W. Brooks, *The English Naval Forces 1199–1272* (London, n.d.), p. 135.

and surprise of seapower that enabled Warwick to cross to Ireland from his stronghold at Calais in 1460, consult with Richard of York, and return unhampered to launch the invasion which led to the capture of Henry VI at Northampton.[1]

But such grand designs were rare, and much of this interest, particularly in strategically-sited or isolated havens, was confined to piracy, with the privateer of good family, or the landed backer of such ventures, already the familiar figures they remained until Jacobean times. In the fifteenth century we have not only the massive and indiscriminate depredations of Warwick himself, or the deeds of ships of West-country squires like John Trevelyan, whose *Edward* was on one occasion involved in the capture of goods allegedly worth £12,000, but also the less spectacular, but still substantial hauls—£200 or so—of the craft of men like Sir Robert Constable of Flamborough.[2] Then with the return of similar opportunities after the death of Henry VIII, Lord Admiral Seymour appears in profit-sharing association with the very pirates he was supposed to suppress, whilst in the 1550's Henry Strangeways of Dorset plied his trade in Irish waters with such zeal and success that two men-of-war were fitted out to bring him in.[3]

Nevertheless, as elsewhere in Europe, high birth, then as later, was no bar to an appreciation of the profits of trade and industry —witness Edward IV and Henry VII—and ships belonging to de Roos, Darcy, Percy, Herbert, Lestrange, Howard and even Warwick, to mention but a few, were all at some time or other engaged in legitimate commerce.[4] In some cases this interest was merely that of a sleeping partner, but it might well be more direct, and indeed the wealth and power of the aristocrat clearly had their advantages in business. John Howard, like Henry Tudor after him, could, if need be, give credit to the charterers of his ships, or like his contemporary, Lord Rivers, get preference in their lading. And in 1472, at issue with the Merchant Adventurers over the

[1] Sir James Ramsay, *Lancaster and York* (Oxford, 1892), ii, pp. 222 ff.

[2] Kingsford, *Prejudice and Promise*, pp. 94–95; *C.P.R., 1467–77*, p. 409.

[3] A. F. Pollard, *England under Protector Somerset* (London, 1900), p. 188; *Victoria County History, Dorset*, ii, pp. 199–200.

[4] *C.P.R., 1452–61*, p. 348; *C.P.R., 1476–85*, p. 366; Cora L. Scofield, *The Life and Reign of Edward IV* (London, 1923), ii, pp. 417–20; Cooper, 'The Dunwich Iceland Ships', p. 172; Thrupp, *Merchant Class*, pp. 243–44.

lack of cargo for two of his craft which they had chartered (for which it would seem he or his agents were to blame), he threatened, if not recompensed, to sue 'utterly as he cowde', and should this fail, to re-imburse himself by force; at which, after 'grete labor', he was duly placated, receiving as well 'a pleasourer' of 20 marks, 'and he to be oure goode lorde and lover'.[1]

Of the importance, then, of English merchant shipping in the century after 1450 there can be little doubt; it must throughout have absorbed a high proportion of the country's industrial capital; like the land or the manufacture of cloth it was equally remarkable as an employer of labour and a field for investment; as an industry it differed in size alone from those of Europe's leading maritime powers. But more than this, or the surprising sophistication of much of its organization, it was, as later publicists never wearied of urging, a 'nursery of seamen', and a potent instrument of policy, supplying transport and fighting vessels for countless ventures both public and private. Later glories, and a quite unwarranted identification of maritime aptitude and consequence with feats of navigation and discovery, have obscured this significance, but none of it was lost on Henry VIII. Far from needing to insist, as has recently been argued, that the officers of his newly-formed navy should be seamen,[2] he was able to tap a reserve of long and varied experience of the sea. Of ten Admirals of England between 1513 and 1550, seven were shipowners, and two, Edward and Thomas Howard, were of a family which had controlled merchantmen, and served with, or commanded, war fleets since at least the 1460's.[3] So, too, many of the most eminent officers and administrators—Thomas Spert, of seafaring stock which can perhaps be traced back to the reign of Edward III, John Hopton, William Gonson—were established and experienced seamen and owners. Nor did such influences cease here. It was from two areas of particularly flourishing maritime activity in the hundred years after 1450—London, and the Thames estuary in its widest sense, and the West country—that

[1] *Acts of Court of the Mercers' Company, 1453–1527*, ed. Laetitia Lyell and F. D. Watney (Cambridge, 1936), pp. 63–65, 87; *Household Books of John, Duke of Norfolk*, p. 112.

[2] Waters, *Art of Navigation*, p. 463.

[3] Scofield, *Edward IV*, i, p. 258; ii, pp. 303–04, 315. See also above, p. 114, n. 1.

there came most of the inspiration, skill and leadership in subsequent oceanic enterprise. Then as every devotee of Tennyson knows, Howards still commanded fleets, as Gonsons still administered them, in the last decades of the sixteenth century; whilst that Robert Dudley, sometime privateer and explorer, who, in Italian service in the early 1600's, wrote so expertly and extensively 'touching Marinerie', was a grandson of Henry's Lord Admiral Lisle, shipowner and protagonist of oceanic ventures. And the Hawkins dynasty, like Wynter, and even the exquisite Raleigh, all came of West-country shipowning families.[1] It was this legacy of generations of war and trade by sea—of piracy, of local, particular, endeavour largely untrammelled and unsupported by royal authority, of fierce individualism—that explains the character, and the strength and weakness, of the maritime achievements of the Elizabethan age.

[1] Johns, 'The Principal Officers'; *Mariner's Mirror*, xlvii (1961), pp. 142–44; F. Braudel and R. Romano, *Navires et marchandises à l'entrée du port de Livourne, 1547–1611* (Paris, 1951), p. 25; Waters, *Art of Navigation*, pp. 83–85; Williamson, *Hawkins of Plymouth*; W. M. Wallace, *Sir Walter Raleigh* (Oxford, 1959), p. 7; M. J. G. Stanford, 'The Raleghs take to the Sea', pp. 18–35. For a *Mary Raley* in 1503, see E.122/41/25, m. 4.

III

British Merchant Shipbuilding, c. 1500-1750[1]

The centuries after 1500 were characterised by the emergence of England - later Britain, following union with Scotland in 1707 - as the world's greatest maritime and commercial power. Why this should have happened has been the subject of much erudite if inconclusive debate. One incontrovertible fact, however, is that such a process demanded ships. How these were provided for the emergent Navy has received, not surprisingly, a great deal of attention. For merchantmen the story is somewhat different, with interest largely focussed on the evolution of builds and rigs rather than on the origins of the vessels. As at most times, some were bought or otherwise acquired abroad. Many, particularly in the course of the Anglo-Dutch wars of the seventeenth century, came into English hands as prizes. But with the passage of time more were built in Britain or in British footholds and possessions overseas in ways which this essay hopes to trace.

For most of the early modern period - and indeed well beyond - and notwithstanding a growth in specialization of function, craft of one sort or another were produced on most of the coasts and rivers of the British Isles, sometimes in unlikely places. All but the smallest were built on stocks, which at their most rudimentary could entail nothing more than a few balks of timber on which the keel could rest, and which could be laid wherever there was access to water and materials, with the growing hull propped up, and if need be surrounded by scaffolding to facilitate work. Hence, ships at various times were said to "lie on" the stocks, to be "building" on them, or to have been recently launched from them.[2] In

---

[1]The author wishes to record his thanks to Professor Lewis R. Fischer for his valuable advice and to two anonymous readers for their stimulating comments.

[2]Great Britain, Public Record Office (PRO), High Court of Admiralty (HCA) 13/2, 12 February 1537/1538; 13/4, 6 December 1541; 13/75, 2 March 1665/1666; and 13/78, 11 September 1678.

This essay originally appeared in the ISMH, Vol. XI, No. 1 (June 1999), 27–52. It is hereby reprinted with the kind permission of the International Maritime Economic History Association.

some instances this could mean that they were quite literally carried to the water in a fashion familiar to those who today frequent yacht marinas. So at Portsmouth in 1675 a forty-two-ton craft built for the king of France was "drawn on a cradle placed on four wheels at least two hundred yards to the seaside where [it] was lifted with tackle...and let down gently on the ooze where the tide came in."[3] For vessels of any size - 100 to 1000 tons in contemporary terms - ways were used. These were ramps down which ships slid, all being well, on the day of their launch. Thus in 1676 we hear of Mr. Boys, "his ways before his yard," at Limehouse, and a few years later of those of Mr. White and Captain Potter nearby.[4] But, as ever, things did not always go smoothly. At Ipswich in 1672 a new East Indiaman was reported stuck "for want of water...half on the ooze, and the other half with her stern on the launch."[5]

Such mishaps greatly added to the attractions of docks - excavated basins with gates or more primitive means of excluding or retaining water. In these vessels could be built, and then floated out, or they could be warped in for repair and kept on an even keel as the water receded, and until shored up, by what were cryptically described as "engines" at Bristol in 1580. The best known in the early 1600s were those on the Thames belonging to the Crown, but already in Elizabeth's reign there were many others privately owned.[6] There was agitation at Ipswich in 1634 for a new (or perhaps additional) dry dock.[7] Many more were dug along the Thames soon after, some economically finished and strengthened with former

---

[3]PRO, Texts and Calendars, *Calendar of State Papers Domestic (CSPD), 1675-1676*, 195.

[4]PRO, HCA 13/78, 24 October 1676; 9 June 1681; and 24 February 1681/1682.

[5]PRO, *CSPD, 1671-1672*, 95.

[6]W.G. Perrin (ed.), *The Autobiography of Phineas Pett* (London, 1918), 115-116; PRO, *CSPD, 1671*, 457-458; Jean Vanes, *The Port of Bristol in the Sixteenth Century* (Bristol, 1977), 8; N.A.M. Rodger, *The Safeguard of the Sea. A Naval History of Britain Vol. I: 660-1649* (London, 1997), 335-336 and 377.

[7]PRO, *CSPD, 1634-1635*, 38.

ships' timbers.[8] The shipwright Thomas Taylor had one at Wapping in 1640 and there were others at Limehouse and Rotherhithe in mid-century, while in 1716 another Taylor was said to have "a great wet dock."[9] A colleague ran an impressive one at Deptford, in which in the same year he built a 1000-ton, sixty-four-gun ship for the king of Sicily. Less than a decade later the indefatigable Daniel Defoe counted three wet and twenty-two dry docks on one stretch of the river alone.[10] The largest, together with their various ancillary buildings, were known as shipyards and were clearly precursors of their modern equivalents.

Alongside such indications of things to come, however, there were abundant signs of a simpler economy. Small boats were commonly built on beaches. Vessels were frequently repaired, to the hazard of fellow seafarers and the wrath of local authorities, in impromptu excavations ("holes") in harbours. Many ships, including some of considerable size by the standards of the times, were constructed in ports and havens where access to the sea was not always easy. Colchester had a significant industry in the sixteenth and seventeenth centuries.[11] Topsham produced a ship suitable for Henry VIII's navy in 1530.[12] Vessels were built at Tintern Abbey (upstream on the Monnow) as late as 1670, while in 1664 Sandwich could manage a "hoy, alias pink" - i.e., a vessel of the latest Dutch fashion.[13] Building was going on at Gainsborough - fifty miles inland from the Wash - when Defoe knew it in 1724. In the early 1600s the little south-coast haven of Shoreham was the base for one of the

---

[8]David Saxby and Damien Goodburn, "Seventeenth-Century Ships' Timbers and Dock on the Thames Waterfront at Bellamy's Wharf, Rotherhithe, London SE 16," *Mariner's Mirror*, LXXXIV, No. 2 (1998), 173ff.

[9]PRO, HCA 13/56, 16 October 1640; 13/85, 17 May 1716; Saxby and Goodburn, "Seventeenth-Century Ships' Timbers," 174.

[10]PRO, HCA 13/85, 4 and 17 July 1716; and Daniel Defoe, *A Tour through England and Wales* (reprint, 2 vols., London, 1928), I, 348.

[11]PRO, HCA 13/4, 22 January 1540/1541.

[12]PRO, Texts and Calendars, *Calendar of Letters and Papers, Foreign and Domestic, Henry VIII (LP)*, IV (3), no. 6490 (5).

[13]PRO, HCA 13/78, 20 June 1676 and 11 September 1678.

country's major builders and even decades later was still turning out vessels for the Yarmouth fishery and the Newcastle coal trade.[14]

The geographical distribution of shipbuilding throughout the British Isles is hard to establish. Impoverished Ireland produced fishing craft and short-haul traders. Like western Scotland it also built those vessels of ancient pedigree required in peace and war by Gaelic chieftains. More remarkably, it could supply large ships of up-to-date design. A 300-ton privateer occurred in 1625, and a still bigger vessel was subsequently (1677) built at Kerry under a London shipwright, its timber provided by the pioneer economist, Sir William Petty.[15] In equally impoverished Scotland, activity for long was on a similarly modest scale. Yet what could be achieved with seemingly limited resources in skill and man-power, and the astonishing potential of primitive economies, was graphically illustrated by a brief outburst of spectacular and innovative naval building under James IV. For his greater power and glory, but at prohibitive cost, he had the 600-700 ton *Margaret* constructed at Leith (1504-1507), followed by the 1000-ton *Michael* (1506-1512).[16] It was to be centuries before the country had either the will or the means to attempt the like again. Various smaller craft were certainly provided subsequently for private owners by Dumfries, Leith and Aberdeen. Inverness produced a vessel of "prodigious," but unspecified, "bignes" in 1643 and another was built for a Glasgow worthy at Greenock towards the end of the seventeenth century.[17] But these were the occasional fruits of an industry of such insignificance that the Scottish Navigation Act (1661) made no attempt to protect it, and most of the vessels the country required were obtained from Holland or Norway. Indeed, so bleak was the scene that it was alleged in 1695 that at Leith the "building of ships...can not now be done through want of skill and art of sawing."

---

[14]Defoe, *Tour*, I, 347; PRO, *CSPD, 1627-1628*, 500; PRO, HCA 13/78, 27 July 1677; and Kenneth R. Andrews, *Ships, Money and Politics: Seafaring and Naval Enterprise in the Reign of Charles I* (Cambridge, 1991), 25.

[15]PRO, *CSPD, 1625-1626*, 201; and PRO, HCA 13/78, 8 December 1679.

[16]Rodger, *Safeguard*, 168-169.

[17]S.G.E. Lythe, *The Economy of Scotland in its European Setting, 1550-1625* (Edinburgh, 1960), 132-133; and S.G.E. Lythe and J. Butt, *An Economic History of Scotland, 1100-1939* (London, 1975), 50-51.

Things began to look up in the early eighteenth century, particularly under the stimulus of the new Atlantic trades. A Hull entrepreneur opened a yard at Kingston-on-Spey and in 1711 Scott's was established at Greenock, where it was to enjoy a long and illustrious history. Nevertheless, for decades it simply turned out fishing and coastal craft, not launching a ship of any size until 1760. Of the great Scottish industry, which in the 1930s was to account for nearly half of Britain's output of ships, there were as yet few signs.[18]

In England the situation was far brighter. Problems there certainly were, with demand for tonnage dwindling in times of recession like the early 1600s, but by and large overseas trade boomed in the hundred years or so after 1650. Furthermore, for much of the sixteenth century, and until the beginning of the eighteenth, building was encouraged by government subsidies on vessels suitable to be employed as men of war. Yet excellent though these might be in such a role, they made a poor showing in many trades in the 1600s against lightly and cheaply built, and economically run, Dutch vessels. But with the aggressive reassertion of English maritime ambitions the industry received a massive fillip. Holland's merchant fleet was dealt some cruel blows in the course of three Anglo-Dutch wars while England's was encouraged by a series of Navigation Acts, commencing in 1651, which reserved whole areas of trade to English-built vessels - a privilege subsequently extended to Scotland after the Act of Union. So cherished, and showing a greater adaptability than it has often been credited with, the English industry was launched on a career which has only foundered in our own times.

Throughout the early modern period vessels of various sorts were constructed at, or in the vicinity of, most of the country's major ports. In the Northeast, along the banks of the Tyne, Wear and Tees, eventually the home of one of Europe's greatest shipbuilding industries, boats and ships had been produced since the Middle Ages, some for the pre-Reformation bishopric and priory of Durham.[19] In 1549 Newcastle was said to be

---

[18]James Grant (ed.), *The Old Scots Navy from 1689 to 1710* (London, 1914), 69; T.C. Smout, *Scottish Trade on the Eve of Union, 1660-1707* (Edinburgh, 1963), 47ff; Henry Hamilton, *An Economic History of Scotland in the Eighteenth Century* (Oxford, 1963), 287; and Lythe and Butt, *Economic History*, 50-51, 145, 216 and 219.

[19]Archives of the Prior and Convent of Durham, Accounts of the Bursar, 1508-1509; Commoner, 1510-1511 and Cell of Farne Island, 1453-1454.

engaged in the "making and mending" of ships.[20] The following century the Tyne was turning out both distinctive coasters and vessels suitable for the new long-distance trades, like that in which Edward Barlow sailed (1677) for Jamaica. And soon after it was one of the main builders of colliers.[21] Much the same happened at Hull, where the industry had an equally lengthy pedigree. The city was producing large vessels, including men of war, in the late 1600s, and by the mid-eighteenth century had ten or so yards, one of which supplied the Navy with eight vessels during the Seven Years War.[22]

On the south coast there was considerable activity in the sixteenth and early seventeenth centuries at Shoreham and in the vicinity of Southampton, yet another ancient and celebrated centre of building. From the Hamble there came in late Elizabethan times Robert Dudley's well-regarded *Bear*, together with the *Galleon Ugtred* of more uncertain reputation.[23] Other vessels were built at Portsmouth or thereabouts, while in 1662 a foreign visitor marvelled at the scale of Benjamin Newland's undertaking at East Cowes, with its "very fine house...warehouses and wharves." Later still the Montagues of Beaulieu, in a notable burst of patrician entrepreneurial zeal, developed yards on their estate which were employed by the Navy in the 1740s.[24]

---

[20]Richard Welford, *History of Newcastle and Gateshead* (3 vols., London, 1885-1887), II, 265; and G.V. Scammell, "War at Sea under the Early Tudors," Pt. II, *Archaeologia Aeliana*, 4th ser. (1961), XXXIX, 179 and 182.

[21]Basil Lubbock (ed.), *Barlow's Journal* (2 vols., London, 1934), II, 327; and Ralph Davis, *The Rise of the English Shipping Industry in the Seventeenth and Eighteenth Centuries* (London, 1962), 62ff.

[22]Gordon Jackson, *Hull in the Eighteenth Century. A Study in Economic and Social History* (Oxford, 1972), 180-183.

[23]George F. Warner (ed.), *The Voyage of Robert Dudley to the West Indies, 1594-5* (London, 1899), xix; and Elizabeth Story Donno (ed.), *An Elizabethan in 1582. The Diary of Richard Madox, Fellow of All Souls* (London, 1976), 114.

[24]Richard Hakluyt, *The Principal Navigations* (12 vols., Glasgow, 1903-1905), V, 292; PRO, *CSPD, 1675-1676*, 195, 197 and 231; Maurice Exwood and H.L. Lehmann (eds.), *The Journal of William Schellinks' Travels in England, 1661-1663* (London, 1993), 140; and H.V. Bowen, *Elites, Enterprise and the Making of the British Overseas Empire, 1688-1775* (London, 1996), 54.

At Bristol, in the vanguard of English oceanic endeavour in the late Middle Ages, there was so much building that in 1475-1476 the city fathers felt obliged to prohibit the unlicensed "breaking of any ground" for the purpose. Events, however, quickly overtook them, with the port's fortunes declining dramatically under the early Tudors. Some building nevertheless continued, and in 1535 a Dartmouth shipwright and twenty carpenters were to "new make" the *Saviour*, belonging to that pioneer of imperial expansion, Nicholas Thorne. But all in all it seems that no more than eight ships of any size (140-300 tons) were launched there during the closing years of Elizabeth's reign.[25] Only in the late 1600s did things begin to look up, reflecting a prosperity stemming from new Atlantic opportunities. There was also some building for the Navy, though after a while the service found the port too remote to allow it to supervise work as it wished. Far more valuable was the impact of Bristol's now burgeoning West Indies trade in which, on the eve of the War of American Independence, nearly half the vessels and tonnage employed were of local build.[26]

In the West Country John Leland had noted a flourishing industry at Bideford in the time of Henry VIII. In the ensuing century and a half, when few were to equal the enterprise and initiative of seamen from the Southwest, Exeter, Barnstaple and Dartmouth all built ships and Devon produced some celebrated big privateers in the closing years of the Elizabethan war against Spain. Thereafter a shortage of timber, in the South at least, cramped the industry, though a Topsham man - of either formidable energy or fertile imagination - subsequently claimed to have built a veritable armada of "near 100 ships and 400 boats" between 1660 and 1711. Be this as it may, when the new Plymouth naval dockyards

---

[25]E.M. Carus Wilson (ed.), *The Overseas Trade of Bristol in the Later Middle Ages* (2nd ed., London, 1967), no. 192; PRO, *LP*, IX, No. 1025; and Vanes, *Port of Bristol*, 8-9.

[26]PRO, *CSPD, 1673*, 5; N.A.M. Rodger (ed.), *The Naval Miscellany, Vol. V* (London, 1984), 106; R.D. Merriman (ed.), *Queen Anne's Navy. Documents Concerning the Administration of the Navy of Queen Anne, 1702-1714* (London, 1961), 62; Richard Ollard, *Man of War. Sir Robert Holmes and the Restoration Navy* (London, 1969), 170; and Kenneth Morgan, *Bristol and the Atlantic Trade in the Eighteenth Century* (Cambridge, 1993), 40.

were being developed in the early eighteenth century additional shipwrights were recruited from as far away as London, Hull and Liverpool.[27]

For most of the early modern centuries, however, the heart of English shipbuilding, as indeed of the country's entire economy, was in the Southeast. The industry was concentrated along the Thames and in those East Anglian ports reaching from roughly Leigh-on-Sea to King's Lynn. Long in a class of its own was Ipswich, second only to the Thames until the outbreak of the Civil War. It built ships for the Spanish trade in the early 1500s and provided some powerful craft for London owners under Elizabeth.[28] In 1614, according to Tobias Gentleman, it was the best place for fishing vessels to compete with those of the Dutch, since it had more (and presumably cheaper) shipwrights than "any other six towns" in England. And certainly it was then launching ship after ship - seventy-six in the reign of James I, and about a sixth of the large vessels licenced to carry artillery in the time of Charles I. Some were for the home port, some for Londoners, and some for provincial owners in places ranging from Exeter to Newcastle. Among them were ships of 200 to 500 tons, while according to Defoe "before the late Dutch wars" Ipswich was the main source of big colliers for the east-coast coal trade, some of them 400 tons or more, and all allegedly likely to last at least half a century.[29]

But by the late 1600s this heroic age was passing. Just when the East Indies and Levant trades required powerful and impressive ships, such as the Thames could easily supply, it was difficult, though as Defoe noticed, not impossible, to get such vessels afloat on the Orwell. A long run of easy prosperity may well have encouraged the familiar complacency of prolonged success, and significantly enough local shipmasters were complaining of the lack of a dry dock in 1634. The Anglo-Dutch wars of the later seventeenth century, largely fought in the North Sea, and often on the East Anglian coast, put the port at risk. The very durability of its products was hardly a stimulus to their replacement. Worse still,

---

[27]PRO, Texts and Calendars, *Calendar of State Papers Spain (CSPS), 1580-1586*, 572; and Samuel Purchas, *Hakluyt Posthumus, or Purchas His Pilgrimes* (reprint, 20 vols., Glasgow, 1905-1907), XVI, 358.

[28]PRO, HCA, 13/2, 12 October 1538; and Andrews, *Ships, Money and Politics*, 24ff.

[29]PRO, *CSPD, 1627-1628*, 108, note 14, 500; Defoe, *Tour*, I, 40 and 42-43; *Victoria County History (VCH), Suffolk*, II, 217.

with the ending of Elizabethan and early-Stuart oceanic privateering, and with the astounding success of the Dutch in the carrying trades, there was an urgent need for ships of less massive proportions than those that Ipswich traditionally built. And certainly the flood of cheap Dutch prizes into the English merchant service and subsequent competition from new Northeast coast yards did the town no good.[30]

Much the same happened in neighbouring Aldeburgh, Brightlingsea, Walberswick and Woodbridge. All were formidably difficult of access, but all continued to launch appreciable numbers of substantial vessels until the mid-1600s. Nor were these solely colliers, which suggests that East Anglia's eventual eclipse was not simply due, as Defoe argued, to the emergence of an alternative source of tonnage for the coal trade.[31] The process, furthermore, was neither sudden nor total. Woodbridge was building men of war as late as 1697. The royal shipwright, Phineas Pett, found it worthwhile to use an Ipswich yard in 1673, and building was flourishing at Lynn at the beginning of the following century.[32] Moreover, according to the Elizabethan veteran, William Monson, in the early 1600s the Dutch, with characteristic duplicity, were having ships constructed at Yarmouth, "according to [their] direction." Perhaps their view of English practice was more favourable than those of contemporary publicists and modern scholars, and perhaps English shipwrights could already produce vessels as good as those from Holland. But whatever the reason, Yarmouth prospered and by Defoe's day was annually turning out a "very great number of ships."[33]

All the same the East Anglian industry as a whole steadily lost ground. One formidable competitor was the Thames, where shipbuilding could tap the resources of an extensive and richly endowed hinterland. Moreover, whatever the navigational hazards of the river and its estuary, they served England's capital and greatest port, allowing easy access, for

---

[30]PRO, *CSPD, 1671-1672*, 95; and Defoe, *Tour*.

[31]PRO, HCA 13/2, 12 February 1537/1538; 13/24, 24 April 1580; Defoe, *Tour*, I, 41 and 147; and Davis, *English Shipping Industry*, 55-57.

[32]PRO, *CSPD, 1627-1628*, 500; 1673, 57-58; and Defoe, *Tour*, I, 347.

[33]M. Oppenheim (ed.), *The Naval Tracts of Sir William Monson* (5 vols., London, 1902-1914), V, 269; and Defoe, *Tour*, I, 67 and 347.

the most part, to necessary raw materials and, more important still, to a concentration of mercantile wealth unequalled elsewhere in the country. Shipbuilding was already well established on the river by 1500.[34] Under the Tudors and early Stuarts Thames shipwrights catered alike for royal demands for men of war and the needs of the capital's merchants for large and powerful vessels to be employed first in oceanic privateering and then in those new trades to the distant and dangerous waters of Asia and the eastern Mediterranean which London for long more or less monopolized.

By the end of Elizabeth's reign a whole string of yards, together with those of the Crown itself, lay along the river's banks in places whose names - among them Shadwell, Limehouse and Blackwall - were synonymous with the greatest days of British seafaring.[35] Here were built many of the ships prominent in various dashing enterprises of Elizabeth's last years - *Ark Raleigh*; Cumberland's 900-ton *Malice Scourge;* the *Dainty* of Richard Hawkins - and here, too, were subsequently built most of the country's East Indiamen.[36] The industry was in the sixteenth and early seventeenth centuries largely in the hands of a small group of leading shipwrights, many of whom also worked for the Crown, and who enjoyed, as many other contractors were later to do, those handsome profits reaped from serving the state or associating with corrupt officials. Among this select band were Matthew Baker, Edward Stephens, Richard Chapman, William and Peter Pett, William Burrell and John Ady.[37] With important consequences for the design and construction of ships, there were close associations between some members of this exclusive confraternity. Phineas Pett was apprenticed to Richard Chapman and thereafter worked

---

[34]PRO, *LP*, XX (I), No. 543.

[35]PRO, HCA 13/2, 4 December 1536; and Andrews, *Ships, Money and Politics*, 25.

[36]Purchas, XVI, 25; and XVII, 57.

[37]PRO, *CSPD, 1581-1590*, 604, and 1627-1628, 48; Julian S. Corbett (ed.), *Papers Relating to the Navy during the Spanish War, 1585-1587* (London, 1898), 314; A.P. McGowan (ed.), *The Jacobean Commissions of Enquiry, 1608 and 1618* (London, 1971), 151 and 235-236; K.N. Chaudhuri, *The English East India Company. The Study of an Early Joint-Stock Company, 1600-1640* (London, 1965), 97; and Brian Dietz, "The Royal Bounty and English Merchant Shipping in the Sixteenth and Seventeenth Centuries," *Mariner's Mirror*, LXXVII, No. 1 (1991), 5-20.

for Matthew Baker. Chapman had in turn learned his trade from yet another Pett.[38] In some cases there emerged dynasties, or at least families of builders, with the Petts active from the sixteenth until well into the seventeenth century, and Henry Johnson and his heirs producing Indiamen at Blackwall from the mid-1600s.[39]

Some Thames shipwrights dealt mainly in small craft, like Thomas Redwood, who in 1609 was said to devote his energies to "ships, carvels or hoys."[40] But the river's industry was best known for, and owed its prosperity to, the building of men of war under contract, together with the construction of such large and powerful vessels as East Indiamen, for which purpose the East India Company maintained its own yards at Deptford and Blackwall for a time in the early 1600s.[41] In these undertakings Thames builders, unlike their East Anglian colleagues, had nothing to fear from foreign competition and very little from compatriots. Then the growth of trade, and better still, the demand of the Navy for ships during the wars of the late seventeenth and early eighteenth centuries, combined with the emergence of a state able, however reluctantly, to pay for them, were incentives to further and rapid expansion. The river, like the capital, sucked in talent and ambitions from the provinces, with Henry Johnson of East India fame abandoning Aldeburgh for the Thames in the mid-1600s. New yards sprang up - nearly forty in 1703 alone. Some were offshoots of established enterprises. Others belonged to new recruits to the industry - Richard Dummer, for example, probably a relative of the pioneer of the West India packet service. In a climate of expectations of easy profit, some undertakings predictably expired at birth, but others, like that of Captain Burchett at Deptford in 1709, developed impressively.[42]

---

[38]Dietz, "Royal Bounty," 11.

[39]Merriman (ed.), *Queen Anne's Navy*, 62; and Davis, *English Shipping Industry*, 55.

[40]McGowan (ed.), *Jacobean Commissions*, 237.

[41]K.N. Chaudhuri, "The East India Company and the Organization of Its Shipping in the Early Seventeenth Century," *Mariner's Mirror*, XLIX, No. 1 (1963), 27ff.

[42]Merriman (ed.), *Queen Anne's Navy*, 62 and 81-83.

By this date, however, there was in progress a fundamental shift of English shipbuilding to the Northeast, which by the end of the eighteenth century was established as its main centre. It was a shift that foreshadowed the North's subsequent industrial pre-eminence. It was also one that did something to counterbalance the rapidly growing maritime and commercial importance of the ports of the Northwest, where by the mid-1700s Liverpool was adding shipbuilding to an already thriving economy fuelled by slaving and allied ventures. In the Northeast the new industry was concentrated in Stockton, Sunderland, Tyneside and most remarkably in the hitherto virtually unknown fishing havens of Whitby and Scarborough. Of the former, which already possessed at least one yard in 1635, Defoe later reported that "they build very good ships for the coal trade and many of them too."[43] The harbour was improved in 1726 to allow the construction of still bigger vessels, and a dry dock added a few years later – a story more or less parallelled in contemporary Scarborough and Sunderland. By this date all these places were specializing in colliers, though they also produced some sizeable craft for other trades. All had easy access to the necessary raw materials and almost all had been building ships or boats since the Middle Ages. The reasons for their dramatic rise are, however, by no means clear. It was not that the North had a sharper appreciation of the opportunities of the time, for already in 1630 Yarmouth was building a 250-ton "round stern ship," which would seem to indicate a Dutch-style vessel of a design soon to enjoy such popularity. Conversely, the Newcastle of the day was well-known for employing – and presumably also building – colliers hefty enough to serve as convoy escorts or men of war. There was thus no sharp distinction between a North acutely aware of a new demand for bulk carriers and a Southeast blithely ignoring it.

To confuse matters further, in the early 1600s Newcastle also employed, and probably also built, both colliers so lightly manned as to arouse the apprehension of Captain Boteler as to their safety, and those handy crompsters or hoys much admired by Walter Raleigh. Possibly of Dutch inspiration, these craft were perhaps the precursors of those the

---

[43]Perrin (ed.), *Autobiography of Phineas Pett*, 159.

Northeast was soon turning out in large numbers.[44] The industry was already stirring at Whitby in the 1620s and 1630s.[45] Opportunities improved with the need to replace tonnage lost in the second of three Anglo-Dutch wars and as East Anglian and Thameside yards concentrated on big ships or were busy with naval building and repairs. They were enhanced further in the late seventeenth century as the Thames came to monopolize the construction of large, powerful vessels, mortally wounding the East Anglian industry in the process. Having thus lost one market to its neighbour, East Anglia lost another with the influx into the collier fleet in the later 1600s of cheap and relatively efficient Dutch prizes. When, around 1700, these reached the end of their working lives, the only yards capable of supplying suitable replacements were in the Northeast.[46] The region enjoyed, moreover, the further advantage of being more remote than others from the regular beat of French privateers in the second Hundred Years War. So, too, its distance from London and consequent virtual exclusion from naval building, encouraged it to concentrate on new opportunities. And it perhaps received an added fillip when momentary stagnation in the coal trade in the late 1600s may have tempted local entrepreneurs to look for new outlets for their capital.

Meanwhile, with the colonization of North America and the West Indies, and with the opening of a direct seaborne commerce to East Asia, the construction and repair of ships for European use took root in many parts of the non-European world. From the seventeenth century, to the accompaniment of talk of redressing the increasing shortage of suitable timber in England, vessels were built in bases belonging to the East India Company, such as Surat and Bombay (Mumbai) in India. Some of these craft were of local design and most spent their entire existence in the

---

[44]PRO, HCA 13/51, 22 August 1634, and 13/78, 14 August 1677; W.G. Perrin (ed.), *Boteler's Dialogues* (London, 1929), 49; Davis, *English Shipping Industry*, 47 and 62-65; and R.H. Boulind, "The Crompster in Literature and Pictures," *Mariner's Mirror*, LIV, No. 1 (1968), 3ff.

[45]PRO, *CSPD, 1627-1628*, 500; Perrin (ed.), *Autobiography of Phineas Pett*, 159; and Davis, *English Shipping Industry*, 55.

[46]Davis, *English Shipping Industry*, 62.

East.[47] Initially it was common for the Company, and its would-be rivals, to send English shipwrights to Asia. There was one in Japan in 1619, who was to be the chief carpenter "to trymme and repaire" ships, and there were others at Surat and elsewhere in the mid-1600s.[48] It was, however, soon appreciated that Asia offered not only excellent timber (teak especially) but also "very expert" craftsmen who cost much less than their European counterparts, but who had no difficulty in adopting their methods and who could build, launch or survey ships as well as any. It was, for example, the East India Company's senior local carpenter - the ancestor, perhaps of the celebrated Wadia dynasty - who at Surat in the 1670s advised that a vessel under construction ought to be "broader and deeper."[49] Increasing English involvement in local trades brought the growth of both English-owned yards, employing Asian labour, and others in Indian hands, but heavily dependent, as in Coromandel, on English patronage. And at the same time there appeared indigenous equivalents of those shipbuilding dynasties that emerged in Britain, notably the Wadias of Bombay. The construction of vessels according to Asian design and technique had many attractions and advantages. Such craft carried their water in tanks, not casks. Carvel-built hulls, with skin planks set into one another and spiked together (as in modern strip-planking) had no need for expensive and, in sun-baked regions, ineffective, European-style caulking. But not all the products of this rudimentary industrial cross-fertilization were unqualified successes. Besides, there was the considerable disadvantage that in Coromandel, it was said, Indian master shipwrights, sharing the supposed addiction of their compatriots to such stratagems, were likely to poison European colleagues to be rid of unwanted competition.[50]

---

[47]W. Foster (ed.), *The English Factories in India, 1618-1669* (13 vols., Oxford, 1906-1927); *1646-50*, 232; *1668-90*, 201.

[48]Foster (ed.), *Factories, 1646-50*, 94; and Sir Richard Carnac Temple and Lavinia Mary Anstey (eds.), *The Travels of Peter Mundy in Europe and Asia, 1608-1667* (5 vols., London, 1907-1935), III, 1 and 141.

[49]Foster (ed.), *Factories, 1668-9*, 79-80; Sir Charles Fawcett (ed.), *English Factories in India, 1670-77, 1678-84* (Oxford, 1952-1955), 223.

[50]Foster (ed.), *Factories, 1651-4*, 154; and Thomas Bowrey, *A Geographical Account of Countries Round the Bay of Bengal, 1669 to 1679* (London, 1905), 102-104.

Less colourful, but of far greater economic consequence, were the beginnings of shipbuilding in colonial North America (especially New England) and to a lesser degree in the Caribbean. From the outset of English settlement vessels were needed to fetch food and supplies, to engage in fisheries vital to survival, and to participate in that vigorous maritime economy which rapidly emerged, linking colonies to one another and to Europe. Then, ironically enough, the protectionist legislation introduced by English governments from the mid-seventeenth century drove the Dutch out of the colonial carrying trade, left it short of tonnage and so provided the northern settlements with a magnificent opening. There was some adaptation of indigenous builds of coastal and river craft, as with the boat-shaped canoes of New England, fashioned from hollowed-out pine trunks. But, at least to start, most seagoing ships were replicas of models from the mother country.[51] The rapidly-growing industry had its problems. The construction of vessels for British customers - of whom there were soon many - entailed, at such a distance, difficulties over supervision, not to mention pay. Then again, even as late as the opening decades of the eighteenth century, rigging, sails and ironwork had to be imported from Britain for craft on the stocks in Nova Scotia and New England.[52] More fundamentally, it was widely, and probably rightly, believed that American ships were inferior to British, being generally built from poor quality and inadequately prepared timber.[53] Nor, since their crews were of the same size, were they any cheaper to run. Nevertheless, before long they had plenty of staunch and influential advocates. The attractions of building in New England, New York or Pennsylvania were being urged by the early 1700s. The merits of Rhode Island and Bermudan sloops were extolled, and the possibility of men of war of North American

---

[51]Paul J. Lindholdt (ed.), *John Josselyn, Colonial Traveller: A Critical Edition of Two Voyages to New Englnad* (Hanover, NH, 1988), 46-47; and John J. McCusker and Russell R. Menard, *The Economy of British America, 1607-1789* (Chapel Hill, 1985), 99.

[52]PRO, HCA 13/88, 30 October 1729; Julian Gwyn (ed.), *The Royal Navy and North America: The Warren Papers, 1736-1752* (London, 1973), 29.

[53]*Gwyn (ed.), Warren Papers*, 28-29 and 37; and Christopher J. French, "The Longevity of Ships in Colonial Trade: Some Further Evidence," *International Journal of Maritime History*, III, 1 (1991), 155ff.

origin was broached at the same date.[54] Essentially such enthusiasm stemmed from the fact that American vessels were cheap, given the huge and accessible wealth of the continent's North Atlantic seaboard in timber, pitch and tar. The American industry was, moreover, strenuously competitive since the building, operation and sale of ships provided colonists, and New Englanders especially, with an income necessary to help with their purchases from Europe. For owners in England colonial-built ships had the further attraction of counting as English for the purpose of the Navigation Acts, while for Scotland, whose Atlantic trade soared from the late 1600s, North America was a supplier of tonnage on a scale, and at a price, few could equal.

Already in the 1630s a Devon fishing station off the Maine coast was providing its own boats and the first New England-built vessel had reached Europe. A century later, when Boston alone had sixteen yards and the export of ships was an important element in Philadelphia's trade, Thames shipwrights were complaining – and probably with justice – that American competition was putting them out of business. London owners had American agents (who might well be recommended by builders from the capital itself) to handle their commissions, and English shipmasters sometimes went out to supervise the work.[55] By 1760 probably one English ship in four was of American origin, and for Scotland the figures were even higher.[56] Less well-known, less significant, but nevertheless of some importance was the industry in Bermuda, and in such Caribbean islands as Barbados, St. Kitts and Jamaica, whose first locally-built ocean-going ship sailed for London in 1660.[57] But most of these craft found

---

[54]Gwyn (ed.), *Warren Papers*, 37.

[55]PRO, HCA 13/88, 5 November 1729; Captain Alfred Dewar (ed.), *The Voyages and Travels of Captain Nathaniel Uring* (London, 1928), xviii; Davis, *English Shipping Industry*, 66-68; McCusker and Mennard, *Economy of British America*, 205; Michael Duffy, *et al.*, *The New Maritime History of Devon. Vol. I: From Early Times to the Late Eighteenth Century* (London, 1992), 146.

[56]Davis, *English Shipping Industry*, 66-68; and Hamilton, *Economic History of Scotland*, 287.

[57]PRO, HCA 13/85, 4 June 1714; 13/88 19 November 1731 and 4 January 1731/2; and Stephen Saunders Webb, *The Governors-General, The English Army and the Definition of the Empire, 1569-1681* (Chapel Hill, 1979), 194-195.

employment, legitimate or otherwise, in home waters or in whatever opportunities wars might offer.

In an economy in which specialization was still in its infancy, ships were designed and built by a rich diversity of individuals. Henry VIII was the alleged "architect" of some oared vessels for his Navy, while in 1609 Sir George Somers, wrecked in Bermuda, had a pinnace constructed "by his owne directions," participating in the task "with his owne hands."[58] Some builders were seamen or former seamen. In the early 1600s the versatile George Waymouth was an experienced sailor, expert military engineer, sometime spy and the author of treatises on maritime affairs. His remaining energies were divided between exploration and, like his father before him, the building of ships.[59] In much the same mould was Captain John Mason, who in 1628 bombastically offered to supply the Navy with vessels of superior design. His career embraced Arctic whaling and the pursuit of pirates, and he was still alive in 1652 at the age of seventy-nine, after half a century of seagoing command. Nor was there any lack of others of similar background. The future Cromwellian admiral, Robert Moulton, set up a yard on the Mystic River in New England in 1629.[60] So, too, in 1716, John Brown, a London seaman, then aged sixty, declared that for many years he had built, owned and commanded ships and was currently a merchant.[61]

Some craft, small boats especially, could be knocked up by ordinary carpenters in any convenient spot, though by the early eighteenth century boatbuilding was a recognized skill in its own right.[62] By and large, however, ships of any size were built by men variously described as ship carpenters or shipwrights. They turn up throughout most of maritime Britain, even in minute coastal villages. But in any individual

---

[58]PRO, *LP*, XVI, No. 1005; Purchas, XVIII, 539-540.

[59]J.F. Coates, "The Authorship of a Manuscript on Shipbuilding c. 1600-1620," *Mariner's Mirror*, LXVII, No. 3 (1981), 285-286; and David B. Quinn and Alison M. Quinn (eds.), *The English New England Voyages, 1602-1608* (London, 1983), 58-62.

[60]Gillian T. Cell (ed.), *Newfoundland Discovered: English Attempts at Colonisation, 1610-1630* (London, 1982), 92; and Purchas, XIV, 78.

[61]PRO, HCA 13/85, 5 July 1716.

[62]Hartlepool Town Books (England, Hartlepool Town Hall), Vol. I, 234ff.

locality – Thameside apart – their numbers were generally so few that for ambitious undertakings reinforcements had to be brought in from a wide area, just as were masons employed on some spectacular country house. Some, both English and Scots, were obliged to seek work abroad, either through lack of opportunity at home – as was said to be the case in late Elizabethan England – or to escape the consequences of incompetence or worse. But some were of sufficient standing to be invited into foreign service. In 1595 William Lambert of Liverpool was in Lisbon building for Philip II "5 such ships as the king had not the like before," while in 1716 the royal master shipwright in the same port was English.[63] The majority of those working in Britain were natives, unlike the large alien contingent in England's textile industry, though under the Tudors there were a number of Portuguese and Italians, usually in royal pay.[64]

Essentially, shipwrights designed and constructed vessels and ensured that all the necessary carpentry was carried out. But their expertise extended much further. They selected the timber, surveyed, measured and valued vessels, and undertook such salvage operations as raising sunken hulls.[65] Their ranks accordingly came to embrace a great range of wealth and status. On the one hand were those master shipwrights in government pay who owned ships and who, with their own yards, workmen, servants and apprentices, undertook naval contracts: skilled men, that is, who like their equivalents in other industries had gained control of their fellow workers and the means of production. Then there were those who merely eked out a modest living as impoverished proletarians – one, for example, declaring in 1681 to have done a spell as

---

[63]G.V. Scammell, "Shipowning in the Politics and Economy of Early Modern England," *Historical Journal*, XV (1972), 385-387; Duffy, *et* al., *New Maritime History of Devon*, I, 117; Martin Bellamy, "English Master Shipwrights to the Danish Crown, 1570-1680," *Mariner's Mirror*, LXXXIV, No. 2 (1998), 215ff; and Rodger, *Safeguard of the Sea*, 386-387.

[64]V.M. Shillington and A.B. Wallis Chapman, *The Commercial Relations of England and Portugal* (London, 1907), 131.

[65]PRO, HCA 13/2, fo. 24, and 13/56, 7 May 1640; and PRO, *CSPD, 1627-1628*, 500 and 588.

a lighterman.[66] True, some used their wits to improve their lot, like the carpenter of a man of war who in 1608 was building a vessel for two Navy officials in the state's time and with the state's materials. Some also alternated, as opportunity offered, between work at sea and work ashore, and some, like other artisans, had small holdings which helped to sustain them in hard times.[67]

Shipwrights were originally organized in guilds in which young recruits, some from comfortable social backgrounds, learned their trade and imbibed inherited wisdom through apprenticeship, which included a stint at sea. But no more than in other crafts did all serve out their full time, with the celebrated Phineas Pett quitting after two years and picking up knowledge and skills as he went along.[68] As London grew in wealth, and as economic change favoured the rise of metropolitan-based chartered companies at the expense of guilds, London shipwrights, encouraged by the impecunious monarchy, sought incorporation. This they eventually achieved in 1605, when they also secured wide powers of inspection, which they interpreted as giving them authority over their provincial colleagues. Such pretensions, like those of other metropolitan companies, were strenuously resisted, and in 1612 the jurisdiction of the Shipwrights Company extended no further than Rotherhithe. But this was no obstacle to its endeavouring to determine what work might be undertaken in the rest of the country, where, however, matters supposedly came to be regulated by local companies.[69]

Like many other industries of the time, shipbuilding ranged from relatively large centralized undertakings, of which in England the Navy's own dockyards were the most remarkable, to the assorted endeavours of independent master craftsmen. With at most a couple of assistants, a man

---

[66]PRO, HCA 13/78, 7 December 1681; and McGowan (ed.), *Jacobean Commissions*, 38.

[67]McGowan (ed.), *Jacobean Commissions*, 150-151; and J.D. Davies, *Gentlemen and Tarpaulins. The Officers and Men of the Restoration Navy* (Oxford, 1991), 21.

[68]Hakluyt, *Principal Navigations*, V, 76; Davis, *Shipping Industry*, 54; and Rodger (ed.), *Naval Miscellany*, V, 2-3.

[69]Welford, *History of Newcastle and Gateshead*, III, 359; and D.W. Waters, *The Art of Navigation in England in Elizabethan and Early Stuart Times* (London, 1958), 296.

might then as now build or repair a small boat, while in the 1530s with twenty or so he could "new make" a sizeable vessel.[70]

Such ventures, and far more ambitious ones, demanded, like so much contemporary industry, little initial capital and less subsequent investment. Yard holders might have to furnish apprentices who had finished their time with a set of tools. Leases for establishments in prime sites could be expensive, and to excavate a new dock - though hardly an everyday occurrence - could be costly. But for the rest cash came in from customers who paid for their ships as the work progressed. Hence, the assets of a yard holder could amount to little more than a collection of mallets, axes, adzes, saws, caulking irons, drills and chisels, together with a few balks of timber on which keels could be laid.[71] As late as 1686 the total stock of one of the most important Thameside yards was worth only a little over £800 at a time when a new 300-ton ship would cost about £1500. Nor, on the whole, were things to change much. Nineteenth-century shipyards building wooden vessels were rarely larger than the workshops of other crafts, while a sample of Scottish shipbuilders in 1790-1800 shows an average insurance valuation of around £1800 - roughly one-tenth the rate for Glasgow weaving.[72]

True, there were exceptions. For a time in the early 1600s the East India Company had its own yards and ancillary industries at Deptford and Blackwall. Elsewhere bigger and more complex machinery came into use, whether for moving timber or bending planks, and some private yards eventually came to rival those of the Navy. Nevertheless, even in the late 1600s, and on the Thames itself, it is hard to find builders who regularly employed more than 100 men or who could construct or repair anything larger than a naval third rate.[73]

---

[70]PRO, *LP*, IX, No. 1025.

[71]John Webb, "Apprenticeship in the Maritime Occupations at Ipswich, 1596-1651," *Mariner's Mirror*, XLVI, No. 1 (1960), 29-31.

[72]D.C. Coleman, "Naval Dockyards Under the Later Stuarts," *Economic History Review*, 2nd ser., VI, No. 2 (1953), 134-155; Davis, *English Shipping Industry*, 56; and Lythe and Butt, *Economic History of Scotland*, 173.

[73]Chaudhuri, *English East India Company*, 99; and Coleman, "Naval Dockyards," 137.

The industry thus had a number of clearly defined features, best revealed in the relatively abundant sources relating to England. The pace of work, notwithstanding long hours, was slow since timber, the basic raw material, was heavy and intractable, with few aids to its handling. And activity was all too likely to be halted by bad weather or failure of supplies. In 1618 Phineas Pett finished a 500-ton ship in nine months, but it took over a year to build one half the size at Yarmouth a little later, and this was probably the usual rate.[74] In the second half of the seventeenth century, even major builders specializing in Indiamen turned out at best one in twelve months, or a couple of smaller craft, which was poor by contemporary Dutch or German standards.

As Samuel Pepys observed, shipbuilding was not an industry in which fortunes were made or from which dynasties sprang, though in this there were more exceptions than he was aware - not only the Petts and Johnsons already noticed, but the Blaydes at Hull in the seventeenth and eighteenth centuries and a succession of Barnards at Ipswich, Harwich and on the Thames from around 1700. It was, furthermore, an industry which in general gave little encouragement to change. Admittedly it accepted, like its counterparts in most of northern Europe, the use of carvel planking and the merits of some Dutch-style freighters. And shipwrights in royal service, whether in the Scotland of James IV or, more influentially still, in the England of Elizabeth, were responsible for major innovations in the design and construction of fighting ships. It was also English royal dockyards that first employed such time and energy saving practices as mechanized sawing and the stockpiling of parts, long familiar to the Dutch. But by and large initiatives were restrained as traditional skills and venerable designs were passed from master to apprentice, or as customers specified their particular, usually unadventurous, requirements.

The industry had other distinctive and occasionally unique features. Like building as a whole, and sustained by similarly exiguous resources, it produced some of the most valuable and impressive artefacts of the day. By its very nature it could hardly be organized on a family-based putting-out system in which, as in textiles, for example, entre-preneurs supplied necessary materials to workers labouring in their own homes. Instead, as in mining or metal smelting, shipbuilding was carried

---

[74]PRO, HCA 13/51, 22 August 1634; Perrin (ed.), *Autobiography of Phineas Pett*, 115-117; and Davis, *English Shipping Industry*, 55-56.

on in centralized units – certainly as yet for the most part tiny – requiring some fixed plant and reflecting the beginnings of a more general move towards capital-intensive undertakings.[75] Unlike most other contemporary industries it appears to have made little or no use of women, though like clothmaking it was a particularly lavish employer of labour, needing a host of specialists to supply, for a vessel of any size, an astonishing variety of parts and fittings, to prepare materials for the shipwrights and to put the finishing touches to their work. Indeed few industries illustrate more graphically the nature of an economy in which small master craftsmen, of an infinity of gradations of wealth and status, proliferated. Hewers and sawyers cut and trimmed timbers which clinchers secured. There were "corkers" who stopped the seams between planks, among them clearly some men of enterprise, with one acting as attorney for a carpenter who was indebted to him in the early 1700s.[76] There were oarmakers who might be able, as in 1676, to provide unspecified fittings from the family yard.[77] There were sailmakers who owned ships, as did also ropemakers, and sometimes on a considerable scale, usually the outcome of foreclosures for unpaid bills for naval stores. There were hempdressers who supplied the ropemakers; pulleymakers; blockmakers; pumpmakers – some of them dealing in timber – and even specialist topcastle makers.[78] Besides which there were gunmakers, anchor smiths and the smiths who produced the nails required in such prodigious numbers, and not least there were ship painters.[79] When a hull was finished the builder might fit it out himself, though it might go elsewhere to be sheathed. Rigging might likewise be entrusted to others. In some cases it was undertaken, at the

---

[75]D.C. Coleman, *The Economy of England 1450-1750* (Oxford, 1977), 76, 87 and 171.

[76]PRO, HCA 13/85, 21 October 1714; and Welford, *History of Newcastle and Gateshead*, II, 6.

[77]PRO, HCA 13/78, 24 October 1676.

[78]PRO, HCA 13/56, 30 September 1640; 13/65, 26 May 1652; 13/78, 4 July 1678; 13/85, 8 March 1714/15, 16 June 1715, and 20 February 1716/1717; McGowan (ed.), *Jacobean Commissions*, 123; and Andrews, *Ships, Money and Politics*, 53-54.

[79]PRO, HCA 13/65, 3 May 1652; HCA 13/78, 24 October 1676 and 4 July 1678; 13/85, 8 March 1714/15; and McGowan (ed.), *Jacobean Commissions*, 142.

owners' cost, by the bosun appointed to the vessel. But for a ship of any size it was usually a job for specialist riggers, who by the early 1700s were commonly former bosuns. They would negotiate a price with the owners and then set their own men to the task, perhaps assisted by the vessel's skeleton crew.[80]

Having a ship built could be a long, difficult and potentially litigious business. Matters were simplest when a would-be owner found some suitable craft in the process of construction.[81] Otherwise he and his partners made their requirements known to a shipwright who tendered a price and, if all went well, agreement - usually written - was reached and a date fixed for the completion of the vessel.[82] Many owners knew what they wanted, which as often as not was a replica of some successful craft. Some even submitted their own plans, with Charles II providing "a draught...by his...own hand" for the highly satisfactory *Fubbs*.[83] Leading builders, dealing with important clients, would produce drawings before work began, as when in 1578 the future *Galleon Leicester* was said to have been "moulded" by the celebrated Matthew Baker and then "framed" by John Ady - though the vessel turned out to be little credit to either.[84] By the beginning of the following century even quite modest provincial shipwrights might work from plans and, as elsewhere in Europe, models might be constructed from preliminary drawings. The same era was marked by the emergence of something of a science of naval architecture, often of considerable sophistication, developed especially by shipwrights in royal service towards the end of Elizabeth's reign. The dissemination of such learning was, however, another matter.[85] Will Adams, ensconced in Japan in the early 1600s, might find there an enthusiastic audience for

---

[80]PRO, HCA 13/85, 5 and 17 July 1716.

[81]PRO, HCA 13/75, 9 March 1665/1666.

[82]PRO, *CSPD, 1627-1628*, 592.

[83]Edgar K. Thompson, "The Yacht *Fubbs*," *Mariner's Mirror*, XLV, No. 2 (1959), 157-158.

[84]E.G.R. Taylor (ed.), *The Troublesome Voyage of Captain Edward Fentom* (Cambridge, 1959), 170; and Donno (ed.), *Diary of Richard Madox*, 114.

[85]Rodger, *Safeguard of the Sea*, 219 and 387-388.

his exposition of geometry and mathematics, while works on shipbuilding began to appear in England in the late seventeenth and early eighteenth centuries. But for most of the early modern period the majority of British shipwrights proceeded according to tradition and by rule of thumb.

Once work on a hull commenced, its progress would be watched by the owners' representative, who was usually a seaman and perhaps the vessel's master-designate.[86] The builder would use his contract as security to obtain the necessary timber, which might well have to be brought from a considerable distance.[87] He might have to take on extra labour, or he might bring in subcontractors or indeed subcontract the work to other yards. Should his own be full he might use one elsewhere, especially if he could get it cheap and with cheaper labour. Hence in 1604 Phineas Pett built a ship in David Duck's yard at Gillingham, while another of the clan was investigating the prospects of Ipswich in 1673.[88] More lucrative still, the select band of builders in royal service could employ the crown's yards and resources for their own business, as was notoriously the case in the heyday of corruption under the early Stuarts.[89] Smaller men, with little or no capital, and paid as work progressed, lived a hand-to-mouth existence, buying timber as each instalment of their payment came in, and in trouble if there was any delay, or if they found they had rashly committed themselves to something too ambitious.

The profits from shipbuilding were nothing like those generated in the great "rich" overseas trades of the time. But if many builders foundered there were plenty who did well enough, though usually by engaging in a variety of enterprises. In the late 1600s – when, however, the fortunes of London commercial tycoons could run into six figures – William Wyatt was able to leave his widow £3000 and some property, the fruits of a combination of shipbuilding, shipowning, naval contracting and

---

[86]PRO, HCA 13/88, 23 August 1731.

[87]PRO, *CSPD, 1665-1666*, 287.

[88]PRO, *CSPD, 1673*, 57-58; and Perrin (ed.), *Autobiography of Phineas Pett*, 23-24.

[89]Perrin (ed.), *Autobiography of Phineas Pett*, 115-117.

timber importing.[90] Some drew steady incomes from their share in the earnings of their apprentices, with John Okill of Liverpool (a considerable trader in sugar as well) receiving in 1752 between fifteen and thirty shillings a month from each of the fifteen in his care. There were colleagues who sailed as masters, traded, or leased out their yards. Many were shipowners, sometimes since they had foreclosed on customers who had failed to pay for work undertaken, sometimes since they built vessels when business was slack in the hope of selling them when things looked up.[91] And of course investors welcomed the association with men who could (or should) have been able to ensure that their vessels were sound and properly maintained.[92] Then there were those who, as in other crafts, traded in raw materials. At the beginning of the reign of James I, William Girdler was importing masts in a purpose-built ship, while many others dealt in timber, or were the close associates, to their mutual benefit, of timber merchants.[93] Some secured useful civic office, like William Burrell, who in 1624 became Master Dredger and Master Ballaster of the Thames.[94] Luckier still were some of those who migrated to royal service, there to enjoy careers often lucrative - at times, as in the early 1600s, scandalously so - and occasionally illustrious.

Humbler colleagues who were working masters could make a passable living. In 1500 they were paid something like three times as much as seamen, and in the early eighteenth century rather more than half the wages of mates in sizeable ships. Besides which they could be the

---

[90]A.J. Holland, "Naval Shipbuilding on the Hamble River before 1815," *Mariner's Mirror*, XLIX, No. 1 (1963), 21ff.

[91]PRO, HCA 13/56, 16 October 1640; and 13/65, 28 May 1652; and Davis, *English Shipping Industry*, 120-121.

[92]Perrin (ed.), *Autobiography of Phineas Pett*, 77; Welford, *History of Newcastle and Gateshead*, III, 11; McGowan (ed.), *Jacobean Commissions*, 238; and Scammell, "Shipowning," 397-398.

[93]R.G. Marsden (ed.), *Select Pleas in the Court of Admiralty. Vol. II. The High Court of Admiralty (1547-1602)* (London, 1897), 185-186; McGowan (ed.), *Jacobean Commissions*, 37-38; and James A. Williamson, *Hawkins of Plymouth* (London, 1949), 252-253.

[94]J.J. and M.F. Packard, "A Missing Part-Owner of the *Mayflower*," *Mariner's Mirror*, LXXIV, No. 1 (1988), 54-55.

recipients of far from negligible increments. Some became yard foremen; the majority had apprentices; and by a liberal interpretation of their customary right to allegedly surplus timber, most could augment their standard of living. They acquired not only free firewood but also, at no cost, the raw materials - rare and expensive in many parts of the British Isles - with which to embellish and furnish their own houses and those of their clients: a cottage industry in every sense of the words.

In the centuries which saw the beginnings of British maritime hegemony the country's shipbuilding industry grew in size and underwent radical relocation. Some yards became bigger and more complex in organization, though rarely approaching the scale that characterized those of the Navy. For the rest the pattern and structure of shipbuilding reflected the general economic trends of the time, from the proliferation of small master craftsmen to the hesitant evolution of relatively large centralized undertakings. The shortcomings of the British industry and its products were much discussed by contemporaries, as they have been since. It was slow, compared with that of the Dutch, to respond to economic challenges in the seventeenth century, just as it was reluctant, unlike that of France, subsequently to learn what science could teach.

All the same, private yards supplemented the output of those belonging to the Navy to provide the service with virtually all the vessels it required. Overall, the industry supplied a substantial percentage of England's - though not Scotland's - merchant and fishing fleets. It employed directly and indirectly an important labour force, enabling the Navy in moments of crisis to press or recruit shipwrights by the hundred, just as it provided the service with a number of distinguished servants. In the late sixteenth century it produced fighting ships second to none and went on to produce others, whether collier brigs or East Indiamen, widely and greatly admired. Not least, it put down roots in North America with the profoundest maritime and economic consequences. Maybe it could have done better. Nevertheless, like the proverbial tortoise, it got there in the end, playing an indispensable role in the genesis of British seapower.

IV

THE MERCHANT SERVICE MASTER IN EARLY MODERN ENGLAND

The safety and success of any sea voyage largely depend on the character and competence of its commander. This was still more the case in those centuries in which Europeans first penetrated to most of the oceans of the world. The voyages themselves were frequently longer and more arduous than hitherto. Ships were often of a construction, or in a condition that left much to be desired, and even if well-found were at the mercy of the elements to a far greater degree than their modern counterparts. Aids to navigation were imperfect. Trade in many areas remained, in the graphic contemporary phrase, a venture. Occasional English patriots might flatteringly depict the country's shipmasters – or some of them at least – as omniscient absolutists in charge of crews unequalled 'under heaven in their profession; and by forreiners compared unto Fishes'. Others were less sanguine. But despite the pioneering studies of Ralph Davis and Peter Earle much remains to be known about those who commanded English merchant ships in that age (c.1550–1750) which witnessed England's eventual emergence as the world's greatest maritime and commercial power. This gap the present paper makes some attempt to fill.[1]

First, however, there is a problem of nomenclature. In the sixteenth and seventeenth centuries especially those in command are often described as captain. Such individuals might well not be seamen, but, in accordance with that ancient tradition which conflated authority with rank, they would be persons of suitably elevated social standing exercising overall control, though with a skilled master as their right hand man.[2] In some instances the titles were employed as synonymous or interchangeable, with a man described, for example, as 'master or captain'. And notwithstanding the resolve of the East India Company in 1640 'to entertain no man with the title of captain again', the rank survived, but with its functions increasingly absorbed into those of the master – the very opposite to what happened in the Navy.[3] Even so, at a time when there was little concern

1. Ralph Davis, *The Rise of the English Shipping Industry in the Seventeenth and Eighteenth Centuries* (London, 1962); Peter Earle, *Sailors: English Merchant Seamen 1650–1775* (London, 1998).
2. London, Public Record Office (hereafter PRO), High Court of Admiralty (hereafter HCA), 13/32, 27 August 1597.
3. Sir Richard Carnac Temple and Lavinia Mary Anstey (eds.), *The Travels of Peter Mundy in Europe and Asia, 1608–1667* (5 vols, London, Hakluyt Society, 1907–1936), II, p.23n; HCA 13/32, 28 May 1596; HCA 13/88, 5 May 1732.

with precision or consistency in such matters, and when in any case multiple social and occupational designations were common, those commanding merchantmen could be variously described as captain and master; master or commander; captain or commander; master and chief commander; commander; captain and commander; master and captain; master and chief commander; or master and commander in chief.[4] But by and large from about 1600 at the least, the military/naval style of captain was assumed by, or accorded to, those in charge of big, prestigious ships like East Indiamen. It was also used by, and of, men who enjoyed some fame and reputation, or, like the most outrageous pirates, sufficient notoriety. Lesser mortals were usually called, or called themselves, master and perhaps captain as well in grander moments.[5]

Captains or masters were commonly appointed to their commands by the owners (usually the managing owners) of the vessels in question, or, less frequently, by their charterers. Many were, of course, themselves owners or partowners of the ships in which they sailed, and some commanded one vessel and had shares in others. The luckiest were those able to succeed their fathers in command, as happened in the East India Company's *Success* in 1677. In most trades masters received a wage and some indeed, like many contemporary craftsmen, were simply workers with nothing to sell but their labour and skills. Their numbers included some unfortunates who having started as partowners ended as wage earners, together with those who, less happily still, eventually found themselves serving as subordinates in vessels they had once commanded.[6]

Masters might manage their ships as their own, or they might merely be the agents of a managing owner. Many were hired for a single voyage, whilst others served in the same trade under different owners or in different ships belonging to the same owner. A fair number were in long and regular employment with some particular owner, sometimes in the same vessel. So, in the early 1700s, Henry Thirkettle spent about 16 years in the *Richard*, whilst at Bristol John Plummer was with the *Jason Galley* for over a decade.[7] As European trades and

4. HCA 13/51, fo.145v; 13/56, fo.186; 13/65, 5 December 1651, 1 March 1651/2; 13/75, 2 June 1666; 13/78, 1 May 1680, 17 February 1680/1, 27 August 1681; 13/88, 18 February 1730/1, 2 March 1730/1; 3 March 1730/1, 5 May 1732.

5. So, for example, the distinguished Elizabethan privateering commander Captain Christopher Newport, or later the versatile Captain Nathaniel Uring. For pirates, the seventeenth-century Captain Walsingham and his contemporary, Captain Salkeld, onetime 'king' of Lundy Island.

6. HCA 13/88, 17 December 1731. See also the career of John Scandret at Bristol in David Richardson (ed.), *Bristol, Africa and the Eighteenth-Century Slave Trade to America*, vol. I, *The Years of Expansion 1698–1729* (Bristol, Bristol Record Society, vol. xxxviii, 1986), pp.99, 106. For a son succeeding his father, see W. Foster (ed), *The English Factories in India, 1618–1669* (13 vols, Oxford, 1906–1927), 1670–1677, p.285. For downwardly mobile masters see HCA 13/78, 27 July 1677; 13/85, fo. 33; and cf. Davis, *English Shipping Industry*, p. 265.

7. HCA 13/88, 17 November 1729; Richardson (ed), *Bristol ... and the Slave Trade*, pp.32, 120.

empires expanded there were increasingly men experienced in seas the world over, like Nicholas Woodcock who in the early 1600s knew alike Asia and the Arctic. Others might work virtually a lifetime in a single trade, accumulating valuable navigational knowledge and building up useful business connections. In 1640 a Hull master claimed to have been 20 years at least in trade to London, whilst nearly a century later colleagues recalled 13 or more years experience of Norway and 15 of Maryland.[8] Many commanders, particularly in the late sixteenth and early seventeenth centuries, alternated as opportunity offered, between commercial voyages and privateering ventures against current enemies. Until the mid 1600s some remained in charge of their vessels when these were hired or pressed by the government as fighting ships, or they might even command men of war. When times were hard or difficult there those who worked for foreign owners, with, for example, Thomas Bowrey captaining a Portuguese ship in the Bay of Bengal in 1676. By this date it was also not unusual for regular naval officers who saw their employment or career prospects blighted by unwelcome periods of peace, to do a stint in charge of merchantmen till things improved.[9]

A master was responsible for the safety and well-being of his ship and her gear and, once he or his deputy had endorsed the bill of lading, for her cargo as well.[10] Any shortcoming could cost him dear. In 1541 two London masters, convicted of the negligent stranding of their vessels, were sentenced to make good the damage, imprisoned and barred from future command.[11] The East India Company fined or demoted a number of its commanders in the early seventeenth century for surrendering to, or fleeing from enemies, indigenous or European, in Asian waters. It similarly punished slackness, poor seamanship or navigation, and cowardice in the face of danger. It held that its commanders could be dismissed at its pleasure, or at the instance of its agents, factors or even seamen.[12]

8. HCA 13/56, 30 May 1640; 13/88, 19 September 1728, 3 February 1728/9, fo.93, 7 November 1729; Earle, *Sailors*, p.47.

9. Sir Richard Carnac Temple (ed.), *A Geographical Account of Countries Round the Bay of Bengal, 1669 to 1679*, by Thomas Bowrey (London, Hakluyt Society, 1905), p.172 and n; Geoffrey Holmes, *Augustan England: Professions, State and Society, 1680–1730* (London, 1982), p.283.

10. HCA 13/56, 24 July 1640.

11. G.V. Scammell, 'Manning the English Merchant Service in the Sixteenth Century', *The Mariner's Mirror*, 56 (1970), pp.131–54 at 144.

12. Foster, *English Factories in India, 1646–50*, p.289; *1651–54*, p.165; *1661–64*, pp.2, 82 and n; HCA 13/88, 18 December 1732.

Others were of the same opinion and Captain Nathaniel Uring was denied his wages in 1707 for having surrendered to the French in the course of the War of the Spanish Succession – though it was in fact his lieutenant who had done so. He was sued on a bond he had given to keep clear of all shipping and only eventually acquitted after he had spent, as he complained, 'a good deal of money'.[13]

A master had, therefore, to get his ship safely from place to place. To do this he needed, for one thing, to keep his crew in order, for which he had considerable and increasing scope. The 'daily controversies', which it was alleged in 1635, arose from men being shipped on vague verbal terms, were alleviated with the introduction from the early 1600s of the practice of their entering into written and sealed agreements as to the nature and conditions of their service. After the passage (1729) of the *Act for the Better Regulation and Government of Seamen in the Merchants' Service* it was obligatory for them to sign on for a voyage by endorsing a printed document specifying their pay, rating and the destination for which they were bound.[14] Even so, a master's authority was still far from being clearly defined, let alone absolute. In moments of peril and in matters of importance crews expected that, like their medieval predecessors, they would be consulted as to what should be done, and were reluctant to see their standing and influence eroded. Caught in heavy weather off Honduras in 1711 Nathaniel Uring 'called all the seamen together and asked their opinions' as to whether they should risk making for a haven he had sighted. In the sixteenth century especially, when many commercial voyages were more like armed incursions, crews expected to have some say as to whether extra freight or passengers should be embarked. And at all times prudent commanders consulted their officers and men and endeavoured to secure their goodwill. Mishandling of a crew could lead to unrest, disorder and worse, as well as the likely overthrow of the whole venture.[15]

Nevertheless, as longer voyages became more common and ships were out of contact with their home ports for greater periods of time than hitherto, the master's authority was strengthened and as early as 1581 a seaman could claim as justification for his actions an order from the master 'whose bidding the company were not to gainsay'. The unprecedented problems arising from lengthy oceanic passages, with little prospect of any resort to local judicatures before the development of those of the English colonies, brought unprecedented measures. John Weddell, commanding an expedition to the East in 1635, was empowered to exercise martial law 'because ... there may bee occasion for more severe

13. Captain Alfred Dewar (ed.), *The Voyages and Travels of Captain Nathaniel Uring* (London, 1928), p.74.
14. HCA 13/51, 26 September 1634; 13/88, 27 December 1729, 17 December 1731, 29 February 1731/2; Earle, *Sailors*, p.30.
15. HCA 13/56, 15 July 1640, fos.127v, 156v; Uring, *Voyages*, p.117; Scammell, 'Manning the Merchant Service', p.144; Earle, *Sailors*, pp.160–1.

punishments than ordinary'. Captains of East Indiamen had authority to imprison and impose capital punishment for mutiny or individual criminal acts, after court martial.[16]

At home or abroad the master hired, directly or indirectly, the men he needed, just as he dismissed those he found unsatisfactory.[17] He determined what food they should receive. They were unable to leave the ship without his permission, and should they do so he might have them rounded up, sometimes joining in their pursuit himself. He kept them at work and in order, often by kicks, blows and beatings accompanied by colourfully abusive language. In an age of endemic violence and disorder, and dealing with men widely considered to be 'despisers of government', the master had to defuse those tensions which built up in complements increasingly confined together in close proximity for long periods and in arduous conditions. He had to decide, guided only by his temperament, experience and commonsense, and by his understanding of the 'custom of the sea', how to deal with disobedience and dereliction of duty, and what punishments to impose. Violence and brutality could be counterproductive, or, as one Elizabethan veteran put it, 'too much cruelty may prove worst of all'. Besides which it might lead to a captain being sued for damages by his victim, or even tried and convicted for his murder. And even if events never reached such a pass, masters too free with their tongues and fists were in danger of being lynched by their men should they be so ill-advised as to cross their paths ashore. Proverbial advice to live and let live had much to recommend it.

A master likewise appointed, disrated or dismissed his officers and often treated them no better than he did his men. The captain of a Bristol slaver demoted his mate to deckhand. The commander of the *Mary Galley*, not finding things to his liking, dragged his second in command round the deck. He might, however, find an experienced mate wished on him by his owners or freighters, though such an appointment would allegedly be with his 'consent and good liking'.[18] He might

16. PRO, CO 77/7, no.9 (1635); Scammell, 'Manning the Merchant Service', p.144; Davis, *English Shipping Industry*, pp.260ff; K.N. Chaudhuri, 'The English East India Company's Shipping, c.1600–1760', in Jaap R. Bruijn and Femme S. Gaastra (eds.), *Ships, Sailors and Spices. East India Companies and their Shipping in the 16th, 17th and 18th Century* (Amsterdam, 1993), pp.49–80, at p.65.

17. HCA 13/75, 17 May 1665, evidence of Cuthbert Chapman; 13/78, 8 September 1675, 23 & 29 January 1676/7, 30 March 1681; 13/85, 8 February 1714/15.

18. HCA 13/56, 30 July 1640; 13/78, 23 August 1677; 13/85, 10 & 19 December 1712, 3 February 1712/13, 15 January 1714/15; 13/88, fo.276, 4 February 1728/9, 31 October 1729; Earle, *Sailors*, pp.148–9, 159.

also find he had to cope with the discontent, jealousy and disloyalty of his fellow officers, some of whom, mates especially, were apt to see themselves as better qualified than their nominal superiors – as indeed they might well be.[19]

Contending with his crew, however strenuous a matter, was nevertheless only a small part of a master's duties. Subject to his owners' or charterers' instructions – or in East Indiamen to those of the Company's agents – he had overall control of his ship.[20] It was his responsibility to ensure she was seaworthy, and he might himself take charge of her fitting out, just as he commonly kept an eye on her building as the owners' representative.[21] It was for him to decide how she came away from anchorage, already in 1549 giving those orders still familiar to seamen – 'full and by', 'luff', 'up helm', 'bear away'. He might take the helm himself.[22] He would decide whether or not a pilot was needed and what sail was to be carried. In danger his skills and ingenuity could save his command, just as his folly or incompetence could lose her. When a ship of the Elizabethan earl of Cumberland was caught in heavy weather the master got her new mainsail off single handed 'when none else would or durst'.

But there was no shortage of colleagues whose drunken brutality lost them officers and alienated their men.[23] Their self-willed idiosyncracies ruinously prolonged voyages and drove up costs, as when in 1724 a master bound for Königsberg (Kaliningrad) via Newcastle put into Hull to visit an old sweetheart. She was quite unmoved by his arrival, but he spent nearly a month pressing his suit besides wasting money on a 'jack and Pendent' for the 'festive occasions' which failed to materialize. Others, in alcoholic stupor, ran down passing vessels or heedlessly pressed on into trouble.[24] Some were not, in the language of the times, 'artists in navigation'. They put ships ashore through careless or incompetent pilotage like that London master who, making for Newcastle in 1547, ran aground in the approaches, having mistaken 'a church steeple five miles off for Tynemouth'. Colleagues got into muddles as to where they were

19. Geoffrey Scammell, 'Mutiny in British Ships, c.1500–1750', in Silvia Marzagalli and Hubert Bonin (eds.), *Négoce, Ports et Océans, XVIe-XXe siècles: Mélanges offerts à Paul Butel* (Bordeaux, 2000), pp.337–354, at p.346.

20. Foster, *English Factories in India, 1646–50*, pp.230–31; *1651–54*, pp.59–60.

21. HCA 13/85, fo.421; Geoffrey Scammell, 'British Merchant Shipbuilding, c.1500–1750', *International Journal of Maritime History*, XI (1999), pp.27–52, at 50.

22. Alan Moore (ed.), 'The Sea Scene from the Complaynt of Scotlande', in Sir John Knox Laughton (ed.), *The Naval Miscellany*, vol. II (London, Navy Records Society, 1912), pp.69–84 at 81; HCA 13/88, fo.256.

23. HCA 13/65, 23 April 1652; Foster, *English Factories in India, 1651-54*, 1, pp.40–41; Scammell, 'Manning the Merchant Service', p.145.

24. HCA 13/78, 12 & 26 January 1676/7, 13 May 1678; 13/88, 1 June 1728.

when out of sight of land and what course they should be sailing. Others gave the wrong orders, or hazarded or lost ships through an admixture of drunkeness, ignorance, stupidity and arrogance.[25]

As such unfortunate instances show, navigation was equally the master's responsibility. This increasingly entailed an ability to employ the new science of determining positions at sea by celestial observation which was spreading from the early sixteenth century. And already at this time there were more English seamen competent to do this than is sometimes assumed – witness, for example, the skills of those who brought the *Barbara* of London home from Brazil in 1540. From the 1570s references proliferate to masters who possessed 'books for navigation', crosstaffs, astrolabes, variation compasses and other 'instruments for the sea'. By the mid-eighteenth century the great majority of those employed in long distance trades could, within the contemporary constraints of the technique, establish their latitude (longitude was another matter) and determine courses with the aid of celestial observations.[26] So equipped, a master decided in what direction he should proceed, though in difficult, dangerous or unfamiliar waters he might have the aid of a pilot or mate with specialized local knowledge. Similarly, in voyages of exploration, with several vessels in company, a master who knew the area might assume responsibility for the navigation of the entire flotilla. On the other hand, when his competence was not all that it might have been, he would usually have with him a mate who was a skilled navigator. Hence in 1732 a coasting skipper, not understanding 'the business of a mariner' – and allegedly a congenital drunkard as well – had a 'helper' to do the navigation.[27]

Such men apart, masters took sights, kept detailed logs (registering courses, currents, compass variations and so on) and on all but the briefest runs recorded their progress and what they thought their position to be. They taught their apprentices navigational skills (as, indeed, according to their zeal and conscientiousness, others relevant to their calling) and they collected navigational information. This was particularly the case with captains employed by the East India Company, which for example in 1668 ordered commanders using the treacherous Hugli river to 'put all persons, from the youngest to the eldest, upon taking depths, sholdings (shallows), setting of tydes, currents, distances, buoyes and making of drafts …'.[28]

But masters were much more than simply seamen. In the sixteenth century in particular those of staunch Protestant convictions would conduct shipboard services and often had with them collections of devotional literature to be

25. HCA 13/85, fo.429v, 12 June 1714 (fo.173v), 27 October 1716, 30 November 1716; 13/88, 27 December 1729; Richard Welford, *History of Newcastle and Gateshead* (3 vols, London, 1885–87), II, p.242.
26. HCA 13/23, fo.141v; 13/25, December 1584; R.G. Marsden (ed.), 'Voyage of the *Barbara* to Brazil, *anno* 1540', in Laughton, *Naval Miscellany*, pp.3–66, *passim*.
27. HCA 13/85, 29 November 1716; 13/88, 16 June 1732.
28. Foster, *English Factories in India, 1668–69*, pp.300–301.

employed on such occasions.[29] When disaster threatened they might lead their crews in prayer, as did John Hawkins when his ship sprang a leak in heavy weather. It was likewise the master who might attempt, or be expected to attempt, to treat his men who fell ill or suffered injury. Surgeons were carried in some vessels – though there was much doubt as to the efficacy of their ministrations – but not in most. Masters might therefore have to do their best with the aid of the ship's medicine chest and, if lucky, a book of instructions. Thus in the 1670s the captain of a vessel bound for Barbados discovered that his surgeon neither knew how to tackle an infected wound nor possessed anything that might be used on it. Danger was averted by his ingenuity in treating the place with balsam obtained from the cook and draining off the poison with a syringe made from a quill.[30]

More arduously still, until a network of overseas commercial agents and contacts emerged as England's trade settled into new and regular patterns, a master commonly acted as his owner's or his employer's business representative, or, if he had a share in his command, as the agent of his fellow partners. He might be assisted by a supercargo or a purser – perhaps his own son – who in some instances took full charge of all commercial transactions. Alternatively, he could combine command with the offices of either purser or joint purser.[31] Hence he might have to handle local taxes and secure passes and safe conducts where necessary. He signed the bill of lading, recorded all business done, and by the early eighteenth century kept a ship's book in which were entered the names of the crew, the date of their joining and the wages for which they were engaged. Should his vessel and her cargo be damaged he would have the details recorded by a notary if possible (his 'Protest against the Seas').[32] In some exotic settings – the East especially – he could appear like the forerunner of some imperial proconsul, entertaining local dignitaries, receiving and dispensing gifts and courtesies, enjoying or enduring gargantuan feasts and coping with the problems of indigenous etiquette.[33] In big ships, or in those of prosperous owners, he would normally have some clerical assistance, but if he commanded his own vessel he would like as not conduct all business himself.

---

29. HCA 13/24, ult February 1581/2; P.E. Hair and J.D. Alsop, *English Seamen and Traders in Guinea, 1553–1565: The New Evidence of their Wills* (Lewiston, 1992), pp.325–7.

30. HCA 13/78, 25 & 28 November 1679; Earle, *Sailors*, p.139.

31. HCA 13/32, fo.lv (1593); 13/85 3 February 1715/16, 20 April 1716.

32. HCA 13/78, 4 June 1675, 5 August 1678, 1 December 1679, 21 September 1680; 13/85, 27 April 1713; 13/88, 19 September 1728, fo.63.

33. Temple (ed.), *A Geographical Account* ... by Thomas Bowrey, p.301ff.

It was, therefore, on a master's character, competence and judgement that the entire success of a venture might well depend. Indeed loss of a trusted man could lead an owner to dispose of his ship, as did the celebrated shipbuilder Phineas Pett in 1612. Hence to secure their best interests owners would grant or sell a share or shares in their vessel to a master in whom they had confidence, with the added attraction that he would then have every incentive to ensure that she was fully and profitably employed.[34] Better still, at a time when, because of slow and unreliable communications, individual initiatives were so important in business, and mutual understanding, knowledge and trust vital, owners would appoint relatives to command. But whatever the case it was up to the master to keep a voyage moving. If his ship was arrested he had to secure her release. If supplies ran out or gear was lost or broken, he had to arrange for their replacement, and raise the necessary funds if need be.[35] His enterprise might get a lading in unpropitious circumstances, as when a rabidly Protestant master, illicitly in Catholic Brazil in 1581, 'set up bills both in the churches and market place' of Bahia, announcing he was sailing for Europe. A colleague finding himself without cargo in Crete some years later sought the advice of the principal local merchants as to what was best to do. Too keen a nose for profit, however, could lead to disaster, as happened with the illegal export of bullion from Spain in the late sixteenth century, or when crews were deliberately misled as to the true purpose of a voyage, like ivory poaching in East Africa in the early 1700s.[36]

For some men such responsibilities proved too much. They might sink into nervous exhaustion or, like one of Joseph Conrad's characters, remain shut in their cabins at sea. Many became hopeless drunks and some killed themselves.[37] But for the rest the rewards, legal and otherwise, could be good. True, there were inevitably those who by accident, folly or sheer bad luck, fell on hard times. In Honduras in 1711 Nathaniel Uring came across a onetime master who had first got into debt and then run off with a married woman. She soon left him, whereupon he set up as a logger, living an arduous frontiersman's existence with an Indian girl to console him. Two years later a colleague was reported to be in that 'privileged place for debtors ... called the Mint' in London, whilst in 1716 a 30 year-old explained that he had once briefly been a shipmaster, but had not worked for the past four years and was supported by friends.[38] The commander of an East Indiaman, lost on the Hugli in 1694, managed to transfer, with what he could save of her cargo, into another ship. She in turn was captured by the

34. HCA 13/56, 1 May 1640, 6 August 1640.

35. HCA 13/78, 24 October 1676; W.G. Perrin (ed.), *The Autobiography of Phineas Pett* (London, Navy Records Society, 1917), pp.96–7.

36. HCA 13/23, fo.113; 13/24, fo.221; 13/32, fo.3; 13/88, 3 & 9 March 1714/15, 17 May 1715.

37. Foster, *English Factories in India, 1655–60*, p.33.

38. HCA 13/85, 4 July 1713, 13 June 1716; Dewar (ed.), *Voyages of Nathaniel Uring*, p.143.

French and he was imprisoned, only to find on his release that his former crew were suing him for their wages. Others did even worse, Robert Crosse, an eminent Elizabethan privateer and sometime comrade in arms of Francis Drake, Raleigh and Essex, ended in penury after nearly 40 years service, petitioning the government in 1611 that if he were not 'befriended' he would be obliged to flee abroad.[39]

Nevertheless, many flourished and some, as we shall see, exceedingly, whilst plenty did well enough. Even if they were merely wage earners – which was seldom the case – they received a great deal more than their men. In the sixteenth century ordinary hands could expect, very roughly, a basic monthly wage of less than £1, and in the seventeenth and eighteenth centuries, between £1 and £2, rising occasionally, as in the wars of the mid-1700s, to £3.[40] Many masters were of course paid by the voyage, but between c.1600 and 1750 those on longer European runs would receive (again, very roughly) between £2-5-0d and £6 a month, and those in oceanic trades up to £10.[41] Comparisons with earnings in other occupations are difficult, if not impossible to make, because (amongst other things), of the differing scales and range of incidentals and perquisites. However, it is worth noting that, for example, in Elizabethan and Stuart times a master in a good grammar school could hope for (approximately) between £1-10-0d and £6 a month. In the mid-1600s many provincial gentry had incomes of less than £100 a month. A naval captain commanding one of the country's biggest fighting ships c.1700 was entitled to between £20 to £30 a month, whilst the 'middling sort' of London merchants and tradesmen earned about £16.[42]

---

39. M. Oppenheim (ed.), *The Naval Tracts of Sir William Monson* (5 vols, London, Navy Records Society, 1902–1914), 1, p.213n; *Reports and Calendars issued by the Royal Commission on Historical Manuscripts*, vol.VI (new series), *The Manuscripts of the House of Lords, 1704–1706*, no.2045.
40. Davis, *Shipping Industry*, pp.135–7; K.R. Andrews, *Elizabethan Privateering: English Privateering during the Spanish War, 1585–1603* (Cambridge, 1964), pp.84–6; K.N. Chaudhuri, *The English East India Company. The Study of an Early Joint-Stock Company, 1600–1640* (London, 1965), p.105; Scammell, 'Manning the Merchant Service', p.146.
41. HCA 13/56, 4 June 1640; 13/65, 12 December 1651; 13/75, 10 August 1666; 13/78, 8 September 1675, 3 March 1675/6, 15 December 1677; 13/85, fo.421, 8 & 24 March 1714/15, 6 December 1715; 13/88, 19 November 1731; Temple (ed.), *Travels of Peter Mundy* II, pp.1–2 & n; Chaudhuri, *East India Company*, p.105; Scammell, 'Manning the Merchant Service', p.146.
42. Geoffrey Holmes, *Augustan England*, p.278; N.A.M. Rodger, *The Wooden World: An Anatomy of the Georgian Navy* (London, 1986), p.252; David Cressy, 'A Drudgery of Schoolmasters: the Teaching Profession in Elizabethan and Stuart England', in Wilfrid Prest (ed.), *The Professions in Early Modern England* (London, 1987), pp.129–153 at 144–7; Peter Earle, 'The Middling Sort in London', in Jonathan Barry and Christopher Brooks (eds.), *The Middling Sort of People: Culture, Society and Politics in England, 1550–1800* (London, 1994), pp.141–158 at 144–5; Felicity Heal and Clive Holmes, *The Gentry in England and Wales, 1500–1700* (London, 1994), p.14.

But a master's wage constituted only a part, and often an insignificant part of his earnings. If he was the owner, or a partowner of his ship he had a share in the profits (and expenses) of a voyage. He was the natural recipient of tips and bonuses for services rendered or anticipated. In 1630 the master of an East Indiaman got a £10 gratuity 'to set him to sea and encourage him to proceed with cheerfulness and alacrity', and the Company subsequently rewarded captains who made fast passages or who displayed zeal and competence beyond the normal call of duty.[43] Masters similarly enjoyed various traditional increments, just as they enjoyed the services, premiums and wages of the apprentices under their care and tuition and had the chance and incentives to engage in schemes, legal or otherwise, to maximise profits.[44]

Some, like the Elizabethan privateer, Christopher Newport, rose to fame and fortune in the risky business of privateering and allied pursuits. Others added to their incomes by building ships, or by leasing them to the government. But the safest, and often some of the most lucrative opportunities, arose from the master's age-old entitlement to engage in private trade and to embark supposedly agreed amounts of goods freight free. In the Newfoundland trade in 1672 this was a ton 'from every port to every port'. In the Bristol slave trade the master's slaves were carried without charge and fed at the ship's expense. The commander of an 800-ton East Indiaman came to enjoy the significantly-named 'outward privilege' of exporting at least 56 tons of goods for his own use and a 'homeward privilege' of importing 30 tons, consisting largely of silks and cottons, or in the China trade, of tea and porcelain. It was furthermore alleged in 1733 that over and above their 'indulgence' captains could also have £100 in foreign coin or bullion per 100 ton of their ship to meet extraordinary demands in Asia. All such considerable and immensely profitable perquisites their holders freely and radically enlarged so that in 1682, according to Edward Barlow, the East India Company obliged its commanders (and other officers) to enter into bonds not to trade in those commodities of which it supposedly enjoyed the monopoly. Undeterred, captains sold hold space and smuggled what they could where they could – arms and gunpowder in Mozambique in 1718, or opium and spices in the Malay peninsular.[45] Such activities were by no means confined to the especially rich trades of the East, and owners repeatedly expressed their concern at the scale and adverse repercussions on their own business of the commerce

---

43. Temple (ed.), *Travels of Peter Mundy*, II, pp.1–2 and notes.
44. Earle, *Sailors*, pp.98–9.
45. HCA 13/78, 3 March 1675/6; 13/88, fo.276v, 5 May 1732, 26 May 1733; Basil Lubbock (ed.), *Barlow's Journal of his life at sea in King's ships, East and West Indiamen and other Merchantmen from 1659 to 1703* (2 vols, London, 1934), II, p.352; C. Northcote Parkinson (ed.), *The Trade Winds. A Study of British Overseas Trade during the French Wars, 1793–1815* (London, 1948), pp.141–156.

conducted by the masters they employed. Nor surprisingly, since one way or another it could be of an impressive order, as when in the 1660s one captain set off for Russia with £450 worth of cloth he intended to sell.[46]

Trade apart, there was an infinity of other opportunities for making money. At Aden in 1647 an East India Company commander proposed to force local vessels to buy safeconducts from him. A less bellicose contemporary, amongst his other misdeeds, financed his purser's illicit commerce in Asia by loans at 28% interest, thereby doubling his capital annually, so it was alleged. Others of more modest entrepreneurial inclinations sold their men rum in the Maryland trade, or in Asia charged them 7/- a gallon for arrack purchased for 4/-. Some shipped passengers on their own account, dealt in indentured servants, lent money to their crews or exacted extra payments from passengers to allow their goods to be landed. In Jamaica in 1675 a master refused to accept a lading unless he was 'refreshed' by a 'present'. Later (1715) another financed his commerce in West Africa by selling the ship's boat and one of her anchors. Others brazenly assembled working capital by such simple expedients as delaying the transmission of their vessel's earnings to her owners or appropriating the fruits of their crew's enterprises.[47]

Masters could thus end as men of wealth and substance. They might trade both in their own commands and in other vessels. They might become successful full-time merchants, perhaps specializing in areas of which they had earlier experience. Some acquired property which could be rented to fellow seamen, and many were large-scale investors in shipping. The Elizabethan Peter Hill controlled an entire fleet.[48] In 1614, in addition to other assets, John Love of Ipswich had shares in six vessels. A few years later James Moyer of Leigh-on-Sea left his widow 17 shares in ships (worth nearly £3000) together with an 'adventure' put at £1100, whilst his sons got legacies of over £2000 between them. Thomas Trenchfield, who died in 1646, after nearly 40 years at sea, bequeathed an unspecified amount of shipping , four houses – one with stables, orchards and outbuildings – and funds for the construction of four almshouses.[49] Nathaniel Uring came ashore in 1721 at the end of a rich and varied seafaring career. He then did a spell as Deputy Governor of St Lucia, in the West Indies, before dieing at the age of 61, leaving an estate to his nephew, a country house and bequests (none to charity) of more than £4000. Above all there were, from

46. HCA 13/75, 10 August 1666.

47. HCA 13/65, 9 December 1651, 3 May 1652; 13/78, 3 October 1676; 13/85, 6 December 1715, 16 May 1716; 13/88, fos.271v, 248; Foster, *English Factories in India, 1646–50*, pp.147–8, 290.

48. HCA 13/28, 23 January 1589/90 (the master of the *Hopewell* owns the *Costly*. The master of the *Flower de Luce* owns the *Bonny Besse*); 13/88, 21 May & 7 October 1729; Scammell, 'Manning the Merchant Service', p.146.

49. K.R. Andrews, *Ships, Money and Politics: Seafaring and naval enterprise in the reign of Charles I* (Cambridge, 1991), p.45.

the late seventeenth century, the fortunes amassed by successful East India Company captains. At a time (c.1700) when £100,000 could constitute a mercantile fortune there were commanders who made as much as £10,000 in a single voyage. Better still, on their retirement they were happily able to sell their posts and thus on the proceeds of trade and privilege to enjoy incomes comparable to those of the upper ranks of the landed gentry, and to be classed, or to class themselves as gentleman.[50]

Many such men, and indeed their far less wealthy colleagues, came to be of considerable local and national importance. The records of the London parish of Stepney, at the very heart of the capital's maritime life, show that between 1579 and 1662 almost all the parochial officials were prominent seamen. So, too, in Scotland half a century later shipmasters from Queensferry, Kirkaldy, Montrose and elsewhere were active in local government and also held their own independent tribunals to settle disputes over such matters as seamen's wages.[51] In England there were families of which several members were likely to be commanding at sea at any one time, and dynasties, like the seventeenth-century Goodlads, who provided masters for decades.[52] Many captains or former captains made their mark one way or another in politics. The veteran Elizabethan privateer, Thomas Best, pushed for the application of similar forceful and well-tried measures to establish England in the rich trades of Asia in the early 1600s. Christopher Newport, whose first and far from creditable appearance was in one of the early English interloping expeditions to Brazil (1580), went on to play a distinguished role in the war against Spain in the Caribbean and eventually in the colonization of North America and in the pioneering voyages of the East India Company. And both, together with others of like parts, were important members of that maritime 'interest' which under Elizabeth and the early Stuarts was instrumental in directing English energies and resources into an aggressive oceanic strategy against Spain. In the Civil Wars of the mid-1600s the above-mentioned Thomas Trenchfield was an eminent naval commander for Parliament, as were others of similar background and experience, such as Roger Tweedy, William Rainborowe and William Batten. In 1699 the old Asia hand, Thomas Bowrey, almost persuaded the East India Company to embark on colonial schemes in Indonesia and some years later was trying, admittedly in vain, to get the British government to seize bases in Spanish South America.[53]

50. HCA 13/85, 16 May 1716; Dewar (ed.), *Voyages of Captain Uring*, pp.xxx-xxxiii; Chaudhuri in Bruijn and Gaastra (eds.), *Ships, Sailors and Spices*, p.66.

51. Cheryl Fury, 'Elizabethan Seamen: Their Lives Ashore', *International Journal of Maritime History*, X (1998), pp.1–40 at 33.

52. T.C. Smout, *Scottish Trade on the Eve of Union, 1660-1707* (Edinburgh, 1963), pp.56–7; Andrews, *Ships, Money and Politics*, p.45.

53. Temple (ed.), *A Geographical Account* ... by Thomas Bowrey, p.xlii; Andrews, *Privateering*, pp.84-86; *id, Ships, Money and Politics*, p..44–46; G.V. Scammell, 'England, Portugal and the *Estado da India* c.1500–1635', *Modern Asian Studies*, 16 (1982), pp.177–92 at 186–7.

Many masters, and especially those working regularly from London, England's greatest port, lived by the early eighteenth century in considerable style. They had houses, some apparently tastefully furnished, by the Thames – as at Wapping and 'Green Bank' – or elsewhere in the capital and its vicinity (Enfield Chase, for example).[54] Some had places in the country and rooms in town and some also had establishments abroad, like that East India captain who in 1731 had a house at Gray's Inn in London and another in Bengal.[55] True, the less fortunate might have to stay with relatives, or take lodgings handy for the sea.[56] But the successful could live and work in comfort and even luxury. In vessels of any size, and especially in East Indiamen, captains had their own cooks and their own staff – some recruited from among seamen; some relatives; and some who claimed to be of gentle birth. By the early 1700s these included the captain's or master's clerk, the captain's steward and quite often the captain's tailor.[57] Ashore or afloat a master also enjoyed the services of his apprentices and he might have in addition an African slave boy as his personal servant and perhaps other African slaves as well.[58] He had his own cabin, situated it was said in1730, on the half deck and commonly, and from an early date, well-appointed.[59] Already in 1548 that of a notorious pirate contained 'a fine featherbed' and a cover to go with it.

In all but the smallest vessels the master rarely stood a night watch. He might occasionally be accompanied by his wife.[60] He could eat and drink well, not to say to excess as it often seemed to his men, though not many captains dined off silver dishes, such as those provided for the 'service accommodation' of the officers and merchants in an expedition to Asia in 1636. The tedium of long passages to and in the East could be broken as commanders entertained, or were entertained by local dignitaries in port. At sea there were junketings amongst ships in company when officers invited colleagues from other vessels to what an observer described in 1673 as 'entertainments', the high spot of which ('the most attractive dish') could be a romp with the 'lovely ladies' on board. Such festivities might be further enlivened by music, with the captain himself among the performers, like that John Lemon who 'blowed a good trumpet'.[61]

---

54. HCA 13/85, 10 March 1712/13; 13/88, 2 November 1728, 7 May 1730; Earle, *Sailors*, p.64.
55. HCA 13/85, 8 February 1716/17; 13/88, 17 & 25 November 1732.
56. HCA 13/85, 4 December 1716; 13/88, 29 June 1728.
57. HCA 13/78, 12 June 1676; 13/85, 11 February 1715/16, 12 March 1715/16, 16 May 1716 (fo.343Bv.), 13 October 1716, 4 December 1716; 13/88, 1 July 1729.
58. HCA 13/78, 27 August 1681; 13/85, 5 & 6 December 1715.
59. HCA 13/88, 12 January 1729/30.
60. HCA 13/56, 30 July 1640; 13/88, 12 January 1729/30 (master and mate taking four-hour watches turn and turn about); HCA 1/34, fo.176v.
61. Temple (ed.), *Travels of Peter Mundy*, I, part 1, p.17; Sir Charles Fawcett and Sir Richard Burn (eds.), Lady Fawcett (trs.), *The Travels of the Abbé Carré in India and the Near East, 1672 to 1674* (3 vols, London, Hakluyt Society, 1947-1948), III, p.685; Earle, *Sailors*, p.93.

Most masters were English even before the requirements of the Navigation Acts of the later seventeenth century. However, in some unfamiliar or illicit trades it was advisable to have expert local knowledge, or to be able to use a foreigner's name to help disguise the true identity of a ship and her cargo. Hence especially in the reigns of Elizabeth and the early Stuarts, in order to keep Anglo-Spanish commerce flowing while wars were in progress, English vessels appear under Dutch, German, French, Portuguese, Breton and other command.[62]

The attractions of the office are reflected in the wide range of occupations from which English masters were recruited. Some, frequently the most successful, came from well-established and well-connected seafaring families in which sons followed in the wake of fathers, grandfathers and other relatives. But many were of very different origins. In a calling which offered remarkable and probably unequalled opportunities for natural talent and abilities there were those who worked their way up from the ranks of ordinary hands. Furthermore, in the century after roughly 1650, when the English economy by and large flourished, but whilst specialization was still in its infancy and multiple skills common, many men moved from one occupation to another, or engaged in several simultaneously according to circumstances. Thus there were masters who were former or practising shipwrights, like the commander of a vessel involved in a collision in 1676 who was able to assess the damage to her and the likely cost of repairs, 'because ... being a carpenter (he) knew ... as well as any man'. So, too, in 1716, John Brown, a London seaman then aged 60, declared that for many years he had built, owned and commanded ships, but was now a merchant.[63] Besides which there were onetime tidesmen, taverners, ironmongers, woodmen, sailmakers and even, to the chagrin of Edward Barlow, 'a former milliner of small wares'. In 1716 the erstwhile commander of a hoy described himself as a victualler, though he had once been a bosun and rigger.[64] More versatile still was an East India Company captain, said in 1669 to be an expert in fortification, gunnery, fireworks and 'playing the granadoes' (grenades). A colleague, of similarly explosive potential, was the Company's former engineer and master gunner at Madras.[65]

62. HCA 13/56, 23 July 1640; G.V. Scammell, 'The English in the Atlantic Islands, c.1450–1650', *The Mariner's Mirror*, 72 (1986), pp.295–317 at 310.

63. HCA 13/78, 26 January 1676/7; 13/85, 5 July 1716; Margaret Pelling, 'Medical Practice in Early Modern England. Trade or Profession?', in Prest (ed.), *Professions*, pp.90–128 at 102–3.

64. HCA 13/85, 8 February 1716/17, 17 July 1716, 30 November 1716; Scammell, 'Manning the Merchant Service', p.147; Earle, *Sailors*, p.162.

65. Foster, *English Factories in India, 1668–9*, p.94; Sir Charles Fawcett (ed.), *English Factories in India, 1670–77, 1678–84* (Oxford, 1952–1955), *1678–84*, IV, p.83.

The pull of London, England's capital, greatest port and rumoured centre of infinite opportunities, is reflected in the careers of those masters who eventually established themselves there after starting their careers in places as different as East Anglia, the West Country, Ireland, Hampshire, the North-East or the Scottish borders.[66] Throughout the entire period with which we are concerned most were literate, though some, unable to read or write, long continued to hold responsible posts, like those in the Newfoundland fishery in 1633 who needed to have the letters they received read to them.[67] But overall, and as with seamen as a whole, the standards are impressive. Of 25 deponents in Admiralty Court Examinations in 1651–52 only one was unable to sign his name. All 12 deponents in 1664–66 were literate. Of 30 in 1675–83 only one was illiterate and none of the 47 in 1712–17. During this time, it is worth recalling, by the same test of ability to sign one's name, 80 percent or more of merchants were literate and the rates of English adult male working class literacy rose from roughly 30 percent to over 60 percent.[68]

From the early 1500s masters regularly appear keeping detailed navigational, financial and business records and sending and receiving letters. Some were men of considerable achievements. A 25-year old with John Hawkins in the 1560s was fluent in Spanish and Giles Penn, grandfather of the Quaker founder of Pennsylvania, spoke Arabic.[69] Richard Whitbourne published in 1622 a *Discourse and Discovery of Newfoundland*, whose literary merits have often been noted, and the versatile Thomas Bowrey later (1701) compile an Anglo-Malay dictionary. In the early eighteenth century Nathaniel Uring left an account of his voyages which abounds in perceptive comments on a great variety of things – the ruins of Carthage, the civilizations of Central America, Moorish influence on Portuguese culture amongst them.[70] From the mid-1600s there were many masters or ex-masters who wrote not only of their own experiences, but on a whole range of maritime, economic and political questions. A handful became men of remarkable and respected erudition, like Christopher Middleton, long in the service of the Hudson's Bay Company, elected a Fellow of the Royal Society in 1737 for his work on magnetic variation.[71]

66. Andrews, *Ships, Money and Politics*, p.47.

67. HCA 13/51, fo.4.

68. HCA 13/65 (1651–52); 13/75 (1664–66); 13/78 (1675–83); 13/85 (1712–17) supply the statistics. See also, K. Wrightson, *English Society 1580 – 1680* (London, 1982), p.190; Paul Langford, *A Polite and Commercial People: England 1727–1783* (Oxford, 1989), p.91.

69. Andrews, *Ships, Money and Politics*, p.171.

70. Dewar (ed.), *Voyages of Captain Uring*, pp.152ff, 189–90, 218; Temple (ed.), *A Geographical Account* ... by Thomas Bowrey, p.xl; Scammell, 'Manning the Merchant Service', p.147.

71. William Barr and Glyndwr Williams (eds.), *Voyages in Search of a Northwest Passage* (2 vols, London, Hakluyt Society, 1994–95), I, p.36n.

Of other aspects of the lives of such seafarers we have only fragmentary evidence. Some, as might be expected, remembered in their wills their places of birth and the trades in which they had served. Thus in 1713 Thomas Bowrey, a veteran of eastern waters, left money to 'poor seamen' in Wapping and especially to those who had been in the East Indies.[72] In the sixteenth and seventeenth centuries in particular there were some whose wills, correspondence and behaviour reveal them as of those stern and often radical Protestant beliefs which then flourished. Stephen Hare of the *Minion* was in trouble in Brazil in 1581 when it was reported what sort of theological literature he had with him. Several London masters who supported Parliament against Charles I were Presbyterians, and Thomas Trenchfield, who self-consciously described himself as 'of honest and religious parents', significantly recalled how his grandmother had been put to death for Christ 'in the time of the persecution in Queen Mary's reign'. But other than in moments of desperate danger such determined godliness waned and in 1719 Daniel Defoe's Robinson Crusoe was of the view that seamen were 'destitute of the fear of God'.[73]

Masters, it would seem, were commonly married, and often to women themselves from seafaring families, who as wives or widows regularly appear successfully handling business and financial affairs. Bonds of affection between spouses were frequently strong, as we have recently come to realize of other strata of early modern society.[74] Wives might accompany their husbands to sea and frequently came out by boat to meet their homecoming ships. The formulae used in wills are, it is well known, a treacherous source, often merely repeating standard wording, but the genuineness of references to such as 'my dear husband', 'my dear wife' or 'my dearly beloved husband' cannot be entirely discounted. And in 1715 the widow of Thomas Bowrey would seem to have combined affection and piety in her wish that the almshouses she founded should bear an inscription to 'perpetuate the Memory of my … dear Husband and me'.[75]

72. Bowrey, *A Geographical Account*, pp.xliv-v.

73. Andrews, *Ships, Money and Politics*, pp.45-6. See also above,, n.29.

74. Fury, 'Elizabethan Seamen', pp.18-19.

75. HCA 13/85, 8 March 1714/15; Bowrey, *A Geographical Account*, p.xlvii.

On the career patterns of masters it is possible to shed a little more light. Admiralty Court records show men in command at the following ages:

	20–30	31–40	41–50	51–60	61
1530–1600	8	14	7	5	2
1651–52	3	5	11	4	2
1664–66	1	4	3	1	3
1675–83	5	9	10	5	1
1712–17	9	18	8	6	6
1728–36	3	8	11	2	1
Totals	29	58	50	23	15

(For sources see note 76)
With the exception of the very young and the very old – one ancient mariner indeed claiming to be 79 in 1652 – the majority (137 out of 175) are between roughly 30 and 50, which is the same age group within which a man might expect a command in the modern industry. It is likewise the age group in which, until the revolutionary changes of our own time, men might have been expected to be at, or near the top of most professions.[77] And so, too, there were plenty of masters in their 20s in charge of oceangoing vessels, just as were some fishing skippers until recently.

Command, as we have already noticed, could be achieved in a variety of ways. The most difficult was for a man to work his way up from common seaman in an industry perhaps unique in the opportunities it offered to those with nothing to recommend them but their natural abilities. Best placed, however, were youths from shipowning and seafaring families who, after serving an apprenticeship, could count on the good offices of friends and relatives to ensure their speedy promotion. In 1729, for example, Thomas Kennet was apprenticed to his brother who commanded the *Young Prince*, whilst two years later Daniel Yeoman was master of a Whitby collier owned by his father.[78] Then there were the cosy arrangements in the East India Company. Commands were bought and sold and

76. Figures from HCA 13/1–5, 23–5, 28, 29, 32; 13/65; 13/75; 13/78; 13/85; 13/88.
77. HCA/13/65, 27 February 1651/2; cf. Earle, *Sailors*, p.45 for a slightly difference conclusion.
78. HCA 13/88, fo.272, 12 March 1729/30.

future captains, according to the somewhat overenthusiastic Abbé Carré (1673), were 'mostly the sons of members of Parliament ... or of noblemen and the richest merchants of London and the principal towns'. In other trades there were those who having shown themselves to be men of parts might be taken on by an owner, and if they had capital or credit, might further be granted, or sold, a share in a vessel. Similarly those who inherited or obtained shares could insist, as happened in 1640, that unless they were given command, the would-be charterers could look elsewhere for the carriage of their goods. And, as always, there was pure luck, with the 27 year old second mate of an Indiaman promoted to her command after the captain had died and the mate had been dismissed by the company.[79]

Even young men who became masters in their 20s had, at least in theory, considerable technical knowledge. Those from families already in shipping would have learned their trade by apprenticeship – the common mode of entry into most crafts and professions – or by some less formal arrangement, in vessels commanded by, or belonging to their kith and kin. Some were, for example, apprenticed to their own fathers, and many masters had their sons at sea with them. Children from non-maritime backgrounds, whose parents could pay the necessary premiums and costs, would be apprenticed to experienced and respected masters. Families with the right contacts and sufficient means might come to so arrangement, not necessarily an apprenticeship, with a successful or even distinguished seaman, to take their son. For most other parents it was a matter of how much they could afford, or who they could persuade to have their offspring, which could end up little better than the blind leading the blind. Hence one way or another, and before they had climbed very far up the educational ladder, sons of ambitious parent or boys eager for advancement, would be sent to sea at the age of about 11 to serve up to a dozen years in apprenticeships formal or informal to learn the mysteries of the seaman's calling. Many less fortunate, and with poorer prospects of promotion, started off as hired servants and picked up what they could from shipboard instruction and helpful shipmates. Some, with whatever savings they scraped together, subsequently became pupils at one of an increasing number of establishments ashore offering instruction in relevant skills, like that in Norfolk whose curriculum included in 1673 ship modelling, navigation, geography, arithmetic and the making of 'all sorts of sea instruments'.[80]

79. HCA 13/56, fo.482v; 13/88 18 December 1732; Sir Charles Fawcett and Sir Richard Burn (eds.), *Travels of the Abbé Carré*, p.682; Earle, *Sailors*, pp.43–4.

80. HCA 13/78, 25 November 1679; Davis, *English Shipping Industry*, pp.124ff; Scammell, 'Manning the Merchant Service', pp.137–9; Cressy, 'The Teaching Profession', p.132; Cheryl A. Fury, 'Training and Education in the Elizabethan Martime Community, 1585–1603', *The Mariner's Mirror*, 85 (1999), pp.147–61.

There was, however, little check on such qualifications, by whatever means obtained. The country's Trinity Houses, essentially gilds of shipmasters founded in the early 1500s to improve the allegedly lamentable skills of English mariners, came to examine the qualifications of those who sought to join them and issued certificates of competence. In the sixteenth century the Muscovy Company enjoined that apprentices and young seamen in its service should be taught navigation, and almost from its inception the East India Company tested the skills of potential deck officers and ensured that its commanders were experienced navigators. And in its heyday it laid down stringent standards of seamanship and navigation and punished captains who failed to maintain them.[81] In less prestigious circles it was well and widely understood, as appears from an inquest of 1536 and from subsequent inquiries, that some masters were considered fit for nothing better than small boats, or could only be employed in coasting voyages, as opposed to colleagues who could undertake 'distant' passages.[82] Otherwise, apart from the natural reluctance of owners to entrust expensive vessels to untried hands, there was little to prevent the foolish or incompetent, provided they were wealthy and well-connected, from getting ships and wrecking them.

On the other hand there was a substantial body of masters who had worked their way to the top of their profession, accumulating a range of skills and experience impressive by any standards. In 1598, at the age of 63, William Croston explained how in his time he had been a bosun, master's mate, commander and owner. There were subsequently plenty of others who could reasonably claim to have served up to half a century as masters.[83] Litigation in 1716 throws valuable light on the careers of a random group of East India captains who belonged to that select body recruited specifically for promotion. One had been apprentice, fourth mate, third mate and chief mate, another had been in turn apprentice, midshipman, second mate, chief mate and supercargo.[84] The massive expansion of the geographic range of England's overseas trade in the early modern centuries meant that ships could be commanded by men whose experience was almost global. William Baffin, Nicholas Woodcock and Benjamin Joseph, for example, much in evidence in the early English voyages to the East,

---

81. HCA 13/85, fo.22; 10 December 1712, fo.17; 14 January 1713; Chaudhuri, *East India Company*, p.106; Scammell, 'Manning the Merchant Service', p.143.
82. HCA 13/1, fos.5v–6; 13/85, 26 January 1713/14, 17 July 1716; Hartlepool Town Books (Town Hall, Hartlepool, England), vol. 1 (Apprenticeships), 1 May 1674 and 302.
83. HCA 13/65, 7 & 27 February 1651/2; Scammell, 'Manning the Merchant Service', p.148.
84. HCA 13/85, 16 May 1716.

were all veterans of Arctic whaling. By the early 1700s Nathaniel Uring had done stints in royal ships and in packet boats, besides sailing in commercial voyages to the Caribbean, West Africa, the Baltic, North America and the Mediterranean.[85] And in 1716 a veteran in his 60s testified that after 40 years in command he was now a royal pilot and a Brother of Trinity House. Nor was such a career by any means unique, constituting ample evidence that youthful promotion, speeded by networks of influence and connection, did not necessarily entail the triumph of mediocrity or the acceptance of incompetence.[86]

In the centuries after c.1550, and by a process similar to that which occurred in other crafts and professions, the English shipmaster evolved from being something like the chairman of a committee of equals, which had once been the case, into an individual of considerable power, responsibility and authority. He knew more, and was expected to know more than his medieval predecessor. As vessels came to work, as a matter of routine, across the Atlantic or to Asia, he had to deal with the opportunities and problems arising from new trades and the complexities of navigation and pilotage in oceanic voyages. The closer definition of his authority and duties, and the increase in the specialized knowledge and skills expected of those who now came to describe themselves as mariners 'by education and profession', echo that growing professionalization which manifested itself elsewhere in British society at the time.[87] So, too, masters who became the owners of their ships, as often happened, had in a sense gained control of their fellow workers and the means of production, as had many of their equivalents in other industries. Their calling grew, furthermore, into one which embraced – as it still does – an exceptionally extensive hierarchy of status, skills and responsibilities. At one extreme was the skipper of some hoy with only a mate as his crew, and at the other the commander of an East Indiaman, exercising an authority, and bearing responsibility for lives and goods of immense value to a degree unequalled in any other non-military profession.

85. Samuel Purchas, *Hakluyt Posthumus, or Purchas His Pilgrimes*, Maclehose edition (20 vols, Glasgow, 1905–7), XIV, p.65; Edward Grey (ed.), *The Travels of Pietro della Valle in India* (2 vols, London, Hakluyt Society, 1892), I, p.3ff; *Voyages of Captain Uring*, pp.ix–xxviii.

86. HCA 13/85, 15 May 1716.

87. HCA 13/65, 7 February 1651/2; Prest (ed.), *Professions*, Introduction.

Command of a ship was similarly a way of life which gave to increasing numbers unparallelled opportunities to know a widening world, just as it would seem to have provided many with a satisfactory way of life. Plenty of masters retired comfortably off and some in considerable affluence. Others remained at sea all their working lives and clearly bound to it by more than the bonds of mere necessity, requesting to be buried there eventually 'after the mariner Custome'. In the discharge of their manifold duties and responsibilities some masters failed abysmally. A minority coped splendidly, whilst the majority – 'careful, fearful (i.e. circumspect) and watchful', as some contemporaries idealized them – managed well enough to meet the demands arising from England's emergence as the world's greatest commercial and maritime power.

V

MUTINY IN BRITISH SHIPS, C. 1500-1750

In 1631 the English High Court of Admiralty condemned all those who uttered "that Pernicious phrase One and All", or who drew up Round Robins, directing that they were to be considered the ringleaders in any mutiny and "severely punished." [1] The problem and its proposed solution were symptomatic of the times. Charles I was ruling without Parliament. Political, religious and social conflict were seemingly endemic. The country's erstwhile shining naval reputation, dating from Elizabeth's reign, was tarnished by a series of debacles. Merchantmen were allegedly at the mercy of privateers from Spanish Dunkirk and easy prey for the even more formidable corsairs of North Africa. A raid on Cadiz (1625) in the course of renewed war with Spain was conducted with farcical ineptitude which led to a humiliating retreat from the scene of the earlier triumphs of the dashing earl of Essex (1596). The outcome, two years later, of an attempt to succour Protestant La Rochelle ended, as contemporaries complained, with the return of the fleet bringing "no little dishonour to our nation (and) excessive charge to our treasury". Next (1639), the Dutch destroyed a Spanish force in the Channel in those very waters over which England ostentatiously claimed sovereignty, and all this to the depressing accompaniment of the repeated collapse of discipline in vessels in crown service, whose crews, and sometimes their officers as well, came ashore to pursue the righting of their grievances in no uncertain way. As the wits quipped, "there were now no more Drakes in England, all were hens".

Mutiny, which may roughly be defined as open revolt against constituted authority, and against which English law as yet offered no adequate procedure, was nothing new. In the sixteenth-century Navy, with

---

1 Kenneth R. ANDREWS, *Ships, Money and Politics. Seafaring and Naval Enterprise in the Reign of Charles I*, Cambridge, 1991, p. 63-4. A Round Robin was a document with the signatures of the participants forming a circle to conceal the order in which they were written, and hence the identities of the ringleaders.

repeated scandals over pay, food and conditions, men frequently and violently refused duty. Part of the fleet returned to harbour in 1554 in contravention of orders, and there detained the Admiral — who had a strong wish to be ashore — on board [2]. Even vessels under commanders as forceful and effective as Francis Drake mutinied [3], whilst in the wars against Spain and France in the 1620's mutinies drove not only individual ships, but on occasions whole squadrons, off their stations [4]. In 1626 and in the ensuing years mutineers marched on London, where troops were turned out to face them [5]. Plymouth had to subdue one lot by force in 1627-1628 and then in the days of the Puritan republic to appease others with drink. At Harwich in 1653 Cromwell's soldiers drove what were described as "drunken and debauched seamen" back on board, whilst the cavalry was let loose against their fellows in the capital [6]. And to all the ancient causes of discontent there was added in the mid-1600's the previously unknown factor of political disaffection. When Charles I and his Parliament fell out most of the fleet refused to serve their royal master. During the Interregnum mutinies took place, or were expected, from the influence of those radical Protestant sects that had long troubled Oliver Cromwell's army. Others were feared from the machinations of the supporters of the exiled royal house and, ultimately, from the activities of foreign agents.

Little changed following the restoration of the monarchy. In a fleet commanded by Sir Thomas Allin some talked (1663) of not standing up to the Dutch — against whom England fought three hotly-contested wars of unprecedented ferocity — through lack of "encouragement", and other subsequently refused to obey orders [7]. The cavalry was out again in 1667 to deal with mutineers who had marched on London to demand

---

[2] Public Record Office, London, Publications, *Calendar of letters, despatches, and state papers relating to the negotiations between England and Spain, preserved in the archives of Simancas and elsewhere*, vol. XII, *Jan.-July 1554*, p. 294.

[3] K. R. ANDREWS, "The Elizabethan Seaman", in *The Mariner's Mirror* 68, 3 (1982), 245-262, at 247.

[4] Public Record Office, London, Publications, *Calendar of state papers, domestic series, of the reign of Charles I, preserved in the State Paper Department of Her Majesty's Public Record Office* (hereafter *CSPD*), vol. II, *Jan. 1627-Feb. 1628*, p. 248, n° 58 ; p. 490, n° 62 ; p. 516, n° 91 ; p. 529, n° 30.

[5] *CSPD* 1627-8, p. 44, n° 9 ; p. 47, n° 37 ; p. 401, n° 48.

[6] J.R. POWELL, *Robert Blake, General-at-Sea*, London, 1972, p. 185, 243-7 ; Austin WOOLRYCH, *Commonwealth to Protectorate*, Oxford, 1982, p. 309.

[7] R.C. ANDERSON, ed, *The journals of Sir Thomas Allin, 1660-1678*, 2 vols, London, Navy Records Society, 1939-40, I, 121, 260.

their pay, putting that ever-nervous naval official, Samuel Pepys, "in great fright." [8] At the turn of the century administrators waspishly complained of their time consumed in dealing with the "great clamours and frequent mutinies" of the marines [9]. Yet though the celebrated episode of Captain Bligh and the *Bounty* (1789) and the more sinister events at Spithead and the Nore (1797) still lay ahead, and though crews might well refuse to put to sea unpaid, or under officers they disliked, large-scale and serious naval mutinies became fewer with the passage of time.

A code of discipline was slowly developed, like as not deriving from those collections of military "Laws and Ordinances" that proliferated in the war-torn Europe of the day, and which were familiar to the generals who commanded Oliver's fleets. Under the Cromwellian *Articles of War* (1652) and the Restoration *Naval Discipline Act* (1661) mutiny was punishable by death. To keep crews in mind of what could lie in store for them the articles were regularly read out to assembled ships'companies. Alleged cases were heard by courts-martial made up from senior serving officers and proceeding according to well-established precedent. Already, for example, in 1627, in what was to all intents a regular naval expedition under the earl of Warwick, a seaman accused of mutiny was brought before a court convened from "chosen officers", six from the flagship, four from the man's own vessel and three from other ships in company. A verdict of guilty was delivered to Warwick, who, empowered by his commission to enforce martial law,imposed the death sentence (soon revoked) and also reduced to the ranks a member of the court who had taken the wrong view.

But there was more to improving discipline than the liberal doling out of draconian punishments. The emergence in the Navy, from about 1700, of an experienced and professional corps of officers with some concern for the lot (and efficiency) of their men did much to reduce the tensions of earlier centuries. It likewise helped to induce in crews a stronger sense than hitherto of loyalty to their ships and the Service. And in any case, with the country now in urgent need of an effective fleet, the demands of seamen (pay especially) were prudently met by governments richer than ever before, and persuaded — in the first half of the eighteenth century at least — of the wisdom of tempering force with humanity when dealing with popular grievances. True, there were genuine attempts to improve conditions in the Navy, but at the same time a blind eye was

---

8 *Diary*, 23 January, 1667.

9 R.D. Merriman, ed, *Queen Anne's Navy*, London, Navy Records Society, 1960, p. 211.

turned to behaviour it was impossible, or inadvisable, to attempt to eradicate.

The Fleet, however — comprising at the height of the Seven Years War in the mid-eighteenth century around 300 ships manned by some 80 000 hands — was only part of the problem. At the same date England alone possessed approximately 500 000 tonnes of merchant shipping requiring roughly as many seamen as the Navy, besides which there were the vessels owned in Scotland and in various overseas settlements. And not least there were vigorous pirate communities, initially based and operating in home waters and later in the Caribbean — their activities magisterially discussed by Paul Butel — and in Asian seas. To observers then and since the manning and working of pirate ships differed little from sheer chaos. There was, it was alleged, "no regular command" and mutiny was endemic. Officers were indistinguishable from crews, by whom they were elected, and by whom they were just as likely to be deposed. To an age so conscious of rank and status such behaviour appeared peculiarly sinister. Nor surprisingly. Pirate vessels often fought one another. Given the chance their crews took other men's loot. Commanders were regularly overthrown, usually since they had failed to deliver the anticipated riches, but sometimes because they were too authoritarian. Hence it was reported in 1607 that in a mutiny on the Irish coast pirates had removed their captain, "the lady Hawkings's brother" and replaced him by "one Roberts of Plymouth", whilst later in the century buccaneering sallies into the Pacific were punctuated by summary dismissals, and occasional reinstatements of commanders [10].

Such apparently perverse behaviour reflected, however, the workings of a radical and democratic form of military organization geared exclusively to the acquisition of loot. When, in the late seventeenth century, some major buccaneering project was in the air in the Caribbean men would assemble, as had the Spanish conquistadores before them, bringing their own weapons, provisions and ammunition. They would then draw up articles — redrafted if the captain was changed — allocating authority, detailing how plunder was to be distributed and discipline maintained. The captain was chosen for his boldness, his navigational skills, and above all for his reputation for luck and success. He was thus, unlike any other fighting commander — apart from those appointed by militias which in the seventeenth century briefly elected, or aspired to elect their officers — the creature of his men. And the radicalism of such crews was

---

[10] Historical MSS Commission Reports, *Calendar of the manuscripts of the Most Hon. The Marquis of Salisbury*, XIX, 1965, p. 229.

further strengthened by the presence amongst them of French *Croquants* and English Levellers, notorious for their strong views on liberty and equality. True, when chasing a prize, or when being chased by others, the captain's authority was absolute. But otherwise ships were run by majority rule, with commanders who failed to come up to expectations not only deposed but often put to death [11]. Yet at the same time restive or disobedient members of the crew incurred such punishments as "the Captain and the Majority of the Company" should think fit, which included marooning the congenitally unruly or mutinous [12].

Piracy, if not eradicated, was at least damped down in the course of the eighteenth century. But mutinies continued in merchantmen and in privateers, whose conduct, thought supposedly regulated by the state that licenced them, was often only theologically distinguishable from piracy, and whose conventions owed much to pirate lore. There were some particularly spectacular episodes in privateers loosed against Spain in the late sixteenth and early seventeenth centuries. With the war at sea in full swing towards the end of Elizabeth's reign crews might, on their own initiative, and without consulting either commanders or owners, "consort" (i.e. enter into partnership) with other vessels. What was charitably described as "great turmoil" commonly broke out over the division of spoil, with the unhappy Dutch captain of a London vessel derided by his men as a "coppernose", better suited to swilling ale than commanding ships, and whom some of his officers proposed to throw overboard. Men sailed off leaving their colleagues marooned. They refused to continue voyages they considered too dangerous, with the poorly-led and ill-organized last expedition of the circumnavigator Thomas Cavendish coming to grief, as he alleged, through the doings of his "insolent mutinous company". Mutineers might demand their ship make for a destination of their choosing (often home), just as they might desert in strength from ventures whose outcome looked uncertain. And so frequent were uprisings occasioned by the quality of food, or its absence, that the instructions for a voyage in 1603 stipulated that in the event of any grievance the crew was not to mutiny, but instead to elect spokesmen to complain "in a civil manner." [13]

---

11 M. REDIKER, *Between the Devil and the Deep Blue Sea: Merchant Seamen, Pirates and the Anglo-American Maritime World, 1700-1750*, Cambridge, 1987, p. 262 ; and the splendid treatment of Caribbean piracy by Paul BUTEL, *Les Caraïbes au temps des Flibustiers, XVIe-XVIIe siècles*, Paris, 1982.

12 REDIKER, *op. cit.*, p. 265.

13 M. OPPENHEIM, ed., *The Naval Tracts of Sir William Monson*, 5 vols, London, Navy Records Society, 1902-14, IV, 196 ff ; K.R. ANDREWS, *Elizabethan Privateering: English Privateering during the Spanish War 1585-1603*, Cambridge, 1964, p. 70, 215.

To little avail. In the earl of Warwick's fleet in 1627 there was "insolent mutiny amongst (the) vulgar sort" when they were issued with cheese instead of butter to eat with their fish. This was merely the prologue to a lengthy saga of disorder in which at various times mutineers dictated the course to be steered, refused to work their ship (neither "trim a sail nor touch a rope") or sullenly withdrew into dumb insolence. Of their many grievances — over-manning, poor living quarters, the wrong captain, inadequate victuals — that most graphically expressed was lack of drink. They were, they claimed, denied beer, though for their officers "can or bottle is supplied in the cabin ... as though there were a spring or brewhouse in the ... hold." [14]

There were similar and added problems in the long wars against Holland in the second half of the seventeenth century and against France after 1689, with some vessels now engaged in voyages measured in years rather than months. The establishment and maintenance of discipline remained as tricky as ever, with the precise extent of a commander's authority far from generally agreed. Francis Drake, on a notable or notorious occasion during his circumnavigation, had already shown what could be done by securing the trial and execution of Thomas Doughty on the strength of a commission he was unwilling (or unable) to produce. In some subsequent equally ambitious undertakings commanders secured or sought powers to enforce martial law, as did the earl of Cumberland under Elizabeth and the earl of Warwick under Charles I. The appropriate procedure against mutiny later came to be specified in the articles drawn up to govern the conduct of a voyage. The accused might be referred to a committee of ships'officers, or, as was the case in pirate vessels, to the entire crew. The celebrated Commodore Walker, for example, convened a court martial in 1747, and mutiny, like certain other offences, might be dealt with according to criminal law. But the course of events was rarely clear or predictable. In Warwick's voyage, though the Admiral had extensive powers, his subordinates can be found struggling to deploy a whole arsenal of expedients against mutineers — duckings, floggings, turning a ringleader out of his ship, handing men over to the earl himself, threatening them with drawn sword.

As of old, if prizes failed to materialize, crews might lock up their officers, seize the ship, hoist the Jolly Roger and turn pirate, as happened with the *King George* of Bristol in 1761. There were disputes as to what or was not good prize. There was further trouble over the distribution of

---

[14] Nelson P. BARD, ed, "The Earl of Warwick's Voyage of 1627", in N.A.M. RODGER, ed, *The Naval Miscellany*, vol. 5, London, Navy Records Society, 1984, p. 28, 62, 69-70, 82-3.

shares in prizes taken, to which, by and large, hands were entitled to a third, or, in contemporary terms, "thirds and pillage". For the most part privateer crews received no wages (it was different in the so-called "Letter of Marque" vessels, which combined trade and privateering), and since they served on terms of "no purchase (prize) no pay", shares were the major, and often the sole and hotly-contested source of remuneration. Officials and owners allegedly swindled crews, crews swindled officers and officers swindled crews [15]. And true enough men often got less than the customary third since, amongst other things, commanders had secured extra allocations of shares for themselves, either at the outset of the voyage or during its course, whilst colleagues augmented their quotas by buying up those of seamen hard-pressed for cash. Hence a common outcome was that once a cruise was under way men were insistent — mutinously as their officers saw it — that shares in prizes should be distributed "as soon as possible" after capture. Otherwise, as they said, they were likely to find themselves paid "not one tenth their due", through the machinations of commanders and the greed of owners [16].

More contentious still, since potentially of far greater value, was pillage — the customary right of the crew to all those things not part of the prize cargo proper [17]. It was a wide and flexible generic, including goods found above deck and the possessions of prisoners, to be divided, like the cargo itself, amongst the complement according to rank, but with officers entitled to various further perquisites. Once a prize had been secured items for pillage were supposedly assembled at the foot of the captor's mainmast and there shared out among the hands, "every man to his deserts". But since pillage was usually acquired in the heat of battle men were adamant that what they had they held, especially "treasure". Disputes and violence inevitably flared up, and such was the confusion that there were demands, as in 1627, that regulations should be set down in print [18]. To little effect, however, and according to that seasoned eighteenth-century Bristol privateer, Woodes Rogers, "disputes about plunder" were the commonest cause of disorders in privateers. And he had reason to know, having been obliged to placate his restive crew by redefining plunder in terms more to their liking as his voyage round the

---

15 *CSPD* 1625-6, p. 407, 417 ; Historical MSS Commission Reports, *The manuscripts of the House of Lords*. New series, XII, *1714-18*, no. 3039. David J. STARKEY, *British Privateering Enterprise in the Eighteenth Century*, Exeter, 1990, p. 186.

16 W.G. PERRIN, ed, *A Voyage Round the World. Captain George Shelvocke*, London, 1928, p. 18 ff.

17 ANDREWS, *Privateering*, p. 41-2.

18 *CSPD* 1627-8, p. 220, n° 44.

world (1708-11) proceeded [19]. To make bad worse there were further difficulties when commodities unfamiliar to traditional lore were encountered, whilst, as with prizes, crews were eager to secure what they considered their due before owners had their say [20]. There were acrimonious confrontations between officers and the "attorneys" nominated by their men over the handling of various items and the value to be put on them, with crews refusing to allow appraisals by owners' agents, and captains fearing they were likely to take the law into their own hands and seize the lot, which often enough they did.

Meanwhile there were mutinies in merchantmen, whether engaged in normal commercial voyage/or employed in extraordinary ventures like exploration. In such vessels, whose crews in Britain, as in Europe as a whole, enjoyed a reputation for violence, drunkeness and indiscipline, the master's lot could well be not a happy one. His ultimate sanction, as we shall see, was no better than commiting offenders to authorities ashore who might (or might not) impose far from intimidating sentences of imprisonment or fines. By the 1640's mutinies were reported anywhere from home waters to the seas of Asia and the West Indies, with their frequency intensified by the political conflicts of the times — the clash between King and Parliament, the eventual outbreak of civil war — with men refusing to serve under those of the wrong persuasion, or endeavouring to hand their ships over to the side they supported [21]. So common was mutiny that the apprehensive were convinced that some sailors were "despisers of government", and nervous travellers feared that any altercation or disturbance on board was the prelude to an attempt to seize the ship. At least 60 mutinies have been identified in the early 1700's alone, and this probably no more than the tip of the iceberg. In about half violence was used or threatened against officers. In about one in five one or more officers were killed. In about half the mutineers secured the ship, and in about a third they turned pirate. The usual cause of trouble was something specific : that men were required to serve for longer than anticipated, or to destinations other than those expected ; that pay was inadequate or not forthcoming ; that victuals were insufficient, inedible or worse ; that officers made life intolerable. And very often all, or several such grievances were involved. Men might refuse, and not without good

---

19 G.E. MANWARING, ed, *A Cruising Voyage Round the World. Captain Woodes Rogers*, London, 1928, p. 23, 170-1, 173.

20 Woodes ROGERS, *Cruising Voyage*, p. 170.

21 Public Record Office, Kew (hereafter PRO), High Court of Admiralty (hereafter HCA), 13/65, 11 July 1651 ; 5 December 1651.

reason, to undertake or to persist in some particularly hazardous passage, with Henry Hudson's company having long since cast him adrift (1611) in "that desolate place" that now bears his name [22]. They could jib at sailing in wartime without provision having been made for their death or disablement. In 1715 the crew of the *Marlborough* were unwilling to leave Yarmouth for the Baltic, doubting their master's intention or ability to get them there. There was a war in progress, they feared for their wages and their safety, and they were hardly re-assured by the sight of their captain landing his own goods and gear [23]. So, too, the hands in the *Joseph Brigantine* were loth to depart from Lisbon. Believing themselves bound for America (1714), they learned to their dismay they were destined for a dubious quest for ivory in East Africa, where, as they put it, their "lives and liberty", not to mention their wages, would be in jeopardy [24]. In a congenitally bibulous age there were seamen who refused duty when drunk, and others adamant that they would not serve under masters who were brutal, incompetent or addicted to the bottle [25]. Should their ship be attacked, hands might refuse to resist assailants considered too powerful, just as they might refuse to continue a voyage in a vessel whose seaworthiness they doubted, or which they considered undermanned. They could balk at extreme danger — tackling the blaze in a ship whose ammunition was about to explode, for example — or they might abandon a vessel in trouble. And like disillusioned privateers they might seize their craft and turn pirate, since, as one articulate sailor put it, they were ill-treated by their officers, swindled by their employers and persecuted in a world governed by "Laws which rich Men have made for their own security." [26]

Some mutinies, like some riots ashore, were well planned and directed. Participants were bound to one another by oaths of loyalty. Grievances were listed in Round Robins. The identities of the organizers were carefully hidden. Weapons in the master's cabin were secured, as when some of the hands in the *Duke of Cambridge* simply burst in and helped themselves. Mutineers might be led by one or more of their officers, the equivalents of the "village notables" much in evidence in

---

22 REDIKER, *Deep Blue Sea*, p. 227-8.

23 PRO, HCA 13/85, 22 February 1716/17, f°s 429-430.

24 PRO, HCA 13/85, 3 & 9 March 1714/15 ; 17 May 1715.

25 PRO, HCA 13/88, 27 December 1729 ; 29 December 1729 ; 12 January 1729/30 ; 9 February 1729/30 ; 15 April 1730.

26 Captain Alfred DEWAR, ed, *The Voyages and Travels of Captain Nathaniel Uring*, London, 1928, p. 67-9 ; SHELVOCKE, *Voyage*, p. 3 ; H.S. VAUGHAN, ed, *The Voyages and Cruises of Commodore Walker*, London, 1928, p. 178 ; REDIKER, *Deep Blue Sea*, p. 228.

Tudor uprisings, or those men of "wealth and status" later influential in the London mob [27].This was the case in Woodes Rogers' flotilla on one occasion, and in that of Commodore Walker on another [28]. The bosun and carpenter were among the mutineers in the *John and Sarah*, returning from Spain in 1715, and the second mate — allegedly in charge — the bosun and the carpenter led the men of the *Socsdyke* two years earlier [29]. In the *St Quinton* it was the bosun who made the going (1728), and who also threatened at various times to throw the master overboard or to damage the ship [30]. More dangerously still, the mate himself could be the leader. He ought, of course, to have been the master's right hand man. But he could be as well qualified as his superior (if not better) and might have been passed over in favour of the very individual under whom he was serving. Hence in 1715 the mate of the *Marlborough* explained to her crew how they should proceed [31]. The mate of the *Young Prince* supported her mutineers in 1729, and the carpenter took no notice of the master's orders to imprison him. Another mate, having argued the unwisdom of his captain's actions with him, improved the shining hour by debating the legality of the doings of the mutineers in his ship with the commander of a naval vessel that intervened [32]. Nevertheless there were plenty of instances in which ordinary hands, like the rank and file of the Army or Navy, raised and directed mutinies themselves. They might follow the lead of some experienced ex-pirate amongst their numbers, as did the crew of the *Dove* in 1736, allocating themselves offices and plunder in accordance with freebooting practice. Otherwise action was usually set in train on the initiative of a handful of seamen displaying those characteristics that posterity has often (if not always rightly) been happy to identify as rugged British individualism. So (1627) in the squadron under that formidable Puritan, the earl of Warwick, it was elected spokesmen who put the company's grievances to their commander. And it was in the same force that men notably rallied to the support of their leaders, threatened with

---

27 PRO, HCA 13/88, 1 June 1732.

28 WALKER, *Voyages*, p. 134 ; Woodes ROGERS, *Cruising Voyage*, p. 9 ; Nicholas ROGERS, "Popular Protest in Early Hanoverian London", in *Past and Present*, 79, 1978, 70-100 ; S.J. GUNN, "Peers, Commons and Gentry in the Lincolnshire Revolt of 1536", in *Past and Present*, 123, 1989, 52-79.

29 PRO, HCA 13/85, 12 June 1714 ; 25 October 1716.

30 PRO, HCA 13/88, 13 December 1731.

31 PRO, HCA 13/85, 20 February 1716/17 ; 1 March 1716/17.

32 PRO, HCA 13/85, 3 March 1714/15 ; 17 May 1715 ; 13/88, 29 December 1729 ; 15 April 1730.

a ducking from the yard-arm, with the cry of "duck one, duck all." [33] Yet notwithstanding pledges of mutual loyalty in the pursuit of their aims, the high hopes of mutineers were often dashed when men failed to back their comrades, or were simply outmanoeuvred by their officers.

The handling of mutiny, actual or incipient, required, as did dealing with riot ashore, considerable skills and tact, which naturally enough were not always forthcoming. Masters could usually find informants amongst their crews, their own stewards, who saw to their food and creature comforts, being particularly well-placed to let them know all that was going on. In 1730, in the *Hume* (familiarly known as *Horsewhip Galley*) the steward was obliged to tell the captain of the men's complaints about food. He was pressed into disclosing who was their ringleader and then obliged to act as their spokesman himself [34]. At the first signs of any stirrings of discontent some captains attempted to bring the full majesty of the law to bear. Having received, in port, a Round Robin from his men, one master had a public notary fetched on board to discover "the resolution of these people", and to have them sign a contract to behave as he wished. At sea help might be requested from any passing British man of war — like calling out the troops for a riot at home. The prudent commander would endeavour to ensure that he controlled all the small arms in his ship, that he had the backing of his officers, and that they kept a close watch on the ship's boats — lest escapes or maroonings were contemplated [35]. The next move was to identify, isolate, and if possible, secure the leaders, either by force or guile. Thomas Cavendish, in his last and ill-fated voyage, momentarily terrified his demoralized and mutinous crew by himself putting a rope round the ringleader's neck, "meaning resolutely to strangle him." [36] Woodes Rogers did even better, managing to inveigle the principal mutineer in his ship to come alone and unarmed into his presence on the quarterdeck, where he had him flogged by one of his fellows [37]. Once secured, leaders would be put in irons and humiliated in ways which destroyed their standing amongst their comrades — Walker, for instance, had (1734) the ringleaders shackled by

---

33 BARD, ed, "Warwick's Voyage", p. 28-9 ; REDIKER, *Deep Blue Sea*, p. 232-3.

34 PRO, HCA 13/65, 13 November 1651 ; 13/88, 26 February 1730/1 ; 1 March 1730/1.

35 PRO, HCA 13/85, 22 February 1716/17 ; 13/88, 27 December 1729 ; URING, *Voyages*, p. 236 ; SHELVOCKE, *Voyage*, p. 4, 6 ; Woodes ROGERS, *Cruising Voyage*, p. 10 ; WALKER, *Voyages*, p. 83, 134.

36 Samuel PURCHAS, *Hakluyt Posthumus, or Purchas His Pilgrimes*, Glasgow, Maclehose ed, 20 vols, 1905-07, XVI, 171.

37 Woodes ROGERS, *Cruising Voyage*, p. 10.

their own mates [38]. Men as dangerous as these, and who in warships would go to court martial, might thereafter remain prisoners. Alternatively they might be handed over, or pressed into British warships, or, in foreign ports passed to the local authorities or the English consul, should there be one. If the mutiny had taken place in vessels in company they could be dispersed throughout the group, or they might be discharged into some short-handed and undemanding foreigner [39]. Then, if all went well, a measure of harmony could be restored. The less culpable prisoners could be released after a while, providing they made "humble submission". [40] Sentences might be annulled. The original demands of the mutineers might be — and often were — to some extent met. Tempers could finally be cooled by some act of generosity, genuine or feigned. Shelvocke doled out brandy to his crew as "the best means of entirely oversetting (their) wicked intentions." [41] Captain Nathaniel Uring, on the other hand, rekindled the zeal of his men with the sight of a cask of money to be dedicated to their needs. But the outcome was not always so happy, or at least as happy as commanders, mindful of their reputations and future prospects, might report. Some officers were killed, others fled at the first whiff of trouble, and the master of the *Duke of Cambridge*, on passage from Spain to England in 1732, having already been assaulted by his mate, gave up the struggle against a restive crew and surrendered his ship to a seaman opportunely travelling in her as a passenger [42].

Mutiny was by no means peculiar to sailors and the sea. It was endemic in a society in which revolts and riots were frequent and commonly violent, and in a world in which those who felt their rights violated and their living threatened would traditionally petition the authorities for redress, sometimes bringing their grievances in person. Should this fail to produce the desired effect they then turned to riot or worse to intimidate early modern governments feebly endowed to confront such risings and apprehensive of the "violence of the beastly multitude", yet willing (or obliged) to condone such tumults where there was no suspicion of radical political ambitions. Mutinies were commonplace in the armed services of England (and Europe) at the time [43]. The

---

38 WALKER, *Voyages*, p. 74 ff.

39 PRO, HCA 13/65, 13 November 1651 ; Woodes ROGERS, *Cruising Voyage*, p. 282.

40 Woodes ROGERS, *Cruising Voyage*, p. 11.

41 SHELVOCKE, *Voyage*, p. 4.

42 PRO, HCA 13/88, 1 June 1732 ; 12 June 1732.

43 S.J. GUNN, "Lincolnshire Revolt", 69-70 ; H.T. DICKINSON, *The Politics of the People in Eighteenth-Century Britain*, London, 1995, p. 125 ff.

ferocity of the London mob was rightly respected. Robbery and smuggling were sizable businesses caried on by organized gangs, whilst bands of adolescents sought to impose by force what they considered a proper morality. Approximately four hundred strikes of varying degrees of severity have been identified in Britain in the century after 1700 — frequently over wages and the price of foodstuffs — and sometimes accompanied by violent outbursts against the existing social order [44]. Issues as different as parliamentary elections, religion, government policies (especially attempts to impose new taxes or to recruit for the armed forces), the suspected ubiquity of foreigners, threats to traditional rights or customs, wages or the sinister influence of witches, sparked off tumults and riots. Popular belief in the legitimacy of such behaviour was further strengthened by the flourishing cult of ritualistic disorder, a manifestation of that widespread urge amongst Europe's less fortunate to turn the world upside down, thereby satirizing the current social regime. Its inspiration was the injustice of the human lot, together with echoes of biblical (and classical) teaching on the transitory splendours of this life and the coming of a time when the exalted would be humbled and the humble exalted. It took the form of a letting off of steam in processions, violent sports, mock executions, burning of effigies, along with the public shaming, in clamorous ridicule, of the violators of sexual or marital norms.

That similar behaviour should occur in ships is therefore hardly surprising. Moreover, by ancient custom sailors had some say in the conduct of a voyage. They were, for example, traditionally consulted in moments of crisis and were naturally loth to see their influence and standing eroded. In the very nature of their calling they were used to acting together and hence frequently showed themselves capable of initiating joint proceedings to recover their wages — including undertaking litigation in foreign courts — or in drawing up and presenting "protests" to the relevant authorities as to what they considered to be the defects of their ship [45]. From such behaviour to the concerted opposition to officers believed to be incompetent, unsuitable or insufferable was but a small step, and one which needs no recourse to Marxist teachings on class conflict for its explanation.

That seamen could be violent, disorderly or worse is true enough. Records are full of stories of brawling and fighting, of officers abused or

---

44 John RULE, *The Experience of Labour in Eighteenth-Century Industry*, London, 1981, p. 148-9, 212.

45 PRO, HCA 13/56, 17 August 1640 ; 13/78, 31 May 1675 ; 13 January 1681/2 ; 13/85, 26 November 1714.

assaulted, of comrades maltreated, of bellicose drunkeness and of assorted cruelty and brutality. The doings of disbanded sailors were likely enough a significant element in that wave of violent crime that swept through Elizabethan and Jacobean England. By the eighteenth century merchant crews were quite capable of overwhelming — and even kidnapping — naval press gangs by armed force, heightening the fears of those in authority as to what such "baptized beasts" might next accomplish.

But this is only part of the story, and what their men could do officers could do as well or better. The master of a seventeenth-century East Indiaman threatened to throw some of his hands over the side. A drunken colleague hurled (1732) his company's possessions into the sea. He beat his men in general and his mate in particular, whose cabin he also had demolished. When the mood took him he ordered the top-gallant mast to be run up, and the minute this had been done ordered it to be run back down [46]. The mate of a slaver had one unfortunate individual manacled (1728) for several days next to the latrines used by the 400 or so Africans on board [47].

Not all, nor most, voyages were of course conducted in such fashion, but many clearly were. The spread of empire and the expansion of seaborne trade to embrace the best part of the globe in the early modern centuries meant ships were out of contact with their home ports for longer periods of time than ever before. Their crews had greater opportunity to get on one another's nerves, just as they were longer subject to the authority and whims of commanders whose powers were on the increase. A master was no more, as in the Middle Ages, something like the chairman of a committee, but now, as was appositely remarked, one "whose bidding the company were not to gainsay". At the same time the insatiable demands of a growing navy and merchant fleet for men brought large-scale impressment for the fleet and a probably overall less rigorous selection of seafarers than hitherto. Nevertheless, many of the grievances of mutineers were undoubtedly legitimate. Lack of pay was a perennial source of discontent, particularly in ships in state service. The growth of the Navy long outpaced the country's willingness — its ability is another matter — to finance it for much of the early modern period, or even to pay the low wages long in force. The aggressive policies of the Cromwellian government, for example, burdened it with formidable liabilities. At its height the first war against the Dutch (1652-1654) cost

---

46 PRO, HCA 13/88, 12 June 1732.

47 PRO, HCA 13/88, 13 February 1729/30.

50 % more than the total revenues of the lately executed Charles I, and already in 1652 it took roughly £ 1 000 000 a year to get fleets to sea, all of which had to be met from an allocation of less than half that amount. Such problems continued, for much of the period with which we are concerned, to be made worse by corruption and incompetence, whilst many senior officers took the view that it was sound policy to withold pay to discourage desertion — men would stay on board, it was argued, whilst there was some prospect of getting their money.

Food and shipboard conditions — which could indeed be terrifying — were equally common causes of mutiny. In warships before the eighteenth century inadequate or inedible victuals were usually the product of contemporary technical shortcomings in the preparation and preservation of food and drink, aggravated by lack of funds, corruption and administrative incompetence. "What", demanded the mutineers in Elizabeth's *Golden Lion* at Cadiz in 1587, "is a piece of beef of half a pound among four men to dinner, or half a dry stockfish for four days in a week", washed down only with "a little beverage worse than pump water". Things eventually, but slowly improved, though there were still allegations at the beginning of the eighteenth century that it was proposed to issue "dead and stinking meat", some "green as grass", the sight and smell of which had overcome even seasoned handlers [48].

In merchantmen the ancient tribulations of seafaring — a "hard cabin, cold and salt meat, broken sleeps, mouldy bread, dead beer, wet clothes, want of fire" — could be intensified by the parsimony of owners who, to maximize profits, provided only the barest minimum of victuals. Nor was the mariner's lot improved by the slow and painful process of discovering what foods and drinks were suitable for voyages of a distance not previously undertaken and to climates not previously experienced. Furthermore, it was often the desire of a master — who usually held at least a share in his vessel — to engage in some lucrative (but possibly dangerous or illegal) trade, that led him to endeavour to get his crew to serve in a voyage to destinations other than those for which they had originally been shipped.

Equally important, venerable traditions and institutions proved ill-suited to changing circumstances. Customary privateering practice on shares and pillage needed, as we have seen, clarification which it only in fact eventually received in the mid-1700's. In merchantmen there was endless debate and confusion as to what exactly men who joined a

---

48 ANDREWS, "Elizabethen Seaman", 247 ; Historical MSS Commission Reports, *The manuscripts of the House of Lords*, New series, V, *1702-4*, n° 1935, p. 269-70.

particular vessel had committed themselves to, and even how much they were expecting to be paid. It was alleged in 1635 that "daily controversies" arose "by reason that owners, masters and pursers ... always hire their common sailors by verbal contracts", which no doubt served well enough when most seamen were illiterate and most voyages no more than short-hauls [49]. But oceanic passages were another matter. Worse still, such agreements were usually entered into in the convivial informality and alcohol-laden atmosphere of coffee houses, drink shops, taverns and the like. Consequently men often found themselves, so it was repeatedly said, expected to serve in undertakings the precise extent of which they had failed to ascertain, or which had not been made clear to them. Only after 1729, following the passing of the *Act for the Better Regulation and Government of Seamen in the Merchants' Service*, did it become the general rule for men to sign on for a voyage by endorsing a printed document ("agreeing articles") which specified their pay, their rating and the destination for which they were bound [50].

There was, furthermore, no adequate machinery by which seamen could secure dispassionate appraisal of their grievances, let alone their speedy redress — no equivalent, that is, to those governmental enquiries into industrial disputes in the early eighteenth century which commonly resulted in remedial action. True, in royal ships they might petition their captain or even higher authorities, and it was by no means unknown for them to be given a hearing. But they might, on the other hand, find themselves flogged for their troubles and temerity. To add to this confusion it was for long uncertain as to within whose jurisdiction the handling of mutiny lay. In royal ships it was outside the competence of the High Court of Admiralty. It might, as happened in the early seventeenth century, be dealt with by martial law, exercised under the authority of the royal council. This, however, entailed the considerable disadvantage that if proceedings came to grief the crown was discredited, whilst if they went well further trouble might be provoked. In Elizabethan and Jacobean times the sole alternative for commanders was therefore to act in accordance with what were vaguely referred to as "the known orders and customs of the sea". These were enshrined in a code loosely based on the ancient Laws of Oleron, so that captains, by whim or desperation, rather than by law, meted out ferocious corporal punishments (flogging, ducking from the yard-arm, keel-hauling), the variety and brutality of which apparently reached unparallelled heights in the early 1600's.

---

49 ANDREWS, *Ships, Money and Politics*, p. 73.

50 PRO, HCA 13/88, 27 December 1729 ; 17 December 1731 ; 29 February 1731/2.

Commanders could dismiss mutinous "inferior officers" (the equivalents of the modern warrant and non-commissioned rates). But the most senior, the master, was beyond their reach, subject at worst to a stoppage of pay till his case could be investigated ashore by what was soon to become the Navy Board.

Only with the introduction of naval *Articles of War* (1652) did there emerge a tentative code of discipline, with the punishment for mutiny defined, and accompanied by the creation of a rudimentary machinery for its enforcement. Potential for naval mutiny was further diminished by improvements within the Service itself, and by such measures as the introduction (1755) of the "divisional" system, whereby each of a ship's lieutenants was made responsible for a section of her crew, looking after their welfare and getting to know their problems [51].

In privateers, as already noticed, there was no such rationalization and mutiny continued to be handled in a venerable tradition of improvisation, with the imposition of draconian punishments inviting the likelihood of retaliation. Hence when a flogging took place in Warwick's fleet in 1627 it was administered "by one disguised". The situation was little better in merchantmen. With any luck mutineers might be brought before the High Court of Admiralty, but only in a civil action (one, that is, that was non-criminal and simply concerned private rights). Alternatively they could be brought before the Brethren of one of England's Trinity Houses. These, as at Deptford, Hull and Newcastle, were essentially gilds of shipmasters, incorporated in the early sixteenth century, and empowered to deal with, amongst other things, the conduct of seamen. So in 1632 a harassed commander warned his restive crew "that he would acquaint the Judge of Admiralty in England of such their abuses and misdemeanours, or the Master of Trinity House, to receive such punishments as their deserts required." [52] These, however, were hardly calculated 'intimidate. They were commonly fines, or at the worst imprisonment, which by the time of the *Merchant Shipping Act* of 1906 had evolved into a sentence of no more than twelve weeks. Faced with mutiny merchant captains could thus be very much on their own, in the most literal sense of the words. At the first stirrings of trouble the commander of the *Young Prince* had (1729) his boy fetch his sword and load his muskets. Thereafter masters would, according to taste and temperament, and with nothing more than their own sense and understanding of custom to guide them,

---

51 N.A.M. Rodger, *The Wooden World. An Anatomy of the Georgian Navy*, London, 1986, p. 216-7.

52 Andrews, *Ships, Money and Politics*, p. 69-70.

work their way through the repertoire of measures likely to restore order: blandishments, threats, abuse, kicks, blows, duckings and floggings, to mention just the commonest.

The early modern centuries saw mutinies in British ships on a scale and of an intensity unapproached before or since. The circumstances in which seamen lived and worked had in many instances deteriorated. The state was long unable or unwilling to pay its sailors, many of whom had to be pressed, against their will, to make up the crews required by fleets of unprecedented size. Commercial and privateering voyages were frequently longer and more arduous than hitherto. The machinery for handling disorders was complex, rudimentary and, the Navy apart, inadequate. The provocations to mutiny were legion: the frequent misery and constant rigours of seafaring; long periods spent in the closest proximity to fellow mortals; indifferent food; illicit indulgence in drink; short tempers induced by fatigue and digestive disorders; the lengthy absence from any authority other than that of a ship's officers. Furthermore, seamen came from a society in which popular wrath was easily stirred and from a state whose resources to maintain public order were feeble. Yet all in all the remarkable thing is not that there were so many mutinies, but that there were so few — less than one hundred reported in the early 1700's when England alone had something like 6 000 merchantmen [53]. Significantly, too, in an age when the harshest of punishments (not least hanging) could be imposed on land for such relatively minor offences as theft, burglary or assault, mutineers were treated comparatively leniently — testimony, perhaps, to the importance of a Navy and a merchant fleet to the country's prosperity and survival.

---

[53] See the discussion in Ralph DAVIS, *The Rise of the English Shipping Industry in the Seventeenth and Eighteenth Centuries*, London, 1962, p. 401-2.

VI

'A Very Profitable and Advantageous Trade'

British Smuggling in the Iberian Americas circa 1500-1750

Hardly had the Spaniards and Portuguese established their first footholds in the newly discovered Americas they claimed as their exclusive preserves than their European rivals and enemies were on the scene. In what came to be known as the Spanish Indies they endeavoured to obtain some of the continent's staggering wealth in precious metals. In Brazil they were after the logwood that could be more or less had for the taking. It produced dyes far superior to those then in use in Europe and in great demand in an expanding textile industry, of which that of England was a considerable part. Besides which there was the pleasing prospect that Brazil's great rivers might give access to the silver mining regions of Spanish South America. Such predatory urges were sharpened as Protestantism took root in Western Europe. Convinced that the military strength of Spain, the continent's leading Catholic power, stemmed from American bullion, zealous Protestants believed that could this wealth only be diverted into the right hands the true faith would be saved, its adherents duly rewarded and Spain, deprived of its lifeblood, ruined. But the implementation of this godly strategy was no obstacle to conducting a lucrative commerce with the arch-enemy. Sugar and tobacco, of which the Iberian Americas were soon substantial producers, could be purchased for sale in a growing European market. Equally appealing was the opportunity to sell to Portuguese and Spanish colonists the African slaves their plantation economies demanded. And no less attractive or rewarding was the chance to supply them with those European goods, both luxuries and necessities, which they were forbidden to produce for themselves and which Iberian industries were increasingly unable to provide, or which, through the inadequacies of the Spanish and Portuguese imperial commercial monopoly, were usually in short supply and invariably grossly over-priced.

In theory the Iberian monarchs forbade any such direct trade with their colonies. They aimed to define – as indeed did their fellow European rulers, though over realms less extensive – where, how and by whom the commerce of their empires could be conducted. But such schemes, embracing as they did whole oceans, littorals extending over thousands of miles and widely dispersed settlements, were beyond the capability of any early modern state. Moreover, in the Caribbean there were islands galore, many of them unoccupied, and with those settled by the Spaniards thinly populated and weakly defended, and hence all ideal bases for smuggling or piracy. Nor, in any case, was it practicable or possible to enforce such ambitious commercial monopolies. They might be breached through necessity – the need for example, to employ foreign shipping in the absence of suitable, or at times any, native tonnage. They could easily be circumvented by bribery, corruption and fraud, so that by the mid 1600s the bulk of the goods loaded in Spain for the Indies was smuggled into the entrepôts first of Seville and then (from 1680) Cadiz. Or they might be abrogated by force, as when in the 1650s Oliver Cromwell's redoubtable navy, in a pioneering demonstration of the efficacy of gunboat diplomacy, exacted extensive privileges for English merchants from the Portuguese.

The Iberian Americas were first penetrated by the French, the Dutch and the English. In course of time they all established colonies there, whose existence was eventually recognised by Spain in the late 1600s, and all, before and since, were engaged in clandestine trade. But by the end of the seventeenth century the English were the most important, brazen and persistent smugglers, joined occasionally by the Scots and soon overtaken by their compatriots from settlements in the Caribbean and North America. From the mid 1600s, however, direct commerce with Brazil was of far less concern to the British than the right, ever more stridently and insistently asserted, of unimpeded access to the resources and products of an increasingly prosperous Spanish America, and the unhindered opportunity to supply whatever goods it required. Such notable and colourful themes, grist to the mills of theorists of imperial growth and decline, have occasioned much excellent scholarship, whose general conclusions this paper does not attempt to dispute. Its intention is rather to show that the geographical range of these trades was more extensive, and their organisation more complex than is usually assumed in the centuries in which they reached their apogee, and at the time at which Britain and North America laid the foundations of their subsequent economic hegemony in so much of Latin America.[1]

The English in Brazil

In the early 1500s the English planned, and occasionally made expeditions to northeastern America, and a handful of the country's merchants, resident in Andalusia, were legitimately able to trade to the Spanish Indies. But initially the call of Brazil was more insistent, particularly since the onetime 'Land of the True Cross' was now economically linked, by Portuguese enterprise, with West Africa. To begin with the English interest was purely commercial, without any aspirations to geographical discovery, and a further expression of that search for new commercial outlets which in the same years brought the country's ships to the Mediterranean, the White Sea and West Africa. The Brazil voyage was relatively short and easy. It was, moreover, free from the hazards which beset those attempting to do business on the Portuguese dominated West-African coast, since there was as yet no Lusitanian military or naval presence to speak of on the immense Brazilian littoral. The inspiration was like as not French. Bretons and Normans, with the backing of Italian capital and Portuguese navigational skills, were trading to Brazil soon after 1500 – and indeed settling there – and shipping home logwood and cotton wool. The English ventures were probably set in train by William Hawkins, founder of the celebrated Plymouth seafaring dynasty, and from a port long in close contact with the harbours of northwest France. As with many who then and since sought to extend the range of the country's trade he had many other irons in the fire, notably dealings in Iberia and West Africa. But in the decade after 1530 his energies were largely directed to establishing a commerce linking England, West Africa and Brazil. His ship the *Paul* made the voyage three times between 1530 and 1532. Relations with the local Amerindians were good, notwithstanding a widespread belief that they were useless savages who whiled away the time painting their bodies and decorating themselves with feathers. On one occasion a Brazilian 'king' was brought home to be displayed at the court of Henry VIII. In the event he died before he could be returned to Brazil. Nevertheless the English hostage left there as security for his safety was well treated and released.[2]

Hawkins' lead was soon followed by others. In 1539 an English vessel, the *Saviour*, in company with the *Wolf* of Dieppe, sailed from the latter's home port, under a French pilot and freighted with daggers, knives, axes, combs, fishhooks, shirts and caps – commodities in urgent demand by colonial pioneers and their indigenous neighbours converted to the merits of European technology. These goods were to be exchanged for logwood in Brazil and the ships were to return by early 1540 at the latest. Not, however, to their original point of departure, but to the small Sussex haven of Rye, clear of prying official eyes, and a notorious centre of piracy. From here the lading was to be forwarded to France. That the trade was far from being a settled one is clear from the arrangements for the venture. The two shipowners each put up half the costs of the other's vessel, and when the voyage was over each sold the other a half share in his ship – no doubt to fog the issue of ownership and to spread the risk should the undertaking run into trouble. So, too, all those involved agreed in writing to the terms stipulated, presumably in an attempt to avoid the disputes and disagreements, which commonly plagued such expeditions. But in vain. A commercial success the voyage may have been, but the partners then fell out over the division of the proceeds.[3]

There were troubles of a different sort with the next voyage of which there is any record. In 1540 the 400-ton *Barbara* of London – a big ship by the standards of the time – was despatched to Brazil. One of her owners was the city magnate John Chandler, a very different figure from the backers of the previous venture. He was a successful practising goldsmith, a long-standing freeman of the Goldsmiths Company, and with five apprentices under his supervision. He also had substantial interests in shipping, with shares in three other vessels. However, in 1539 he was claiming that without royal financial assistance he would be obliged, for lack of funds, to sell the *Barbara*, 'which is, for a merchant ship, one of the noblest of the realm'.[4] What result, if any, such pleas had is unknown, but in late March 1540 the *Barbara* left Portsmouth for Brazil under a French pilot and with a large complement of about hundred, including ten merchants, a dozen Frenchmen and an interpreter fluent in some native Brazilian tongue. Ostensibly she was to load logwood and cotton wool, but at a time when there was more or less open maritime war between England and the Iberian kingdoms, some of her company had other ideas.

She headed for Pernambuco (Recife) via the Canaries and the Cape Verde Islands, eventually making a landfall at Cabo de São Roque on the northeast shoulder of Brazil. Some Iberian ships were attacked and plundered en route, and one small Spanish vessel was taken to serve as a pinnace. Finding no logwood, the *Barbara* and her consort, after various mishaps, coasted towards the Caribbean. Somewhere between Cabo de São Roque and Trinidad they came across locals happy to do business with them. A base was set up and a cargo of cotton wool, parrots and other exotic goods and creatures was assembled. But then things began to go wrong. The English clashed with the French and Portuguese already established in the area and were eventually attacked by Amerindians who destroyed most of what they had obtained. Some of the French contingent in the *Barbara* saw that it was now clearly time to desert, as did some of her English seamen. After such losses in goods and men the survivors decided to burn the Spanish prize and to make for Trinidad and the Caribbean. There were further scuffles with Spanish craft – a valuable indication of the volume of local seaborne commerce – and one vessel received the full blast of an English broadside. In one of the earliest references to such a use of artillery the *Barbara* was said to have discharged her 'whole side' of ordnance against her victim. The episode is recorded almost as a matter of course, though she was a merchant ship and not a man-of-war, and strongly suggests that those skills in gunnery that were later to stand the English in such good stead were already well-developed. More remarkable still is that soon after she got a taste of her own medicine when she encountered a Spanish galleon that gave an even better demonstration of the destructive power of the same tactic. First the Spaniard 'shote of his hole syde of ordynaunce' at her and then 'caste aboute on thother syde' and gave her 'all his hole syde [...] agayne'.[5] By now, not surprisingly, the *Barbara* was in a poor way, though with the help of a passing Spaniard she managed to reach Jamaica.

Here her French pilot deserted and some captured Amerindians escaped, so adding to the island's already rich ethnic diversity. The *Barbara* was then left to her fate, together with about half her lading, most of which was loot. The survivors put the rest into a Spanish ship they had seized – the very one that had helped them – and in which they set off for home in August 1540. They were, that is, presumably reasonably confident that they could find their way back across the Atlantic without their pilot, at a time when English oceanic navigational skills are still often thought to have been in their infancy. They hoped to reach Ireland, a safe haven for pirates, but being, as was not unusual, somewhat out in their reckoning, arrived instead off Ushant. From there they eventually got into Dartmouth with only thirteen (thirty-eight according to another version) of the crew still on their feet. It was not a homecoming calculated to inspire others. But neither, at least for some, was the voyage a downright disaster. Iberian ships had been looted, and those of the *Barbara*'s crew who had any strength remaining managed to make off with some of the plunder.

The Spaniards subsequently began proceedings against Chandler and a number of his associates in the English Admiralty Court. But he certainly came to no harm, nor very likely did they – a pattern of events to become even more familiar under Elizabeth I. The venture had other equally significant features. That more than peaceful commerce was originally envisaged is suggested, despite the presence of merchants in the *Barbara*'s complement, by Chandler's financial embarrassments and his presumable need for quicker and larger returns than trade alone would provide. Furthermore the ship was lavishly manned and her crew was to be paid, as was the practice in privateers, by 'thirds' – i.e. not a wage, but a third part of the monies arising from any prizes taken. And hardly had the voyage begun than the *Barbara* acquired a consort to serve as her pinnace, the employment of such tenders again being common piratical and privateering usage. No less remarkable are the indications of the navigational learning of the *Barbara*'s officers. Her English master had a chart, and her French pilot a full range of the latest tools of oceanic navigation – an astrolabe, a chart, a cross-staff and an instrument belonging to 'th'office of a pilotte for the nyght'. Moreover, one of the English merchants had a chart showing not only most of western Europe, but also Africa, Brazil, the Straits of Magellan, 'the emperor's Indians' and much else besides, which he sold to one of the junior officers.[6]

Despite, however, such obvious awareness of the nature and potential of the Iberian overseas empires there were, for the time being, no more London ventures to Brazil. Chandler's experiences were hardly encouraging and the capital's overseas trade was in any case thriving. But in the West Country Plymouth, already a celebrated seat of piracy and similar enterprise, continued to send out ships, some again with French pilots. So, too, did Southampton, where among the merchants involved was that Robert Reneger who in 1545 pulled off the first English capture of a Spanish treasure ship. A fellow citizen had a trading post built (1542) near Bahia (Salvador), and Brazilian produce was re-exported from Southampton. Indeed the trade reached a sufficient scale for the emperor Charles V (Charles I of Spain) to endeavour to secure from Henry VIII in 1541 assurances that English vessels sailing 'for Brazil or similar countries' would refrain from attacking these of his subjects.[7]

Then for a time, and for reasons not clear, the trade may have stopped, as the protagonist of English oceanic endeavour, Richard Hakluyt, implies, or may have been greatly reduced, just as English voyages to the Mediterranean and West Africa dwindled. Energies were perhaps diverted into lucrative Channel privateering – mostly piracy in fact – supposedly directed against France in the last years of the reign of Henry VIII, in which both William Hawkins and Robert Reneger were involved. Possibly, too, enthusiasm waned in the mid-sixteenth century when the economic fortunes of the provincial ports were depressed as London engrossed most of England's overseas trade. And maybe, as was the case in West Africa, ambitions were damped by staunch Portuguese opposition, with the Lusitanian crown now taking a much livelier interest in the fortunes of its American colony. But this may not be the whole story. In the 1570s there were English seamen, by no means ancient mariners, who knew Brazil. And when in 1581 an English ship arrived in Bahia the Spanish authorities in Europe (Portugal now being under Spanish rule) were outraged that she had not gone to those parts of the Brazilian coast to which the English were confined.[8] All of which suggests continuing, if not necessarily flourishing contacts.

Meanwhile the economy and society of Brazil were undergoing radical change. Faced with the prospect that the country might well fall into French or Spanish hands the Portuguese monarchy encouraged its settlement and, with enormous consequences for the future, sugar planting was introduced. Before long Brazil had a staple product to market and a small but wealthy colonial population demanding familiar European luxuries and necessities. The situation was cogently explained in a letter written in June 1578 by the Englishman John Whithall, settled at São Vicente in southern Brazil, married into a rich Genoese plantation owning family and about to acquire a sugar refinery from his father-in-law. Catholic he doubtless was, but he remained in touch with his mother country with which his bonds were clearly as strong as with his Latin co-religionists. He thus urged the merits of Anglo-Brazilian trade on a group of influential London merchants, whilst prudently whetting their appetites with talk of newly discovered gold and silver mines. He envisaged a multi-lateral commerce in which, amongst other things, English textiles would be traded for wine and hides in the Spanish Canary Islands, and these then sent on to be exchanged for sugar in Brazil.[9]

The recipients of these glad tidings, transmitted via the English merchant community in Lisbon, were Bartholomew Holder, Richard Staper (apparently a personal friend), Edward Osborne, John Bird and Robert Walkden.

Holder had long lived and worked in Lisbon, and seems to have been Whithall's channel of communication with England. Staper was one of London's most substantial merchants and an old associate of the notoriously anti-Spanish earl of Leicester. He was also a shipowner and a future privateering magnate in the Elizabethan war against Spain, which was, however, no obstacle to his supplying the enemy with munitions in 1588. Osborne was another important Londoner, and both was involved in bold schemes for the expansion of English trade to the eastern Mediterranean and beyond.[10] Bird was a man of similar parts, engaged in dealings in Iberia and the Iberian Atlantic islands and soon another major figure in privateering, whilst Walkden traded to North Africa. Whithall clearly knew who was who in capital, just as his detailed listing of the varieties of English cloths shows a close knowledge of the country's textile industry.[11]

At this stage events took an unforeseen turn when late in 1578 (or early 1579) there arrived on the Brazilian coast the English ship the *Elizabeth*, commanded by John Winter. She had been with Francis Drake at the outset of his epic circumnavigation of the world, but had lost contact, and turned back at the Straits of Magellan. Winter explored the Brazilian coast and got in touch with Whithall, with whom he discussed commercial prospects.[12] In London these seemed all the brighter following Winter's return home (June 1579), especially when after Spain's annexation of Portugal and her empire (1580) England for a time supported Dom Antonio, the pretender to the throne. He in turn, with the desperate largesse of his kind, promised concessions in his country's overseas empire. Hence in response to the invitation from Whithall and, intriguingly, from a fellow countryman in Pernambuco (Recife), a voyage to Brazil was set in train. It was to be undertaken by the *Minion* of London, which possibly belonged to the ubiquitous and aggressive Winter seafaring dynasty, and in which one of Antonio's agents was to sail.[13] In the event he stayed behind when in late 1580 she left for São Vicente, with a cargo consigned to Whithall. At this time the Hawkins family, old Brazil hands, were also reported to be fitting out ships for the same destination.[14] Notwithstanding protestations to the contrary, the likelihood of peaceful commercial exchanges was fairly remote. Instead there began what was to turn into a colourful, and at times almost farcical undertaking that graphically showed, as did so much other Elizabethan maritime enterprise, the English proclivity to shoot themselves in the foot, and the hazards of disorganised Protestant incursions into Catholic lands.

The investors in the venture came from an even wider group than the one originally approached by Whithall. They included Christopher Hodsdon of London, a member of the Russia Company and related by marriage to the city tycoon Sir George Barnes, 'a principall doer' in many such projects.[15] He was joined by Christopher Carleill, soldier, shipowner, naval commander, colonial protagonist and relative of the fiercely anti-Catholic royal secretary, Francis Walsingham. Besides these weighty figures there were also the Iberian trader and privateer owner, Thomas Bramley, John Bird (whom we have already met), a Hawkins (possibly), William Elkin and Anthony Garrard or Goddard of Plymouth, who was one of Richard Hakluyt's sources for the early Brazil voyages he records, and who may well have sailed in the ventures sent out by the William Hawkins of Henry VIII's days.[16] All shared an interest in trade with Iberia and a conviction of the merits of forceful commercial expansion. Embracing alike metropolitan and West Country backers, the *Minion* partnership eclipsed in terms of wealth, experience and influence, any previous English foray to Brazil.

The ship's master was Stephen Hare, accompanied by one Christopher Hare, who subsequently re-appeared in the service of the circumnavigator Thomas Cavendish, and who, like the master, had the same surname as one of the officers of the *Barbara* in 1540.[17] Some of the complement (Edward Cliffe and Thomas Griggs) had been in Brazil with John Winter. Some were there again later, and some could speak Portuguese.[18] The *Minion*'s cargo comprised basically textiles, which were to be traded for sugar, wax and saltpetre (used in the manufacture of gunpowder). Stephen Hare, seemingly a weak but stiff-necked character, had with him a collection of Protestant theological works, presumably for his own edification, but possibly as insurance against any inadequacies in his seamanship. And as events were to show, some of the company regarded the voyage less as a commercial venture than as an armed reconnaissance in the course of which they sought to learn all they could about gold and silver mines, about routes to the treasures of Spanish Peru and about relations between the Spaniards and the Amerindians of the interior.[19]

The *Minion* safely reached São Vicente in January 1581 and contact was made with Whithall and his family. The following month she moved on to the neighbouring Santos, and there loaded some sugar, gaining local goodwill in the meanwhile by lending weapons to be used against an anticipated French attack. Then, however, the Portuguese authorities were outraged to discover that some of the heretical English had attended a Catholic funeral, compounding their sins by getting a priest who came on board drunk. In March the *Minion* accordingly departed for Bahia (Salvador), where there was an English factor, but an inefficient one who had failed to secure a cargo for her. The master was thus obliged to advertise for a freight for Europe, which, staunch Protestant though he was, he did by putting up a notice on a convenient Catholic church door. Such initiative was, however, somewhat premature, since his command was now in so poor a way that he had to discharge what lading she had and put it into bond. Even so, he apparently managed to raise the promise of a cargo of sugar. This, it was later alleged, had been obtained in the course of transactions involving the enormous sum of £4000 – which would have bought a large and well-found ship in England. So far all had gone reasonably well. Notwithstanding some of her crew's indiscretions, the *Minion*'s presence had been welcomed. Business had been conducted in a more or less normal fashion.

Portuguese officials in Brazil had not objected, provided the appropriate dues were paid, and even in Spain the authorities were chiefly exercised that the English were trading outside that part of the Brazilian coast open to them.

Then, however, the tide turned. There had already been the usual friction in the ship over such matters as food and discipline. This was now aggravated by political tensions, ending in the dismissal of one of the factors, Thomas Griggs, from office because of his association with Francis Drake and John Winter. Next, the pilot, Edward Cliffe, unsettled perhaps by this event and swayed by the eloquence of a visiting Jesuit, decided to join the Order. His shipmates, not caring for so untimely a call, sought to restrain him. Threats and counter threats flew and word was passed to the ecclesiastical authorities that the master and gunner had heretical books on board. These the former refused to surrender. Nor, on the advice of a friendly Portuguese, would he come ashore. He was thereupon denounced as a heretic and supplies to the *Minion* were cut off. In such discouraging circumstances some of her crew, amongst them Abraham Cocke, subsequently much in evidence, deserted, whilst a number of the factors, impressed by what Bahia could offer, decamped with the goods entrusted to them by merchants in England, intending to settle in Brazil. Part of a posse from the ship that went after these entrepreneurs ended in the hands of the Inquisition, but was eventually released. The Portuguese authorities then made a botched attempt to seize the *Minion*, which, despite her feeble condition, escaped, taking with her a number of Portuguese hostages but leaving seventeen of her own men and a stock of goods behind. Yet even in the course of this final scuffling one of her company attempted to get a letter for Lisbon aboard a Portuguese craft lying nearby, loading sugar and cotton for Portuguese and – significantly – Dutch merchants.[20]

Despite all her troubles, when the *Minion* eventually returned home there were many, as the Spaniards complained, eager to risk a Brazil voyage, their hopes raised by the prospect of treasure and access to Peruvian silver. In Spain the advice to Philip II was that any ships attempting the passage should be sunk.[21] But this did little to cool English ardour. By now the country and the Hispano-Portuguese empire were drifting towards open war. Bellicose Protestants, influential in shaping Elizabethan foreign policy, like their French co-religionists earlier, saw the potential of Brazil in a grand anti-Catholic, anti-Iberian strategy. Spanish agents reported expeditions in preparation for assaults on Luso-America, and Richard Hakluyt had already urged the capture of São Vicente, to serve as a forward base for the occupation of the Straits of Magellan.[22] Nor, despite the confusions in English policy, were these idle threats. Drake himself, after contemplating some venture to the southernmost tip of South America, had a ship out in 1582. She was part of a badly-organised and unsuccessful foray, supposedly destined for the Pacific and commanded by Edward Fenton. But this degenerated into a piratical cruise in Brazilian waters under a pilot who had been with John Winter. Contact was nevertheless once more established with John Whithall at São Vicente. Any hopes, however, that he may still have entertained of normal business were dashed by Fenton's lunatic behaviour – he thought first of setting up as king of São Vicente and then of St Helena – and the arrival of a Spanish fleet. All the same, some trade apparently continued, by channels unknown, with the Spaniards complaining in 1582 that Brazil's entire sugar crop was 'promised to certain London merchants'.[23] Maybe, but nevertheless eight vessels were said to be preparing to sail from England for Brazil, and the elder William Hawkins, of the Plymouth family long interested in the country, had a voyage in hand. He was, however, diverted to Caribbean privateering by Spanish counter-measures.[24]

The following year Southampton, another pioneer of Brazilian ventures in the time of Henry VIII, re-appeared in the trade. An expedition was planned by Edward Cotton, a future privateering magnate and an urgent advocate of forward policies. He was one of the town's leading merchants, involved alike in Newfoundland and the Mediterranean, and at some stage allegedly engaged in selling slaves to the Ottoman Turks. The ship, the *Edward*, was his own, sailing under a pilot who had been with John Winter on Drake's great 1577 voyage. She was to load salt in the Portuguese Cape Verde Islands, which was then to be traded in Santos and São Vicente for seal skins, whale oil, amber, sugar, cotton wool, parrots and much else besides, including the mysterious 'beast called serrabosa' and oysters, to see if they contained pearls. The care that had clearly been taken assessing the commercial possibilities of Brazil – incidentally throwing interesting light on its nascent whaling and sealing industries – unfortunately did not extend to the conduct of the voyage, with the *Edward* lost, so it was said, 'through mere dissolute negligence'.[25]

Less ambitious but better organised was another 1583 expedition, that of the *Merchant Royal* of London. It was backed by the city merchants Thomas Cordell and William Garraway and their associates. Cordell was influential in both the Levant trade and privateering and Garraway was another major figure in Mediterranean commerce. The ship was commanded by Robert Flick, Portugal trader and future privateering magnate. The *Merchant Royal* arrived safely in Olinda (Pernambuco) where she stayed for six months (not an inordinate delay by contemporary practice) loading sugar. She then sailed for home, leaving behind three factors (amongst them William Ivette, formerly of the *Minion*) together with goods and debts valued at over £4000. The factors carried on business satisfactorily until the appearance of a Spanish fleet, whereupon, because of the doings of Edward Fenton (as noticed above), they were arrested and the goods confiscated. Cordell and his partners suffered a further setback when another cargo also came to grief, sent out from Viana, a Portuguese haven much favoured in illicit endeavours, in the Portuguese *St John* and with a Portuguese factor on board. This, so it was later alleged, cost Cordell and his associates total losses of over £8000. Nevertheless they persisted, and wisely so if the sums reputedly involved bear any relation to reality. Should a mere couple of cargoes be worth so much at a time when England's annual imports came to no more than about one million pounds the prospects of Brazil were indeed alluring.

Hence Cordell was still doing business in the country in 1584-1585, now in partnership with the London sugar magnate Henry Beecher, and with members of the metropolitan and Ipswich King family – the latter veteran Iberian traders, with their own factor in Brazil and active in Lisbon after the outbreak of the Anglo-Spanish war.[26] Also involved, showing the drift away from peaceful commerce, were the future Lord Hunsdon, the politically influential Sir George Carey – shipowner, privateer par excellence and backer of colonial projects – and the undeterred Edward Cotton of Southampton. Once again the *St John* of Viana was used, sailing this time (1584) from Southampton, presumably at Cotton's instance. She had a cargo of metal goods, textiles, gunpowder and foodstuffs – of which Brazil, like the mother country, was frequently in urgent need. These commodities were to be traded for sugar and logwood in Pernambuco (Recife), and such goods as the *Merchant Royal* had left behind were to be recovered. The ship had a Portuguese master and carried Portuguese factors, one of them experienced in working for the English. But Cordell had his own man, the old *Minion* hand William Ivette on board, and most of the crew were English. They also controlled the arms on board, to let foreigners know who was who and to ensure the *St John* returned to London and nowhere else. There was the usual friction endemic in such multi-national ventures from the outset. Some of the hands had to be restrained from deserting in Southampton and the prospects of a successful voyage were not increased by the master's insistence on informing all and sundry that the whole undertaking was English. In the event so much sugar was acquired that it caused alarm as to its likely effect on prices in England. But such worries were premature. On her way home the *St John* was captured by an English privateer.[27]

So far the trade, though strictly speaking illegal, had in general been tolerated in Brazil and Portugal, with troubles chiefly arising from gratuitous English violence or from the tactless flouting of Portuguese religious sensibilities. But there were other and growing difficulties. Direct English commerce with Brazil in England was not popular with merchants still trading to Portugal itself – as they were able to do for nearly a decade after its annexation by Spain – since their imports of Portuguese colonial produce from Iberia were undercut by such competition. Then from 1585 to 1604 England was at war with the Hispano-Portuguese empire. To most of the horde of English privateers loosed by the conflict this meant that English ships or English merchants trading to Iberian colonies were fair game. It also meant that they made such massive hauls of Brazilian sugar as to swamp the English market and depress prices. And in the longer term, and more unfortunately, English devotion to the pursuit of the spoils of war allowed the Dutch to engross much of the business of carrying Brazilian sugar across the Atlantic.

With war came attacks on the coast and ports of Brazil. The privateering grandee, the earl of Cumberland, contemplated taking Bahia in 1586. Pernambuco was raided in 1595 yielding 'wonderful great riches'. In 1601, in the course of a cruise along the Brazilian littoral, a Dartmouth expedition acquired a Jesuit description of the country, which its commander later sold to Richard Hakluyt. Meanwhile fleets, flotillas or individual ships, under some of England's most celebrated privateering captains, operated off the Brazilian coast, as also did Abraham Cocke, once of the *Minion*, and for a time in Portuguese service. Nor were things made any easier by the blossoming of English projects (as in 1589) for the occupation of parts of the country, their likelihood and importance duly magnified by Spanish intelligence.[28] Nevertheless some trade continued, usually by design, but occasionally by accident and doubtless more than has left any record. In 1586 a flotilla under Thomas Cavendish, its pilots allegedly provided by the Portuguese pretender Dom Antonio, and with Christopher Hare, late of the *Minion*, amongst its complement, made yet another attempt to contact John Whithall.[29] The following year, in a further venture in co-operation with Antonio's supporters, two English ships furnished with English safe-conducts left for Brazil. They were 'coloured' as Portuguese, under Portuguese command and with part Portuguese crews. They were to make for the Lusitanian Atlantic islands and there exchange the textiles they were carrying for wine, which was to be used for the purchase of slaves in either Guinea or Angola. These were in turn to be traded for sugar in Brazil, from where the vessels were to sail directly to England.[30] The outcome of the voyage is unknown as is that of an even more remarkable one, planned in 1588 as the Spanish Armada was launched its luckless 'Enterprise of England'. Elizabeth I's physician and master spy, the Portuguese New Christian (i.e. Jewish convert to Catholicism) Hector Nuñez, already busy interloping in Portuguese Asia and Africa, now had some Brazilian scheme in mind. Meanwhile Richard May – probably also a New Christian – who had earlier invested in one of the *St John* of Viana's trips, was again sending English goods to Brazil, now in partnership with the Levant merchant Richard Cobb, but wisely this time in a captured Iberian vessel. Besides which there are hints of further New Christian involvement, in Brazil, in other parts of the Iberian overseas empires, as indeed in the Iberian kingdoms themselves.[31] Then in 1592, after Thomas Cavendish's fleet had failed to pass through the Straits of Magellan, one of the ships seized the opportunity of the ensuing demoralisation and confusion to put into Santos, load a cargo of sugar and run for home.[32]

One important consequence of these spasmodic contacts was to bring into being a body of English seamen familiar with Brazilian waters and a group of merchants conversant with the country's commercial life. The

English acquired Portuguese charts, maps and descriptions of Brazil, just as they picked the brains of those Portuguese pilots who, by fair means or foul, they employed.[33] There was also a growing number of Englishmen who, by the late 1500s, had first hand knowledge of Brazil, much of it soon in wide circulation. Commercial factors, in the country from about 1580 if not earlier, were joined, especially after the outbreak of the privateering war, by men abandoned by their compatriots, captured by the Iberians, marooned by disaster, or who, having succumbed to the attractions of Brazil, had simply deserted. An expedition of 1586 came across Abraham Cocke, left behind by the *Minion* in 1581 and thereafter employed by the Portuguese, as were others, either on land or sea.[34] More dramatic was the story of his contemporary Peter Carder. The sole survivor from a boat belonging to Drake's flagship that foundered in the Straits of Magellan, he got ashore in Patagonia. From there he made his way to Bahia – some 3000 miles – where at various times he worked for the Portuguese as a seaman or as a plantation foreman before being returned to England in 1586. Less fortunate was Anthony Knivet, who sailed in Thomas Cavendish's disastrous last voyage. He, too, came ashore in the Straits of Magellan, and after horrendous struggles eventually reached Brazil. There he was employed as a soldier, lived wild amongst the 'cannibals' and was held prisoner in chains until he managed to escape to Angola, only to end in gaol in Lisbon.[35] Others had very similar tales to tell. In 1612 Andrew Battell, onetime associate of Abraham Cocke, recounted to Samuel Purchas, the chronicler of imperial endeavour, the colourful history of his adventures as a Portuguese prisoner in Brazil and Angola (1589-1609). And at around the same time Purchas also talked to two other veterans of Brazil (and of much of the rest of the world), Thomas Turner (whom Knivet had met in Pernambuco) and John Pountis.[36] Then there are some more shadowy figures, like John King, who was still in Santos where he may have been for the previous fifteen years, in 1591, and the erstwhile pilot of one of the ships of the London privateering tycoon, John Newton, who turned up in Pernambuco. Nor, apparently, were these the sole Englishmen in these ports and there were others besides in Rio de Janeiro in 1600. Their lot, moreover, was not necessarily one of unalleviated hardship. Those who were, or could pass themselves off as Catholics, might lead a reasonable existence, with the above-mentioned Thomas Turner undertaking a venture to Angola on Knivet's advice.[37]

The Anglo-Spanish war ended in 1604, ushering in something like half a century of peace, in European waters at least, disrupted only by renewed conflict in 1625-1630. Nevertheless the English supposedly remained as firmly excluded from direct trade with Portugal's colonial empire as ever. However Portugal, still embroiled with Holland and struggling from 1640 to break free from Spain, made some concessions to obtain aid. Then in 1650-1656 England exacted by naval force from Portugal the right for her subjects to trade to Portugal's colonial possessions on the same terms as the Portuguese themselves. Needless to say, necessity did not engender affection. The treaty was indeed revised and renewed in 1661, but this was not to the liking of the Portuguese, who did their best to ensure that its conditions were ignored. There was, furthermore, the considerable obstacle that Holland, moving inexorably from trade to dominion and rapidly replacing Spain as England's arch-enemy, attacked Bahia in 1625, and by the mid-1640s controlled the best part of the great sugar-producing region of the north-eastern littoral of Brazil. Gloom, however, was not unrelieved, since Dutch aggression rendered the English more acceptable to some Portuguese and Luso-Brazilians.

Interloping accordingly continued. After the vast captures of sugar cargoes by Elizabethan privateers England was irredeemably addicted to a commodity now launched on its way to becoming one of mass consumption. Rich colonials in Brazil demanded European luxuries, whilst with the onset of the Dutch invasion the country urgently needed arms, all of which Portugal notoriously lacked, as also the shipping for their carriage. But the English ventures at this date rarely involved, for reasons which will soon be apparent, men of the wealth and standing of their Elizabethan precursors, nor were they on the scale of those of the Dutch or more surprisingly, the French. They included, however, for the first time, some half-hearted attempts at colonisation. In the early 1600s there were abortive Anglo-Irish settlements in the Amazon delta, which lasted till the Portuguese destroyed them in the 1630s, and to which, in 1618, were being despatched such vital items of frontier life and trade as spades, beads and thimbles.

Meanwhile, for an English textile industry in the familiar throes of crisis and reorganisation, logwood was being illicitly loaded at Ilhéus (Bahia) in 1614. The following year five vessels were attempting to ship a similar cargo from Cabo Frio (Rio de Janeiro) and to establish a trading post there, whilst some optimists were reported to be searching for pearls in Amazonia in 1616.[38] All the well-tried stratagems were used to sustain such a commerce. Venturers might employ an English ship, but under a Portuguese master and pilot. So in 1632 the city merchants Robert Priestly and Roger Corbett sent the *Angel* of London to Santo Antonio (Bahia). She sailed from Viana, whose role in such undertakings has already been noticed, and successfully loaded sugar, tobacco and green ginger, only to be captured by the Dutch.[39] Some more cautious (or ingenious) owners claimed their vessels were Portuguese, or even Brazilian. Others bestowed suitable Portuguese names on their ships, with the *Dolphin* of London thus becoming the *Santa Helena* of Aveiro. Merchants might pass their goods off as Portuguese by using (quite legitimately) partners well-integrated into Portuguese business circles by long residence in the country, or come to some arrangement with an obliging local entrepreneur (often a New Christian).[40] Many simply ignored the restrictions in force, as when in 1635 the *George*, belonging to Sir William Courteen and commanded by Robert Moulton – later a distinguished officer in the navy of the English Republic – sailed for Brazil. There she was to dispose of a miscellaneous cargo of cloth, cutlery and such like goods, and on her arrival met another London ship similarly engaged. Many other owners and merchants, in time honoured fashion, paid the appropriate Portuguese officials to turn a blind eye to their activities.[41]

The need for such expense and subterfuge dwindled from the 1630s. The truce (1609) between Holland and the Spanish empires expired in 1621, leaving Portugal, desperately short of shipping, to wrestle with Dutch attacks on its trade and empire. Like Spain it turned to England, a country that could easily provide food and munitions and, more important still, large, powerful and well-armed merchantmen, famed for their ability to look after themselves. And England was all the more attractive as it was neutral (except for a brief conflict with France and Spain in the late 1620s) in the Thirty Years War, whereas Holland, Spain and (after 1635) France were all involved by land and sea.[42]

Hence, under royal licence, Portuguese merchants employed English ships in their trades with Brazil (and elsewhere). And the situation became rosier still for English owners with the creation in 1649 of a Portuguese Brazil Company, which was to enjoy a partial monopoly of the country's trade with its colony. But it too, in addition to all its other shortcomings, lacked suitable vessels. So, with royal permission it chartered English vessels for the fleets by which its commerce was conducted, their hire so lucrative to owners that in 1663 Charles II lent his brother James three English warships to be used for this purpose. Furthermore, membership of the Brazil Company was open to foreigners, and consequently to foreign, and thus English, investors. So the ranks of its backers came to include such English merchants as the Bushells, Londoners long involved in business in Iberia. In 1649 they reputedly had £5000 sunk in the Brazil trade, and over £20,000 in the 1650s – sums whose magnitude becomes apparent when it is remembered that at that time it cost the English government roughly one million pounds a year to get its formidable navy to sea.[43] A somewhat different but equally significant figure was Samuel Vassal, another rich city merchant and shipowner, and a Parliamentary naval commissioner in the 1640s. His interests ranged from colonial ventures in the West Indies and North America to attempts, in association with the celebrated Maurice Thompson, to break into the West African slave trade.[44]

For such men, able to operate within the frameworks of the Brazil Company, interloping became pointless. Not all, however, were so well placed, and in any case old habits died hard. There were, therefore, those who continued to conduct, by the freest of free enterprise, a Brazil trade of a scale and value it is impossible to determine. Hence, for example, two English ships arrived in Bahia in 1648, one from Newfoundland carrying fish, and the other from London with guns. Four years later Andrew Rand of London, who served as an officer in the Cromwellian navy, sailed for Brazil in his own *Thomas and Lucy*. It was a trade in which she was to continue for at least a further decade, but on this occasion she was in company with another Brazilian veteran, the *Scipio*, also of London, and in a voyage that appears to have been as much directed to plundering the Dutch as to the pursuit of commerce.[45]

Then, of course, there was no guarantee that English vessels chartered or licensed by the Portuguese would not take the opportunity to pursue, one way or another, their own business. Those sailing under Portuguese licence were supposed to call at Lisbon, outward bound, to obtain the necessary clearance, and on the return journey to pay the dues levied on their cargoes. But some ships made straight for Brazil from home, squaring any Portuguese officials they encountered in such ports as they put into. Others returned directly to England from Brazil, thus evading payment of Portuguese customs. So in 1661 four English vessels on charter to the Portuguese arrived in the Thames loaded with tobacco, sugar and logwood, after a direct run home. More colourful were the doings of the *Alexander* in 1660. She arrived in Bahia with her commander claiming to be in possession of a privateering commission from Portugal against the Dutch and a licence to trade. When these were rejected by the Brazilian authorities he anchored his ship nearby and entered into a brisk nocturnal commerce with local planters and the monks of a wealthy monastery. He then departed to Barbados and there topped up his cargo of Brazilian sugar with a further lading of that from the island. On his eventual return home he endeavoured with brazen effrontery to pass the whole lot off as English colonial produce, and so entitled to a preferential rate of customs.[46]

Unlike the contemporary interloping trade then developing with the Spanish Americas, with its wide West Indian and North American, as well as English involvement, that to Brazil in the middle decades of the seventeenth century was largely in the hands of a group of affluent London merchants and shipowners. Their activities, particularly in the time of Charles I, brought a reversion – albeit short-lived – to the pattern that had prevailed in the latter part of the reign of Elizabeth I, just as these involved were, like their Elizabethan predecessors, simultaneously engaged or embroiled in ambitious colonial and overseas commercial ventures. Sir William Courteen, owner of the *George* in 1635, was a businessman, financier and strenuous opponent of the monopoly of eastern trade enjoyed by the English East India Company. Roger Corbett and Robert Priestly, backers of the *Angel* in 1632, were at the same date also operating in the Portuguese sugar island and slaving base of São Tomé, as was their associate John Thierry, another Londoner but of Walloon and Huguenot origins, and a member of a powerful Anglo-Dutch merchant and ship-owning dynasty.[47] John Bushell was from a similar background. He was a city merchant based in Lisbon and belonged to a family prominent in trade in Portugal and amongst the first investors in the Brazil Company. The Bushells were also involved in Jamaica, and in many undertakings in Portugal's Atlantic possessions, which may have been perfectly legitimate, but over which there nevertheless hangs a cloud of suspicion. Notwithstanding deteriorating

Anglo-Dutch relations in the mid-seventeenth century John Bushell had an agent in the great entrepôt of Amsterdam. In 1651 the family, as investors in the Portuguese Brazil Company, were part owners of a Portuguese ship carrying sugar and tobacco from Brazil to Lisbon, and also had cargoes of sugar in four other Portuguese vessels. Meanwhile John and a brother were shipping slaves from Portuguese Angola (where they had a Portuguese factor) to their agents in Brazil. They used a nominally Portuguese vessel, and the family were still engaged in the trade in 1658.[48]

From the mid-seventeenth century direct English voyages to Brazil became increasingly rare. The Portuguese were as determined as any other European power to deny foreign ships and merchants such access to their colonies. Apart from some momentary concessions to obtain aid in the struggle against Spain and Holland, which continued until the 1660s, the privileges secured by the Cromwellian state and confirmed in 1661 were either disputed, ignored or whittled away. The English were repeatedly forbidden, as for example in 1711 and 1735, to trade to Brazil in their own ships. As a rule they came to accept these prohibitions, though not from any respect for an ancient ally that had successfully broken free from Spain, and with whom friendly relations were re-established. In the context of other opportunities available the smugglers trade became too difficult, risky and unrewarding. The Brazilian coast lacked that abundance of convenient footholds that made the Caribbean an ideal base for interloping in the Spanish Americas. Nor were there locally and easily available such a variety of products as the West Indies and North America could contribute to a commerce of this nature, just as there was no comparable range and diversity of markets to handle them, or customers for their purchase. And there was little point in the English engaging in hazardous clandestine operations when their ships were legitimately chartered in large numbers to carry Brazilian products to Portugal, escorted if need be by English men-of-war.[49]

Equally important was the changing nature of the Atlantic, and indeed the whole European imperial economy. From the mid 1600s English merchants (and after the Union of 1707 their Scottish colleagues and competitors as well), could get all the sugar and tobacco they needed from the country's own West Indian and American colonies. The Brazilian industry was, moreover, in difficulties in the late 1600s whilst its sugar was in any case dearer in England than that from the English plantations because of the higher duties it attracted. So, too, the English could now get dyes from Asia, and logwood, without too much difficulty as we shall see, from the Spanish Caribbean. But of prime importance was the discovery of gold in Brazil in the late seventeenth century, turning the country into a large-scale producer of wealth in its most convenient and acceptable form. Some of this gold the English obtained through smuggling, which soon became widespread, either in Lisbon (where it was commonly loaded into British warships), or in Brazil itself.[50] Returning East India Company ships, joined on occasion by vessels of the Royal Navy, put into Brazilian ports on one specious pretext or another, and proceeded to carry on a brisk trade. In 1711 for example, the Portuguese authorities complained that there were eight of them in Bahia and Rio de Janeiro, exchanging European and Asian goods for tobacco and gold. And so lucrative were the opportunities that some naval captains, ingenious and intrepid as ever in the augmentation of their pay, allegedly arrived with their ships full of textiles they intended to sell.

Most Brazilian bullion was, however, simply funnelled, legitimately or otherwise, through Portugal to England to pay for the manufactures demanded by a prosperous Brazil and its reinvigorated mother country. With a trade of impressive value now flowing – thought to be worth around half a million pounds per annum in 1761, when England's gross total trade was of the order of twenty million pounds – and with the wealth of Brazil thus so agreeably to hand, there was little incentive, for the time being, for British ships to run unnecessary risks, or for Britain to seek to change things.[51] Not that some Britons did not entertain, as the Portuguese generally suspected, other ambitions. In 1670-1671, at a time when English interest in South America was once again stirring, the English Consul-General in Lisbon urged his compatriots to colonise the southernmost regions of the country (claimed, but not yet settled by the Portuguese) where, he predicted, the prospects were far rosier than in New England. His advocacy fell on deaf ears, but Brazilian wealth attracted English pirates in the late 1600s, just as Brazil figures largely in Daniel Defoe's *Robinson Crusoe*.[52] There were those, too, who attempted to participate in the flourishing business of supplying the African slaves required by Brazil's plantation and mining economy. The celebrated Bristol privateer Woodes Rogers had made a colourful visit to the country in the course of his circumnavigation of the globe (1708-1711). He was back before long with slaves acquired during a further voyage (1714-1715). They were from Madagascar, a recently opened additional source of labour for the Atlantic world, whose resources were soon tapped by fellow Bristolians, and had been obtained in exchange for weapons and ammunition, at a premium in this hub of Indian Ocean piracy. Some of his slaves Woodes Rogers disposed of in East Africa, Batavia and at the Cape of Good Hope. The rest – six hundred or so, and thus remnants of a very large cargo – he hoped, Portuguese prohibitions notwithstanding, to sell 'by stealth' in Brazil, though with what success is not known.[53]

Interloping in Spanish America

Whilst such voyages more or less died out, those to Spanish America grew at a prodigious rate. Since the middle decades of the seventeenth century access to the riches of the Spanish Indies had been a prime object of English ambitions. And to this legendary wealth Brazil came to provide yet another route. That Peru could be reached from the Río de la Plata had long been known to the English. But events took a gratifying if belated turn when in 1713 Spain ceded Nova Colónia do Sacramento, on the north bank of the river, to Portugal. A clandestine commerce with Spanish America, as vigorous and profitable as any, quickly sprang up. Its focal points were Lisbon, Nova Colónia and Buenos Aires. The merchants handling business in Brazil were either locals or Portuguese, though in fact they were for the most part merely agents for firms in Portugal, which in turn were fronts for British enterprises. So blatant was British interest in the well-being of the trade that when in 1735-1736 Nova Colónia was besieged by the Spaniards the British government, amongst whose priorities the advancement of trade now ranked high, refused to help its Portuguese allies lest Spain should be offended. Friendship was good, but profit was better: dealings through Nova Colónia were probably running at about half a million pounds a year at a time when total British imports were worth roughly eight million pounds.[54]

Elsewhere in Spanish America – in those lands, that is, discovered, subjugated and in varying degrees subordinated to the European economy by Columbus and his successors – interloping was of a greater volume, complexity and variety than to Brazil, just as it employed far more ships and involved many more merchants. In its early stages the English predominated amongst the participants from the British Isles, but were soon joined – as again was not the case with Brazil – by Scots and then by compatriots from settlements in North America and the West Indies. Trade came to be conducted largely through entrepôts seized from Spain in the attempted pursuance of colonial grand-strategies. It enjoyed almost universal local support, not to say encouragement, in the Indies. It was also accompanied, as smuggling often was, by much armed violence and by a growing and vociferous British pressure for the opening of the markets of Spanish America by force if need be. And it was, though this cannot be examined here, part of a competitive international business, in which the French and the Dutch were for long formidable rivals.

Already in the early 1500s, when their country was still Catholic, some members of the English community in Cadiz and Seville could lawfully own or invest in ships working to the Indies, trade there or even back or participate in voyages of exploration. But once radical Protestantism took root in England and Catholic Spain was identified as the country's mortal enemy, the English, like their French, Scottish and other coreligionists launched plundering expeditions against Spanish America. Their main inspiration was the hope of securing bullion, and by the mid 1500s the English government was toying with the possibility of conquering Peru. Early in Elizabeth I's reign John Hawkins, of a family long engaged in attempts to broaden the scope of England's overseas commerce – embracing, as we have seen, Brazil – made an abortive attempt to break into the lucrative Iberian slave trade between West Africa and the Spanish Indies. His failure was little deterrent to others. In 1570 a ship belonging to the influential

Winter dynasty – associates of the Hawkins clan and similarly involved in Brazil – was reported trading in Spanish Jamaica. Three years later the outright onslaught on the flow of American bullion to Europe, now increasingly seen as the source of Spanish strength, began with Francis Drake's celebrated attack on Nombre de Dios. Schemes were aired for English seizure of bases in the Americas anywhere from the Straits of Magellan to the future Virginia, and the Spaniards feared that the English were aiming at 'a regular annual trade' with the Indies.[55] Radical Protestants, and those who from convenience or conviction supported them, envisaged the beneficial diversion of American treasure into more deserving hands and the consequent destruction of that Spanish power which was at the root of all Europe's troubles. The eventual outcome was open warfare (1585-1604), in the course of which the English sacked ports in the Indies and momentarily secured strongholds, but at the same time carried on an extensive commerce, plundering with one hand and trading with the other, as outraged Spanish officials somewhat infelicitously complained. Indeed, such was their alarm that they were unwilling to exploit the potential of islands like Puerto Rico and prohibited the production of tobacco in Venezuela and adjacent lands to discourage further interloping. All the same, in one way or another, the English, like the French and Dutch obtained hides, silver and the sugar and tobacco for which a craving was now developing. In exchange they supplied much sought after textiles and metallurgical goods, together with other European manufactures, not to mention two shiploads of captured papal privileges they were trying to dispose of on one occasion.[56]

A further consequence of such activities was that, as in Brazil and for the same reasons, some Scots, Englishmen and Irish found themselves domiciled for longer or shorter periods in the Spanish Indies. Here they were sometimes able to be of service to compatriots, and from the Americas they might also pass on information, which, however, rarely conferred that power the modern adage assumes. It could be that John Rut, who in 1527 commanded one of Henry VIII's ships which sailed down virtually the entire habitable coastline of Atlantic North America and ended as a Spanish conquistador in Paraguay.[57] About the same date there were others, and not only Catholics, well-established and even married in Mexico, like that Scot, said in 1557 to have lived there for twenty years. A decade later Robert Sweeting, son of an English father and a Spanish mother, was able to ease the lot of some fellow Englishmen imprisoned near Mexico City. There were compatriots in Hispaniola, whilst in 1576 an Irish 'captain' was reported to have been domiciled in the Indies for fifteen years.[58] There were also prisoners, usually, as in Brazil, survivors from bold schemes that had miscarried. Some were men who had been with John Hawkins in the fiasco of his final slaving voyage. Others, like John Drake, nephew of the celebrated Sir Francis, and held in Paraguay in 1583, had come to grief in the course of Edward Fenton's antics (noticed above) off the Brazilian coast. Then there were men cast away in even remoter places, with some seeking safety in the 1590s among the Indians of the Mosquito Coast (Nicaragua). From choice or necessity many such worked for the Spaniards, commonly as seamen. Several endured lengthy exile, as did John Chilton, who only returned to England in 1586 after nearly two decades of wandering and trading in the Indies. And some accomplished fearsome itineraries, like those survivors from an expedition to Guiana (1605), who trekked to safety through Venezuela and Colombia.[59]

This British presence in the Indies was soon notably strengthened. The Anglo-Spanish peace of 1604 was interpreted by James I to mean that the English were at liberty to colonise those parts of the Americas not settled by the subjects of other Christian princes, but that they traded to Spanish possessions at their peril. Nor, for the moment, was interloping particularly attractive. Force was debarred, Dutch competition was increasing and Spanish reaction could be sharp and effective, killing off the nascent tobacco smuggling industry from Venezuela in the early 1600s. Hence for the time being poaching in the Caribbean was chiefly undertaken by small provincial merchants, with the London magnates, so much in evidence in the Elizabethan war, now largely absent. Most English energies were, instead, like those of the French and the Dutch, deflected to areas clear of Spanish reach – to North America and the Lesser Antilles on the one hand, and to the 'Wild Coast' of South America on the other. This was the region between the deltas of the Orinoco and the Amazon, inhabited by primitive indigenous peoples and far removed from any major Spanish bases. It was also handy for trade with Spanish Trinidad, an important clandestine supplier of the much-desired tobacco, until this traffic too was nipped in the bud in the interests of that Anglo-Spanish rapprochement dear to the heart of James I.

There were abortive attempts to establish footholds in what became known as Guiana, none more celebrated than that of Walter Raleigh (1617), whose chief outcome was to ensure his own death and the demise of what remained of tobacco smuggling.[60] Subsequent ventures in the Amazon delta were quickly destroyed, as we have seen, by the Portuguese, whilst a promising settlement in Surinam (1651) was soon lost to the Dutch. But bold spirits were undeterred, with, from the early 1600s, zealous Puritans pressing for a vigorous anti-Spanish and anti-Catholic oceanic and colonial strategy, which the crown so manifestly failed to provide. As they saw it the faith was everywhere in danger whilst England was deprived of her fair share of the world's trade. What was needed was a West India Company on the lines of that of the Dutch, then enjoying such success, or Anglo-Dutch or even Anglo-Swedish assaults on the might of Spain. The English should push into the Spanish Indies, where, as was said, 'honey was to be had', and, as of old, the life-giving flow of silver from America was to be diverted from Spanish into English hands. As under Elizabeth such policies were advocated by members of a far from cohesive group. Amongst them were Dudley

Digges, whose interests spanned alike Asian trade and the colonisation of North America, and John Pym, the strenuous parliamentary opponent of the Stuarts. There were London merchants, like the ubiquitous Maurice Thompson, and there was that formidable Puritan grandee, the earl of Warwick, together with his clients and relatives. He was to be Parliament's Admiral at the outbreak of the Civil War, whilst during the Anglo-Spanish war of 1625-1630 he commanded a privateering flotilla of his own ships. He was a major figure in renewed efforts to colonise North America and a prime mover in schemes embracing Bermuda, Trinidad, Tobago and West Africa. In best Elizabethan style he envisaged godly projects of profit and expansion to be brought to fruition through a self-financing war against Spain, whose pernicious power and activities the crown so blindly refused to confront.[61]

Inspired by reports of the potential of the island of Santa Catalina, off the Nicaraguan coast, and in the very heart of the Spanish Caribbean, Warwick and his associates set up the Providence Island Company (1630), dominated by aristocrats and squires, some of them veterans of other colonial ventures. Santa Catalina, now renamed Providence, was occupied to form the core of a British Caribbean empire and to provide a home – or, in the language of the day, 'a warmer Diverticulum and Receptaculum' – for the Puritans of New England, whose future then seemed far from assured. A staple crop and some subsidiary industry would, it was assumed, sustain the colonists, though the island never managed to produce anything more than poor quality tobacco and small amounts of cotton. Undismayed, fertile minds sought other opportunities. There was a search for silver in Darien (Panama). The possibility was aired of settlement on the neighbouring Mosquito Coast, of whose resources there were great hopes and where the native people were already sufficiently versed in European ways to offer to trade slaves (probably escaped Africans) for weapons. But given the tenets of the Company's major backers, and the island's superb situation, right on an important Spanish shipping route, privateering was soon in full swing. Honduras was attacked in 1638, whilst another expedition, sent out by the London merchant, Maurice Thompson and his partners, embarked on a triumphant plundering cruise round the Caribbean, in the course of which Maracaibo (Venezuela) and Trujillo (Honduras) were taken and Jamaica briefly occupied. Part of the resultant loot (cotton, tobacco and slaves especially) was sold in New England. All this was more than Spain could stomach. The island was attacked and eventually (1641) recovered, when some of its English inhabitants departed to join a handful of their compatriots already living on the Mosquito Coast.[62]

England's aggressive expansion was more purposefully renewed under Oliver Cromwell, an admirer of the ways in which the Elizabethans had sustained the godly cause. With Charles I executed and the first Anglo-Dutch war brought to a satisfactory conclusion, Cromwell controlled impressive armed forces. It was, however, sound policy that these should be employed well away from the mother country, and preferably in ventures which offered the likelihood of wealth to help restore the regime's shattered finances, and not least to enable it to pay its navy. The Protector inherited from the Elizabethans ideas of a godly and profitable war against the forces of Catholicism. Fact and fantasy – some of it inspired by the experiences of the Providence Island Company – circulated in England as to the condition of Spain's empire and the opportunities it could provide. So, in 1654, an expedition was launched against Hispaniola. It was undertaken by the state itself, and not, as in earlier forays to the Indies, by an admixture of private and government forces, and, for the first time, it was the preparatory step in the mooted invasion of the mainland of Spanish America. But, as so much subsequent imperial history was to teach, the optimism of metropolitan strategists was an unbeatable recipe for disaster. The attack was ignominiously repulsed. Then, however, the force regrouped and secured instead the consolation prize of Jamaica (1655). Many thought the island not worth the candle. Yet it was at the heart of the Spanish Caribbean, and soon to become the major entrepôt in a huge and valuable clandestine trade with a vast segment of the Spanish Indies – a role much like that of the Dutch island of Curaçao, which it eventually eclipsed. It was also, before very long, to become an important producer of sugar. But initially, and spectacularly, it was a notorious centre of the piracy that Europe had brought to the Caribbean. The association was strengthened by the trade in logwood, which sprang up with the neighbouring Spanish mainland in Yucatán, along the shores of the gulfs of Campeche and Honduras, and on the Mosquito Coast of Nicaragua. These were regions barely touched by Spanish colonisation and difficult of access by land. Trees producing that logwood which the English had earlier sought in Brazil grew in wild proliferation, whilst in Honduras there was similarly to be had the mahogany increasingly in demand for the making of fashionable and expensive Spanish-style furniture. Parts of this forbidding littoral had been known to Elizabethan privateers, with Campeche taken by William Parker in 1596, and the Providence islanders had subsequently pioneered a trade to the Mosquito Coast.[63]

The early history of the commerce in logwood is obscure, but soon after the mid-seventeenth century timber was being supplied by English loggers settled along the northern shores of the Central American isthmus. Most of them were men who for one reason or another wished, or found it advisable, to eschew civilised society. There were pirates and seamen, temporarily or permanently unemployed, together with the usual unfortunates unsuccessful in business, love or life. The setting was not idyllic. Alligators abounded, together with 'infinite Numbers of Sand-Flies and Muskitos, [an] unsufferable Plague and Impediment to Sleep'. But such an existence had its attractions, quite apart from escape from the restraints imposed by European rules and conventions. The trees required no attention. Their actual felling occupied only part of the year, and the cut timber could be stored in the open for months without deteriorating. Loggers were thus left ample time for idleness, inebriation and fornication, which ensured they were known then and since, and doubtless rightly, as 'a rude drunken crew'. Some lived in Crusoe-like isolation, others in settlements. Most had their native women, together with African and Indian slaves to support them. Like pirate communities in the Caribbean and elsewhere they sometimes developed rudimentary political organisations. Thus, for example, in Honduras in the early eighteenth century, they had their own king 'chose from among their Body, and his Consort is stiled Queen, agreeing to some Laws by common Consent, as a Guide to them'. The survival of these exiles, outlaws and renegades largely depended on their control of a valuable commodity. By the late seventeenth century, when logwood imported into Europe through legitimate channels sold at around one hundred pounds a ton, the English were taking timber allegedly valued at the very considerable price of twenty-five to forty pounds a ton – it would, for instance, cost six to seven pounds a ton to build a new ship in England at the time. The logwood trade was familiar to the notorious pirate Henry Avery, who, however, abandoned it for his old vocation when his wife ran off with another man.[64] It was similarly known to that remarkable explorer and erstwhile buccaneer William Dampier, who in 1679 sailed from Jamaica to Campeche, where he had previously spent a number of years. In Port Royal (Jamaica) he had traded English goods for such necessities of frontier life as rum, sugar, saws, axes, shoes and stockings, with which he intended to purchase timber.[65] Against such blatant and persistent encroachments on what they considered to be their preserves, the Spaniards occasionally reacted with vigour, especially in the early 1670s and again during the years of worsening Anglo-Spanish relations in the first half of the eighteenth century. Meanwhile trees were being felled at such a rate that in many parts of the Central American isthmus timber had to be fetched from over thirty miles inland. Nevertheless the trade continued and flourished. Ships from New England joined in soon after 1660. In 1671-1674 Spain seized seventy-five English vessels in Honduras alone. By 1715 nearly 6000 tons of logwood were being imported into Britain, and in mid-century fifty ships were reported to be loading in the Bay of Campeche. And with growing trade came increasing settlement, so that by 1700 it was reckoned that there were some 5000 North Americans living in various parts of the region.[66]

The reasons for so buoyant a trade are not far to seek. There was a lively European demand for logwood, and the English claimed that in any case they had every right to take it in Honduras by the terms of the Anglo-Spanish treaty of 1670. Furthermore, timber provided a useful freight for ships working in the now important sugar trade that often failed to secure a full lading, or indeed any at all. Nor were they alone in seeking to augment their incomes. British naval officers on the West Indies station, with the entrepreneurial zeal of their calling we have already noticed, found the timber trade a useful way of increasing their earnings. Hence in 1712 Captain Nathaniel Uring, whose long seafaring career included many years as a master and merchant in the business, was given command of a large (three hundred ton) ship in Jamaica, commissioned to fetch logwood. She belonged to Commodore Littleton, the senior officer and in his day a staunch opponent of such doings. Meanwhile, many other vessels owned by less illustrious colleagues were engaged in carrying logwood from Campeche and Honduras to Jamaica. In wartime such ventures might be combined with privateering, and at most times with piratical or semi-piratical cruises.[67] They might be of considerable complexity, and some, of uncertain value and volume, involved direct passages between Central America and Europe. So in 1699 the *Seaflower*, almost certainly an English ship, was chartered in Venice by an Englishman living there, to sail to Guinea – like as not to pick up slaves – and thence to Honduras. At the end of the War of Spanish Succession (1713) Captain Uring knew of Honduran and Mexican logwood destined for either Livorno (Leghorn) or Lisbon. Two years later some London optimists were planning to send a vessel to the West Indies to search for treasure. Should this prove abortive she was to go to Campeche and load timber for Venice. In 1725 the *Fame*, probably yet another London ship, was despatched to Jamaica, from where she crossed to Campeche carrying thirty slaves, provisions and miscellaneous goods. There she exchanged her cargo for logwood to be taken to England or Holland, only to be obliged by unseaworthiness to return to Jamaica. Then, once repaired, she set off again for Campeche. Meanwhile there was an equally, if not more vigorous flow of traffic from Central America to the English settlements on the North Atlantic seaboard of the continent, and from there to Europe. It was, for example, estimated in mid-eighteenth century that in peacetime between 1000 and 1500 tons of Honduran logwood were sent annually from New York, Boston and Rhode Island to Holland in a trade whose significance will be noticed below.[68]

By this date interloping was so well-established as to have developed its own particular organisation and conventions. There was, for instance, a standard rate of pay for seamen working between Jamaica and the Isthmus. So, too, in Honduras, as probably elsewhere, timber was felled in the dry season and then floated down to the coast by canoe or similar craft when creeks and valleys were flooded by seasonal rains. By the late seventeenth century the trade was so much a matter of routine that loggers would contract in advance to provide a given lading and their representatives would accompany the Jamaican shippers, who came out to the coast to pick up what they had purchased. Should it be known in Jamaica that there were large numbers of vessels in the vicinity seeking freights for Europe, groups of seamen would go by boat from the island and cut sufficient timber to load a ship. They would then signal vessels passing along the coast and come to terms with their masters, securing for themselves 'a certaine share [...] of the profit of the logwood when sold in Europe'. After this they helped to load the ships and took passage in them back to Jamaica, before they cleared for home. By such means some men were able to work their way up from being labourers employed by others to financial independence, whilst skippers like Captain Uring moved on from seagoing command to become considerable merchants, chartering vessels to engage in the trade.[69] To protect so valuable and important a commerce, organised settlement of the Mosquito Coast was projected in 1739, and a decade later some North Americans were sent out from Jamaica to colonise an island in the Bay of Honduras to ensure its safety. Persistence paid, and in 1763 Spain recognised British logging rights in Honduras. But by then timber was being felled with such abandon that the European market was saturated and logwood once fetching thirty pounds a ton was now selling at only four. The British soon after withdrew from the Mosquito Coast.[70]

The shores of the Central American isthmus, however, accounted for only a fraction of Jamaica's flourishing Indies trade. It was in the closest contact with neighbouring Spanish islands – as also indeed with those of the French, with which it had no hesitation in doing business, even in times of war. Spanish Cuba, the source of mules, horses and silver amongst other things, was less than one hundred miles away and consequently of prime importance. In 1719 a Spanish prisoner in Port Royal (Jamaica) counted one hundred and forty-three ships leaving for Cuba in the course of only nine months, with the cargo of one of them allegedly worth more than Havana's entire trade. Jamaica was likewise used by vessels that came out directly from Britain to sell goods in such Spanish possessions as Florida, and then called at the island for a freight home. It similarly carried on a roaring trade with the Spanish mainland anywhere from Veracruz (Mexico) to Caracas (Venezuela) and Río de la Hacha (Colombia) – the latter in touch with Peru. In the early eighteenth century in particular this southern littoral of the Caribbean enjoyed – if this is the right word – a massive upsurge in smuggling when Anglo-Spanish war damped down the activities of the British South Sea Company, then, as we shall see, the would-be monopolist of the country's direct commerce with the Spanish Indies. Its relatively isolated ports gave access to a hinterland with some one million consumers, and Spanish officials reckoned that such harbours as Santa Marta, Rio de la Hacha and Cartagena (all now in Colombia) accounted for half, by value, of the whole Spanish Caribbean smuggling trade.

Jamaica directed into Spanish colonial markets a flow of British exports and re-exports (chiefly manufactures, textiles especially), together with African slaves and the products of a rapidly expanding Atlantic economy, such as North American flour and Madeiran wines. In exchange it received hides, dyes, cotton, coffee, livestock, tobacco, slaves (occasionally), and above all bullion, including by the 1700s some that had worked its way through from Brazil.[71] To this rich assortment were added its own products (notably sugar and rum), those of the Central American isthmus and the fruits of piracy and privateering, including in 1664 a cargo of mercury. Most of these commodities were then shipped to England in a commerce whose worth strained contemporary resources in hyperbole and which made it the country's most valuable overseas colony. Its interloping trade with the southern littoral of the Caribbean was alone thought to amount to around £250,000 a year in 1706-1713. A subsequent careful estimate reckoned that in 1748-1765 Britain received from her colonies Spanish bullion worth over £3,250,000, the bulk of it from Jamaica. The mother country's total annual peacetime naval and military expenditures at that date totalled £2,250,000.[72]

Jamaican interloping was carried on in ways ranging from the primitive to the comparatively sophisticated. In some cases it was conducted, as was slaving on parts of the African coast, from ships lying offshore. Thus in 1710 Captain Uring sailed from Jamaica to Portobelo (Panama) with one hundred and fifty African slaves (obtained, it might be noted, from what is now the Ghanian coast in exchange for textiles from the Cape Verde Islands). There he anchored whilst a Spanish-speaking intermediary went off to negotiate with local merchants.[73] In some places there were even resident English factors. This seems to have been the case at Veracruz (Mexico) in 1664, when one took passage in a Spanish ship carrying log-wood, tobacco, cochineal and silver. At sea she was intercepted by an English man-of-war, whereupon the Spanish owners of her cargo collusively transferred it to the factor, with the predictable result that when she arrived in Jamaica he claimed it as his own.[74] There were, however, other more assured forms of contact, as between, for example, members of the Jewish communities in London and Jamaica and their coreligionists in the Spanish possessions. And by the beginning of the eighteenth century Jamaica's dealings with the neighbouring mainland were so frequent and well-established that the island was firmly integrated into a complex international economy. Hence in 1709 the Bristol privateer Woodes Rogers, having disposed of some slaves ('Useless Negroes') in the Pacific, arranged that payment should be made to his owners at home through Portobelo, and thence transmitted to Jamaica 'with the English trading sloops'.[75]

To some extent Jamaica owed its dazzling success to its superb geographical location, helped by the general absence of Spanish naval forces sufficient to check its activities permanently, and by the eclipse of any serious competition. The trade of the even more favourably sited Dutch entrepôt of Curaçao had passed its peak by circa 1700, whilst other routes to the Spanish Indies (as for example from French Louisiana) could be closed by British naval power. But the prime driving force was that of supply and demand. Jamaica served the needs and interests of the wealthy citizens of an empire whose mother country remained industrially feeble (as was also the case with Portugal and her colonies) and hence unable to supply their wants from its own resources. And the problem was exacerbated by Spain's insistence on conducting imperial commerce – despite occasional modifications – through the cumbersome and unreliable monopoly of the Indies fleets. England on the other hand (and Britain after 1707) had since the mid-seventeenth century possessed Europe's most formidable navy. Its merchant fleet and industrial output were likewise growing, and manufactured goods were of increasing importance in its export trade.

In Jamaica itself opportunities were avidly pursued by merchants (and others) whose acquisitive urges were sharpened by descent from, or long association with, members of one of the most fearsome pirate communities of the time. Their enterprise was on the whole supported by British governments except when, from the late seventeenth century, they were attempting to ensure that Spain and its navy were not driven into the arms of the now arch-enemy, France. So in 1704 interloping trade was allowed to continue – admittedly at Dutch insistence – notwithstanding that the War of Spanish Succession was in progress. And such was the wealth and influence of Jamaican merchants that they could demand naval protection for their goods going to Spanish harbours and immunity from seaborne attack for the places in which they conducted their business. And not least Jamaica had all the ships and seamen needed to keep the trade flowing. Ironically enough this was in part the unforeseen outcome of Britain's own naval policies. Large-scale pressing for the fleet from the late seventeenth century meant that many sailors fled to, or deserted in Jamaica, (as elsewhere) to avoid such a fate and to enjoy the high wages that wars assured those serving in merchantmen. Meanwhile long experience of piracy and smuggling had provided the island with a fleet of distinctive small and fast sloops, propelled by sail and oars, of which circa 1700 there were about two hundred, with over one thousand hands, regularly reinforced by Mosquito Indians, to man them.[76]

What Jamaica could do other colonies could do as well or better. By the mid 1600s there was in existence a chain of English Atlantic and Caribbean islands stretching from Bermuda to the Lesser Antilles, and a growing string of settlements along the Atlantic seaboard of North America. All were well-placed and eager to participate in clandestine trade with the Spanish Indies, and before long names such as Barbados and New England were added to that of Jamaica by Spanish authorities in their complaints as to the scale of smuggling in progress. The survival of the once promising traffic to Venezuela is suggested by the capture by a French privateer in Caracas in 1650 of the three hundred ton *Civil Society*, which had apparently come from Barbados to load hides, tobacco, ivory and salt. A decade earlier a group of Spaniards had hired a London ship in Bermuda to take a cargo of jewels and precious metals to England. The freight rate was to be two per cent of the value of the lading – which suggests this was no novelty – whilst the passengers were to pay between five and twenty pounds a head, according to their means. And clearly for some money was no object, as they allegedly whiled away the tedium of the voyage by gambling for stakes of ten to twenty pounds a time, which again suggests little apprehension as to embarking on such a venture. Less colourfully, Bermuda was also engaged in fetching logwood from Honduras and selling English cloth in Puerto Rico, another favourite entrepôt for smugglers.[77] Some years later

(1696) it was reckoned that settlers in the Bahamas, recently reinforced by an influx of pirates for whom the Caribbean was now too hot, could 'gain a great trade' with Spanish Florida.[78] The extent and complexity of such dealings appears in the account of a venture in 1711, when a thirty-ton sloop made the passage from Barbados to Hispaniola. She carried ninety slaves, and in the space that was left cider, drinking glasses, hats, paper, combs and lace, which were to be exchanged for coin, indigo and Madeiran wine – now presumably past its prime.[79]

It was, however, the merchants and shipowners from the British North American settlements who eventually proved to be the most adept, determined and successful interlopers in the Spanish Indies. The New England colonies in particular sought incomes that would help to pay for the imports their growing populations and expanding economies required. The Americans could provide at much lower cost than Europe, and in better condition, the food of which the monoculture Caribbean islands stood in urgent need. In turn the inhabitants of the British mainland quickly developed an insatiable craving for Caribbean sugar and its alcoholic derivatives. But most remarkably North American success reflected, in addition to impressive entrepreneurial zeal and skills, the rapid emergence of a colonial shipping industry, protected by the English Navigation Act, and benefiting from the shortage of tonnage those same Acts had occasioned by clipping the wings of the Dutch.

By the late seventeenth century there was in existence a vigorous North American maritime economy reaching from Newfoundland to Louisiana, and embracing most of the Caribbean. Irrespective of relations prevailing between the various European colonial powers, Americans traded alike to English, French, Dutch, Spanish and Danish islands. They provided, as the English did, slaves and manufactures (chiefly British), together with the foodstuffs, livestock and timber they produced themselves. In exchange they received bullion, sugar, rum, molasses and assorted local specialities, such as mules from the Spanish islands. The trade with Spain's possessions was initially conducted through the same bases, and along the same routes, as those employed by the English. But in due course familiarity brought innovation and the opening of new channels of contact and the use of new methods of business.

Already in the mid-1600s ships from New York (and like as not from New England as well) bound for Europe or England would top up cargoes such as furs with Yucatán logwood and Honduran mahogany. During the War of Spanish Succession, when British energies were for the most part otherwise engaged, the trade increased and also now involved vessels from other North American ports, most notably Philadelphia.[80] But by this date the traffic was primarily in foodstuffs, and soon on such a scale that the Americans were provisioning both Florida (which was in close touch with Carolina) and Cuba, and according to some disgruntled British officials sustaining the entire Spanish Caribbean. Commerce continued to flow throughout the War of Austrian Succession and the Seven Years War. Indeed, these conflicts with the obstacles they presented to the pursuit of profit were a stimulus to ingenuity, just as by removing British competition they were a boon to American entrepreneurs. Hence trade with Spain's colonies could be conducted through those of the French (Louisiana for example), with which the Americans had long done business, not withstanding that they belonged to the mother country's mortal enemy, and that the French royal house had also established a line in Spain in 1701. Or if the worst came to the worst, goods could be loaded in ships sailing under flags of truce, supposedly engaged in repatriating prisoners of war.[81] The North Americans were equally prominent is slaving, supplying chiefly Africans, together with a sprinkling of Mexican and Brazilian Amerindians. Some of their vessels worked directly between Africa and the Indies, discharging their cargoes in Campeche, Costa Rica, Cuba, Florida and Hispaniola, whilst others took their slaves to Jamaica for redistribution. Should the political situation render this interloping too blatantly obvious the traffic might be diverted – commonly to Curaçao, which had the added attraction of being a plentiful source of sugar and rum. Nor were these in any sense the limits of American enterprise. At the close of the seventeenth century New York, Charleston, Philadelphia and Rhode Island were all receiving a rich assortment of exotic products from the pirates of Madagascar, some of which commodities appearing to have found their way to the Spanish Indies through Jamaica and Curaçao.[82]

North American interloping in Spanish America was probably at its peak in the mid-eighteenth century, with the Americans then the main agents in British smuggling in the Indies. In the years between the ending of the War of Austrian Succession (1748) and the beginning of the Seven Years War (1756) they increasingly worked directly to Spanish possessions rather than through such British entrepôts as Jamaica. And when, after 1757 British seapower effectively excluded French shipping from American waters there was another rewarding opportunity for the colonists to seize. This they did with such efficacy, handling the bulk of the contraband trade to both Spanish and French territories, that one dispirited British admiral attributed Spain's relatively good showing in the War of Austrian Succession to the resources provided by American interlopers. In the Seven Years War it was Pitt's opinion that only this same commerce kept Spain afloat.[83]

Outside the Caribbean there were other routes by which interlopers might reach the Spanish Indies. One was via the Río de la Plata, and thence by river and land to Chile and Peru, as Richard Hakluyt understood in the late sixteenth century. There was, as we have seen, some English activity in the gigantic estuary of the Plate at this time. Ships belonging to such familiar figures as Edward Cotton of Southampton and the earl of Cumberland appeared to the alarm of the Spanish authorities, whilst in England information about Spanish settlements in the region was disseminated by escaped English prisoners or repatriated deserters.[84] There is no evidence of subsequent commercial voyages, but the route came to carry a trade of considerable volume and value, in which the bulk of the goods imported was British, but handled as noticed above by Brazilian and Portuguese intermediaries. This pattern was briefly modified with the appearance of the English South Sea Company in the early eighteenth century, which having secured a base in Buenos Aires was soon much involved in smuggling. The Company, however, abandoned trading in the mid-1700s, whilst the route lost its importance and activity rapidly dwindled, chiefly because of incessant Hispano-Portuguese frontier wars.

An arduous alternative was the passage round the tip of South America, pioneered by Magellan and Drake, and promising direct access to the Pacific coasts of Spanish America. How this might be accomplished was discussed in England in the 1570s, with talk of a colony in the vicinity of the Straits of Magellan and alliances with indigenous opponents of Spanish rule.[85] That such schemes were not fanciful was shown by the French in the early eighteenth century. But the English attempts were less purposeful and usually no more than buccaneering expeditions in search of fresh pastures. One such, however, encountered a London ship off the Peruvian coast in 1684, fitted out by 'very eminent merchants' and laden with a suitable and 'very considerable' cargo, yet soon reduced to piracy. English enthusiasm was tepid; the resources employed inadequate; the voyage particularly long and difficult; Spanish reactions sharper than anticipated; and English ambitions for the region soon in any case deflected to grander schemes for the Pacific.[86]

Other prospects were tried, with ships working directly from Britain to wherever a profitable welcome was expected, whether in Florida, Cuba or Puerto Rico. Other possibilities were likewise aired. From the mid-seventeenth century English publicists increasingly portrayed Spain's American empire as rich, inadequately exploited, feebly defended, full of disaffected natives and ripe for the taking, or at least for being forcibly opened to English merchants. In the early eighteenth century Spain was concerned that the British intended to seize ports on the Pacific coast for commercial or strategic reasons. They had their eye on Buenos Aires, and in the 1720s the taking of Guatemala, Puerto Rico and even Peru were all mooted. By mid-century the same anti-Catholic, anti-Spanish message had been taken up in North America, from where there now issued calls for conquests and for new markets for American merchants. But the only direct intrusions into Spanish territory after the mid 1600s were some settlements on the Mosquito Coast and thereabouts, and the disastrous Scottish attempt (1695) to get a foothold in jungle-engulfed and disease-ridden Darien (Panama), which soon collapsed through a combination of English hostility and the political and economic inability of Scotland to mount and sustain such an undertaking unaided.[87]

Old-style British interloping then, however, took on a new and institutional form with the founding (1711) of the South Sea Company. This was intended to exploit whatever commercial concessions could be extracted from Spain at the end of the War of Spanish Succession, confidently expected to be of such an order as would make the Company a pillar of the London financial establishment. In the end England settled (1713) for the acquisition of the *asiento* – the contract to supply slaves to the Spanish Americas – for thirty years, with the implication that in the Company's interests smuggling would now be stopped. But given its scale and profitability this was widely opposed, and in any case the Company itself was well aware that slaving was of little consequence compared with dealings in British commodities, and was quickly transformed, as was said, into a 'shield for illicit trade'. Allowed to send an annual shipload of merchandise to Portobelo or Veracruz, the Company did its utmost to make the best of the opportunity by such artful measures as repeatedly refilling the vessels on their arrival in Spanish waters. The rest of its goods were transmitted one way or another through the bases it now had in Buenos Aires, Campeche, Cuba, Caracas and Jamaica, with an inner ring of directors running contraband in imposing amounts in ships nominally carrying slaves, and Company officials pursuing their own illicit businesses. Not surprisingly the Company offended many and pleased few. For a time it sent slaves from Jamaica to the Spanish possessions at such a rate that the island's planters reckoned they were being starved of labour, just as its agents cut into what had once been a lucrative business for local merchants. Some of its ships were certainly worked intensively, like the *Prince of Asturias* which in 1725 sailed from Ostend to Jamaica and was then engaged in shuttling between the island and Veracruz. Such passages were momentarily so routine that British seamen could be hired in Veracruz and Company vessels would casually moor themselves to the walls of the town's castle. Nevertheless the Company's performance as a slaving enterprise failed to come up to expectations. It was obliged to provide a set number of Africans irrespective of the state of the market. And for such as it did supply it had great difficulty in securing payment. Its operations were undermined by the private entrepreneurial zeal of its employees, by the smuggling that continued unabated, and by the existence of rival routes, notably that through Nova Colónia in southern Brazil. Hence it was soon reduced to being a 'mere money corporation', dropped out of trade, and in 1750 surrendered the *asiento*. Not that this was the end of the smuggling of slaves or anything else, though from the 1760s activities were on a much-reduced scale. Spanish commercial policies became more liberal, encouraging direct trade and diminishing the attractions of contraband. Meanwhile, as a result of its experiences in the Seven Years War, Britain set its navy to stamp out illicit traffic. Combined with the subsequent decline of the Río de la Plata link with Chile and Peru this marked the end of a spectacular chapter in the long history of smuggling.[88]

Conclusion

From the early 1500s England (and later Britain) maintained a flourishing clandestine trade to the Iberian Americas. The country was not, of course, alone in such endeavours. It competed with France to start with, was initially outstripped by Holland, and was eventually joined and ultimately eclipsed by its own North American colonies. The trade went on in peace and war alike, with the English, for the most part, encouraged by their governments till the mid-eighteenth century, except when it was thought prudent, for political and strategic reasons, to seek Spanish goodwill. After strenuous resistance in the sixteenth and early seventeenth centuries it was similarly tolerated by Spain (unless it became too blatant), usually in the hope of securing British support in Europe. Political and economic weaknesses likewise obliged Portugal to make concessions, but never on the same scale, with direct English interloping rendered superfluous as England came, for a time, to dominate so much of Portugal's overseas trade through sheer economic strength. Hence, following the South Sea Company's acquisition of the *asiento*, there was the curious paradox that British governments were committed to upholding those very Iberian monopolistic trading systems so many of their subjects had risked, and were risking, so much to undermine.

Smuggling to Portuguese and Spanish America reached its apogee around the middle of the eighteenth century. Thereafter economic and political change in both the Old and the New World brought its reduction: Spanish commercial policies became more liberal; routes through southern Brazil were blocked by war; and Britain's navy made strenuous efforts to curb illicit trade, particularly that of the North Americans, in the later stages of the Seven Years War. But in its heyday interloping was of remarkable volume and variety and a significant part of a flourishing global smuggling industry. So, whilst early-modern governments helplessly looked on, American tobacco flowed to Europe, French spirits to England and Spanish-American bullion to Asia. The conduct and organisation of the British trade are eloquent testimony to the zeal, tenacity and ingenuity of the British and North American merchants involved, just as they graphically reveal their assumptions as they came to see the world as their oyster. To eighteenth-century North Americans any interference with their dealings with the Spanish Indies, even in wartime, became a violation of fundamental freedoms. In similar spirit, their British counterparts demanded the enforcement of discriminatory regulations and navigation codes against fellow Europeans, whilst pressing for access to the consumers and sources of supply in the Iberian Americas, and urging that if necessary force should be used to attain these desirable objectives.

In such a spirit were the foundations of British and North American economic preponderance in Latin America laid. In the meanwhile the rewards of the trade were impressive, and its benefits, for some at least, undeniable. Britain and North America supplied the Iberian colonies with those things which, through the frailty of the metropolitan economies and the vagaries of the commercial systems of the mother countries, were either unobtainable or in expensive short supply – textiles, metallurgical goods, fashionable clothing and books of recent vintage amongst others. American foodstuffs helped to keep Caribbean populations, and particularly their African slaves, alive, just as British and American interlopers helped to ensure that sufficient black labour was available. One recent estimate is that about twenty-five per cent of the African slaves shipped across the Atlantic in the eighteenth century in British and colonial vessels were landed in foreign possessions.[89] Areas of the Indies once depressed revived under the stimulus of smuggling, with Honduras and Cuba flourishing as satellites of Jamaica. Meanwhile some British planters in the Caribbean urged dramatically, and not entirely improbably, that they had 'no other way of getting one shilling of ready money for their commodities but by [...] trade to the coast of New Spain'. Enterprise of this order helped to ensure that by the eighteenth century Jamaica was Britain's wealthiest colony, whose riches made a notable contribution to the financial well-being of the mother country. So, too, interloping played an even more fundamental role in the economic development of the North American colonies, and especially in the growth of their merchant fleet. Such indeed was the value of smuggling that when, in the course of the Seven Years War, Britain sought to curb it, there was colonial outcry against so serious a threat to 'liberty and rights'. For Britain, the Iberian Americas were an excellent market for, and a consequent stimulus to, industries like the manufacture of textiles and metallurgical goods. In return they could initially, and comparatively cheaply, supply tobacco, sugar and dyes, until Britain had its own sources for such commodities. Later they could offer fashionable hardwoods at lower rates than these commanded when imported via Iberia. And best of all they were a constant source of ever-welcome bullion.[90]

Nor was the impact of interloping solely economic. Its sheer scale and success was an added reason for the Iberian monarchies to reform their imperial systems in the eighteenth century. In England it was for centuries a potent factor in the shaping of colonial projects and in the making of foreign policy, whether under Elizabeth and Oliver Cromwell, or in the subsequent agitation to secure the opening of Spanish American markets to British merchants. Men who had traded to, or lived and worked in the Iberian Americas, made their views known, or were consulted, when the possibility of expansion into the region was mooted. So, as ambitious strategies revived in Augustan and early Georgian England, information and advice were sought from those veteran practitioners of the interloper's arts, William Dampier and Woodes Rogers.[91] Rarely can smuggling have been so profitable and influential.

Notes

1 For good surveys of recent scholarship see Stanley L. Engerman and Robert E. Gallman eds, *The Cambridge Economic History of the United States* I: *The Colonial Era* (Cambridge 1996); John R. Fisher, *The Economic Aspects of Spanish Imperialism in America, 1492-1810* (Liverpool 1997); Nicholas Canny ed., *The Oxford History of the British Empire* I (Oxford 1998); P.J. Marshall ed., *The Oxford History of the British Empire* II (Oxford 1998).

2 Richard Hakluyt, *The Principal Navigations* I-XII (Glasgow 1903-1905) (hereafter Hakluyt) XI, 23-25; Kenneth R. Andrews, *Trade, Plunder and Settlement: Maritime Enterprise and the Genesis of the British Empire, 1480-1630* (Cambridge 1984) 59-60.

3 Public Record Office, London (PRO), High Court of Admiralty (HCA), 13/4, fos. 274v-276v.

4 PRO, James Gairdner and R.H. Brodie eds, *Texts and Calendars, Letters and Papers, Foreign and Domestic, of the reign of Henry VIII, Addenda* I-II (London 1929-1932) no. 1430.

5 R.G. Marsden ed., 'Voyage of the *Barbara* to Brazil, anno 1540' in: Sir John Knox Laughton ed., *The Naval Miscellany* II (London 1912) 31, 51.

6 Marsden ed., 'Voyage of the *Barbara*', passim; G.V. Scammell, 'Shipowning in England c. 1450-1550', *Transactions of the Royal Historical Society* 12 [5th series] (1962) 113.

7 Hakluyt, *Navigations* XI, 23-25; PRO, G.A. Bergenroth et al. eds, *Calendar of Letters, Despatches and State Papers, Relating to Negotiations between England and Spain* (hereafter *Cal. Sp.*) *1538-1542* (London 1868) no. 148; Andrews, *Trade, Plunder and Settlement*, 59-60.

8 Hakluyt XI, 25; *Cal. Sp. 1580-1586*, 302, 357; Andrews, *Trade, Plunder and Settlement*, 137.

9 Hakluyt XI, 26ff; *Cal. Sp. 1580-1586*, 64; E.G.R. Taylor ed., *The Troublesome Voyage of Captain Edward Fenton: Narratives and Documents* (Cambridge 1959) L and notes; Gilberto Freyre, *The Masters and the Slaves* (London 1956) 198; Andrews, *Trade, Plunder and Settlement*, 160.

10 Hakluyt XI, 26ff; *Cal. Sp. 1587-1603*, 186-187; Kenneth R. Andrews, *Elizabethan Privateering* (Cambridge 1964) chapter 10.

11 HCA 13/24, 16 January 1581/2; Andrews, *Elizabethan Privateering*, chapter 10.

12 Andrews, *Trade, Plunder and Settlement*, 160.

13 *Cal. Sp. 1580-1586*, 55, 64.

14 *Cal. Sp. 1580-1586*, 3, 64, 302; Andrews, *Trade, Plunder and Settlement*, 161.

15 Andrews, *Trade, Plunder and Settlement*, 20.

16 Hakluyt XI, 33; E.G.R. Taylor ed., *The Original Writings and Correspondence of the Two Richard Hakluyts* I (London 1935) 18.

17 HCA 13/24, fo. 218; Hakluyt, XI, 295; Marsden, 'Voyage of the *Barbara*', 8.

18 HCA 13/24, ult. February 1581/1582, 8 December 1582; Hakluyt, XI, 162; Taylor ed., *Correspondence of the Two Richard Hakluyts* I, 18 and note, 146; Andrews, *Trade, Plunder and Settlement*, 161.

19 HCA 13/24, ult. February 1581/1582 at fo. 226; Andrews, *Trade, Plunder and Settlement*, 164-165.

20 HCA 13/24, ult. February 1581/1582, 2 November 1582, 24 November 1582, 8 December 1582; Hakluyt XI, 34-35; *Cal. Sp. 1580-1586*, 302, 356-357; Andrews, *Elizabethan Privateering*, 201-202; Idem, *Trade, Plunder and Settlement*, 164-165.

21 Hakluyt XI, 38; *Cal. Sp. 1580-1586*, 356-357.

22 Taylor ed., *Correspondence of the Two Richard Hakluyts* I, 18; Andrews, *Trade, Plunder and Settlement*, 138, 160-161.

23 Taylor ed., *Troublesome Voyage of Edward Fenton*, L, 126, 128, 195; idem, *Correspondence of the Two Richard Hakluyts* I, 18; Andrews, *Trade, Plunder and Settlement*, 164-165.

24 *Cal. Sp. 1580-1586*, 385, 413-414; Andrews, *Trade, Plunder and Settlement*, 162-163.

25 HCA 13/32, 22 November 1595; Hakluyt VI, 411; Taylor ed., *Correspondence of the Two Richard Hakluyts* I, 18; David Beers Quinn ed., *The Voyages and Colonising Enterprises of Humphrey Gilbert* II (London 1940) 426-427; Elizabeth Story Donno ed., *An Elizabethan in 1582: The Diary of Richard Madox, Fellow of All Souls* (London 1976) 109.

26 HCA 13/25, 4 September 1585, 6 and 7 December 1585; PRO, Robert Lemon et al. eds, *Texts and Calendars, Calendar of State Papers, Domestic Series, of the Reigns of Edward VI, Mary*

Elizabeth and James I, 1547-1625 (hereafter *CSPD*) *1601-1603*, with Additions *1547-1565*, 102-103; Andrews, *Elizabethan Privateering*, 205-206.

27 HCA 13/25, 4 September 1585, 6 and 7 December 1585; Samuel Purchas, *Hakluyt Posthumus, or Purchas His Pilgrimes* I-XX (Glasgow 1905-1907) (hereafter Purchas) XVI, 145. Hakluyt XI, 43, 53, 208.

28 *CSPD 1581-1590*, 640, no. 97; *CSPD 1595-1597*, 77, no. 32; *Cal. Sp. 1587-1603*, 572, no. 582; Purchas XVI, 243, 417ff.

29 *Cal. Sp. 1580-1586*, 610; Hakluyt XI, 295.

30 G.V. Scammell, 'The English in the Atlantic Islands, c. 1450-1650', *The Mariner's Mirror* LXXII (1986) 310.

31 HCA 13/25, 6 December 1585; *Cal. Sp. 1587-1603*, 222; G.V. Scammell, 'England, Portugal and the Estado da India c. 1500-1635', *Modern Asian Studies* 16/2 (1982) 182-185.

32 R.F. Hitchcock, 'Cavendish's Last Voyage: The Charges against Davis', *The Mariner's Mirror* 80 (1994) 265-266.

33 Taylor ed., *Troublesome Voyage of Edward Fenton*, xxxviii; Quinn ed., *Voyages of Sir Humphrey Gilbert* II, 415.

34 Hakluyt XI, 208. For Abraham Cocke see: Andrews, *Elizabethan Privateering*, 88.

35 Purchas XVI, 144; D.B. Quinn ed., *The Hakluyt Handbook* I (London 1974) 123-124.

36 Purchas XVI, 244, 290; L.E. Pennington ed., *The Purchas Handbook; Studies of the Life, Times and Writings of Samuel Purchas, 1577-1626* I (London 1997) 337-339.

37 Purchas XVI, 182, 232, 243-244, 290; Freyre, *The Masters and the Slaves*, 199.

38 A. da Silva Rego and Elaine Sanceau eds, *Documentação Ultramarina Portuguesa* I (Lisbon 1960) 62; Frédéric Mauro, *Le Portugal et L'Atlantique au XVIIe Siècle, 1570-1670* (Paris 1960) 140; Andrews, *Trade, Plunder and Settlement*, 299.

39 HCA 13/51, 5 March, 11 and 18 June 1634.

40 HCA 13/45, 8 June 1626; HCA 13/51, 11 and 18 June 1634; HCA 13/56, 1 May 1640.

41 Kenneth R. Andrews, *Ships, Money & Politics: Seafaring and Naval Enterprise in the Reign of Charles I* (Cambridge 1991) 89-90.

42 HCA 13/56, 1 May 1640; C.R. Boxer, 'English Shipping in the Brazil Trade, 1640-1665', *The Mariner's Mirror* 37 (1951) 199ff.; Andrews, *Ships, Money & Politics*, 22; L.M.E. Shaw, *The Anglo-Portuguese Alliance and the English Merchants in Portugal, 1654-1810* (Aldershot 1998) chapter 9.

43 Boxer, 'English Shipping in the Brazil Trade', 214-215; Mauro, *Le Portugal*, 459-460.

44 HCA 13/65, 23 March 1651/1652; Andrews, *Ships, Money & Politics*, 59-61; John C. Appleby, 'A Guinea Venture c. 1657: A Note on the Early English Slave Trade', *The Mariner's Mirror* 79 (1993) 85.

45 HCA 13/65, 11 March 1651/1652; R.C. Anderson ed., *The Journals of Sir Thomas Allin, 1660-1678* I (London 1939-1940) 53; Boxer, 'English Shipping in the Brazil Trade', 204; J.R. Powell, *Robert Blake, General-at-Sea* (London 1972) 319.

46 C.R. Boxer, *Descriptive List of the State Papers, Portugal, 1661-1780 in the Public Record Office, London* I: *1661-1723* (Lisbon 1979) 20, nos. 45, 47, 48; Boxer, 'English Shipping in the Brazil Trade', 219-220; Shaw, *The Anglo-Portuguese Alliance*, 117.

47 HCA 13/51, 11, 18 and 20 June 1634, 6 July 1634; Maurice Exwood and H.L. Lehmann eds, *The Journal of William Schellinks' Travels in England 1661-1663* [Camden Society, 5th series, volume 1] (London 1993) 9ff; Andrews, *Ships, Money & Politics*, 52.

48 HCA 13/65, 25 August 1651; 23 March 1651/1652; 20 May, 2 July, 15 July, 20 July 1652; J.C. Whitebrook, *Edward and John Bushell, Puritans and Merchants* (London 1915) passim; Appleby, 'A Guinea Venture', 85; Andrews, *Ships, Money & Politics*, 59-61.

49 Anderson ed., *Journals of Sir Thomas Allin* I, 99; J.S. Kepler, 'Fiscal Aspects of the English Carrying Trade during the Thirty Years War', *The Economic History Review* XXV [2nd series] (1972) 261; C.R. Boxer, *The English and the Portuguese Brazil Trade, 1660-1780: Some Problems and Personalities* (Bundoora 1981) 5.

50 José Jobson de Andrade Arruda, 'Colonies as Mercantile Investments; The Luso-Brazilian Empire, 1500-1808' in: James D. Tracy ed., *The Political Economy of Merchant Empires: State Power and World Trade, 1350-1750* (Cambridge 1991) 388.

51 A. da Silva Rego ed., *As Gavetas da Torre do Tombo* I (Lisbon 1960) 550-551; Andrade Arruda, 'Colonies as Mercantile Investments', 393; Boxer, *The English and the Portuguese Brazil Trade*, 5-6; Shaw, *Anglo-Portuguese Alliance*, 118.
52 Boxer, *State Papers, Portugal* I, 250, no. 138; idem, *The English and the Portuguese Brazil Trade*, 3-4.
53 HCA 13/85, fos. 279, 283.
54 H.E.S. Fisher, *The Portugal Trade: A Study of Anglo-Portuguese Commerce, 1700-1770* (London 1971) 33; D.C. Coleman, *The Economy of England, 1450-1750* (Oxford 1977) 133; Boxer, *The English and the Portuguese Brazil Trade*, 5; Peggy K. Liss, *Atlantic Empires: The Network of Trade and Revolution, 1713-1826* (Baltimore/London 1983) 83.
55 *Cal. Sp. 1568-1579*, 242-243, 264; *Cal. Sp. 1580-1586*, 585-586; Andrews, *Trade, Plunder and Settlement*, 140, 161.
56 M. Oppenheim, *A History of the Administration of the Royal Navy and of Merchant Shipping in Relation to the Navy* I (London 1896) 398-399. For the privateering war see Andrews, *Elizabethan Privateering*.
57 Tom Glasgow Jr., 'The Mystery of Juan de Rute of Asuncion, Paraguay', *The Mariner's Mirror* 52 (1966) 78-79.
58 Hakluyt IX, 347, 421; *Cal. Sp. 1568-1579*, 526.
59 Hakluyt IX, 360ff; Hakluyt XI, 208; Purchas XVI, 6, 324ff; Karen Ordahl Kupperman, *Providence Island, 1630-1641: The Other Puritan Colony* (Cambridge 1993) 280.
60 Purchas XVI, 309ff; G.V. Scammell, *The World Encompassed: The First European Maritime Empires, c. 800-1650* (London 1981) 484, 492.
61 J.C. Appleby, 'An Association for the West Indies? English Plans for a West India Company, 1621-1629', *The Journal of Imperial and Commonwealth History* XV (1987) 213-241; Andrews, *Trade, Plunder and Settlement*, 325; Kupperman, *Providence Island*, 109.
62 Kupperman, *Providence Island*, 97-99, 167-169, 280, 335-339, 346.
63 Purchas XVI, 134.
64 Alfred Dewar ed., *The Voyages and Travels of Captain Nathaniel Uring* (London 1928) xxiv, 125, 240-246; Arthur M. Wilson, 'The Logwood Trade in the Seventeenth and Eighteenth Centuries' in: Susan Socolow ed., *The Atlantic Staple Trade* II: *The Economics of Trade* (Aldershot 1996) 477-491.
65 William Dampier, *A New Voyage Round the World* [ed. Sir Albert Gray] (London 1927) 7.
66 Liss, *Atlantic Empires*, 26; Wilson, 'Logwood Trade', 480-481.
67 HCA 13/85, 13 July 1714; Dewar ed., *Voyages of Captain Uring*, xxiii, 165, 169, 246.
68 HCA 13/85, 13 October 1716; 13/88, 26 October 1728, 18 November 1728, 28 March 1729; Dewar ed., *Voyages of Captain Uring*, xxiv-xxv, 179; Nigel Tattersfield, *The Forgotten Trade: Accounts of the Slave Trade from the Minor Ports of England, 1698-1725* (London 1991) 8.
69 Cf. Wilson, 'Logwood Trade'.
70 Dewar ed., *Voyages of Captain Uring*, 167, 171, 241-242, 246; Wilson, 'Logwood Trade', 482, 487, 490; Liss, *Atlantic Empires*, 28-29.
71 HCA 13/85, 13 July 1714; Dewar ed., *Voyages of Captain Uring*, xxii; *Reports and Calendars Issued by the Royal Commission on Historical Manuscripts*. New series vol. VII, *The Manuscripts of the House of Lords, 1706-1708* (London 1921) no. 2402, 316; John Robert McNeill, 'American Ports and Imperial Trade' in: Socolow ed., *The Atlantic Staple Trade* II, 683; Liss, *Atlantic Empires*, 75; Fisher, *Economic Aspects of Spanish Imperialism*, 120-121.
72 Boxer, *State Papers, Portugal* I, 41, no. 220; Wilson, 'Logwood Trade', 483; *The Oxford History of the British Empire* II, 22.
73 Dewar ed., *Voyages of Captain Uring*, xix-xxii.
74 HCA 13/75, fos. 388ff.
75 Woodes Rogers, *A Cruising Voyage Round the World* [ed. G.E. Manwaring] (London 1928) 187; Ian K. Steele, *The English Atlantic 1675-1740: An Exploration of Communication and Community* (Oxford 1986) 176-177.
76 Dewar ed., *Voyages of Captain Uring*, 165; Liss, *Atlantic Empires*, 76; Jonathan I. Israel, *Dutch Primacy in World Trade 1585-1740* (Oxford 1989) 325, 369-370, 374; G.V. Scammell, *The*

First Imperial Age: European Overseas Expansion c. 1400-1715 (London 1989) 440.
77 HCA 13/56, 6 August 1640; 13/65, 15 January 1651/1652.
78 *Reports and Calendars Issued by the Royal Commission: On Historical Manuscripts.* New series vol. II, *The Manuscripts of the House of Lords, 1695-1697* (London 1903) 440.
79 HCA 13/85, 4 June 1714.
80 Liss, *Atlantic Empires*, 26, 28, 257; *Cambridge Economic History of the United States* I, 234.
81 Liss, *Atlantic Empires*, 28; *Cambridge Economic History of the United States* I, 351.
82 *Manuscripts of the House of Lords, 1695-1697*, no. 1115, 440ff; *Manuscript of the House of Lords, 1699-1702* (London 1908) no. 1634; Liss, *Atlantic Empires*, 30.
83 Liss, *Atlantic Empires*, 28-30.
84 Taylor ed., *Troublesome Voyage of Edward Fenton*, 286-287; Hakluyt XI, 39ff, 208; Purchas VI, 367; XVI, 231.
85 *Cal. Sp. 1568-1579*, 242-243, 264; Quinn, *Voyages of Sir Humphrey Gilbert* I, 29.
86 Dampier, *A New Voyage*, 100.
87 Jeremy Black, 'Anglo-Spanish Naval Relations in the Eighteenth Century', *The Mariner's Mirror* 77 (1991) 242; Liss, *Atlantic Empires*, 32, 53; Glyndwr Williams, *The Great South Sea: English Voyages and Encounters, 1570-1750* (New Haven/London 1997) 202.
88 HCA 13/88, 18 November 1728, 21 May 1729; Jean O. McLachlan, *Trade and Peace with Old Spain, 1667-1750* (Cambridge 1940) 122; Liss, *Atlantic Empires*, 31, 75-76.
89 *Oxford History of the British Empire* II, 459.
90 Wilson, 'Logwood Trade', 488; McNeill, 'American Ports and Imperial Trade', 685-686; Liss, *Atlantic Empires*, 40.
91 Williams, *The Great South Sea*, 118, 202.

VII

THE ENGLISH CHARTERED TRADING COMPANIES AND THE SEA

Companies: Origins, Nature and Functions

Between roughly 1500 and 1800 the nature and pattern of Europe's overseas trade were radically transformed. At the close of the fifteenth century the Portuguese opened a sea route to Asia. Soon after, the conquest and settlement of the immense and recently-discovered American continent was begun, and before long there had come into being a vast new oceanic economy. In Asia Europeans penetrated existing trades and created new ones. In east and west alike colonies traded with one another – Africa with the Americas, Mexico with the Philippines, New England with the West Indies – and with a Europe whose centre of wealth and power was no longer, as for centuries past, the Mediterranean, but the countries of the north-west.

In this transformation the behaviour of England was like that of the proverbial tortoise. The Tudor kingdom undertook some modest voyages of exploration in the early 1500s, but by the mid-sixteenth century had neither founded colonies nor discovered any source of such wealth as Asian spices were believed to be bringing to Portugal, or American silver to Spain. By 1800, however, it was a very different picture. An empire had been won (and in part lost) in North America; the Indian sub-continent was passing into British control; British ships sailed the oceans of the world; Britain was Europe's greatest commercial power; and after Trafalgar British naval hegemony was unchallenged for the best part of a century. In this process an important role, though as we shall see not always a conscious or willing one, was played by a handful of chartered corporations, each enjoying (at least in theory) the monopoly of the trade of some generously defined area. Many are now remembered only by ardent researchers in the backwaters of English commercial history, but others, like the East India Company and the Royal African Company, are names evocative of imperial might and grandeur.

Companies of one sort or another had long been known in Europe. At their most rudimentary they merely consisted of a couple of partners sharing the risks and costs of a single trading venture. Sometimes, and from an early date, they were more elaborate and enduring, as when a number of investors held shares in a ship. And by the end of the Middle Ages there were in existence, as in the remarkably precocious commercial and banking city of Florence, companies which were permanent associations of capital. Meanwhile, as happened in late medieval England, groups of merchants might be incorporated by royal charter to control a given trade, or bodies of artisans similarly organised to regulate their standards of workmanship and conditions of employment. Nor was the use of companies in colonial commerce and government any novelty, since already in the fourteenth century the impecunious Genoese republic had handed over most of its Mediterranean possessions to joint-stock corporations known as *mahones*. But the hundred years or so after about 1550 saw the proliferation in Europe of companies which, like the United Dutch East India Company (1602), were of a size and strength hitherto unknown. Such associations were used where costs, and more especially risks, were high – which commonly meant in attempts to open routes to some Eldorado. They were likewise used in endeavours to penetrate trades considered particularly valuable or important, to wrest them from undesirable hands – which for the English increasingly entailed trying to break the grip of 'those Horse-turds' the Dutch – and to impose a monopoly for the benefit of the members of the company in question. And they were widely used in trades to distant lands, where expenses were in any case abnormally heavy, the more so since in England and Holland the state long left to private initiative the provision of the forts, factories and naval protection which in the empires of Portugal and Spain were supplied, however imperfectly, by the crown.

Some of the English companies (such as the Levant Company and the Eastland Company) were, in the terminology of the time, 'regulated' – their members, that is to say, themselves engaged in trade, either individually or in partnership with their fellows. Hence they or their agents are to be found travelling by sea, or doing business in those foreign ports with which their company dealt. But the company itself did not trade. Instead, it defined to where, within the terms of its charter, members might carry on business, what ships they might use, and how much of a particular commodity they might export.

Of a fundamentally different nature were joint-stock companies like the Russia Company, the Hudson's Bay Company, the Royal African Company and the East India Company. These traded themselves as corporate bodies, supposedly on behalf of the shareholders who had subscribed their capital. Business was handled by salaried employees under the general supervision of a board of directors, and so (at least in theory) members of such associations did not, unlike those of 'regulated' companies, trade within the area of their company's charter. Joint-stock financing, familiar in hazardous undertakings such as shipowning and privateering, was favoured in trades in which, as was said, a 'single or sudden voyage' would not suffice, but where, as in the Far East, West Africa or the remote fastnesses of northern Canada, forts and trading posts were required to assemble cargoes, to hold off European rivals, to permit 'a constant correspondency' with indigenous peoples, and to provide, if need be, a refuge from their hostility. All this cost money, and money which being tied up in buildings could earn no profits. Furthermore, in a commerce conducted over thousands of miles by sailing ships, returns on investments came – if they came at all – inordinately slowly. Combined with the well-attested perils of the deep, and the dangers of dealing in far-off lands with societies whose conventions were not those of Europeans – those 'infidels and Barbarous nations' as contempories were apt to dismiss them – all this meant risks of such an order that investors preferred to spread the burden to many pockets, and individually to put up only relatively modest amounts. Before the close of the seventeenth century few companies had share capitals of more than £100,000 at a time when, for something less chancy, an investment of £10,000 was within easy reach of a small partnership or even a single plutocrat.

The incorporation of such companies by royal charter had many powerful advocates and admirers. To rulers, and especially to those of the Stuart dynasty, the very issue of a charter was an exercise of that kingly prerogative they cherished so highly. The resultant corporation could, moreover, be an outlet for the interests and ambitions of members, legitimate or otherwise, of the royal house, and Charles II, James II, prince Rupert and the duke of Monmouth were all at some stage involved in undertakings of this sort. Better still, companies meant money for invariably impecunious sovereigns, and this without recourse to the uncertain generosity, and exposure to the uncertain temper, of the House of Commons. They could be tapped for loans, as was particularly the case with the East India Company, or they could be bullied into making substantial grants by threats of withdrawal of their privileges. Alternatively they could be saddled with responsibilities and burdens the state alleged itself unwilling or unable to shoulder. Hence in 1618 there was talk of financing an expedition against the pirates of North Africa – ubiquitous enemies of English trade and shipping – with £40,000 to be provided by the chartered companies. Nor was this all. A monopoly corporation conducting an important trade through a single entrepôt overseas could be a useful lever in any dealings with the host country. Such associations could similarly enforce government orders and directions on their members, just as they could ensure that their doings abroad were not of such a nature as to provide friction, reprisals, or worse. Furthermore, by confining particular trades to those supposedly of suitable skills and standing, statesmen felt themselves to be strengthening the existing social fabric, in which harmony, so it was believed, would be maintained by all occupying their ordained station. And if companies could be obliged to use English ships, and to export English manufactures – which meant, in fact, and even to the most improbable destinations, woollen textiles – the poor would be 'set on work', and the likelihood of their rioting or rebelling averted, or at least diminished.

Incorporation was equally attractive to influential members of the business community. The recipients of charters were almost invariably select groups of London magnates. They obtained the monopoly, usually couched in the most lavish terms, of some specified trade, together with promises of the exclusion of rival compatriots and royal support against foreign competitors. Once constituted, chartered companies could sue, own property, tax and discipline their members, and secure legal and fiscal privileges abroad. Equally vitally, they could determine not only who should trade within their monopolies, but how they should do so. By limiting their commerce to specified ships, very often sailing in seasonal convoys, they offered their members the prospect of the secure carriage of their goods, enabled them to further reduce risks by distributing cargoes amongst several vessels, and supposedly ensured that no one should enjoy any unfair advantage over his fellows by having his goods on sale before theirs. In dealings with foreign rulers, and more especially with such capricious potentates as Ivan the Terrible of Russia, it was believed that companies could exert greater pressure than individuals, particularly since in the last resort they could threaten to boycott markets where conditions were not to their liking. Moreover, given the widely-held and long-enduring assumption that overseas demand for goods was rigidly fixed, and international trade accordingly 'an unending war', it was argued that monopoly companies were most likely to secure for the mother-country the best selling price for its products and the biggest share of business and profits. Besides which, wealthy corporations, allegedly dedicated to the national well-being, and with the government's eye on them, were soon discovered to be useful clients by shipowners. Already in 1579 Olyff Burre of London, who claimed to have made a living for forty years 'cheefely by the maynteyninge of shippinge and the navygacon', finding his fleet unemployed, petitioned the crown that a chartered company be persuaded to give it work. Hence before the end of the seventeenth century some three dozen major companies had been established in England. The pace was particularly brisk in the early 1600s when, with the country in grave economic difficulties – trade contracting, Dutch competition and seapower seemingly ubiquitous – it was believed that the success of the Netherlanders in part stemmed from their use of such associations. But in any case parliamentary condemnation (1624) of royal grants of monopolies to individuals encouraged the crown to create corporations to whom they could be sold or leased. There were companies to establish or revive English sea fisheries, not to mention those to further a wonderful assortment of industrial and manufacturing ventures. There were others to explore unknown waters, to bring the riches of the New Worlds to England, or, like the Virginia Company (1606), the Bermuda Company (1612), and the Massachusetts Bay Company (1628), to found colonies. Still others were entrusted with various long-distance trades, amongst them the Russia Company (1553); the Spanish Company (1577); the Eastland Company (1579); the Levant Company (1581); the East India Company (1600); the Hudson's Bay Company (1670); and the Royal African Company (1672). Some died almost as soon as they were born, and the careers of the majority were both brief and undistinguished. But the East India Company was to become one of Britain's most powerful financial institutions and to lay the foundations of the country's rule in the sub-continent, whilst the Hudson's Bay Company is, uniquely, still in business.

Whatever their form of organisation, whether joint-stock or 'regulated' – and some started as the former and ended as the latter – the trading companies had many features in common. In all of them a tightly-knit and closely-defined group of London plutocrats was long pre-eminent. Thus at the end of Elizabeth I's reign one of the great names in the Levant Company was alderman John Watts, a major figure in oceanic privateering against Spain and a shipowner whose nine vessels were known to contemporaries as his 'fleet'. His colleagues included the equally important shipowner alderman Thomas Cordell (likewise of the Venice, Spanish, Mercers' and East India companies), and Francis Cherry (also of the East India and Russia companies), whose craft were to be found alike trading in the Mediterranean or fishing in the Arctic, where indeed Bear Island was for a while named after him. With the passage of time the network grew tighter and the affiliations closer. Over 30 of the founding members of the East India Company were from the Levant Company, whilst in 1675 practising merchants in the latter controlled 25% of the stock of the Royal African Company. And so it went on, with some of the city's most opulent and influential men in the late seventeenth century simultaneously involved .in several major companies, and Hudson's Bay profits invested to earn good interest in East India stock.

A concentration of power and affluence as narrowly-based as this attracted sustained and growing hostility. Manufacturers complained that companies restricted the volume of exports,. bought their produce cheap and supplied their raw materials dear. The East India Company was blamed for introducing inexpensive Asian textiles into the country to the detriment of the English cloth-making industry, and exporting scarce silver, thereby weakening the state. Non-company merchants, and especially those from the provinces, alleged they were ruined by the misdeeds of London-based monopolists, and (1604) that 'the whole trade of all the realm is in the hands of some two hundred persons at the most'. As perhaps it was. The business of the Russia Company was thought to be carried on by only 15 members in 1604, and the Eastland Company was run by some 30 individuals at roughly the same date. A century later though the Levant Company had almost 200 members only about 50 were trading, whilst the Hudson's Bay Company had no more than 35 shareholders. Power and profit, that is to say, were concentrated in the hands of a rich minority, or, in the language of the time, trade was 'stinted . . . and restrained of pourpose . . . for the benefit of soom fiew'. These, who had no hesitation in violating company rules when it suited them, not only excluded non-members but their fellows – usually the younger and less affluent – not accepted into some inner coterie. The outcome – as was regularly, vociferously and in general rightly urged by those 'interloping' merchants theoretically debarred from the various monopoly trades – was a regime of complacency, idleness and inefficiency. The British West Indies were short of slaves in the late seventeenth century because the Royal African Company failed to supply them. The unwillingness of the Russia Company to expand markets in the realms of the Czar was said to have let the Dutch in, and whilst the Hudson's Bay Company 'slept at the edge of a frozen sea' France was penetrating far and wide in Canada. Parliament received countless petitions against the iniquities, real or imagined, of such bodies, and from the late 1600s steadily diminished their privileges. Indeed, after another century or so the companies had few defenders. Publicists, scholars and statesmen all condemned the 'useless and injurious restrictions' they imposed on trade and the 'negligence and profusion' that allegedly characterised their conduct of affairs.

By then, however, few were still in existence. At best they handled no more than a fraction of England's overseas trade, with, for example, the Russia and Eastland companies between them accounting for a mere 12% of the cloth leaving the country c.1600, and the Royal African Company never responsible for more than three per cent (by value) of English exports. And even this modest share was soon eroded as trade increasingly passed into the hands of merchants operating singly or in partnerships wherever they reckoned a profit could be made, and free from company control. The Eastland Company was to all intents extinct by 1673, the Russia Company at roughly the same date, and the Royal African Company in the mid-eighteenth century. The Levant Company, after a spectacular resurgence in the exceptional circumstances of the Napoleonic wars and their aftermath, was abolished in 1825. Others had long since gone, leaving only the Hudson's Bay Company, a minute enterprise engaged in a small but highly specialised traffic to regions so remote and hostile as to attract few rivals, and the very different East India Company. After a precarious first 50 years this indeed went from strength to strength. In the late 1680s it was paying annual dividends of 20% and bringing in about 14% of the country's imports, whilst by the time of George I nothing but that of the Bank of England could surpass the solidity of its stock. Not even this could last however. Province after province in the sub-continent fell to its servants, but its trading position weakened and its monopoly was finally dissolved early in the nineteenth century.

Successes and Failures

There were, therefore, fairly closely defined circumstances in which chartered companies could survive and prosper. Faced with the varied and fluctuating opportunities of the new and expanding maritime economy of the Atlantic almost all, irrespective of nationality, failed, and usually sooner than later. There were no such prospects of personal fortunes as the Far East offered – the lucrative 'country trades' for example – to attract able and ambitious employees into their service. The companies themselves, hampered by poor communications and the lack of adequate administrative organisation, generally responded lethargically to changing circumstances. And all too often they were crippled by onerous and unnecessary expenses and burdens, like the Royal African Company's forts and factories in Gambia and elsewhere. Added to which were the blows inflicted by the accidents of political change, so that following the fall of James II (1688) both the East India and Royal African companies, previously closely associated with the Stuart court, found their privileges either radically modified or entirely withdrawn. And by the beginning of the nineteenth century a more complex and self-conscious English state was not prepared to see private bodies – such as the Levant Company with its own consuls in Mediterranean ports – exercising powers thought more appropriate to itself.

But companies were far from synonymous with failure. They could succeed at a time of economic recession, when few compatriots had the wealth or inclination to challenge them, and when their resources and influence allowed them to undertake ventures would-be competitors thought too risky. They could flourish, too, where foreign states were indifferent to, or incapable of resisting their aspirations. They could likewise flourish, at least for a time – as did the Eastland Company in the Baltic – when some foreign ruler or community was willing or even eager to welcome them, or when, as with the East India Company in the Orient, indigenous authorities could in one way or another be persuaded to receive them. And as both the Dutch and English East India companies were to demonstrate, they could do astonishingly well when, in Asia, they encountered an ancient and well-established maritime economy. Into this they could insert themselves, linking it to the homeland in a commerce in which the inescapable overheads – factories, costly dealings with local potentates and their officials – were, together with the very distance from Europe, long sufficient to deter interlopers.

Fisheries

The worst and most embarrassing company failures were in purely maritime undertakings. A sequence of attempts to oust the Dutch from their lucrative herring fishery, blatantly conducted in what were considered British waters, came to nothing. The Society for the Fishery of Great Britain and Ireland (1632) was bankrupt within two years of its foundation, its misfortunes attributed to incompetent management and the unreasonable refusal of herring to surrender to its vessels. The later and grandiosely entitled Society of the Free British Fishery (1750) – which, as a satirist quipped, was to 'drag up oceans of gold from the bottom of the sea' – likewise foundered after an equally brief and ignominious history. Nor did companies do much better in whaling. The experience of the Russia Company was, as we shall see, uniformly unhappy. In the 1690s the Hudson's Bay Company undertook some short-lived and abortive ventures in the waters under its jurisdiction, whilst the Company of Merchants of London Trading into Greenland (1692) collapsed without a single profitable voyage to its credit – though some of its skippers were alleged to have done well for themselves on the proceeds of illicit deer hunting in Spitsbergen. Later still, the affluent South Sea Company was inveigled into whaling by a plausible and seemingly omniscient entrepreneur. A dozen new vessels were laid down for the 1725 season, followed by another dozen the next year, and money was poured out in all directions. But by 1733 this enterprise had failed too, incurring in the process what amounted to a huge net loss of £1,000 a year per ship. Such debacles, apologists and critics in some measure agreed, were the outcome of hopeless management and the country's lack of suitably-equipped vessels and seamen of appropriate skills – harpooners, if they could be got at all, had to be hired abroad. Not surprisingly England found it impossible to withstand, let alone overcome, the well-entrenched dominance of the Dutch.

Voyages of Exploration and Discovery

In exploration the record was rather better, though naturally enough monopoly companies were not eager to seek and reveal to all and sundry new ways of reaching the sources of their profits, actual or potential. They might, however, from time to time, and with varying degrees of enthusiasm, follow up rumours of unknown lands, or investigate routes which only incidentally related to the main purpose of their existence. In 1676 ships of the Hudson's Bay Company were sent to search for 'Busse Island', long alleged to lie somewhere off the coast of Labrador, and said to be prolific in whales 'easie to be struck, Sea-horse, Seal and Codd'. Nearly a century earlier, and far more ambitiously and significantly, a number of Russia Company magnates had backed a projected voyage to exploit those opportunities in the Far East revealed by Francis Drake's epic circumnavigation of the globe. The newly-knighted hero was himself a subscriber, and the planning of the venture was in part undertaken, in best city style, over 'a great dynner' at the Pope's Head Tavern in London. But the sole outcome of these prestigious and convivial preparations was a piratical cruise by Edward Fenton off Brazil (1582).

Nevertheless the pull of the Orient, with its legendary wealth, was unremitting and irresistible. And since the route via the Cape of Good Hope was in Portuguese hands, and that through the Straits of Magellan more or less in those of the Spaniards, and since both were of formidable length and hazards, there was every incentive to seek ways both shorter and easier, and also beyond the reach of Iberian pretensions. One possibility, said by experts of the mid-1500s to present no great difficulties, was to sail round northern Norway and then eastwards along the Russian coast and so to China. Thus it was that in 1553 members of the future Russia Company sent out an expedition to open this passage to the riches of Asia, and to open as well, with any luck, a new market for English woollen textiles, whose traditional outlets were at this time 'waxing cold and in decay'. The whole venture was carefully prepared under the supervision of Sebastian Cabot, erstwhile Pilot-Major of Spain, including sheathing the ships employed with lead to protect their hulls from the ravages of boring worms. It was commanded by Sir Hugh Willoughby, a fighting man whose 'singuler skill in the services of warre' had been displayed in campaigns at sea against the Scots, and its navigator was the learned and versatile Bristol seaman Richard Chancellor, who some years before had proposed to go 'toward the New Found Lande at merchaunte adventure'. On passage the little flotilla, only three strong, was scattered in a storm. Two of the vessels ended in Lapland, where their entire complements froze to death in the long hard winter 'for want of experience to have made caves and stoves'. But Chancellor, in the *Edward Bonaventure,* eventually reached the mouth of the Dvina from where he made his way to Moscow and to a favourable reception by the Czar, thus opening for England an Arctic trade with Russia.

Of China, however, there was no sign. The company, formally incorporated in 1555, instructed its agents to 'use all wayes and meanes possible to learne howe men may passe from Russia, either by land or sea to Cathaia'. The answer was only with the greatest difficulty. Stephen Borough, an able member of an outstandingly able seafaring family, reached as far east as Vaigach Island in 1556. But whatever the confident pronouncements of sages at home, the route, barred by ice, was impossible for the ships of the time. In the late 1550s another way was tried, and one which was to flourish for a while. Company servants descended the Volga, as the Vikings had done centuries before, and then crossed the Caspian Sea from Astrakhan to Persia. One such voyage (1565), using a 30-ton boat specially built for the occasion, produced a modest amount of silk and spice eventually sold in England. But the route was so long, and its difficulties in the Caspian and Russia alike so many, that it was abandoned and the search for a northern passage resumed. In the 1580s there was some interest in what the islands of Novaya Zemlya might offer, and in what lay beyond the vast Gulf of Ob, whilst in 1603 – though for his own rather than the company's benefit – Francis Cherry sent a ship to Lapland, from where she was to 'proceed upon some discoverie'. And as England became increasingly apprehensive as to the doings of the Dutch in both Asian and northern waters, activity was intensified. The company employed Henry Hudson to seek that 'passage by the North Pole to Japan and China' thought to lie between Spitsbergen and Greenland (1607). The following year he tried again, this time through the Barents Sea. But all in vain. Nevertheless his crew had been cheered by the sight of mermaids; the more sceptical had noticed a potential fishery off Spitsbergen; and Novaya Zemlya had been explored. For some years, therefore, company efforts were concentrated on whaling from

Spitsbergen and on hunting walrus and prospecting for lead on Bear Island, with ships under Jonas Poole regularly in these forbidding waters in the opening decade of the seventeenth century. There were still hopes too – though rapidly dwindling ones – of ways 'to the East Indies', or of 'a trade or passage' at the North Pole, and encouraging rumours circulated of Chinese commerce in the Laptev Sea. The main concern, however, as we shall see, was with a whale fishery, but one in which, as was so often the case, the Dutch were in the end to prevail.

The east could also be reached, according to some influential sixteenth-century cosmographers, through a strait which ran north-westwards into the Pacific from somewhere above the modern Labrador. It was of course by such a way that John Cabot had earlier proposed to sail to Asia. Interest in the strait revived in England in the 1570s for a variety of strategic and economic reasons. It provided further justification for the colonisation of North America – a major attraction of which was the founding of a base handy for attacking Spanish bullion fleets leaving the Caribbean – and it would mean too that the arduous route to India via the Cape of Good Hope could be left to Portugal, an ally, and for a time a member, of the Habsburg world empire. In pursuit of this north-west passage some of England's ablest seamen sailed year after year into ice-ridden and formidably hostile waters: Martin Frobisher in the 1570s; John Davis in the ensuing decade. And from the end of the century amongst the expeditions were several financed by the major chartered companies, or by some of their influential members.

In 1596 Michael Lok of the Levant Company – himself Frobisher's former backer, and a scion of a London merchant family long involved in similar ventures in Africa and Russia – was trying to tempt to England the aged Greek pilot Juan de Fuca who, in Spanish service, had explored the west coast of America. There his name is perpetuated in a strait to the south of the modern Vancouver Island, through which he claimed to have reached the Atlantic. But of this no more was heard. Six years later the East India Company, having raised the necessary funds by a five per cent call on shareholders, sent out George Waymouth with two ships to search for the eastern end of the passage. In persistent freezing fog, and to the accompaniment of the terrifying sound of grinding ice-floes, 'very loathsome to be heard', he reconnoitred Hudson Strait until forced back by mutiny. But worse was to come. The 40-ton *Hopewell,* jointly backed by the Russia and East India companies (1606) lost her rudder in Labrador on a similar quest. The master and some of his crew mysteriously disappeared on shore, and the survivors were attacked by allegedly cannibal Eskimos. Only after further tribulations did they return home, their ship's rudder patched up with 'iron bands off the master's chest to make fast two pick axes for two pintels, and to bind it withall'. Then in 1610 some magnates of the East India and Russia companies financed a voyage by Henry Hudson of north-east passage fame. Sailing in Waymouth's old *Discovery,* he reached what was to become known as the 'bottom' of that great bay which now bears his name. Frozen in, he wintered there, his men surviving on such birds as they could shoot. When, in the following year, the ice broke up and he prepared for further exploration his crew mutinied and sent him and six others to their deaths in an unprovisioned open boat. *Discovery* herself eventually got back to England with only eight of her hands still alive.

Nothing deterred, and despite complaints from the East India Company (1614) of the vast sums (£900 in fact) laid out in such futile ventures, there was established in 1612 the optimistically entitled company of the Merchants of London Discoverers of the North-West Passage, prominent amongst them that grandee of the Levant and East India companies, Sir Thomas Smith. Its first expedition, under Thomas Button, traced the western shores of Hudson Bay. Efforts were then once again turned to Hudson Strait, to where in 1615 there sailed the veteran *Discovery,* commanded by Hudson's old shipmate Robert Bylot, and with that remarkable seaman and navigator William Baffin — who had already been whaling in Spitsbergen for the Russia Company, and who was to meet his death commanding an Indiaman in the Persian Gulf (1622) — as her pilot. Having drawn a blank in 1615 Bylot and Baffin set out the following year with the intention of making for Japan through the Davis Strait. They reached 78° N in waters between Greenland and Canada, and in what is now Baffin Bay found Jones Sound and Lancaster Sound which lead, though they failed to appreciate that this was so, by a north-west passage into the Arctic Ocean. But this was not for tiny wooden sailing ships, and all that Baffin could offer his backers was the 'probabilitie or hope of profit' from whaling. Soon after voyages under other sponsors removed from contemporary maps any representations of a western outlet from Hudson Bay to the Pacific and Asia.

Interest in the north-west passage was, all the same, to revive in the later seventeenth century, and one of the objectives of the first Hudson's Bay Company expedition (1668) was to look, if opportunity offered, for some way to the South Sea. But once established the company was reluctant to become involved in any activities which might attract interlopers to its preserves. Nevertheless, inspired by the views of its servants, and encouraged by rumours of gold, it did from time to time make some generally halfhearted and usually abortive efforts. In 1719 two vessels set out at what was ruefully calculated to be the cost of a year's trading were lost, and their crews massacred by the Eskimos, whilst seeking 'the Straights of Anian . . . and . . . the Gold and Copper Mines'. Later in the century, sensitive to attacks on its whole position and notable lack of achievement in discovery, the company undertook the investigation of the western side of the formidable landmass of the Labrador peninsula, and sloops from its post at Churchill resumed the search for that westward passage from the Bay whose non-existence was at long last proved by the remarkable overland journey of one of its employees to the Arctic Ocean (1770–2).

Companies and Trade

The fundamental purpose, however, of a chartered trading company was to establish and maintain to the best of its ability the monopoly of some particular commerce. Occasionally this might be accomplished peacefully, at least to begin with, as when, quite accidentally, the search for a north-east passage to Asia brought the opening of relations between England and Russia through the White Sea. But more commonly force was needed, especially if the company had to break into an already established trade. Hence not even the Russia Company was without its troubles. A direct commerce between England and Russia affected many interests, the more so since the company soon aspired to become western Europe's sole supplier of Russian products, amongst them some of the vital materials used in the building and rigging of ships. English vessels sailing past the North Cape, so the Danes alleged, violated their sovereignty over the waters between Norway and Iceland. Even worse, a trade with Russia, conducted outside the Baltic, meant a loss of revenue for Denmark from those tolls her kings levied on ships entering and leaving the sea. Thus there were threats, occasionally implemented it would seem – as in 1582 – to sink all company craft bound for 'the Frozen Sea'. Further difficulties arose when Russia took (1558) the Baltic port of Narva, which was thereupon included in the company's monopoly. Sweden and Poland actively opposed England's dealings with the unpredictable Ivan the Terrible as both detrimental to their own commercial aspirations and as fostering, so they claimed, dangerous Russian ambitions by the supply of arms. Trade accordingly had at times to be conducted by armed convoy, as when in 1570 a Narva-bound Russia Company fleet under the distinguished veteran sailor William Borough destroyed the best part of a Polish flotilla it encountered – 'burnt the same and slew the people'.

These difficulties were quickly resolved by Sweden's capture of Narva (1581), removing it from the Russia Company's orbit, and since in any case the company's northern monopoly soon disintegrated. Not so, however, the problems of the Levant Company. This was concerned with the infinitely more lucrative opportunities of the Mediterranean, and in particular with the import of those oriental luxuries which could be obtained from its eastern shores, where they arrived by a variety of land and sea routes. Such a commerce the English had long and enviously eyed, and by the late 1500s, with the decline of the Venetian republic, its former monopolist, the moment for its penetration seemed at last to have come. But easier said than done. Spain, the champion of the Catholic cause and western Europe's greatest military power, controlled alike the straits giving access to the Mediterranean and the strategically vital south of Italy. Her rulers, furthermore, were only too well aware of the dangers inherent in an alliance between their arch-enemies the Protestant English and the Moslem Turks, and in the easy acquisition of western weapons by the

Ottoman sultans. Besides which the Mediterranean itself abounded in pirates and privateers, Christian and Moslem, working from bases anywhere from Morocco to Constantinople (Istanbul). Consequently the early annals of the Levant Company's trade are a chronicle of pitched battles, sudden arrests and daring escapes, many recorded with patriotic fervour in the writings of Richard Hakluyt, the Tudor protagonist of English imperial expansion. In the closing decades of Elizabeth's reign the *Susan,* bound for Constantinople, forced her way out of trouble in Mallorca with trumpets and drums sounding, and her guns traversed muzzle to muzzle with those on land. One of her sisters, returning from Tripoli (Syria) had to be extricated from the grip of the Maltese inquisition by diplomatic exchanges at the highest level. Another, caught whilst surreptitiously attempting to escape from the same port carrying a stowaway wanted by the Turks, had her master executed and some of his crew sent to end their days in the Ottoman galleys. Still others, like the *Centurion,* or that celebrated 'hot shippe' the *Solomon* – veteran of many a campaign – and their consorts fought off whole Spanish squadrons in regular actions.

The following century it was the French, with fleets based in both the Atlantic and the Mediterranean, who were the enemy. From 1650 onwards, and for the most part successfully, the growing and powerful British navy provided escorts for company convoys. But in 1693, through a series of errors and misunderstandings, there occurred the worst single disaster suffered by English merchant shipping in modern times. A joint Anglo-Dutch convoy, over 400 strong, and said to have been 'the richest that ever went for Turkey', was surprised off southern Portugal by the combined Brest and Toulon fleets after its escort had been withdrawn. About 80 ships were captured or destroyed, 29 more pursued into Iberian ports and burned or taken, and others scuttled at Gibraltar. Nor was this the end of a sorry story. The survivors, re-attempting the voyage, were caught in a violent storm. Four were sunk and the remainder took refuge in Cadiz, where it was reckoned that the costs of their stay would swallow up the entire value of their cargoes.

The early history of the East India Company was much the same. It was founded (1600) at a time when the enormously valuable trade between Asia and Europe was in the hands of Portugal, a satellite of Spain. Amongst its begetters, and providing something like a quarter of its initial capital, were many experienced in, and enriched by, the Elizabethan privateering war against Habsburg Iberia. Thus though the company forbade its captains to attack the subjects of any Christian power, and whilst James I and Charles I attempted to pursue a policy of friendship with Spain, English East Indiamen set about the Portuguese in the Orient in the old familiar privateering style until the growing threat from Holland brought reconciliation in 1635. There were pitched battles, skirmishes, and captures of Portuguese prizes in waters anywhere from East Africa to South China. Alliances were formed, where opportune, with Portugal's eastern enemies, and so it was that a squadron of Indiamen joined the Persians in the capture of Kishm (1622), where their artillery played a major role, and where William Baffin of Arctic fame was killed whilst ranging his guns – or as Samuel Purchas puts it, 'trying his Mathematical projects and conclusions'. Company ships similarly helped the Persians to take the vital entrepôt and stronghold of Hormuz the same year, where once again their artillery was of deadly effect, destroying or damaging six big Portuguese vessels. But though in the ensuing pillage one East India master – yet another Arctic veteran, Nicholas Woodcock – allegedly secured for himself 'a million of royalls *(reales)*', the company as such had to pay James I £20,000 to obtain his pardon for its supposed piracy. At the same time Portuguese carracks on passage to and from Europe were attacked, and Portuguese naval forces engaged and more often than not worsted. Off Mozambique in 1616 a flotilla of Indiamen under Benjamin Joseph – who for years had commanded Russia Company whaling fleets in the Arctic – met the sole survivor of a quartet of outward-bound carracks, eventually forcing her ashore in a bitter struggle which cost Joseph his life. Six years later, in the same waters, three Indiamen and their Dutch consorts were in action for two days against a powerful Goa-bound armada, with, in the end one big (1,600-ton) Portuguese ship sunk, another ashore and a third capsized.

Meanwhile, and in the face of vigorous Portuguese opposition, the English were endeavouring to establish themselves on the north-west coast of India – an area of prime commercial importance under the rule of the Mogul emperor – and in the trade with Persia. In 1612, off the port of Surat, and in full and admiring view of a Mogul army, the Indiamen *Hosiander* and *Dragon* beat four large galleons and their escorts in a lengthy and hot action. Three years later the onetime privateering captain Nicholas Downton gave a repeat performance by worsting six galleons, two galleys and some assorted lesser craft. But the English were far from being the predestined victors in such engagements, and near Gombroon in 1625 the 45-gun, but sluggish *Lion* was taken by a flotilla of small vessels whilst reloading between broadsides. And so it went on, combined with English attacks on indigenous shipping whose behaviour offended company pretensions. Yet another former privateering magnate, Christopher Newport, bombarded and pursued two local craft which refused him a pilot in the Gulf of Oman (1613). Malabar shipping was attacked off Surat in 1618, and Chinese junks pillaged in Indonesia, 'for debts owing. to your Worships', it was reported to the company.

But the English were, for a time, to meet more than their match in the rapidly-growing Dutch East India Company. Disaster after disaster inflicted by the Hollanders in the first half of the seventeenth century drove them out of Japan and much of Indonesia, whilst Indiamen were lost in a series of well-publicised humiliations. Two of a flotilla surprised whilst loading in Indonesia surrendered to the Dutch without firing a shot. When the *Swan was* captured (1616) in the Bandas the Hollanders used some of her crew as forced labour for fortress-building. Other prisoners were put in cages and carried 'bound in Irons from Port to Port amongst the Indians'. Ultimately, as is well-known, the picture changed dramatically. French ambitions made Holland and England allies. Dutch seapower dwindled and that of Britain and of the East India Company grew, though not before an attempt to extract concessions from the Mogul emperor by force had ended in total failure (1686).

Commodities and Cargoes

On the whole the commodities handled by the chartered companies, once established, were of a nature which might be deduced from their names. The Russia Company imported the products of a notoriously primitive economy, of which the most important were those lumped together under the generic of 'naval stores' – cables, cordage, tar, hemp. It also brought to England seal oil – ever willing to leak out and foul other goods – furs, wax and small amounts of caviar, esteemed, like so much else at that date, for its supposed aphrodisiac qualities. In exchange the company shipped out the inevitable English woollen textiles – which right to the end of the seventeenth century accounted (by value) for the best part of the country's total exports. To these there were added from time to time modest quantities of commodities obtained elsewhere in Europe, and, so it was regularly alleged, munitions. A trade of this sort was not new, but prior to 1553 it had been conducted through the Baltic, and very largely by members of the German Hanseatic League.

Other companies were similarly engaged in the exchange of manufactures for primary products. In the little Polish port of Elbing, through whose mud-silted harbour a ship moved 'like a plough upon land', the Eastland Company sold woollen textiles for a good part of its life and bought there, and in Königsberg and Danzig, flax, hemp, tar, timber and grain. From northern Canada, in an archetypal colonial commerce, the Hudson's Bay Company imported immense quantities of beaver furs – tens of thousands a year in the early eighteenth century – source of a felt used in the making of the then fashionable and head-warming beaver hat. Indeed the whole purpose of the company's foundation had been to gain easier access to the source of furs than the French enjoyed from their posts on the St Lawrence, further south. Besides beaver the company also sent home lesser amounts of fox, otter and other skins, paying the Indians who brought them to its trading stations with guns, ammunition, blankets and such potent firewaters as brandy, rum and raw gin.

Of a very different order was the commerce of the Levant Company. It, too, of course exported woollen cloths. It likewise imported primary products, amongst them those currants from the Greek islands, without which, according to an eminent Jacobean diplomat, his compatriots could 'hardly digest bread, pastries, broths and bag-puddings', and from which the company was once reputed to be making an annual profit of over £11,000. But at the same time it was sending fish, metals, munitions and bullion to the eastern Mediterranean, and importing from there both raw silk and cotton, and such manufactures as oriental silken textiles. And ironically enough, it was able to ship into the Mediterranean spices from the Far East purchased from the East India Company, so supplying the Levant with those very luxuries it had itself once provided for western Europe. In addition, Levant Company vessels, whose size, strength and armaments gave them a well-deserved reputation for security, were widely employed by Christians and Moslems alike in local trades, and were even attempting – though in vain – to extend their operations into the Black Sea in the early 1600s.

More complex still, and undergoing several fundamental changes in the course of a life of over two centuries, was the East India Company's trade to the Orient via the Cape of Good Hope. Its essence was the westward shipment of Asian produce, which in the earliest years largely meant the high-quality spices of Indonesia and Malabar, much in demand to improve, amongst other things, indifferent wines and to make salted dried meats palatable. But by the late 1600s spices had lost their pre-eminence, and the greater part – 70% to 80% – of the value of homeward cargoes was accounted for by cotton textiles. These ranged from exquisite muslins and fine calicoes – for which, it was said, there was 'an ungovernable female passion' – to coarse cloths used in the purchase of slaves in West Africa. Later again, in the second half of the eighteenth century, there came yet another major shift with the growth of a European taste for Mocha coffee and China tea – of which, by 1760, the company was importing some 2,500,000 lbs annually. For these products, and many others besides, the west offered Asia little it wanted or could afford. Imports were accordingly paid for either from earnings made in local trades or with cash. Hence outward-bound Indiamen sailed virtually in ballast. They had on board the vital bullion – preferably silver coin – which occupied next to no space, together with small amounts of the inescapable woollen textiles and some metal goods. The rest of their very considerable spare capacity was only in part filled with extra victuals – to be consumed on the voyage or passed to sister ships in Asia – arms, ammunition and whatever else Europeans in India might require.

Much shorter-lived, but equally complex, were the trades of the Royal African Company, founded to establish England in that highly lucrative commerce, which had grown up since the early sixteenth century, of supplying West African slaves to the new European settlements in the Americas and the Caribbean, where they were used as plantation labour. In its heyday the company acquired Africans from its agents in Gambia or on the Gold Coast in exchange for textiles (some of them Asian), metals (some from the Baltic), firearms and liquor. Beyond the river Volta, where there were no company posts, vessels lay offshore and cargoes were assembled by their masters haggling with local rulers as to what they could supply and at what price in the so-called 'ship trade'. Thus it was that between 1672 and 1713 (that is between its foundation and the effective ending of its monopoly) the company delivered 100,000 Africans to the West Indies, some for use in British colonies, some in those of other powers. But these wretches were all that remained of far larger initial ladings. The company urged that so valuable an investment should be carefully watched. The decks of slavers were to be swabbed regularly with vinegar to keep down disease, and the slaves themselves put in good heart 'with some sorts of musick and play'. Nor would it pay except on the basis of those delivered alive. Even so, the brutality and cupidity of its agents and captains were such that in the late 1600s about 25% of every cargo was lost on average, and the company's clients, to their great annoyance, regularly short of labour.

The company's monopoly further embraced, at least in theory, England's commerce with West Africa, from where it shipped home gold, together with ivory, dyewoods and wax obtained in Gambia and Sierra Leone. Company vessels, having delivered their slaves, could also load cotton and sugar in the West Indies for carriage home. But this was not the best of trades. The company enjoyed no privilege, exports from the islands being outside its monopoly, and with planters notoriously reluctant payers, agents and masters could find themselves without the means to make purchases. Sugar was, moreover, not a particularly attractive cargo, since only when the crop was abundant could a full freight be obtained other than by taking up lot after lot from different plantations. Nor, before the end of the seventeenth century, did it or any other island product command a good price in Europe, so that the company preferred as a rule to be paid in specie or by bill, and the entire proceeds of the sale of a cargo of slaves might be returned to England in an envelope containing nothing more than a handful of papers. Only as prices — and especially of sugar — rose, which was in the years immediately preceding its collapse in the early 1700s, were the company's ships commonly engaged in that notorious triangular traffic linking England — West Africa — the West Indies — England.

Interport and Country Trade

In many trades the goods in which companies dealt were obtained in the ports where they enjoyed concessions, and beyond which, for either economic or political reasons, English merchants were unable to penetrate. Throughout most of its existence the Eastland Company conducted its business from Elbing or Danzig. In the eastern Mediterranean it suited the Levant Company to attempt, from the late seventeenth century, to confine its commerce to Alexandretta (for Aleppo), Smyrna and Constantinople (Istanbul). But in some cases it was possible, and indeed imperative, for merchants or company employees to assemble cargoes from, or deliver them to, destinations far beyond any entrepôt. For a time, in the late 1500s, and until the obstacles became too many and too great, the Russia Company in its attempts to trade with the Far East, sent ships down the Volga to Astrakhan – like the 70-ton *Thomas Bonaventure* in 1569– bound for the Persian ports of the Caspian Sea. In the following century the Royal African Company employed half a dozen or so small sloops and yachts (40-ton at the most) on the West African coast. There they worked up river, and between the company's fort at the mouth of the Gambia and its chief places of business, assembling for its ships cargoes of anything from ivory to slaves. In much the same way the Hudson's Bay Company used sloops and shallops to maintain communications between the posts which, by the mid-1700s, it had at both the head and foot of the Bay. Others were sent out annually from the base at Churchill to sail up the coast delivering gifts to ensure the goodwill of local chiefs, and trading weapons and beads to the little-known and much-feared Eskimo in exchange for whale oil and blubber.

But any such commerce was eclipsed by the wealth and variety of the great 'country trades' of Asia. There the English, like other Europeans, found on their arrival an immense maritime economy stretching from the shores of East Africa to those of South China and beyond. From the profusion of commodities it offered – silks, spices, precious stones, artefacts from China and Japan – the company's employees assembled at its factories the cargoes of whose shipment to England it enjoyed the monopoly. But it was soon realized that there were magnificent profits to be made from trading and other ventures within Asia itself, and before long English-owned vessels were carrying Moslem pilgrims from northern India to Jidda, or exporting Indian textiles to the Red Sea and the Persian Gulf, from where they returned, it was enviously reported, laden with 'vast quantitys of pearl and treasure'. Many of these trades were ancient and well-established, but others were modified, extended or created by Europeans, with the English, for example, taking, from the eighteenth century, Indian opium and cottons to China to be exchanged for tea. For a time the company maintained that its monopoly embraced not only commerce to and from the east, but within Asia as well, and Indiamen indeed continued to make occasional 'country' voyages. But such was the extent of the Asian economy, and such its opportunities and rewards, that whole areas came to be dominated by English private traders. Some were company servants, but the majority were not, and since the company found it impossible to suppress their activities it eventually accepted and licenced them. Furthermore, there sprang up in its major bases at Bombay, Madras and Calcutta English-owned merchant fleets, and amongst those investing in them its own officials, such as the governor of Calcutta who, in the eighteenth century, had vessels trading to the Red Sea and the Persian Gulf, whilst those of a colleague at Madras were working to the Philippines. From these and similar enterprises many men grew exceedingly rich, often at the expense of the company, whose capital they used in their own affairs, or whose ships went unladen to the benefit of those of its employees. Nevertheless the company was not always the loser, and it was the specie remitted to China by private traders that helped to pay for its purchases of tea there. And such was the importance of the 'country trades', which in part fed its long-distance commerce, that for their defence the company maintained its own naval force, the Bombay Marine, whose galleys and bomb-ketches were employed in the Arabian Sea and on the west coast of India against pirates and unco-operative local potentates.

Whaling

Finally there were those rare occasions on which a company itself, rather than its uncontrollable members or employees, vigorously pursued some new opportunity. The Russia Company's long search for a northern passage to China brought to light the prospects for whaling in the Arctic, and for thus obtaining, amongst other things, the oil used in the manufacture of soap. Fortified by an astonishing grant (1577) of the monopoly of 'the killing of whales within any seas whatsoever', the company backed some spasmodic ventures towards the end of Elizabeth's reign. More ambitious expeditions were sent out in the early 1600s, first to Bear Island and its environs, under Jonas Poole, and then, following the return of Henry Hudson, to Spitsbergen. All, however, to little avail. Competitors, English and foreign, were soon on the scene, unimpressed by the company's pretensions. It, in turn, burdened itself with the expense of supporting battle squadrons rather than fishing fleets, commanded by the like of the bellicose Benjamin Joseph, and empowered to drive off interlopers or to force them into company service. Proceedings of this nature, combined with the hanging from yardarms of those allegedly guilty of 'peremptorie speeches', brought Dutch and Danish men-of-war to the aid of their compatriots and cost the company more than it could afford, especially since its own hauls of whale were so poor. After some mergers and re-organization, which at one stage involved the intervention of the East India Company, there finally emerged the Greenland Company (boasting four active members), a semi-independent offshoot of the Russia Company. For a while it did a great deal better than its parent, and some of its fleets – usually seven to 12 vessels – returned home with as much as 2,000 tons of oil. But that all was not well is reflected in reports of ships wrecked, or whalers lost when harpoon lines ran out foul. Besides which there was the persistent competition of old interlopers like Hull, now joined by such new ones as London, York and Yarmouth, with whose ships those of the company fought regular battles. But it was the presence of the far more efficient Dutch – using better harpooners and more vessels, and tapping much bigger markets – that was fatal, and by the 1670s the company had foundered.

Ships and Shipping

All such enterprises required ships, of which the companies, taken together, were considerable employers. Naturally enough, not all were involved to the same degree. The Hudson's Bay Company annually sent across the Atlantic only two or three vessels of modest size, and the fleets of the Russia Company comprised, by 1600, no more than a dozen craft. But with others it was a different story. Towards the end of the sixteenth century the Eastland Company despatched something like 100 ships a year into the Baltic. The Levant Company convoy destroyed by the French in 1693 numbered over 400, and by the end of the eighteenth century the East India Company had about 90,000 tons of shipping in its service. Even so, with the great expansion of English merchant tonnage from the late 1600s, company shipping only accounted for a small fraction of the country's total resources – Indiamen, for example, for just over two per cent at best.

Often enough company vessels were of no more than average size for the time, and only rarely were they specialized craft in the sense that, for instance, modern tankers are, though in 1693 the Hudson's Bay Company's newly-purchased *Royal Mary* was given a double bow of three-inch planking to withstand ice. But some company ships were, as critics and apologists agreed, remarkable in that they were of exceptional size and weight of armament – as indeed they were by the standards of the pre-Victorian centuries when anything approaching 1,000 tons passed for a leviathan. Some were employed in trades in which armed opposition was to be expected. Some, in the Elizabethan age, were the property of privateering magnates. And some, like Indiamen, were designed alike to fight, to impress orientals, and to provide tolerable living conditions in voyages of enormous distance and duration – six months to India, or the direct run home from China. Thus in the late 1500s, when English merchantmen of more than 200 tons were rarities, amongst those in the service of the Levant Company were alderman Thomas Cordell's 300-ton *Edward Bonaventure,* his *Centurion* – 'a very tall ship of burden' as she was known – and his 400-ton *Merchant Royal,* a veteran of trade, war and privateering. Such traditions the company long maintained, stipulating the size of crews and the amount of artillery to be carried, or the maximum age (18 in 1664) at which vessels were acceptable to it.

Even larger and more powerful were the ships of the East India Company. Some of the first, like the 600-ton *Dragon,* were erstwhile privateers. Others, notably the 1,000-ton *Trade's Increase* (1609), were of an unprecedented size since merchants expected she 'would make return of their goods at far cheaper rates than any small shipping'. Indiamen were to continue in this formidable style, and in the early 1600s commonly had more (and better served) guns than the bigger Portuguese royal galleons they encountered in Asia. Later years saw them of lesser tonnage, flush-decked (under Indian influence), but also, very often, crank as a result of long, deep and narrow hulls. Then towards 1800 size again increased, with some ships for the China trade reaching 1,500 tons. Copper-sheathed, well-armed (38 pieces in the largest) and relatively well-manned they were, in the right hands, as good as many men-of-war. In 1804 a French regular squadron, encountering the China fleet under the company's senior commander, Commodore Dance, turned and fled when he bore down on them. And despite appearances Indiamen could be fast if they had to be. A few years later another China fleet astonished the shipping world by arriving in the Channel 109 days out from Canton.

Ships were occasionally owned by companies themselves, like those sloops and similar craft which the Royal African and Hudson's Bay companies stationed at their overseas posts. But even the biggest might belong to a company, especially in some new or dangerous trade, or where other circumstances made owners reluctant to provide tonnage. The Russia Company, which owned all its first vessels, was still talking as late as 1567 of 'our . . . shipe' the *Harry*. When struggling to survive the abrogation of its charter, the Royal African Company bought vessels for itself — 44 between 1720 and 1724. And most remarkably, the East India Company, unable in its early years to charter what it wanted, commenced in 1607 to build its own ships in its own yards on the Thames, and was responsible, in the decade after 1610, for the construction of some 60 large vessels.

Once trade settled to a more or less normal pattern, however, and with an increasing volume of English tonnage available, it became usual for companies to charter. But this was a business with rules of its own. With a 'regulated' company it could amount to no more than a merchant notifying the relevant officials of the vessel he intended to employ, and paying them the appropriate dues. Alternatively, a company, having decided on its requirements, might hire the necessary craft itself, usually from a fairly constant body of owners who, hardly surprisingly, were also of its fellowship. The whole process was most highly developed with the East India Company once it abandoned building for itself. By the eighteenth century most of its vessels were constructed in a small group of Thameside yards for a ring of owners who had established their sole and hereditary right to tender for charters. They excluded outsiders, never competed with one another, and as 'the shipping interest' hired their vessels to the company for given periods — 12 to 16 years as a rule after the introduction of coppering, 'which', as was said, 'is as long as (they) will last'. Nor did the ramifications of oligarchy and monopoly end here. Masters, in the early days of the Russia Company, might be company members, or even, as with the Levant and East India companies, on the board of management. In the great days of the East India Company the builders who built its ships, the managing owners who ran them, and the captains who commanded them almost all held company stock, whilst amongst that very select band with shares in company ships were such grandees of its service as the governors of Madras and Bengal.

Given that the prime concern of companies was to maintain their monopolies of particular trades between particular ports, ships in their employment sailed at specified times, under specified conditions and, as a rule, in convoy, with masters sometimes even required to enter into bonds to keep together. In the vessels of a 'regulated' company – known as 'general' or 'joint' ships – cargo space was allocated by the company to those of its members intending to trade. In the holds of the craft of joint-stock companies, on the other hand, went the freights assembled by their agents and servants in England for carriage to their opposite numbers overseas, and vice versa. The basic ladings were, of course, of those goods which fell within the monopolies of the respective companies. But a great deal else was carried as well. Outward-bound ships might take gifts for foreign potentates, like that pair of lions sent to the Czar of Russia in 1557. They might return, as was regularly the case with those of the Levant Company, bearing the choice loot amassed by discriminating diplomats – oriental manuscripts, classical artefacts and remains, like the celebrated Elgin marbles – or they might carry back, as did Hudson's Bay craft in the eighteenth century, specimens and data for the scrutiny of scientists.

Passengers and Private Cargoes

An assortment of passengers was regularly embarked too – sightseers, ambassadors, or personnel destined for overseas posts, such as those crofters and fishermen (together with the sheep and cattle to sustain them) taken from the Orkneys by Hudson's Bay ships. But the most variegated company was to be found in Indiamen, amongst whose crews there were also, and from an early date, Asian seamen. The fleet in which Sir Thomas Roe sailed as ambassador to the court of the Mogul emperor (1615–19) carried, in addition to 11 Japanese and 14 Gujaratis, 19 ex-convicts who were to be deposited en route 'for the discoverie of unknowne places'. By about 1800, when much of India was in British hands, and as the ranks of Europeans were constantly and radically thinned by the ravages of disease and drink, outward-bound company ships might have on board re-inforcements on their way to join regular army units, or recruits for the company's own forces, together with cadets and writers destined to enter its establishment of officers and civil servants. There could be high-ranking soldiers returning from leave, merchants going out under company licence, wives re-joining their spouses and unattached ladies in pursuit of husbands. Occasionally the long months at sea were whiled away watching or participating in plays –Shakespeare's *Hamlet* and *Richard II* were even staged by the crew on one early voyage – or in learning an oriental language. But such high intellectual endeavour was rare, and the usual round was one of card-playing, dancing and flirting, with goodwill and harmony induced and sustained by a liberal flow – for private travellers alone of course – of madeira and champagne. In this way captains sought to establish for their ships a reputation which would attract rich passengers – 'nabobs' like William Hickey – for the homeward passage, and with any luck a fortune for themselves.

Finally there was the cargo privately loaded, legally or otherwise, by anyone from merchants to the vessel's own officers and crew. Returning Indiamen carried, for a fee, 'fine goods' and those things in which the company itself did not trade. Pre-eminent amongst these were diamonds, often the property of Portuguese Jewish dealers, though Robert Clive, the victor of Plassey, alone sent home a consignment worth the enormous sum of £30,000. Part of the hold space in its ships – the evocatively designated 'old indulgence' – the company also, for a time, allocated to the goods of its employees, whose private commercial activities it had early come to accept. Officers and seamen enjoyed similar and more durable concessions, carefully graduated according to rank. The 'outward privilege' of the commander of an 800-ton vessel in the late 1700s meant 56 tons at the least for his own use, chiefly taken up with marine stores. For 'homeward privilege' he was allowed 30 tons, largely devoted to silks and cottons, though the officers of China ships could bring in tea, and were in addition given in effect a monopoly of the import of chinaware. All these very considerable and highly lucrative perquisites their holders freely and radically enlarged, selling hold space, and smuggling what and where they could. Hardly surprisingly the commanders of Indiamen, who were also happily able to sell their posts on retirement, were often men of enviable wealth.

Conclusion

The shortcomings of the chartered companies were, as their opponents frequently and forcefully re-iterated, many and obvious. They were all too commonly remarkably inept and unenterprising. Rarely could they eradicate the competition of those who openly violated their supposed monopolies, whether they were fellow companies, outright interlopers, or – as was embarrassingly common – some of their own most influential members, like those notoriously 'disorderly brethren', Sir Francis Cherry of the Elizabethan Russia Company and Lionel Cranfield of the Jacobean Eastland Company. Equally rarely could they check the vast and unquantifiable private dealings of their employees, with the Russia Company apprehensive almost from its inception as to the scale of its seamen's ventures, and the Royal African Company later bemoaning that there were 'few or none' of its captains not engaged in smuggling slaves to the West Indies. Even so, the companies between them opened and exploited some new trades (through the White Sea to Russia, through Hudson Bay to North America), and successfully established

England in others, most notably to the Levant and the Far East. For that great growth, in every sense, of English overseas commerce from the late 1700s onwards, they could claim little responsibility. Nevertheless multilateral trading – where exports are exchanged not against imports, but against commodities to be resold elsewhere, and the sign of an expanding and more sophisticated English commerce – received a further extension in the seventeenth century from their activities. Asian textiles provided by the East India Company, and Baltic metals in part supplied by the Merchant Adventurers were, for example, used by the Royal African Company in its purchases of gold and slaves. In the same way that growth of re-exports, marking a revolutionary change in the nature of England's overseas trade from the mid-1600s, was in some measure fuelled by the East India Company, whose spices and cotton textiles commanded a lively market almost everywhere in Europe.

In things purely maritime the record varies from company to company. After prolonged troubles in its early years with incompetent, drunken and dishonest masters, the Hudson's Bay Company maintained for centuries a link with the formidable waters of northern Canada. But obsessed as it was with secrecy and with warding off any infringement of its monopoly, it did its uttermost, until the late 1700s, to prevent the diffusion of information about the geography and trade of the Bay and the sea routes leading there. The Russia and East India Companies, however, either corporately, or through the interests of their members, contributed substantially to the early exploration of the Arctic. Furthermore, the Russia Company for a time employed – and included amongst its fellowship in its pioneering days – some of England's ablest seamen, and made serious if short-lived attempts to ensure the competence of others in its service. It enjoined that accurate observations be taken and recorded by its ships, and that apprentices and young sailors be taught navigation and 'the science of cosmography', to which end, at a date when celestial navigation was in its infancy in England, a standard Spanish text was translated for their benefit (1561). The East India Company pursued similar policies, laying down in its heyday stringent standards of seamanship and navigation, and punishing any captains who failed to maintain them. And all to good effect. After six months at sea its outgoing fleets seldom arrived in Asia more than a fortnight later than expected, and Indiamen were widely regarded with admiration and respect. No doubt the achievement could have been improved, but it remains a considerable one all the same.

Further Reading

The background to the rise of the chartered companies is discussed by G. V. Scammell, *The World Encompassed: The First European Maritime Empires c.800 – 1650* (1981). Their significance in the English economy of the time is admirably treated in D. C. Coleman, *The Economy of England, 1450 – 1 750* (Oxford 1977). Current approaches to, and interpretations of, company history are indicated in L. Blussé and F. Gaastra (eds), *Companies and Trade: Essays on Overseas Trading Companies during the Ancien Régime* (Leiden, 1981).

There is a rich and extensive literature on the history of the companies as a whole, together with many studies of individual associations. Still invaluable, despite its size and intimidating title, is W. R. Scott, *The Constitution and Finance of English, Scottish and Irish Joint Stock Companies, 1558 – 1 720* (3 vols, 1910 – 12). Of the histories of particular companies or trades the following are especially useful. R. W. K. Hinton, *The Eastland Trade and the Commonweal in the Seventeenth Century* (Cambridge, 1959), now supplemented by J. K. Fedorowicz, *England's Baltic Trade in the Early Seventeenth Century: A Study in Anglo-Polish Commercial Diplomacy* (Cambridge, 1980). The standard work on the Hudson's Bay Company is that by E. E. Rich, *Hudson's Bay Company, 1670 – 1870* of which vol 1(1961) covers the years 1670 – 1763. For the Levant Company there is A. C. Wood, *A History of the Levant Company (Oxford,* 1935), to which new information on the earliest period is added by S. A. Skilliter, *William Harborne and the Trade with Turkey, 1578 – 1582: A Documentary Study of the First Anglo-Ottoman Relations* (Oxford, 1977) T. S. Willan, *The Early History of the Russia Company, 1553 – 1603* (Manchester, 1956) is an excellent example of the work of an acknowledged master of the history of English commerce in the early modern centuries, and K. G. Davies, *The Royal African Company* (1957) is a book of fundamental importance for the understanding of English trade and finance in the seventeenth century, written with admirable vigour and clarity.

The East India Company has been, and currently is, the focus of a great deal of scholarly attention. Its origins are examined by K. N. Chaudhuri, *The English East India Company: The Study of an Early Joint-Stock Company, 1600 – 1640* (1965), which, in addition to its other merits, is particularly good on the building and operation of the first English Indiamen. The company's attacks on the Portuguese in the Persian Gulf and its participation in the capture of Hormuz can be followed in C. R. Boxer's edition of the *Commentaries of Ruy Freyre de Andrada* (1930), and are further studied by G. V. Scammell, 'England, Portugal and the *Estado da India,c.* 1500 – 1635' *(Modern Asian Studies,* 16, 2 (1982), 177 – 192. The subsequent history of the company is magisterially discussed in Holden Furber, *Rival Empires of Trade in the Orient, 1600 – 1800* (Oxford, 1976), and in K. N. Chaudhuri's vast and erudite work on *The Trading World of Asia and the English East India Company 1660 – 1760* (Cambridge, 1978). Invaluable information on 'country trades', and on English-owned private shipping in India is to be found in P. J. Marshall's excellent *East India Fortunes:The British in Bengal in the Eighteenth Century* (Oxford, 1976). The role of the companies in the search for the northwest passage to Asia is discussed in W. P. Cumming, R. A. Skelton and D. B. Quinn, *The Discovery of North America* (1971), and W. P. Cumming, S. Hillier, D. B. Quinn and G. Williams, *The Exploration of North*

America, 1630 – 1776 (1974) — both lavishly illustrated and documented. See, too, the illuminating article by G. Williams, 'The Hudson's Bay Company and its critics in the eighteenth century', in *Transactions of the Royal Historical Society*, 5th ser, 20 (1970), 149—171.

The abortive whaling ventures of the companies are outlined in Gordon Jackson, *The British Whaling Trade* (1978). The role of London shipowners in early company history, and the wealth and influence of London merchants in Elizabethan and Jacobean times are examined by K. R. Andrews, *Elizabethan Privateering: English Privateering during the Spanish War, 1585 – 1603* (Cambridge, 1964), and by G. V. Scammell, 'Shipowning in the economy and politics of early modern England', *The Historical Journal*, xv (1972), 385-407.

For the ships of the East India Company it is well worth starting with the excellent contribution of C. Northcote Parkinson, 'The East India Trade', to the volume of essays he edited under the title of *The Trade Winds: A Study of British Overseas Trade during the French Wars 1793 – 1815* (1948). This is now supplemented by Jean Sutton *Lords of the East, the East India Company and its Ships* (1981). Authoritative on the vessels of the companies, and the ways in which they were employed, is Ralph Davis, *The Rise of the English Shipping Industry in the Seventeenth and Eighteenth Centuries* (1962). For the concern of the companies with navigation and seamanship, see the definitive work of D. W. Waters, *The Art of Navigation in England in Elizabethan and Early Stuart Times* (1958).

There is a mass of information,most of it eminently readable, on the early history of the companies in the great collections of those pioneer advocates of English imperial expansion, Richard Hakluyt (*The Principal Navigations*, Maclehose edition, 12 vols, Glasgow, 1903—5) and Samuel Purchas (*Hakluyt Posthumus, or Purchas His Pilgrimes*, Maclehose edition, 20 vols, Glasgow, 1905—7).

VIII

THE GREAT AGE OF DISCOVERY, 1400–1650

Ladies and gentlemen, the subject I am going to discuss is as vast and limitless as the oceans seemed to those who first sailed them in the rightly-named Great Age of Discovery. All I can hope to do is to touch superficially on a number of important and contentious themes, conscious, if you will pardon the confusion of figures of speech, that this is like attempting to arrange some Wagnerian epic for comb and paper.

Our period opens with the English re-discovery of Iceland, and with Portugal undertaking in North Africa and the Atlantic islands the first conscious imperial expansion outside the continent of Europe since classical times. It ends in the mid-seventeenth century when the tentative world economy created by Spain and Portugal was slipping into the hands of the Protestant maritime powers of the north, Holland and England.

What set this whole process of exploration, conquest and colonization in train we cannot go into on this occasion. But a major factor was the desire to reach Asia where, as had been known since Antiquity, there were riches beyond Europe's wildest dreams, and, as was equally well known, women 'hot and lascivious', as the sages reported. Ironically enough, it was in the Mediterranean, notably in Florence, Genoa and Venice, that this ambition found some of its most ardent protagonists. The merchants of these great commercial and financial centres had dealt directly or indirectly with the Orient in the high Middle Ages and (very largely) by so doing acquired a wealth unknown elsewhere in the west. A high proportion of the names prominent in the first wave of Europe's expansion overseas are from these cities – Columbus, Cabot, Verrazzano, Toscanelli, to mention merely the most familiar. But of course once their dream was realized, and the east was reached from Atlantic Europe, the Mediterranean's age-old economic pre-eminence in the continent was doomed.

In pursuit of Asia, and of the opportunties revealed en route, Europeans established the outlines of the gigantic African land-mass, discovered and in part conquered the Americas, opened a sea route to the Far East via the Cape of Good Hope, and established themselves in the great and ancient maritime economy of Asia. They marched across the Andes, reached the Rocky Mountains, were ship-wrecked in the Seychelles, climbed Table Mountain, sought to look into the crater of Popocatepetl, froze to death in the Arctic, gazed with wonder on the great buildings of China, and examined with a mixture of awe and horror those of Aztec Mexico and Inca Peru.

All this was accomplished in feats of seamanship and campaigns which for centuries have strained the resources of those contemplating them for adequate superlatives of admiration or condemnation. The first voyage of Columbus was of a distance and duration in open seas unequalled since Viking times. That of Vasco da Gama, pioneering a way to the east, involved an initial leg of 6,000 kms, lasting ninety-three days without sight of land and in unknown waters. The circumnavigation of the world, begun by Magellan and completed by Elcano, entailed a passage from the west coast of South America to the Moluccas of ninety-eight days on an ocean seemingly devoid of land and 'so vast', it was bitterly remarked, 'that the human mind can scarcely conceive it'.

Navigational techniques were such that only latitude could be established, and not even this with too much confidence. Hence seamen as good as Francis Drake could find themselves quite literally going round in circles, or, as unkind critics put it, sailing for days on land. Passengers listened with amazement and alarm as masters and pilots debated with all the acrimony of an academic seminar just where in the world they might be – which all too often was far from where they thought. Sailing ships, the biggest hardly larger than those dhows still to be seen in the Indian Ocean, were at the mercy of the vagaries of the weather to a degree now hard to appreciate. There were no barometers to indicate what (meteorologically at least) lay in store for seamen. And there was no equivalent to modern weather forecasting, and even if there had been, no way of transmitting its predictions, however fallible, to vessels at sea. True, there was a certain amount of folklore in such matters, often garnered by scholarly voyagers from the yarns of ancient mariners. Brother Domingo Navarrete, whose travels and tribulations have been excellently edited for our Society by Professor Cummins, learned, amongst other wonders, that in Far Eastern waters a stiff blow could be expected when the cockroaches that infested ships were 'restless' and the pigs on board 'run and tumble about'.[1] And of course the prudent were able to gather from the careful observation of natural phenomena some indication of what the elements might be about to do. Portuguese sailing directions warned that a dead calm and a long oily swell, or birds settling 'like flocks of sheep' on the water, meant trouble. A colleague of Humphrey Gilbert's recorded (1583) that in the north-west Atlantic porpoises 'passing through the ocean in heardes did portend storme'.

Then again, with consequences which need no elaboration, most ships were hopeless performers except with a following wind. The Elizabethan *Galleon Leicester*, built on the lines of the celebrated *Revenge*, could, as her officers reported, make no headway when tacking, but merely struggled to and fro on a broad reach, 'E on ye on boord and W on ye other, for (she) wold ly no nyer'. And such indifferent qualities were aggravated, and sailing speeds reduced, by rapid and luxuriant marine growth on underwater hulls. Against weeds, barnacles and such like, current nostrums, ranging from coatings of fish oil or tallow to dressings of concrete and ground glass, were of no avail. Voyages were accordingly of prodigious length and duration, generating all those problems inseparable from having (very often) several hundred men cooped up in a confined space for months on end.

[1] J. S. Cummins (ed.) *The travels and controversies of Friar Domingo Navarrete, 1618–86*, 2 vols (Hakluyt Society, Cambridge, 1962), II, 356.

Ships became so insanitary that crews and passengers fainted at the stench released when hatches were opened. Food, where it lasted, was almost invariably unsuitable; disease and death were commonplace. As the chaplain of one English expedition pathetically wrote, 'I was seasick, and no marvel, having changed at once both ayr, exercyse and diet, rummatique I was and exceedingly costyve and trobled with hartburning, which be appendixes of ye sea'.[2]

Such conditions aggravated the tensions inevitable amongst cosmopolitan complements, and in vessels whose crews worked whilst, as Drake's famous words remind us, their social superiors looked on. So it was that the standing orders for any expedition were largely taken up with attempts to remove the sources of friction or worse. The first Portuguese viceroy of India banned all drink in his ships, though allowing (o happy thought!) an issue of olive-oil in cold weather. The redoubtable Martin Frobisher, preparing to sail over the North Pole to China, denied his men the inflammatory pleasures of 'swearing, dice . . . card-playing and filthy conmunication' (*sic*). The commander of a Spanish flotilla about to be launched into the Pacific (1605) forbade swearing and blasphemy, under pain of loss of rations for the first offence and imprisonment and fines for any recurrence. There was to be no dice or card-playing, and if the seemingly innocuous draughts and backgammon led to disputes, they too would be prohibited. Nor was there to be any 'loose or disrespectful' talk about royalty.[3] And even in the fleets of England's Puritan republic of the mid-seventeenth century punishments had to be stipulated for profanity, irreligion, cursing, drunkenness and 'uncleanness', whilst Admiral Nehemiah Bourne was obliged to 'banish strong waters' from the vessels of his command. So fine was the line between peace and disorder. Not surprisingly, under the pressures of coping with their men and the elements commanders had nervous breakdowns – as would seem to have been the

[2]E. G. R. Taylor (ed.), *The troublesome voyage of Captain Edward Fenton* (Hakluyt Society Cambridge, 1959), p.166.

[3]Celsus Kelly, OFM (ed.), *La Austrialia del Espíritu Santo*, 2 vols (Hakluyt Society, Cambridge, 1966), 1, 140ff.

case with Columbus on his last voyage – or went completely mad, as did Thomas Cavendish. The progress of the expeditions of more rugged leaders, whether the plebeian Drake or the patrician Albuquerque, was punctuated by summary trials, hangings and executions. As the author of a memorandum for Walter Raleigh put it, 'the general (is) to Commaund absolutly'.

The wider world to which Europeans penetrated after such tribulations was by no means everywhere to fall under their control. They could succeed when – terrain, climate and disease permitting – they enjoyed some element of surprise. The horse, previously unknown in South America, was vital in the Spanish conquest of Mexico and Peru, just as it was vital in establishing Portuguese authority in Angola. Here, so it was said of cavalry armed with lances in a land where once again the horse was a stranger, 'one man on horse-backe is of more worth then a hundred Negroes, because the Horsemen doe afright them greatly'.[4] Similarly, where, as in the highly developed societies of Aztec Mexico or Inca Peru, Europeans could extract advantage from civil war or inter-tribal rivalries, the outcome could again be total conquest. They could also do well, at least for a time, as the Portuguese did in the Congo and Japan, where for some reason – usually hopes of European weapons, tools or aid – potentates were willing to welcome them. And indeed a measure of indigenous co-operation was essential in the establishment and exploitation of any empire. The behaviour of the Portuguese on their arrival in the Indian Ocean and western India was radically affected by their association with Hindu seamen, mercenaries and merchants. It was the pirate and general military entrepreneur Timoja who suggested to Albuquerque the desirability of taking Moslem Goa, the eventual capital of the Portuguese *Estado da India*. And we can see why. War between Moslems and Hindus was endemic, and to sustain war cavalry was vital. But since horses were unable to flourish in southern India the upkeep of such forces was dependent on the import of mounts from Arabia and Persia. One of Timoja's

[4]Samuel Purchas, *Hakluyt Posthumus, or Purchas His Pilgrimes*, 20 vols (Robert Maclehose, Glasgow, 1905-7), VI, 440.

duties was to prevent these cargoes from reaching the Moslem opponents of his Hindu masters. As he rightly saw, with Goa in the hands of the Portuguese – then, so it seemed, the implacable enemies of Islam – his lot would be much improved. And so it was on his advice, and with the aid of his troops and those of his fellows, that Albuquerque took Goa.

Intriguingly enough, not all these indigenous collaborators were in fact genuinely indigenous. One, whom the Portuguese met in 1501, and who had spent the previous quarter of a century sailing the seas of Asia, retained his Italian name, Benvenuto de Abano. Another, Coge Çofar (Khoja Safar Salmâni) was a renegade Genoese or Albanian. He was also a Moslem. More remarkably still, a few years later, and at the very time the rulers of Portugal and their bellicose clergy were breathing out fire and smoke about the destruction of the accursed sect of Mahomet, their government in Asia was in close relations with one Khoja Shams-ud-Dîn, reputedly the richest merchant in India. Although a Moslem he continued, in the 1530s and 1540s, to trade from the west of the sub-continent to Cairo, Jidda and Mecca (that is along routes Portugal had supposedly closed), sometimes in partnership with an opulent Catholic businessman from Goa. Besides which he provided the Portuguese with ships, money and military intelligence as to the doings of the Ottoman Turks. Meanwhile the Sultan's officers were apparently receiving similar information from him about the Portuguese.[5]

Europeans made no conquests to speak of in regions such as western Africa, where the climate was hostile, or where, as in North-West Africa, India and most of Asia, they were up against powers well able to look after themselves. They also had great difficulty with primitive nomads, like the Araucanians of the southernmost tip of South America, whose tribal societies offered no central authority which could be seized and manipulated to an invader's advantage. Europeans might also be deflected from con-

[5]Geneviève Bouchon, 'A propos de l'inscription de Colombo (1501): Quelques observations sur le premier voyage de João da Nova dans l'Océan Indien', *Revista da Universidade de Coimbra*, xxviii (1980), pp.233-70, at p.253. Information on Khoja Shams-ud-Dîn from a forthcoming study by Luís de Albuquerque and Inácio Guerreiro.

quest, as were the English Puritans in North America, by their own beliefs. The extreme Protestant sects – we know from Dr Porter's recent erudite study – had little wish to associate with the local Amerindians, let alone dominate or convert them.[6] Similarly, they could be deflected where, as in Asia, they were confronted not only by powerful states and civilizations, but by a rich maritime economy. By plundering it, taxing it or participating in it they could become, almost effortlessly, exceedingly rich and so able to live in style – as it was generally agreed that Christian gentlemen should – without working.

Of the vast consequences in Europe and the non-European worlds of the events of the century and a half after 1400, time permits us to say very little. The bounds of Christendom were massively enlarged. Whole indigenous states and empires were overthrown, most notably in Mexico and Peru. Indigenous peoples were in part or totally wiped out, as in the Caribbean. Another awful dimension was added to the slavery endemic in Africa, Asia and the Americas by the shipment overseas of Africans to serve as anything from field labourers in the plantations of the Americas to soldiers or seamen in Portuguese Asia. In Europe royal authority was momentarily enhanced by empire. Theorists, such as Richard Hakluyt and Walter Raleigh in England, argued that colonization was a matter for governments; that it was something too great and risky to be left to private individuals. In Spain and Portugal absolute royal authority was established over the new colonial churches, and control of imperial trade was exercised through new and specially created departments of state – the *Casa da Mina*, *Casa da India* and *Casa de la Contratacíon*. Colonies absorbed the ambitious and unruly, and the control and exploitation of such possessions, all too prone to reproduce on a grander scale the failings of the European world that had engendered them, demanded more institutions; more officials. But then, as empire became the crippling burden it always ultimately is, money had to be raised by one desperate expedient after

[6]H. C. Porter, *The Inconstant Savage: England and the North American Indian, 1500–1660* (1979).

another. Titles and offices were sold, so that in seventeenth-century Castile individuals and communities were able to purchase back privileges of which they had earlier been deprived, and society was thus re-feudalized. This is merely one instance of the strains imposed on early-modern Europe by overseas expansion. Another is the chronic shortage of ships and seamen as the oceans swallowed them more rapidly than the continent could produce them. Already in the early 1500s the Portuguese were using in their vessels Asians, African slaves and country bumpkins who needed some familiar vegetable lashed to the rigging to enable them to distinguish port from starboard. And when in 1636 England assembled a fleet, it was alleged of one vessel that virtually none of the 300 or so men on board knew how to steer; of another that apart from her officers she possessed hardly a seaman; and of yet another that no more than a third of her crew had ever been afloat before and that only a dozen were fit to take the helm.

With conquests and colonies there came into being, as is well-known, the first tentative global economy. American silver was exported to China; Asian spices shipped to Europe; English cloths sold in Africa; and lead stripped from the roofs of English abbeys during Henry VIII's Protestant Reformation ended as ballast in fleets sailing from Catholic Seville to the Spanish, and equally Catholic, Indies. By the early decades of the seventeenth century wine from the Canary Islands was being drunk in India; English settlers in Barbados had a notorious addiction to that of Portuguese Madeira; and the indigenous inhabitants of Spanish America would, it was said, 'sell their wives and children' for the white man's drink. More pleasingly, that lord of the world, Philip IV, ruler of the combined empires of Spain and Portugal, ordered that wild animals and birds from East Africa, Iran, Arabia and India – amongst them a female rhinoceros, Sri Lankan elephants and Cochin tigers – be sent to him 'as an ornament for my court'.[7]

Another consequence of this Great Age of Discovery was the birth of a new race of seamen, soldiers, bureaucrats and mission-

[7]A. da Silva Rego, 'The Monsoon Codices at the National Archives of the Torre do Tombo', in John Correia-Afonso (ed.), *Indo-Portuguese history: sources and problems* (Bombay, 1981), pp.68–9.

aries who had sailed every ocean or served in every land. That learned and well-travelled Jacobean, Sir Thomas Roe, was at various times ambassador to the Mogul Emperor ('The Great Mogul'), the Ottoman Sultan ('The Great Turk'), and the kings of Poland and Denmark, besides being a close friend of the Protestant hero, Gustav II Adolf of Sweden, and the Orthodox Patriarch of Alexandria. That remarkable English pilot, William Baffin, spent some of his seafaring life pursuing whales off Spitsbergen, was then employed to sail past the North Pole to Asia, eventually had command of an East Indiaman, and was finally killed in action in the Persian Gulf in 1622. But to have seen, enjoyed or endured so much – always assuming, that is, that one survived – did not necessarily entail any broadening of intellectual horizons. Castilian experience of the Americas persuaded a Spaniard holding high office under Philip II in the Habsburg possessions in Italy that his tiresome charges would be best brought to order by a whiff of true imperial government, and 'that although they are not Indians (they) have to be treated as such, so that they will understand that we are in charge of them . . .'.[8] Which is to say that empire did not stir the human mind to new ideas and new ways of thinking. But the voyages of exploration, and the subjugation of hitherto unknown lands produced, particularly in Iberia, a geographical literature of incomparable richness. Of this we have impressive testimony in the collections of Richard Hakluyt and Samuel Purchas, and in the publications of our Society. This literature was little regarded in its own day, and much perished as soon as it was born. But what survives, published or unpublished, is now recognized as invaluable to scholars working not only on European subjects, but on such questions as the history of Indian caste, Asian commerce, or African tribal society. And so is vindicated, though not quite in the way he meant it, the view of the great sixteenth-century Portuguese humanist and historian, João de Barros, that culture is the most enduring monument to empire. But now my time is spent, and there I must end.

[8]H. G. Koenigsberger, *The practice of Empire* (Ithaca, U S A, 1969), p.48.

EUROPEAN SEAFARING IN ASIA C.1500 - 1750

'No kinde of men ... passe their yeres in so great and continuall hazard ... and ... of so many so few grow to gray heires',

SO WROTE RICHARD HAKLUYT OF THE SEAMAN'S LOT IN 1598.[1] AND the longer the voyage and the more time spent in tropical waters, the greater the likelihood, it was well understood, of a speedy demise. It was also widely agreed that there were few more dangerous and arduous sea passages than that between Europe and Asia opened by the Portuguese at the end of the fifteenth century. For an unlucky ship the round trip could take as long as two years or more.[2] It entailed facing the unpredictable weather of the North Atlantic – a particularly formidable obstacle once the English and Dutch, and then the Scandinavians and Ostenders began to trade to the East. It meant risking all those shipboard and tropical diseases against which contemporary medicine had little or no remedy. And with the establishment of European footholds in Asia Westerners were drawn into further ventures in climates where, as the saying went, 'two monsoons are the age of a man'. Nevertheless the new maritime link between East and West endured and strengthened. Europeans not only survived in the Orient but many enjoyed a cosy imperial affluence there, like those Portuguese at Goa and Macao in the early seventeenth century much given to the delights of boating.[3]

---

1 E.G.R. Taylor (ed.), *The Original Writings and Correspondence of the two Richard Hakluyts*, 2 vols, (London, Hakluyt Society, 1935), II, p. 429.

2 Contributions by Vitorino Magalães Godinho, K.N. Chaudhuri, Ph. Haudrèe, Erik Gøbel, C. Koninckx, K. Degruse, J. Parmentier, F.S. Gaastra and J.R. Bruijn in Jaap R. Bruijn and Femme S. Gaastra (eds), *Ships, Sailors and Spices. East Endia Companies and their shipping in the 16th, 17th and 18th Centuries* (Amsterdam, 1993), pp. 12-13, 84, 193.

3 G.V. Scammell, 'European shipowning in the Estado da India, 1500-1700', *Indica*, 26 (1989), 119-34 at pp. 133-4. Reprinted in *Ships, Oceans and Empire. Studies in European maritime and colonial history, 1400-1750* (London, 1995).

How many Western seafarers there were in Asia at any given moment is difficult to say. Clearly, however, the numbers were, by contemporary standards significant, notwithstanding that the East employed far fewer European ships than the home and Atlantic trades. Nascent colonial powers sent out troops to defend or extend their possessions. There were sizeable contingents of passengers of one sort or another. Disproportionately large crews were needed to work clumsy and inefficient gear. Commanders, given the chance, embarked far more men than were required in the expectation (thus rendered self-fulfilling) of losses through disease. Hence the biggest Portuguese Indiamen of c.1600 might be carrying as many as 1200 men and women apiece when they left Lisbon, while Portuguese expeditions mounted in Asia to save some outpost of empire could include 12,000 or so fighting men of assorted race and religion. This was the equivalent of the population of a modest European town of the time; or put another way, of the complements of a half a dozen large Arab or Gujarati ships.[4]

By the early 1700s European Indiamen were on the whole smaller than the leviathans (1500 - 2000 tons) of Portugal's imperial heyday. Their crews were also smaller, especially those of Scandinavian and Ostend ships which, sailing in the service of owners whose aspirations were purely commercial, could make do with less manpower than the vessels of more ambitious rivals. Thus while the Dutch rate of manning (troops included) was on average twenty-three men per hundred tons in 1600-1750, some Ostenders could manage with just under nineteen in the early 1700s. However, if crews were smaller ships were more numerous, with Dutch sailings for the East rising from seventy-six in 1600-1610 to nearly three hundred in 1750-1760, and English from seventeen to one hundred and ninety-one in the same period.[5] Assuming that two thirds of those embarked survived the passage, this would have brought roughly 12,000 men to the East in English ships and another 53,000 or so in Dutch vessels in the decade after 1750 alone.[6] From among these were recruited not only crews for the homeward journey, but some of those seamen who, in various European footholds, provided commanders – precursors of a gallery of Conradian heroes and villains – and a few hands for craft working in the country trades. Others turned to the alluring prospects of piracy, like those Portuguese and Indo-Portuguese particularly active in and around the Bay of Bengal in the sixteenth and early seventeenth centuries. And by 1700 there was a flourishing community of buccaneers in Madagascar, 1400 of whom sought the protection of the Swedish crown in 1714, having, as they said 'amassed enormous riches'

---

4 *The Voyages of Francois Pyrard, of Laval, to the East Indies, the Maldives, the Moluccas and Brazil*, trans, and ed. by Albert Gray assisted by H.C.P. Bell (2 vols, London, 1887-1890), I, p. 258; II, Pt. 1, p. 186; G.V. Scammell, 'The pillars of empire. Indigenous assistance and the survival of the Estado da India c.1600-1700', *Modern Asian Studies*, 33, 3 (1988), pp.453-489, at p. 486. Reprinted in *Ships, Oceans and Empire*.

5 Bruijn (ed.), *Ships, Sailors and Spices*, pp. 107, 134, 143, 182, 198.

6 Bruijn, *op. cit*, p. 201.

and now wishing to retire.[7] Still others, often renegades, served in Asian-owned ships, usually as masters, pilots or gunners, while a handful became fully-fledged naval *condottieri*, like that erstwhile officer in an English Indiaman who, in the late 1600s, was commissioned by the Marathas to raise a squadron. There were also those Europeans who, usually from necessity, or like as not sheer desperation, took passage in local craft. Fr Jeronimo Lobo, fleeing from Ethiopia in 1634, made an amicable, if not pleasurable trip in a Muslim boat, followed by an uncomfortable crossing from Suakin to western India in a vessel carrying pilgrims returning from Mecca.[8]

Hence there was added to an already astonishingly polyglot and cosmopolitan seafaring community in Asian waters still further diversity. Among Europeans there were blue-blooded grandees, like the viceroys sent out to govern Portugal's empire. There were gentlemen, officials of the various East India companies, merchants of many nationalities, convicts, missionaries and even sightseers. There were officers on their way to or from colonial postings. There were soldiers, whether those half-dead and half-naked wretches seen embarking at Lisbon in 1629 or the burly Germans and Scandinavians the ever-prudent Dutch recruited to bear the heat of their battles.[9] There were Africans and Asians being brought, often unwillingly, westwards, or returning home. There were Asian merchants and pilgrims travelling in the comparative security of European ships. There were the slaves and retainers serving men of rank and wealth, like the Korean, Japanese and 'Mozambique Negro' who waited on the sixteenth-century globe-trotting Florentine merchant, Francesco Carletti. There were also women, and probably more than is usually assumed. Some were grand dames *en route* to join their husbands in the East, while others were ladies who intended to net themselves suitable spouses either in Asia or on the way there. There were less fortunate sisters shipped out to become the wives of rank and file Europeans. There were the prostitutes smuggled aboard, and in country ships there were the women of their Asian crews.[10]

The social and ethnic mix among seamen was equally rich. Until the eighteenth century Portuguese Indiamen were usually commanded by aristocrats

7 Charles Dawson, 'The Madagascar affair: A little-known Swedish project of colonisation', *The Mariner's Mirror*, 81, 2 (1995), pp. 210-12.

8 M.G. da Costa and C.F. Beckingham (eds), *The Itinerário of Jerónimo Lobo* (Hakluyt Society, 1984), pp. 281, 286-7; G.V. Scammell, 'European exiles, renegades and outlaws and the maritime economy of Asia c.1500-1750', *Modern Asian Studies*, 26, 4 (1992), pp.641-661, at p.649. Reprinted *Ships, Oceans and Empire*.

9 Anthony Disney, 'The world of long-distance voyaging in the seventeenth century: The Lisbon-Goa fleet of 1629 as a case study', in K.S. Mathew (ed.), *Studies in Maritime History* (Pondicherry, 1990), pp.143-158, at p. 148; C.R. Boxer, *The Dutch Seaborne Empire, 1600-1800* (London,1965), p. 80; Jan Lucassen, 'The Netherlands, the Dutch and long-distance migration in the late sixteenth to early nineteenth centuries', in Nicholas Canny (ed.), *Europeans on the Move. Studies on European Migration 1500-1800* (Oxford, 1994), pp. 169-73.

10 C.R. Boxer (ed.), *The Tragic History of the Sea 1589-1622* (Hakluyt Society, 1959), p. 20; Francesco Carletti, *My Voyage Around the World*, (ed. and trans.) Herbert Weinstock (London, 1965), p. 228; Scammell, 'Pillars of empire', p. 487.

or gentlemen, while English vessels were as a rule entrusted to members of a select body of captains who frequently achieved wealth, standing and rank. There were many artisans (carpenters, caulkers, coopers) since in long-distance voyages crews had to maintain as well as sail their ships. Not least there were musicians to bang and blast defiance at enemies, arouse the martial valour of colleagues and greet friends in suitable style. Their skills could, however, also be employed to enhance festive occasions, while in Portuguese Indiamen fifers blew by the hour to prevent the duty helmsmen from dozing off.

The greater part of the crew comprised the foremastmen who worked the ship. A nucleus would be from her country of origin, but the rest, in a calling always short of manpower – and hence always cosmopolitan – were recruited wherever they could be found. In Asia they might be deserters from other Western vessels. Some were hopefuls drawn by curiosity or desperation from much of Europe to ports like Lisbon or London. Rich and tolerant Holland attracted men from Germany and Scandinavia especially, together with many from England, Scotland and elsewhere. Force was commonly added to persuasion. In seventeenth-century Lisbon crews of Portuguese Indiamen were brought up to strength with criminals rounded up locally, or with English seamen shanghaied from Irish and English-owned brothels in the city. Meanwhile the Dutch – as indeed their rivals – would press men out of enemy ships if occasion offered. So, in one way or another crews of remarkably diverse origins were assembled. In some Ostend Indiamen of the early 1700s, for example, 4.5 per cent of the hands were English, 52 per cent French, 7.5 per cent Irish, 8 per cent Dutch, 4.9 per cent German, 14.3 per cent south European and 7.5 per cent Scandinavian.[11]

Such, however, was the growth in the volume of shipping in the early modern centuries, such the rate of loss of men, and such the extent of other European demands for labour, that what the home countries failed to provide had to be made good from the resources of the rest of mankind. And nowhere were these more suitable, abundant and accessible than in maritime Asia. Locals and Western pioneers alike quickly appreciated what could be done and before long Portuguese ships working to and from the East, and more especially in Asian waters, were manned in greater or lesser degree by Indians and Chinese; by pagan Africans; by assorted Christians (Indians, Japanese, Goan, Ethiopian, freed-black Brazilian), but above all by Muslims, reflecting the pre-eminence of Islam in much of the maritime economy of Asia. Such eclecticism had its problems, not least that self-styled paladins of Christendom could find themselves at sea in what were to all intents Muslim ships. There were outbursts of ethnic discord, just as there were European allegations of the general uselessness of native seamen. But necessity overcame, even if it never

---

11 L.M.E. Shaw, *Trade, Inquisition and the English Nation in Portugal 1650-1690* (Manchester, 1989), pp. 123ff; W. Foster (ed.), *The English Factories in India, 1618-1669* (13 vols, Oxford, 1906-27); Sir Charles Fawcett (ed.), *English Factories in India, 1670-1677, 1678-1684*, new ser. (4 vols, Oxford,1952-55). [Hereafter *Factories*]. *Factories, 1651-4*, p. 177; Bruijn (ed.), *Ships, Sailors and Spices*, p. 144.

eradicated jingoism. Portugal's policies were followed by others, with England eventually employing Indians in such numbers that the names of their sarangs crop up frequently in the records of the East India Company.[12]

For the rest, as in the Atlantic, crews could be made up with slaves, used spasmodically by the English (as in 1650) and systematically by the Portuguese, in whose homeland slavery had long been an integral part of the economy. Barely had they arrived in Asia than slaves were being employed afloat as well as ashore, so that, as one imperial proconsul ingenuously remarked, 'our men will not die from overwork'. In the end most of those used at sea were not Asians but the so-called 'Kaffirs' of East Africa, 'on whom', declared a Portuguese viceroy in 1728, 'we usually rely', together with fellow unfortunates from the west of the continent.[13]

When we turn to the lot of the seafarer it is clear that ships and those who sailed in them were at risk to a degree now hard to appreciate and imperfectly reflected in figures for craft lost, which take no account of hazards often overcome only at appalling human cost. Vessels were the victims of European wars in Asia. They were endangered by the clashes between monopoly companies and intruders into their preserves and by indigenous reaction to such conflicts. Even the biggest ships might be lost to pirates, as when in 1721 a Portuguese Indiaman bringing home an ex-viceroy and some of his impressive fruits of office was taken at Reunion. So, too, they might fall into the hands of local marauders or naval forces, with an English vessel, inopportunely becalmed, captured by Maratha rowing craft in 1735.[14]

Moreover, although European ships could now accomplish the arduous passage to and from the East, and undertake long and dangerous voyages there, they still had fundamental weaknesses of design, construction and performance. Masts and rigging failed, seams opened, hulls were weakened by marine borers, rudders fell off, anchors gave way. Furthermore, despite the undoubted accomplishments of many navigators, some of whom successfully made and remade the round trip to Asia and back for years, their art remained rudimentary.[15] There was, for example, no adequate way as yet of determining longitude, just as there was no shortage of pilots of lethal incompetence. Moreover, ships sailed in general ignorance of the weather they were likely to encounter. True, they might get some idea of what was coming from vessels they met on passage. As at all times, the prudent were able to gather from careful observation of natural phenomena some hint of what lay in store, while from an early date the seasonal pattern of eastern monsoons was understood.

12 Scammell, 'Pillars of empire', pp. 486-7; Bruijn, *op. cit.*, p. 68.

13 C.R. Boxer, 'The Carreira da India, 1650-1750', *The Mariner's Mirror*, 46, 1 (1960), pp. 35-54, at pp. 40-1.

14 C.R. Boxer, 'The Count of Ericeira and the pirates', *History Today*, XXIV (1974), pp. 854ff.

15 C.R. Boxer (ed.), *Further Selections from the Tragic History of the Sea*, 1559-1565 (Hakluyt Society, 1968), p. 43; cf. P(ublic) R(ecord) O(ffice, London), H(igh) C(ourt of) A(dmiralty), 13/85 (16 May 1716), fols 327ff.

And in the last resort there was the curious wisdom of the lore of the sea, with some mariners claiming that in oriental waters the likelihood of bad weather could be predicted from the behaviour of the ship's cockroaches: 'the more restless they are, the higher the wind'.[16] For the rest there were few instruments for most of our period capable of giving any indication of what might be expected, just as there was no equivalent of weather forecasting and even if there had been, no ways of transmitting its predictions, however fallible, to vessels at sea. Hence ships were regularly caught unawares by squalls or surprised by storms. Hence, too, the sense of human inadequacy in face of the fury of the elements. 'If you want to learn how to pray, go to sea', as the Portuguese said.[17]

To the blows inflicted by nature were added those dealt by human folly, ignorance and incompetence. Vessels were wrecked, involved in collisions or otherwise lost for no better reason that those in charge of them were drunk, asleep, or both.[18] Many went up in flames when their tarred gear, canvas sails and wooden hulls were ignited by hands who disregarded reiterated restrictions on smoking and lighting of fires. An English vessel was set ablaze off Surat in 1633 by the antics of her drunken master who then in panic cut the anchor cable, so allowing her to drift onto a sister, with the consequent loss of both.[19] Earlier a Dutch ship was burned out near Djakarta after some of her crew, 'which had beene at dice all night' – clearly at the liquor too – set fire to their arak.

Not surprisingly publicists, merchants and intending passengers anxiously debated with whom it was safest to travel. The general conclusion, supported by some patchy statistics, was that before about 1700 the Dutch (Europe's leading maritime nation) were probably the best bet, and after that date the English (who succeeded them in the role). Between 1500 and 1630 – after which their voyages to the East dwindled dramatically – the Portuguese lost from four per cent to twenty per cent of their outward bound Indiamen a decade, and from two per cent to forty-one per cent of those returning. In the early 1700s the rate for the Danes and Ostenders ranged from thirteen per cent to twenty-nine per cent of the vessels employed, just as in the same period the English East India Company was losing ten per cent of its tonnage annually. The Dutch, on the other hand, lost only two per cent to three per cent of their outward bound ships between 1692 and 1795.[20]

---

16 J.S. Cummins (ed. and trans.), The Travels and Controversies of Friar Domingo Navarrete, 161886, 2 vols, (Hakluyt Society, 1962), II, p. 356.

17 J. Wicki (ed.), *Documenta Indica* (18 vols, Rome, 1948-88), Vol VI, pp. 306.

18 PRO, HCA 13/85, fo. 17v.

19 M.L. Baumber, 'An East India captain: The early career of Captain Richard Swanley', *The Mariner's Mirror*, Vol. 55, no. 3 (1967), pp. 265-279, at pp. 271-2.

20 Bruijn (ed.), *Ships, Sailors and Spices*, pp. 7, 102, 156, 179.

But the survival of a vessel was not in itself any guarantee of a prosperous and peaceful voyage. Violence might erupt at any time among those on board, as Carletti tells of a passage from Japan to Macao. He and a number of Portuguese embarked (1598) in what was to all intents a Japanese ship, under a Luso-Japanese master, and with a Japanese crew. Trouble started when, in time-honoured fashion, one of the Portuguese kicked a Japanese and was thereby considered to have insulted the entire Japanese people. The vessel was left to her own devices as violence threatened, with the Japanese Christians allying with their unconverted compatriots against their non-Japanese co-religionaries. Carletti was rightly apprehensive as to the likely outcome of a pitched battle, and the day was only saved by the diplomatic skills of some Jesuits on board.[21]

More widespread was unrest among European crews, recruited almost exclusively from young men, who in their own continent were regarded as a class particularly given to 'Insurrections and Mutinies'. On the long passage to and from the East they were alternately exhausted by bouts of unremitting arduous labour, or bored to distraction by spells of dull routine and idleness. Tempers deteriorated among men crowded together, without privacy, and for months on end, in conditions barely tolerable even by the standards of the time. Matters were not improved by food which induced gastric disorders and consequent demoralisation and irritability. Passions were inflamed by drink which, particularly in Dutch and English ships, flowed freely, prohibitions notwithstanding. Nor were tempers cooled by the convention, as Francis Drake's celebrated words recall, that seamen toiled while their social superiors looked on. Trouble arose among bored and fractious hands from such age-old inflammatory pleasures as 'swearing, dice ... card-playing and filthy conmunication' [*sic*] to quote the terse summary of one English commander.[22] Not least, men were deprived of female company, yet often as not able to see passengers, or their own officers, in hot pursuit of those on board. The inevitable frustrations found outlets in sodomy – usually with young boys – in lurid, blasphemous and provocative language, in brawls and in the persecution of weaker colleagues.[23]

Meanwhile Catholic missionaries from different Orders, thrust willy-nilly into one another's company, became embroiled over the finer points of ascetic correctness. Passengers in a junk belonging to the English East India Company marooned their pilot in the Maldives in the 1640s. Drink-sodden, disease-ridden or overwrought commanders might have breakdowns, commit suicide or set about their crews. Lesser ranks fought among themselves, with the mate of an English Indiaman having the quarter master strung up in the rigging in 1728.[24]

21 Carletti, *Voyage*, pp. 136-8.

22 Cf. Celsus Kelly, OFM (ed.), *La Austrialia del Espíritu Santo*, 2 vols (Hakluyt Society,1966), Vol I, p. 140ff.

23 *Voyages of Pyrard*, Vol II, pp. 2, 396-7, 400.

24 J.H. Arrowsmith-Brown (ed.), *Prutky's Travels in Ethiopia and Other Countries* (Hakluyt Society, 1991), p. 435; Bruijn (ed.), *Ships Sailors and Spices*, p. 65; PRO, HCA 13/88, folios 115, 128, 223.

There were confrontations, to put it mildly, between merchants, officers, gentlemen and the rest. In Portuguese ships and fleets there was discord between aristocratic commanders of notorious individuality, and clashes in Dutch Indiamen between German soldiers and Netherlands seamen. Worst of all, in the desperate circumstances of storm and shipwreck discipline might go by the board, with crews endeavouring to save themselves regardless of the passengers, drinking, fighting and plundering the ship. There are indeed many stories of heroic attempts to save vessels and of amazing voyages to safety in open boats. But often enough morale collapsed and ships drove to destruction to the accompaniment not only of the roar of the sea and the howling of the wind, but also to a chorus of recriminations and of 'groans, shrieks, moans and prayers to God for mercy'.[25]

Nevertheless a fair percentage of vessels completed their voyages and seafaring life was something more than a re-enactment of primeval Hobbesian anarchy. Notwithstanding various blatant exceptions crews had an obvious interest in ensuring their ships stayed afloat. Moreover, they pursued their calling in ways determined by age-old custom and confirmed by the stabilising weight of tradition. Hands were divided into watches that worked the vessel turn and turn about. Specialists had clearly defined functions. The entire complement was consulted as to what was to be done in some crisis, when all on board were expected to turn to. Religious services were frequent, attendance at them compulsory, and exhortations to good living and dutiful behaviour the order of the day. In short, seamen were subjected to a disciplined, formalised and regular pattern of work so often assumed to have been an outcome of the Industrial Revolution. Untimely individualism and mutual mayhem were also in some degree restrained by a form of 'mateship', with all those in French Indiamen, for example, paired off and enjoined to aid one another 'like brothers'.[26] In most ships the keen and efficient were rewarded with bonuses, while defaulters were subjected to a discipline whose ferocity reflected the views of a society in which life was cheap, consciences rarely troubled by the infliction of humiliation or pain, and sailors regarded as barely human.

In Dutch ships, in which the regime was notoriously brutal, most of those convicted of murder, mutiny or sodomy were put to death and the rest sent to life-long hard labour on the ill-famed Robben island off the Cape of Good Hope. Any who wounded their fellows with a weapon had a hand pinned to a mast with a knife which they had to withdraw themselves to get free. Those who struck officers were keel-hauled (dragged under the ship from one side to the other) three times, while beatings with a rope's end were routine for other offences. The picture was much the same in other vessels and there are references galore to floggings; to men ducked from yard arms; to prisoners manacled and chained or left hanging in the rigging. In ships of all nations

---

25 Boxer (ed.), *The Tragic History of the Sea*, p. 58; *Voyages of Pyrard*, Vol I, p. 55ff; PRO, HCA 13/65, 30 July 1651.

26 *Voyages of Pyrard*, Vol II, pp. 2, 396.

sodomy brought fearful retribution, the Dutch tying offenders back to back and throwing them over the side.[27]

But despite, or more likely because of such draconian codes, men deserted so regularly that the English East India Company required crews to enter into bonds to stay with their ships; to little avail.[28] Life in the East might be short for Europeans, but it could be good while it lasted. There was the chance to throw off the restraints of Western custom. There was wealth to be had from trade. There were offices and riches on offer in native service, and not least there was piracy. No sooner had the English begun their brief stay in seventeenth-century Japan than there were complaints of men jumping ship to devote themselves to 'idleness' and similar vices.[29] Nor did those left on board, recruited from a society in which revolts and riots were frequent and often violent, suffer in silence. By the mid-1600s mutinies at sea were so common as to convince the apprehensive that some sailors were 'despisers of government', and that any disturbance was the prelude to a crew's seizure of their ship.[30] Friction was intensified as, with voyages longer and with vessels out of contact with their home ports for greater periods of time, the authority of commanders was radically strengthened, allowing them almost limitless opportunity for imperious and oppressive behaviour. And with an insatiable demand for manpower heightened by more ships working in worse climates, the selection of men became less rigorous.

The commonest causes of mutiny were specific grievances about brutal officers, demands for service beyond that expected and, especially, food or the lack of it. A crew's basic victuals comprised bread, biscuit, oil, water, wine (beer in Dutch and English ships), vinegar, together with low-grade salt meat and fish. These staples were supplemented in vessels of various nationalities with local products: onions, sugar and honey for the Portuguese; butter and bacon for the Dutch. In theory at least the Hollanders got three meals a day and meat two or three days a week, whereas in 1740 the unfortunate Portuguese were reduced to one meal a day.[31] Such a diet, lacking fresh fruit and vegetables, was as fine a recipe as any for digestive disorders: for the heartburn and constipation generally regarded as the inescapable accompaniments of seafaring. Worse still it was useless against scurvy, while heavily-salted

27 Boxer, *Dutch Seaborne Empire*, p. 71; *A Cruising Voyage round the World, Captain Woodes Rogers*, Introduction and Notes by G.E. Manwaring (London, 1928), p. 307; *Voyages to the East Indies. Christopher Fryke and Christopher Schweitzer*, with Introduction and Notes by C. Ernest Fayle (London, 1929), pp. 7ff, 113; *Factories, 1646-50*, pp. 193-4; *Factories, 1651-1654*, pp. 11, 77; PRO, HCA 13/85, fos. 17v, 213v.

28 *The Travels of the Abbé Carré in India and the Near East, 1672 to 1674*, translated by Lady Fawcett and edited by Sir Charles Fawcett with the assistance of Sir Richard Burn, 3 vols (Hakluyt Society, 1947-8), Vol III, p. 683; PRO, HCA 18/85, fos. 192. 242.

29 William Foster (ed.), *Letters Received by the East India Company from its servants in the East*, 1602-1617, 6 vols, (London, 1896-1902),Vol. IV, p. 55.

30 *Factories, 1661-1664*, p. 79; PRO, HCA 13/85, fo. 317v.

31 *Voyages ... Fryke and Schweitzer*, pp. 7ff, 176, 197-8; Bruijn (ed.), *Ships, Sailors and Spices*, p. 90; Boxer, *Dutch Seaborne Empire*, p. 83.

provisions aggravated perpetual thirst in the tropics. Nor did preparation do much for what was on offer. Portuguese Indiamen were still without specialist cooks in the seventeenth century. In many other ships the post went to some maimed veteran less as a tribute to his culinary skills than as a convenient and inexpensive recompense for past sufferings. Supplies were frequently insufficient since commanders economised on what was issued in order to profit from the sale of the surplus. They were also commonly of so poor a quality – through corruption and inefficiency – that they were rotten before a voyage had barely begun. Relief was provided from time to time by gifts from wealthy passengers of some of their own choice fare; by fresh food (which came to include such oriental produce as mangoes and coconuts) acquired in ports of call; and by fish and turtles caught at sea. There were efforts, only eventually efficacious, to understand and control scurvy. Lemon juice was carried by a pioneering English expedition to the East and limejuice was in large-scale use in English Indiamen by the early 1700s. The French attempted to emulate Chinese practice by growing vegetables on board, and by the beginning of the eighteenth century oranges, lemons, apples and potatoes appeared among standard rations.[32]

Poor and potentially lethal food was not all that seafarers had to endure. In the early centuries outward bound vessels (especially those of the Portuguese) were grossly overcrowded, just as many making the return voyages were dangerously overloaded. There was little space for passengers (other than the rich and influential) and less for seamen, who were housed in damp, confined, vermin-ridden and fetid quarters where what little air there was was rendered even fouler by the stench of sweat, sickness and disease. Clothing was usually unsuitable, and in such short supply that it often had to be worn damp and dirty, with the inevitable corollaries of aches, pains, fleas and lice – not that these were any novelty to Europeans. There was, as in the West in general, a reluctance to wash, and a willingness, allegedly most marked among Latins, to treat a ship as one great cesspool. The record of many voyages is hence a chronicle of death related in the forthright language of the day. Crews and passengers succumbed to 'ship fever', 'the bloody runs', 'the bloody flux' (typhus and dysentery) or to scurvy, dropsy, smallpox, various pulmonary conditions and those diseases (notably syphilis, cholera and malaria) contracted ashore. Besides which there was the toll from accidents. Men were killed or disabled by falls from aloft. Others ignominiously met their end by slipping from the 'seats of convenience' slung outboard for use as lavatories.[33]

Even by the standards of the time the death rate was staggering, maybe five to ten times as high as in mainland Europe. It might indeed be as low as one and a half per cent of the complement of an outward bound Portuguese

---

32 A. Jan Qaisar, 'From Port to Port; Life on Indian Ships in the Sixteenth and Seventeenth Centuries', in Ashin Das Gupta and M.N. Pearson (eds.), *India and Indian Ocean, 1500-1800* (Calcutta, 1987), pp. 331-49, at p. 342; Bruijn (ed.), *Ships, Sailors and Spices*, p. 203.

33 Bruijn, *op. cit.*, pp. 110ff.

ship, but it could equally be as high as fifty per cent. In French and Swedish Indiamen the average was perhaps between thirteen per cent and twenty per cent. It was a less awesome seven-eight per cent in Ostenders, while in eastward bound Dutch vessels it was as low as 6.7 per cent in the seventeenth century, rising to 7.3 per cent in the eighteenth.[34] But these fragile statistics disguise a reality bluntly depicted by an English commander in 1723: 'Our people fall down very fast of fevers and fluxes'. The paucity and ineffectiveness of medical services meant that sickness was generally synonymous with death. Orders for a Portuguese fleet of 1505 required all who became ill to be confessed and to make their wills directly. And in lengthy voyages there were few rituals more familiar than those for the burial of the dead at sea.[35]

But this is not the whole picture. Official records are in their very nature concerned with reports of, and investigations into disasters. Travellers' tales highlight alarums and excursions. Calm seas and prosperous voyages, on the other hand, elicit little comment, at least from passengers, other than complaints of boredom. True, for many the best day in any trip was that on which it ended. 'We were', wrote an eighteenth-century Franciscan on landing, 'like men reborn'. So, too, presumably were the crew of a Portuguese ship newly arrived in Japan c.1600 and depicted by a local artist as euphorically cavorting in the rigging.[36] Passengers could wash, eat decent food, and were at last freed from the perpetual motion of the ship. For many there was the chance to get on with private trade which was one of the prime attractions of sailing to or from Asia. Seamen and others could swarm into brothels, drink themselves into oblivion, or settle down to serious gaming. In the East this left them with little time or inclination to contemplate the surroundings in which they found themselves. Some were so indifferent that they never once set foot ashore in voyages lasting nearly three years. Many simply classified local peoples as reliable or otherwise.[37] Others reacted with rude vigour against what they considered undesirable native customs, like those English sailors who in late 1600s saved a young Indian girl from the flames of *sati*.[38] Some endured with barely contained impatience what they regarded as fatuous foreign conventions. Plenty conducted themselves in the time-honoured style of conquering heroes. At Mocha in the early 1600s the English fell to drinking, fighting all and sundry, chasing women and urinating on mosques. Yet even as such deeds were perpetrated there were those who explicitly acknowledged the merits of non-

---

34 Bruijn, *op. cit.*, pp. 42, 91, 111, 134, 147, 202; Boxer, 'Carreira da India', pp. 41. In the notoriously disease-ridden Levant of the seventeenth century the death rate for Western merchants was 5 per cent - 10 per cent according to Richard Grassby, *The English Gentleman in Trade: The Life and Works of Sir Dudley North, 1641-1691* (Oxford, 1994), p. 260 n. 17.

35 A.B. de Bragança Pereira (ed.), *Arquivo Português Oriental, Nova Edição*, 11 vols (Bastora-Goa, 1936-40), Vol 4.1.1, p. 55.

36 *Prutky's Travels*, p. 396; Japan, Kobe City Museum, Namban Screens.

37 *The Travels of Peter Mundy in Europe and Asia, 1608-1667*, (ed.) Sir Richard Carnac Temple, 5 vols, (Hakluyt Society, 1907-1936), Vol III (2), pp. 421-2; Baumber, 'An East Endia captain', p. 266.

38 *A Geographical Account of the Countries round the Bay of Bengal. 1669 to 1679, by Thomas Bowrey*, (ed.) Sir Richard Carnac Temple (Hakluyt Society, 1905), p. 40.

Europeans, while many more did so tacitly, deserting to serve Asian merchants or potentates, or acquiring Asian or Eurasian wives or mistresses.[39]

Clearly then, some seafarers were more than the 'baptized beasts' most of their contemporaries were wont to call them, and ships not merely floating dens of violence and iniquity. In vessels on lengthy passages duties were discharged within a framework of religious observance. There were prayers or services daily, during and after storms, at other times of crisis, and on completing some vital leg of a voyage. In Iberian ships there was also the preaching and teaching of any missionaries on board. True, the ideal might exceed the reality, with services conspicuous by their absence from the official record of some Portuguese voyages. Nor were pious exhortations necessarily gladly received by seamen, and Jesuits travelling in Portuguese Indiamen were well aware of the dangers that could arise from attempts to impost too strict a regime. Hence sailors might shirk their duties, drink, fight, swear and gamble on anything from the next day's weather to the outcome of a cockfight. But in a calling in which the rate of literacy was high – particularly in Protestant countries – some kept journals, some learned navigation and some read.[40] Their taste, predictably enough, was rarely for such edifying tracts as the *Holy Meditations* the English East India Company commissioned (1618) for its crews.

More to their liking were works condemned by the authorities as frivolous (chiefly romances of chivalry) or indecent (such as the tales of Boccaccio, which to the consternation of the pious, were the choice of some discriminating sixteenth-century Portuguese seamen). A happy (or hapless) minority might become involved with female passengers. Hours could be passed, and rations improved by fishing, and if sharks were taken they might be, as in some Portuguese ships, hauled on board, blinded, and used as mounts in mock bull fights. There was much singing of sea shanties, embellished with derogatory impromptus about unpopular officers. So, too, as had long been the case in Europe itself, there was much spinning of yarns, held by some connoisseurs to be every bit as good as the enormously popular *Arabian Nights Entertainments*.[41] And with prompting crews could be involved in more ambitious undertakings. Shakespeare's plays were put on from time to time in English ships. In 1688, under a tropical night sky, a drama was staged on the quarterdeck of a Portuguese Indiaman. Earlier, in South-East Africa, the shipwrecked Fr Lobo had been impressed by 'a comedy presented very beautifully by the (Portuguese) sailors', preceded though it was by the somewhat incongruous spectacle of a bull fight against cows.[42]

---

39 Samuel Purchas, *Hakluyt Posthumus, or Purchas His Pilgrimes*, Maclehose edition (29 vols, Glasgow, 1905-7), Vol. IV, p. 555; Boxer, *The Tragic History of the Sea*, p. 198.

40 Cummins (ed.), *Travels of Domingo Navarrete*, 1, 21 n. 2; Fawcett (ed.), *Travels of Abbé Carré*, Vol. III, p. 682.

41 *Doc. Indica*, Vols III, V, VI, XVI, *passim*; PRO, HCA 13/85, fo. 19v; Boxer, *Dutch Seaborne Empire*, p. 93; Bruijn (ed.), *Ships, Sailors and Spices*, pp. 89-90; Peter Burke, *Popular Culture in early modern Europe* (London, 1978), pp. 44-5.

42 Boxer, 'Carreira da India', p. 48; *Lobo, Itinerário*, p. 366.

There are occasional and intriguing glimpses of popular culture, like the election, at Whit, in Portuguese ships, of a boy emperor who ruled for a day and who was served in his brief moment of glory by those of the highest social rank on board: another manifestation of that widespread European urge to turn the world upside down, thereby satirising the social order. The inspiration for this ritualised letting off of steam was the injustice of the human lot, together with classical and biblical teaching on the transitory splendours of this life and the coming of a time when the exalted would be humbled and the humble exalted.[43] There were similar doings, 'in imitation of the Portuguese', in French Indiamen, and in all ships there were boisterous ceremonies on crossing the equator, when those who had not previously done so were – yet another parody of ecclesiastical ritual – 'baptized'. Or as an eighteenth-century Franciscan stiffly put it, the sailors fought, fell about and soaked one another with water.[44] Different roots are hinted for other beliefs and practices. Just as classical (and Hindu) seafarers performed rites to placate the sea, the crews of Iberian ships would endeavour to calm it by casting holy relics overboard. French sailors, threatened by a waterspout, held up swords in the form of a cross to deflect the approaching danger. Portuguese, and doubtless many other seamen, worshipped St Elmo's Fire as it flickered awesomely on the yards of their ships. Men refused to sail with those they considered Jonahs. Many were convinced that vessels in which sodomy occurred would be overwhelmed by divine wrath. And coming from a popular culture in which misogyny was strong, many were uneasy about taking women to sea, to whose presence (and the 'deadly sins' it could occasion) foul weather was attributed.[45]

To some extent such views were shared by officers and well-heeled passengers. But this was about all they had in common with their fellow voyagers. In most vessels they had their own cabins and were waited on by their own servants – one English captain even had his own tailor with him – while in some ships they were accompanied by their own slaves and prostitutes. If all went well, which was by no means unknown, a voyage could be an enjoyable experience, inspiring in some a measure of that affection all true seafarers have for their ships.[46] Passengers could chat, debate, gamble, reflect and read – as did on a heroic scale the celebrated Sir Thomas Roe, like the equally celebrated Macaulay after him. They might write journals – hence the invaluable collection of Jesuit narratives – learn oriental languages, compile dictionaries, engage in amours or visit persons and places of interest on route. Meanwhile officers, and in Protestant vessels the chaplains too, collected and

---

43 *Doc. Indica*, Vol. V, p. 366-7; Vol. XII, p. 881; Stuart Clark, 'Inversion, misrule and the meaning of witchcraft', *Past & Present*, 87 (1980), pp. 98-127.

44 *Voyages of Pyrard*, Vol. I, p.19; *Prutky's Travels*, p. 434.

45 *Voyages of Pyrard*, Vol. I, p. 11; Boxer (ed.), *Further Selections from the Tragic History of the Sea*, p.46; *Factories, 1635-6*, p. 310-11; *Prutky's Travels*, pp. 424-5; G.V. Scammell, European seamanship in the Great Age of Discovery', *The Mariner's Mirror*, Vol. 68, no. 4 (1982), pp. 357-376, at pp. 373-4, reprinted in *Ships, Oceans and Empire*. See also the remarks of Guido Rugiero, *The Boundaries of Eros. Sex, Crime and Sexuality in Renaissance Venice* (Oxford, 1985).

46 PRO, HCA 13/85, fo. 317; Boxer (ed.), *The Tragic History of the Sea*, p. 20; *Lobo, Itinerário*, p. 348.

recorded navigational information. This same élite could live extremely well. Not for them old salt fish and rotting meat, but select cuts from livestock carried in the ship – and replenished on passage – slaughtered as required, and served to the affluent and influential on silver plate specially embarked for the purpose. And such repasts were rounded off with candied fruits, preserves and other delicacies and accompanied by choice wines. High living at the captain's table became proverbial, especially once the commanders of English Indiamen sought to establish for their vessels a reputation which would attract the richest homeward bound passengers and with any luck secure a fortune for themselves.[47]

Voyages were further enlivened by what the Abbé Carré described in 1673 as the 'entertainments' offered by the officers of one ship to those of others, and which might include ('the most attractive dish') a romp with the 'lovely ladies' on board, and all prudently screened from prying eyes. And there could be still better things to come. In many Eastern ports the locals greased the wheels of commerce by receiving Western notables in regal style, showering them with gifts and entertaining them to gargantuan feasts – like that at Mocha in the early 1600s when the aperitifs were so lavish that the English mistook them for the meal itself.[48] Furthermore, as was appreciatively recorded, such hospitality commonly extended to the provision of women, and not just prostitutes such as could be found in the brothels of any European seaport, but the daughters of men of rank. Above all there were the boundless opportunities for lucrative private trade, universally plied so openly and vigorously that, as royal and private monopolists alike bemoaned, their officers were hardly to be distinguished from merchants and bankers, not to say usurers.[49]

A very similar picture could be painted of Western seafaring in other distant waters. We can see at what cost, and with what imperfect means Europe penetrated the oceans of the world. We have a remarkable insight into some less familiar aspects of the continent's popular culture revealed by the crises and stresses of this endeavour. In the process of expansion there was a modest European acceptance of local technology, most notably the incorporation, following Chinese practice, of the stern gallery into the design of ships. There was a general willingness to employ local vessels; an inescapable need to use local seamen; and an avid Asian acceptance of European maritime techniques. There was the usual inter-racial tension and violence, paradoxically accompanied by pragmatic tolerance and even friendship. Not least there was the unambiguous message that for Europeans with the will, means and luck life in the East if short could none the less be good. For the rest it was only marginally worse than had they stayed at home.

---

47 *Travels of Peter Mundy*, Vol. III, pp.1, 17; *Prutky's Travels*, p.427; Boxer, *Dutch Seaborne Empire*, p. 84.

48 Fawcett (ed.), *Travels of Abbé Carré*, Vol. III, p. 685; *Prutky's Travels*, p. 376.

49 William Dampier, *A New Voyage Round the World*, with an Introduction by Sir Albert Gray (London, 1937), pp.268-9; *Factories, 1646-50*, pp. 289-90.

X

England, Portugal and the Estado da India c. 1500–1635

IN January 1635 there arrived in Goa a delegation from the English East India Company. The affluent air and dignified behaviour of its members, not to mention the obviously well-gunned and well-equipped ships that had brought them, greatly impressed the Portuguese, according to the then viceroy, the redoubtable Conde de Linhares. After the solution of the usual niceties of protocol, and after the viceroy had expatiated on the iniquities of England's erstwhile allies, the Dutch, a truce was agreed. So ended something like half a century of war at sea as the English had pushed—and surprisingly slowly, considering their reputation in Europe—into Portugal's Asian preserves. The peace did not, as Linhares had hoped, lead to the downfall of the Dutch, who went on to inflict grievous blows on Portugal in east and west alike. Nor did it establish England and Portugal as '*senores de tudo*'.[1] Nevertheless it opened an era of generally amicable relations between the two countries in Asia, and so forms a convenient point from which to survey their previous history, and to indicate what may be learned from English sources as to the condition and affairs of the *Estado da India.*

In the early search for a maritime route to the east, England had taken an active, though not particularly rewarding role. Whilst da Gama's epic voyage opened a way by the Cape, and whilst Columbus found a New World, the English-backed Cabots attempted to reach China by sailing north-westwards through polar waters. A superabundance of cod there might be in such regions, but of 'the country of the Grand Khan' there was no sign. Under Henry VIII (1509–47) there were some further desultory searches, and then enthusiasm waned. All the English had found was the inhospitable coast of north-east America, notably lacking

[1] *Diário do Terceiro Conde de Linhares, Vice-rei da India* (Lisbon: Biblioteca Nacional, 1937–43), pp. 264, 266–7. For an excellent survey of the events of these years see A. R. Disney, *Twilight of the Pepper Empire: Portuguese Trade in Southwest India in the Early Seventeenth Century* (Harvard University Press, 1978).

in gold, silver or the legendary riches of Asia. Even so, the spendthrift king was sufficiently impressed by reports of the wealth flowing to Portugal from the east to request (though without success) in 1541 that he might send out a man with the India fleet.

Information of this sort could reach England by a number of ways. Henry's ambassador in Rome saw there (1514) the exotic plunder and tribute—silks, jewels, gold, a splendidly-accoutred Persian horse and an even more impressively-bedecked Indian elephant—displayed by a Portuguese embassy.[2] In the early 1500s Antwerp, the centre for the redistribution of Portuguese spices in northern Europe, was also the focus of most of England's overseas trade. At this time, too, and as before and after, there were Portuguese merchants in England and English merchants in Portugal. Henry himself employed Portuguese shipwrights; Portuguese ships were sold to English owners.[3] Around 1500 there were joint Anglo-Portuguese expeditions into the North Atlantic, and thereafter, and whatever the Portuguese crown might say, Portuguese pilots fled, or were attracted to England. Furthermore, to such information as might be gathered through these comparatively peaceful contacts, there was soon added that acquired by force. Tudor clashes with France in mid-century loosed a horde of English pirates and privateers against shipping in the Channel. Before long their attention had turned to that of the Portuguese working to and from Antwerp, producing, as was complained in Lisbon, a state of affairs 'worse than open war'. Thus, and intriguingly, we hear of the capture of a carvel (1549), from which, amongst other things, the English removed 'a navigation chart'.[4]

But not all knowledge of the *Estado* and its commerce in England in these years was second-hand. A report from Portugal (1537) to the emperor Charles V, dealing with matters of the east, mentions 'the Englishman who went thither some time ago'.[5] In 1555 a group of London merchants, probably with Antwerp connections, are to be found insuring a cargo coming from Portuguese India to the west.[6] And when in 1582 an English expedition to Asia was in preparation, amongst

[2] António Alberto Banha de Andrade, *Mundos Novos do Mundo* (Lisbon, 2 vols, 1972), II, 661–2.

[3] G. V. Scammell, 'Shipowning in England *c.* 1450–1550', *Transactions of the Royal Historical Society*, 12 (1962), 105 ff, at p. 107.

[4] *C(alendar of) S(tate) P(apers) Sp(anish), 1547–49* (London, Public Record Office Texts and Calendars), p. 352.

[5] *CSPSp*, 1536–8, no. 144.

[6] R. G. Marsden (ed.), *Select Pleas in the Court of Admiralty* (London: Selden Society, 2 vols, 1894–97), II, 49–50.

its members, the Spanish ambassador in London alleged, were 'six men who . . . have already been in the Moluccas, and . . . lived . . . eight years in the Portuguese Indies'.[7] Indeed by the reign of Elizabeth I there were those amongst her subjects who felt themselves well qualified to pronounce on the affairs of the *Estado*. In 1571, when the two kingdoms were on particularly bad terms, the community of English merchants trading to Portugal urged their government that commerce with the Lusitanian state was of far greater value to England than that with the Far East—'often attempted . . . [but of] small effect'—from which nobody had made any money in the past decade and a half. It was therefore plain that an understanding should be reached with Portugal. England would promise to leave the Orient alone and in exchange would be allowed to do business in Portugal itself.[8]

Such views were not, however, to prevail. Bad for most of the sixteenth century, Anglo-Portuguese relations once again deteriorated after a short-lived improvement in the early 1570s. The English had their eye on Portuguese West Africa. Worse still, they came to regard Portugal as the client of their arch-enemy Spain, by whom the kingdom and its possessions were annexed in 1580, and under whose rule they were to remain till 1640. True, Philip II confirmed the privileges of English merchants in Portugal (1584), and they were not (in theory) expelled from Lisbon until five years later. But from the 1570s onwards, and especially after the Habsburg seizure (1585) of English shipping in Spanish ports, Portuguese vessels were considered fair game in England's privateering war against Spain which lasted until Elizabeth's death (1603). Sometimes cargoes of obviously oriental origin—precious stones, textiles, spices—were taken in craft re-exporting them from Lisbon. Indeed by the end of the century such hauls, combined with the East India Company's own imports, left the English with more pepper than they could sell.[9] But appetites were whetted for the far more tempting prize that the ships of the *Carreira* (the sea voyage, via the Cape of Good Hope, from Portugal to India and back) offered in western waters. The first to be taken (1587), and the first Indiaman lost in action, was the carrack *São Felipe*. The English thought her cargo to be worth £100,000—equivalent in value, that is, to about 10 per cent of their country's annual imports at the time—and the capture, according

[7] *CSPSp, 1580–86*, p. 340.

[8] M. Oppenheim, *A History of the Administration of the Royal Navy and of Merchant Shipping in relation to the Navy from 1509 to 1660* (London, 1896), p. 170.

[9] Sir William Foster, *England's Quest of Eastern Trade* (London, 1933), p. 161, and for the war at sea, Kenneth R. Andrews, *Elizabethan Privateering: English Privateering during the Spanish War, 1585–1603* (Cambridge, 1964).

to the Tudor protagonist of empire, Richard Hakluyt, persuaded his compatriots that the great *naos* were not impregnable, and opened their eyes to the true scale of Asian wealth and Portuguese weakness.[10] Maybe, but it was five years before anything similar was accomplished. Then (1592) a loosely-allied squadron of English ships forced the *Santa Cruz* ashore in the Azores, their crews making off with such goods as the Portuguese failed to remove from her burnt-out hull. They also took her purser and two foreign gunners who, under the threat of torture, revealed that there were other carracks in the offing. So it was that after a fierce struggle the *Madre de Deus* was captured. Her astounding lading of jewels, spices and silks was worth perhaps £500,000, or in other words as much as half of England's annual imports. But so thoroughly was she ransacked by the seamen who took her, now completely out of hand, that by the time she reached England all that remained of her cargo to be divided amongst the backers of the expedition was a mere £140,000.[11]

The coup was never repeated. True, in 1602 the *São Vallentim* fell into the hands of William Monson and his associates. In her they found a mass of calicoes (over 27,000 'bookes' alone) and a fine range of carpets, hangings and canopies. But since many were 'rotten and unserviceable', and since there was little spice the net profit, further eroded by corruption, was no more than £30,000.[12] For the rest, a carrack was burned in the Azores (1597), and the departure of the India fleet from the Tagus prevented the following year. In 1594 ships of the privateering magnate, George Clifford, earl of Cumberland, sank the *Cinco Chagas*, alleged to have been carrying the richest cargo ever sent home from the east. But after the pounding they had received they refused to engage her consort.[13] Whatever the confident assertions of diplomats and men of letters as to Portugal's maritime decline, the view of English seamen was that it needed a whole flotilla to take on a carrack, even as she struggled home on the last leg of the world's most arduous voyage. Hence the prominence in such actions as there were of the vessels of the earl of Cumberland—not a professional sailor, but an amateur, and in the end an impoverished one. And hence, too, eastern cargoes account for only about 10 per cent of the total value of the price goods acquired

[10] Richard Hakluyt, *The Principal Navigations* (Glasgow: Maclehose edn, 12 vols, 1903–05), VI, 443; Andrews, *Elizabethan Privateering*, p. 94.

[11] Andrews, *Elizabethan Privateering*, pp. 73, 128, 132.

[12] M. Oppenheim (ed.), *The Naval Tracts of Sir William Monson* (London: Navy Records Society, 5 vols, 1902–14), II, 341ff.

[13] Hakluyt, VII, 118ff; C. R. Boxer and Frazão de Vasconcellos, *André Furtado de Mendonça, 1558–1610* (Lisbon, 1955), p. 37; Andrews, *Elizabethan Privateering*, p. 219.

by the English in the course of their privateering war against the Hispano-Portuguese empires.[14]

But war meant not only loot, but the capture of information or of those who, like the purser of the *Santa Cruz*, could provide it. In the *Madre de Deus* the English found correspondence, maps, an account of China and its riches, and what was described as 'the Portuguese register of the East Indies', all of which, as was said at the time, revealed 'secret trades' previously 'strangely hidden and cunningly concealed'. From the *São Vallentim* they subsequently removed letters (dating 1600–01), detailing, amongst other things, happenings in Malacca and Cochin—including the rate of inflation—and reporting, ironically enough, the view of the viceroy's own commercial agent on the profits that would accrue from a trade with Zealand. Within a short time this material was translated into English for the benefit of the London East India merchants.[15]

Nor were these the only channels through which knowledge of the *Estado* was now flowing into England. When, in 1608, the English first arrived in Surat they found there a fellow-countryman who 'had long lived amongst the Portugals', and from whom they learned of recent Portuguese reverses at Malacca.[16] Shortly after, one William Carmichael appeared in England. He had, he said, a wife and family in Goa. He claimed to have been in Portuguese service for about 30 years, to know China, and to be ready to reveal all concerning the 'forts, ports and creeks' of the *Estado*.[17] In addition there were one or two English-born ecclesiasts in Portuguese Asia, though they seem to have had little or no contact with their mother-country. Not so a number of English prisoners in Iberian hands. William Monson himself, the future captor of the *São Vallentim*—and incidentally a future pensioner of Spain—was taken in 1591 and held for a time in Lisbon. From there he managed to communicate, through English intelligence agents, with his compatriots, suggesting where the incoming ships of the *Carreira* might be intercepted, and reporting (1592) that those that had left Goa on January 12 were carrying over 34,000 quintals of pepper and more than 900 packs of linen cloth.[18] Then by the early 1600s some of the English

[14] Andrews, *Elizabethan Privateering*, p. 132.

[15] D. B. Quinn (ed.), *The Hakluyt Handbook* (London: Hakluyt Society, 2 vols, 1974), I, 211, 305; *C(alendar of) S(tate) P(apers) Col(onial, East Indies, China and Japan)*, II, 1513–1616 (London; Public Record Office Texts and Calendars), nos 275, 283.

[16] Samuel Purchas, *Hakluyt Posthumus, or Purchas His Pilgrimes* (Glasgow, Maclehose edn, 20 vols, 1905–07), IV, 21.

[17] *CSPCol, 1513–1616*, no. 980.

[18] *Naval Tracts of . . . William Monson*, II, 376–8.

newly-arrived in Asia, and who had there either deserted to the Portuguese or been captured by them, were making their way back to their fellows, as did John Alkin, returning in 1613 with news of the assaults on the *Estado* by the 'Decannes and other Moores'.[19]

Furthermore, even during the worst years of the open war that followed Spain's annexation of Portugal, English merchants traded to the kingdom and to its overseas possessions, including on occasions—and before the foundation of the English East India Company (1600)—those in Asia. Such behaviour was not of course unusual, high ideals rarely being found good for business. So in difficult times men of enterprise passed themselves off as acceptable neutrals, conducted their commerce through acceptable partners, and shipped their cargoes in ostensibly neutral vessels. Amongst the English living in, or trading to, Portugal *c.* 1600, and whose activities included the provision of food, textiles and munitions, were some from west-country ports, Francis Drake's own Plymouth amongst them. But the majority were Londoners, such as those veteran Iberian traders and agents of English espionage, William Holliday and William Resould.[20] Some were also naturalized Portuguese *marranos*, in evidence from time to time (as were Richard May and Benjamin Ames) in ventures to Brazil, or engaged in the redistribution of oriental produce in the capital.[21]

The doings of this community are of particular concern to us. Its members were 'New Christians', that is Jewish converts to Catholicism. Some were descendants of those who, in the later Middle Ages, had been expelled from, or had found it advisable to leave, Iberia. Often the victims of this diaspora were merchants, and often they reverted to Judaism. Settled in eastern Europe, North Africa and the Levant they traded with their fellow Jews in western India, importing oriental goods by the age-old ways. The Portuguese opening of a maritime route to Asia, the rise of Antwerp as northern Europe's greatest entrepôt (and centre for the marketing of Portuguese spices there), and renewed persecution in Iberia brought an influx of New Christians to the Low Countries. And by the reign of Henry VIII there were some in England selling spices. As the Spanish hold on the Netherlands tightened, and as

[19] Raymundo António de Bulhão Pato (ed.), *Documentos Remettidos da India ou Livros das Monções* (Lisbon, 5 vols, 1880–1935), III, 82; Purchas, IV, 166.

[20] London, P(ublic) R(ecord) O(ffice), HCA 13/23, fos 198–198v; 13/24, fos 208–208v.

[21] PRO, HCA 13/25, fos 300ff; *CSPSp, 1587–1603*, p. 222; Lucien Wolf, 'Jews in Elizabethan England', *Transactions of the Jewish Historical Society of England*, xii (1924–27), 1ff; H. Kellenbenz, *Unternehmerkräfte in Hamburger Portugal–und Spanienhandel 1590–1625* (Hamburg, 1954).

Spanish repression there intensified, *marranos* were increasingly attracted to an England now irrevocably Protestant, where they found natural allies in the intransigent Puritans to whom Catholic Spain was the root of all evil. Already in the 1560s they were, according to the Spanish ambassador at Elizabeth's court, encouraging the English to attack 'a very rich part of the Portuguese Indies', just as in the ensuing decade they urged them to support Dom Antonio, the pretender to the Portuguese throne after Sebastian's death, and the only hope of averting Spanish rule.[22]

Similarly in English eyes the New Christians had many virtues, or at least many uses. Expert businessmen, fluent in the tongues of Iberia, bitterly hostile to Spain, and with friends and relatives scattered through most of the major centres of commerce and finance—the Low Countries especially—they were the ideal agents of English espionage in Spain and Portugal during the wars of the last years of Elizabeth's reign. There were about a dozen in her service, carrying on, so the officials of Philip II complained, a correspondence 'with persons in Portugal, Flanders and elsewhere' to the detriment of their master.[23] The operations of these spies were conveniently combined with, or to some extent disguised by, trade. In the 1590s they and their English counterparts regularly went to Iberia under royal licence, usually in allegedly neutral vessels, and sometimes equipped with Habsburg safe-conducts. From Lisbon, under the guise of loading, as Portuguese merchants, some innocuous cargo, like salt or fruit, they despatched to England—though without any incriminating bills of lading—spices, bullion, dyes and coded letters.[24]

In London this intelligence, together with many of the cargoes, was delivered to Hector Nuñez. This Evora-born doctor, English since 1579—though he could still refer to Portugal as 'my country' three years later—became physician to Elizabeth herself, and lived in some style with his devoutly Jewish wife. In 1590, the year before his death there were rumours that his loyalties had not been undivided—no rarity in the realms of spying—and he does in fact seem to have been in contact with Spanish espionage in the end.[25] All the same he enjoyed the complete

[22] *CSPSp, 1558–67*, pp. 666–7. And for what follows, Wolf, 'Jews in Elizabethan England'.

[23] *CSPSp, 1587–1603*, p. 326.

[24] *CSPSp, 1587–1603*, 221; C(alendar of) S(tate) P(apers) Fo(reign), July 1577–May 1578 (London, Public Record Office Texts and Calendars), no. 17.

[25] *C(alendar of) S(tate) P(apers) D(omestic), 1581–90* (London, Public Record Office Texts and Calendars), no. 48; *CSPFo, May–December 1582*, no. 240; *CSPFo, July 1590–May 1591*, no. 694.

confidence of the English government, and not surprisingly if, as was alleged, it was he who had alerted them to the intentions of the Armada. Over the years he brought his adopted homeland a steady supply of information from Flanders and Iberia, practised medicine—his enemas moving some of the mightiest in the realm—and grew rich in trade. In 1571 he was contemplating a venture to Portuguese West Africa. The next two decades saw him dealing in anything from Caribbean hides and African ivory to Spanish wool and English cloth, and contemplating in the very year of the Armada some enterprize in Brazil. He traded to Portugal from at least 1568, and by the 1580s had interests in Iberia reaching from Seville to Lisbon. His associates included magnates of European high finance and fellow New Christians, and the scale of his undertakings may be gathered from references to the despatch of six vessels to the peninsula in 1587 alone and to his goods and debts there valued at £1,400.[26]

But these were not the limits of his dealings. In 1585 he had £300 of cargo coming from India to Lisbon in a ship of the *Carreira*, and destined to his brother.[27] Two years later he was engaged in something similar, writing to the English government about the incoming *naos*—by no means the first time they had received such information.[28] The only arrivals, he announced, were the *St Thomas* and her consort 'called *oure Ladie*'. Of the ladings of both he gives lengthy and precise details. Amongst other things the former was carrying over 30,000 quintals of pepper together with 683 of cinnamon and 198 chests of 'callacout cloth' and silk; the latter had on board 20,000 odd quintals of pepper in addition to 257 of cinnamon and 323 ounces of pearls. And this, he concluded, was all that was expected this year (1587). That being so the price of pepper, cloves and mace had risen by 25 per cent in Lisbon. In Antwerp pepper was up by nearly 100 per cent, and in Hamburg by 20 per cent. The queen, he concluded, would be well advised to hold on to the spice she had got from the *São Felipe*, since it would now rise in value 'to a grete reckninge'. And he himself had an interest in this same ship, taken by Francis Drake. One 'Lewis Farnandis' of Antwerp—'an honeste man'—had had in her six chests of silks and two of 'Calicut cloth', directed by his factor in Asia to his agent in Lisbon. These were now in English hands, and Nuñez—possibly a partner of Fernandes—

[26] J. W. Blake, *European Beginnings in West Africa 1454–1578* (London, 1937), p. 188; *CSPSp, 1587–1603*, pp. 222, 253; *CSPD, 1591–94*, pp. 359, 556; *CSPFo, July 1577–May 1578*, no. 560(4); *CSPFo, August 1584–August 1585*, p. 712; PRO, HCA 13/25, fos 281, 291v; Wolf, 'Jews in Elizabethan England'.

[27] PRO, HCA 13/25, fos 275, 291.

[28] *CSPCol, 1513–1616*, no. 157.

requested that they might be 'presed with sume fauvor' (i.e. that not to high a price be put on them), and that he be allowed to redeem them.[29]

Amongst the many Nuñez agents in Europe was a group of particular importance in Lisbon, including his brother Pero Freyle, his brother-in-law Bernardo de Luis, and another relative Jeronimo Pardo. By 1588 Pardo's involvement in the shipment of spices, bullion and dyes to England was well known to Philip's government, as were the apparently more extensive dealings of Luis, and according to an informant in London the pair, who travelled regularly between England and Iberia, were the traitors who 'have sold Spain'. Luis, like Nuñez, traded from Portugal to India (in 1585, for instance), and three years later he is described as yet once more engaged in importing oriental goods into London, working in association with such fellow New Christians as Richard May. Arrested and interrogated by the Spaniards in 1588—they had warned him to keep clear of England the previous year—he admitted all this, and admitted, too, how he transmitted information to London via Paris and Rouen. In mitigation he pleaded that he had secured the release of captured Portuguese cargoes in England, and achieved much else of benefit. But it was not merely his ingenuity and plausibility that saved his neck, for about this time he became, though not for long, a double agent. Denounced on the one hand for his friendship with English merchants in Lisbon, and on the other as one of Spain's ablest spies in England, he suddenly, and not surprisingly, disappeared in the early 1590s.[30]

The death of Nuñez (1591), and the break-up of his circle by no means ended the flow of information to England. The government heard (1602) of the ladings of two ships just in from India, and knew in the following year of the arrival of four more. More remarkably still they had in 1604 a correspondent in Goa, by whom they were told—presumably via Lisbon—of Portuguese weakness in the east.[31] Just how this communication was maintained is uncertain. But of the possibilities we have a tantalizing glimpse. The Iberian peninsula was chronically short of grain by the late 1500s, and one of its regular suppliers was eastern England. Dr Nuñez himself and some of his associates dealt with various local squires and merchants engaged in the trade, pre-eminent amongst whom was Francis Shaxton, chiefly celebrated for his rise to wealth and honour on the proceeds of smuggling impressive even by the standards of

[29] London, PRO, SP 12/204, fos 60–2.

[30] PRO, HCA 13/25, fos 275, 280v–281; 13/28, fo. 131v; SP 12/204, fo. 60; *CSPSp. 1587–1603*, pp. 221–2, 601.

[31] *CSPCol, 1513–1616*, nos 309, 327, 337.

the age. By the 1580s he was a well-established Lisbon trader, and half-owner of a ship which passed herself off as the *Green Dragon* of Hamburg.[32] She was used from time to time by Freyle, Pardo and Nuñez, and significantly enough when in 1592 William Monson, imprisoned in Lisbon, wrote to England, it was the *Green Dragon* that was to carry his letters.[33]

One way and another, therefore, there were some Englishmen well-informed about the *Estado* by the end of Elizabeth's reign. And for the wider reading public there was the material—admittedly scrappy—assembled by Richard Hakluyt (*Principall Navigations*, 1589; *Principal Navigations*, 1598–1600), and soon amplified by the labours of his successor, Samuel Purchas (*Purchas, his Pilgrimage*, 1613; *Purchas, his Pilgrimes*, 1625). But in any case there was by now an influential group in England who saw Asia in general, and the *Estado* in particular as potential sources of enormous wealth. In 1580 Francis Drake, the arch-privateer and the arch-protagonist of a Protestant maritime onslaught on Catholic Iberia, returned loaded with booty from his epic circumnavigation of the world. In the course of his triumphant progress he had secured a cargo of cloves in Ternate, and demonstrated to those who shared his convictions that the Pacific was open to England and that the claims of Portugal in the east could be ignored. A plethora of grand schemes was concocted, but nothing of consequence accomplished until the arrival of the Dutch in Asia precipitated the foundation of the English East India Company, granted (1600) a 15-year monopoly of commerce 'beyond the Cape of Good Hope and the Strait of Magellan'.

In the establishment of the company, and in its early years a vital role was taken by those experienced in, and enriched by, Atlantic privateering. They provided about 25 per cent of the initial capital, large and powerful ships perfected in the course of operations in the west, and many of the officers to command them. Hence though directors at home might forbid their captains to attack the subjects of any Christian power, and whilst the inept monarchs of the new Stuart dynasty attempted to pursue a policy of peace and reconciliation with Spain, the company's commanders in the east vigorously set about the shipping of the *Estado*, with Thomas Best calling for the general issue of letters of marque in the

[32] HCA 13/25, fos 53–56v, 75v; 13/28, fos 132v, 149–149v; N. J. Williams, 'Francis Shaxton and the Elizabethan Port Books', *The English Historical Review*, lxvi (1951), 387ff.

[33] HCA 13/28, fos 131vff; *Naval Tracts of . . . William Monson*, II, 376.

good old way.[34] In 1602 Captain Lancaster, a veteran of the Atlantic wars, and commander of an earlier and disastrous expedition to the east, took, in conjunction with the Dutch, a 900-ton Portuguese craft sailing from Bengal to Malacca, laden with 950 packs of calicoes and *pintados*.[35] Thereafter there are mentions of pitched battles, skirmishes and the capture of prizes anywhere from Macao to Mozambique. So intense was this onslaught that a visitor to Morocco in the early 1600s there encountered the son of a Portuguese viceroy of India held prisoner for 16 years since his ransom had never arrived from Asia, having been twice taken by the English and once by the Dutch.[36] But whatever else these actions demonstrate, they throw an invaluable light on the nature of the commerce moving along the maritime arteries of Portugal's Asian empire. Off Dabul (western India), for instance, in 1611, the English seized a 300-ton ship bound for Chaul, laden with dried coconuts, tin, sugar, porcelain, alum and coir, together with a 60-ton vessel from Chaul carrying rice to Hormuz.[37] Five years later two craft (one as much as 500 ton) were intercepted near Quilon bringing grain, textiles and butter from Bengal and Burma.[38] Even more remarkable was the taking (1620) near Jask (on the southern coast of modern Iran) of a 200-ton Portuguese ship on passage from Muscat to Chaul. Her cargo consisted of 42 Arabian horses, together with some dates and raisins. The enormously valuable horse trade to India is well known, but the degree of its specialization is revealed by the remark that the vessel in question was 'built for that purpose'.[39]

Nor were English attacks confined to the 'country' trade. Off Mozambique in 1616 a well-equipped outward-bound East India flotilla met the sole survivor of a quartet of carracks on passage from Lisbon to Goa. After a long and bitter struggle the 1,500-ton ship, 'weakened by gunfire', was blown ashore. There her crew fired her and took to the land, abandoning—so it was said—a cargo of 'divers fabriques' and over 300,000 *reales*.[40] At this stage, and indeed for many years to come, the English were chronically short of the silver vital for trade in the east, where there was little demand for European goods. Hence the sinking of another carrack in 1618 and the seizure of her

[34] Andrews, *Elizabethan Privateering*, pp. 218ff; Bulhão Pato (ed.), *Documentos Remettidos*, III, 73ff.
[35] Purchas, II, 424. *Pintados* = painted or coloured cloths.
[36] Purchas, VI, 84.
[37] Purchas, III, 276.
[38] Purchas, IV, 299.
[39] Purchas, V, 243.
[40] Purchas, IV, 363, 461; Purchas, V, 107; Purchas, IX, 10.

treasure. Four years later, and once again near Mozambique, a joint Anglo-Dutch force, including the Indiamen *Royal Exchange, Ann* and *Diamond*, fell in with a Goa-bound armada of three carracks and a galleon. After a two-day battle the 1,600-ton *St Joseph*—more than twice the size of the *Exchange*, and carrying 800 men as opposed to her 140—was sunk. One of her consorts was forced ashore and another capsized, leaving the victors with loot including over 68,000 *reales*.[41]

Meanwhile the English were attempting, and with considerable difficulty, to establish themselves on the north-west coast of India and in the Persian trade. In a stream of bellicose missives from Iberia the viceroys in Goa were urged to ensure, either by diplomacy or force, the expulsion of these pirates and bandits.[42] Seen from Madrid the matter was simple. The English arrived exhausted after the long voyage from Europe, and being merchants concerned only with profit would not persist if their trade was disrupted.[43] But rarely are man and money so easily parted. Off Surat in 1612 the *Hosiander* and *Dragon* under Thomas Best defeated four big galleons and their consorts in a prolonged and hot action—the English firing 3,000 'great shot'—and in full and admiring view of a Mogul army.[44] In a repeat performance three years later Nicholas Downton—a onetime captain of the privateering magnate, the earl of Cumberland—worsted six galleons, two galleys and their numerous supporting craft.[45] But despite these, and even more serious reverses (the loss of Hormuz amongst them), the war at sea was far from being an unbroken chronicle of Portuguese disasters. In 1625 the redoubtable Nuno Álvares Botelho gave three English Indiamen such a pounding off Surat that their compatriots and allies sheltering in Swally thought it best not to come out, and as long as he remained on the coast both the Dutch and the English moved with marked circumspection.[46]

And so it went on. These campaigns, however, have been admirably discussed by distinguished historians of Portuguese Asia from Alfredo Botelho de Sousa to Charles Boxer, and need no further examination here. But this same English push to the east brought into contact with the *Estado* merchants, travellers and seamen who, like their counterparts elsewhere, have left reasonably accurate and dispassionate descriptions

41 Purchas, X, 499; PRO, HCA 13/46, fos. 144ff.

42 Pato, *Documentos Remettidos*, II, p. 275.

43 Pato, *Documentos Remettidos*, III, No. 444; IV, pp. 346ff.

44 Purchas, IV, 158; Pato, *Documentos Remettidos*, III, pp. 78ff, 85ff.

45 Purchas, IV, 316.

46 C. R. Boxer (ed. and trs.), *The Commentaries of Ruy Freyre de Andrada* (London, 1930), p. 317.

of what they encountered. Already in 1558, when the English had dreams of trading to the Orient across Russia, Anthony Jenkinson had reached Bokhara. From there, at a time when the Portuguese royal spice monopoly is generally accepted to have been failing, he reported its continuing efficacy in that no such products were available in this ancient market since Portugal had sealed off their flow from the east.[47] Later in the century John Newbery, Ralph Fitch and others arrived in Asia by those routes leading through the Levant. They noticed (1581) the extent to which the commerce of the Persian Gulf was in non-Portuguese hands, and they were transported from Hormuz to Goa in a ship belonging to the captain of the fortress engaged in the horse trade.[48] On things further east Fitch, who admittedly jogged his memory by plagiarizing the writings of an earlier traveller, nevertheless has some useful information, remarking, for example, the weakness of the Portuguese hold on the territories around Diu and Daman, and the extent of Malabar piracy against their shipping in coastal waters everywhere 'from Ceylon to Goa'.[49]

After the turn of the century, with English voyages more frequent, accounts are more numerous and specific. There are occasional attempts at an overall appraisal of the *Estado*. Following the run of English naval victories in the early 1600s a common view—and one with which the imperial government in Goa would certainly have agreed—was that the Portuguese empire in Asia was fatally weakened and impoverished. Sir Thomas Roe, England's ambassador to the Mogul court, reckoned the *Estado*'s days were clearly numbered, ruined, he thought (1615–16), by the intolerable expense of attempting to maintain too many forts and posts. 'No way ingage your selves but at sea' was the lesson he drew.[50] But this was not the whole story. To many Englishmen, including Roe himself, the Portuguese were, for instance, too well dug in in northern India to be shifted. They were able to interfere with indigenous trade to the Red Sea, whilst their dealings in precious stones gave them a far greater hold than the English were ever likely to achieve with their woollen textiles. In short, here as elsewhere the Portuguese 'caused good by trading', and the Mogul emperor was unlikely to take the first steps

[47] Hakluyt, II, 472. Many of the narratives of English travellers, merchants and seamen are printed in some form by Hakluyt and Purchas. For a useful survey of subsequent editions see the lavishly-documented study by Ram Chandra Prasad, *Early English Travellers in India* (Delhi, 1965).

[48] Purchas, VIII, 459–60; IX, 499.

[49] Purchas, X, 202.

[50] Purchas, IV, 445–7, 462–4.

against them without the encouragement and aid of the East India Company.[51]

In the course of such discussions and debates, and during attempts to discover how England's parlous position in the east in the early 1600s might be improved, various facets of the complex maritime economy of the *Estado* were examined and described in the hope of inspiring similar English undertakings. It was learned that in East Africa the Portuguese acquired slaves—victims of inter-tribal wars—for nine or ten *reales* and resold them in Europe for 100.[52] It was also learned that frigates from Diu brought oriental goods to the Horn of Africa from where they were shipped up the Red Sea by Portuguese country traders to be exchanged for gold and silver.[53] There are likewise illuminating comments on the commerce of the Portuguese in western India. At Diu they were believed to make the equivalent of £10,000 a year—enough to establish a dozen metallurgical works of the latest pattern in Jacobean England—from customs and the profits of letting out ships 'to Guzerates and Banians'.[54] The flow of convoys, sometimes over 200 strong, from south-western ports to Cambay to load goods for the long-distance carrack and galleon trades was noticed, as was the importance of Portugal's hold on the Indus delta. From here indigenous commerce between India and Persia could be taxed. From there also the Portuguese had formerly sent spices to Lahore to obtain the goods needed in their own trade with Persia, where even in 1622 the customs levied at Hormuz were thought to yield 140,000 *reales* annually.[55]

Portuguese imperial policy and practice were similarly remarked. The *Estado* was in contact with Europe not only by that formidable route sailed by the spice fleets, but overland through Persia, the Levant and the Mediterranean. In 1603 John Cartwright travelled from what is now Esfahan (Iran) in company with 'an Armenian Portugall or Portugall Armenian, and one Christophero a Greeke' carrying the viceregal mail from Goa to Madrid.[56] At Diu it was noticed that most of the imperial officials were banians, many of them fluent in Portuguese—a further instance of that well-known Lusitanian utilization of indigenous skills.[57] The English also reported the comparatively effective functioning of the *cartaz* system in the Arabian Sea—the

51 Purchas, IV, 162ff, 339, 463–5, 501.
52 Purchas, IV, 292.
53 Purchas, IV, 564.
54 Purchas, IV, 206. Bania—an Indian merchant, particularly a Hindu from Gujarat.
55 Purchas, IV, 128, 134, 268ff, 501; Boxer, *Ruy Freyre de Andrada*, p. 271.
56 Purchas, VIII, 516–17.
57 Purchas, IV, 204.

licensing, that is, of native shipping, which had to pay dues at specified Portuguese posts and whose cargoes and routes had to be cleared with the Portuguese authorities. In Surat the English, when they first arrived, found to their disgust the local inhabitants in 'slavish awe' of Portugal, and at Diu the trade of the 'Moors' to the Persian Gulf and the Red Sea under strict Portuguese supervision. Yet though at sea the English often encountered local skippers who could produce a duly authenticated *cartaz*, they also noticed those enterprizing Gujaratis who in the very vicinity of Surat loaded 'great ships' (900–1,500 tons) and set sail unbeknown to the Portuguese.[58]

And there is much more in similar vein, whether news from Ceram (Indonesia) that the locals would roast alive any Christians they could catch in revenge for Portuguese misdeeds, or from Japan of futile Iberian attempts to enlist imperial aid to round up Portuguese and Spanish nationals illicity living there and have them despatched to defend the Moluccas against the Dutch.[59] But of particular interest are the views of English seamen, widely respected in the Europe of *c.* 1600 for their skills and fighting capabilities, on the maritime qualities and resources of their Portuguese opponents. Certainly the officers of the *Estado* might bewail their compatriots' shortcomings and a chronic lack of ships, men and munitions, just as court wits might polish their epigrams—'one Portugal to three moors, one Englishman to three Portugals' said Roe.[60] But others thought otherwise. The captains who fought the *Cinco Chagas* (1594) indeed remarked how little sail she carried for a vessel of her size, but were surprised by how lively she was even at the end of a long voyage when the marine growth on her hull must have slowed her. And in their refusal to engage her consort they showed a healthy respect for Portuguese fighting power.[61] Furthermore, even in the direst straits the Portuguese long continued to assemble formidable fleets in Asia, with the English fearing as late as 1622 that they would 'beate our Englishe shipps oute of their seas'.[62] Seven years before an East India Company flotilla had encountered off western India a Portuguese squadron of six galleons, two *naos*, one pinnace, two galleys and 60 small craft. The biggest galleon was 800 tons, and the remainder anything from 400 to 700, and all manned on the usual lavish scale for warships anywhere —on average one man to four tons. They were, however, relatively weak in fire-power, with a 600-ton ship carrying as few as 18 guns as opposed

[58] Purchas, III, 89; IV, 25–6, 189ff, 296.
[59] Purchas, III, 105, 469.
[60] Pato, *Documentos Remettidos*, IV, p. 348; Purchas, IV, 517; IX, 35–6.
[61] Hakluyt, VII, 118ff, 123.
[62] Boxer, *Ruy Freyre de Andrada*, p. 266.

to over 20 in a much smaller English vessel.[63] But this again was not always so. The fleet against which Thomas Best fought (1612) his men considered well-armed, with one of the galleons mounting 38 pieces and the rest 30, and all 'very good Ordnance'. And time and again, in Asian as in other waters, the English complained that their own heavily-built and heavily-armed craft were outsailed by their opponents' lighter vessels.[64] Ironically enough, too, the Portuguese who were frequently worsted through the inept and idiosyncratic behaviour of their aristocratic commanders in the face of those of less elevated birth but greater natural talents, blamed their reverses on the cowardice of the indigenous seamen they used in such large numbers. But to the English, who were soon to organize things in similar fashion, the fact that Portuguese ships were worked and fought by slaves 'and inferiour sea-people' gave them an advantage over their own in which Europeans had to do all such things themselves under the blazing tropical sun 'which greatly quells their courages'.[65]

By 1635 the heyday of the Portuguese empire in Asia was over. The possessions of the *Estado* were fewer and its revenues drastically diminished. That this was so reflects less English attacks than unremitting Dutch and indigenous pressure. The newly-founded English East India Company lacked the capital and the business and maritime resources of its Dutch counterpart. Even more fundamentally it lacked any equivalent overall direction. Nevertheless the English arrived in Asia better informed than is often assumed, so that as early as 1600 Fulke Greville could draw up sensible proposals as to where it was best to trade.[66] The materials available for such an analysis, this paper has suggested, whether the reports of English spies, the narratives of English travellers or the journals of English seamen, throw an incidental but valuable light on the history of the *Estado da India*, and throw light, too, on an Indo-European trade which finds little mention in the records normally consulted by historians of commerce.

63 Purchas, IV, 263; Pato, *Documentos Remettidos*, III, p. 80; G. V. Scammell, 'Manning the English Merchant Service in the Sixteenth Century', *The Mariner's Mirror*, 56 (1970), 131ff; *id.*; 'Shipowning in the Economy and Politics of Early Modern England', *The Historical Journal*, xv (1972), 385ff.

64 Purchas, IV, 158.

65 Pato, *Documentos Remettidos*, IV, p. 162; Purchas, IV, 232.

66 *CSPCol, 1513–1616*, no. 266.

XI

SEAFARING IN THE *ESTADO DA ÍNDIA* C. 1500-1700

The sea was the lifeblood of the *Estado da Índia*. The empire was established to enable Portugal to control the shipment of the fabled riches of the Orient to Europe. It came to be sustained by the profits of that Asian interport commerce somewhat disparagingly known in the West as the «country trade». By accident and design it developed into a series of footholds, few of which dominated any appreciable hinterland, scattered along the shores of maritime Asia. Hence in the heyday of the empire these forts and factories were linked to one another, and to Europe, almost exclusively by sea, just as at all times they were largely dependent on the sea for supplies of everything from food to weapons and for the arrival of royal officers to govern them and, with decreasing likelihood, troops to defend them.

The object of this paper is to examine life on board vessels actually or nominally, but not exclusively, Portuguese, operating roughly within the confines of the *Estado*. There have of course been many studies of various aspects of Lusitanian maritime endeavour in Asia from such eminent scholars as Alfredo Botelho de Sousa, António da Silva Rego, Josef Wicki, A. J. R. Russell-Wood, Charles Boxer, Anthony Disney and Geneviève Bouchon.[1] Their attention has, however, for the most part been focussed on the ships which attempted the formidable oceanic voyage via the Cape of Good Hope, from Portugal to India and back (the *Carreira*). Here I hope to survey wider horizons, taking in, for example, the colourful experiences of those Europeans who for one reason or another travelled in native craft, and examining the reactions of members of widely differing social, ethnic and religious groups to one another when cooped up together on board ship for lengthy periods of time, usually in arduous, not to say terrifying, circumstances. How many people were at sea in the *Estado* at any given moment is impossible to determine, though we know that in the sixteenth and seventeenth centuries Indiamen might have anything up to 1200 on board whilst expeditions to reinforce threatened pillars of the empire could be 12,000 or so strong.[2] Such complements comprised a rich social and ethnic mix, particularly in vessels engaged in lucrative long-distance voyages, like those between Asia and Europe, or, until their abandonment in the early seventeenth century, between Macao and Japan. They included Europeans, chiefly, but by no means exclusively, Portuguese, of every class from grandees proceedings to, or returning from, high offices of state to luckless convicts destined to be dumped wherever seemed best. There were sharped-eyed travellers and adventurers from many parts of Europe, like Pyrard de Laval or Jan Huyghen van Linschoten. There was that great multitude who had purchased berths or posts from the crown.[3] There were merchants, often foreigners, like the ubiquitous Florentines in the sixteenth century or those indigenous Asian traders who travelled in the convoys of inshore craft organised by the Portuguese. There were bureaucrats and clergy. There were also, and more often than is assumed, women. Some were so-called «orphans of the crown», shipped to the East as potential brides. Some were prostitutes, embarked for their pleasure by the wealthy or cunning. Others were slaves. A few were the spouses or daughters of magnates, and many more Asian women accompanying the Asian seamen who manned Portuguese ships.[4] In the vessels of the *Carreira*, or in those participating in some military venture in the East, there were the assorted servants, slaves and henchmen of grandees, whose social standing was measured by the number of their retainers. There were likewise those employed by opulent merchants, with the homeward-bound Francesco Carletti attended by a Korean, a Japanese and a «Mozambique Negro».[5] And of course there were soldiers, whether the feudal retinues embarked in the East by men of consequence in the heroic days of the *Estado*, or those who subsequently came out from Europe in Indiamen to defend the empire. With the passage of time it was increasingly felt that such warriors were of a quality more calculated to depress compatriots than intimidate enemies, being largely recruited, as an Italian Jesuit reported in 1629, straight from goal and carried on board in Lisbon penniless, more or less naked and like as not infected with syphilis or something equally unpleasant.[6]

Like their equivalents elsewhere Portuguese Indiamen and men of war shipped an imposing range of officers and those that we would now know as petty officers – captains, pilots, masters, mates, quartermasters, master gunners, chaplains and, not least, in the ships of the *Carreira*, those royal clerks to whose authority even captains were subject. Until the eighteenth century the latter were not salaried professional seamen, and strenuously resisted any suggestion that, as was more and more the case in the vessels of other European powers, they should be so. Instead they were gentlemen of high social rank, appointed by the crown in return for services rendered or anticipated, and allowed, to their immense financial benefit, lucrative trading privileges. True to the ethos of their class they were prickly about their honour and, as a contemporary put it, «unwilling to yield to one another in anything», thereby precipitating countless mishaps and worse.[7] Smaller craft could be under foreigners, such as the Florentine merchant Francesco Corbinelli, the great Albuquerque's onetime supporter,[8] whilst in Asian waters there were many commanders who, like the heroes or villains of some Conrad novel, might be the only white men, other than perhaps one or two compatriots, in their ships.[9]

Vessels of any size usually carried, as was the general European practice, a range of skilled artisans – carpenters, coopers, caulkers – since in long distance voyages it was vital that crews could maintain and repair, as well as sail their ships. They also often had on board, like the vessels of most other European powers, a number of musicians, chiefly trumpeters and drummers. The prime functions of these ensembles were to bang and blast defiance at opponents, to arouse the martial valour of colleagues and to greet friendly ships and fortresses in suitable style. Their skills, however, could be employed, when opportunity offered, to enhance festive occasions, whilst in the *Carreira* fifers blew by the hour to ensure that helmsmen stayed awake on watch.

The best part of the crew, numerically at least, consisted of the foremast hands who worked the ship. In an Indiaman there would be 60 or so, aided by the apprentices. As in the ships of other seafaring nations crews were astonishingly cosmopolitan. There were, for example, Biscayans in some of the earliest Portuguese expeditions to the East where one, together with two Greeks, deserted Albuquerque in his hour of need at Hormuz. At this date too, given the well-known Portuguese shortcomings in such matters, gunners were commonly Germans or Flemings. Subsequently we hear that the Lusitanian flotilla in action against that of the English East India Company in the Persian Gulf in 1625 had on board more than 200 English, Scottish, Irish and Dutch sailors, whilst the well-travelled Abbé Carré later met 20 French deserters serving Portugal at Kung – though without much enthusiasm.[10]

Ships sailing to and from Europe, or employed in military expeditions in Asia generally carried a nucleus, albeit a decreasing one with passage of time, of Portuguese seamen. These were commonly regarded by compatriots (and others) with that same contempt their fellows endured elsewhere in Europe, though probably, in view of Portugal's difficulties in raising sufficient manpower, with more justification. So, for example, those newly arrived in the East in 1518 were written off as no better than «muleteers and thieves», whilst some decades later many gunners were alleged to be shoemakers, tailors and the like, entirely innocent of martial skills. In the late 1500s competent foreign observers thought Portuguese sailors lacking in seagoing experience, so unskilled that not one in five could take the helm, and for the most part illiterate – and this at the time when, for instance, English seamen were amongst the most literate members of an emergent working class.[11] And as, with difficulty, standards were raised elsewhere, Portugal sank deeper into trouble. By the mid 1600s a good percentage of the hands for the *Carreira* were recruited directly from the country's gaols, with the crown writing annually to all judicial districts ordering them to send convicts to Lisbon to be embarked in the India fleet should this fail, as it usually did, to attract sufficient volunteers. Still more radical solutions were therefore required and deficiencies in European manpower had to be made good from the rich resources of the rest of humankind. This willingness, not to say eagerness, to employ all and sundry was not peculiar to Portugal. In its very nature seafaring is cosmopolitan, and this was never truer than in those centuries in which Europeans first penetrated the oceans of the wider world. In the West Amerindians served in Spanish and English ships just as Asian and African seamen crop up in most European vessels in the East. But Portugal was unique among European powers in the sheer extent to which it came to rely on non-European muscle and skill. Its own resources in manpower were modest and dwindling; its imperial commitments seemingly growing and limitless. So it was impelled to that pragmatic employment of whoever it could recruit which was such a hallmark of its policies. Moreover, its ships worked a network of routes extending from Europe to China, adding to the ethnic variety of their crews by picking up hands wherever they could be found to replace those who died, deserted or became incapacitated. And of course the Portuguese entered, and were eventually absorbed into a vast and ancient Asian maritime economy long accustomed to employ seamen of many races and religions.

Thus the crews of Portuguese ships in the East came to resemble a United Nations in miniature, down to the discord endemic in such gatherings. Vessels might be commanded by Christian Arabs and manned alike by pagan Africans, pious Muslims, Japanese Christians and an astonishing assortment of other indigenous seamen. Some, as slaves, had no choice but to serve. Some were recruited by force, like those Goans sent to the galleys in 1646 for objecting to the conversion of Hindus.[12] But large numbers served for wages and were obtained by the Portuguese in traditional local ways, mostly through the offices of those *nakhudas* who provided men and handled their pay.

Surveys starting in the sixteenth century reveal the resultant admixture of races and religions. So, for example, there could be mustered for the defence of Barcelore in 1570 the mariners – presumably Portuguese or Indo-Portuguese – of the various small craft together with the «free mariners» of the galleys – probably of the same ethnic groups. In addition there were the lascars (Indians) of the sailing ships, together with other lascars, convicts and galley slaves. At Goa, at roughly the same date, there were Arab seamen, local Marathi-Konkanis, Malabar Christians and sailors of mixed Arab and India nor Arab and Persian descent.[13] Francesco Carletti similarly records among the crew of the Portuguese ship in which he sailed (1599) from Macao to Goa those he identifies as Arabs, Indians, Turks and Bengalis. Other sources mention Arabs (often as pilots), Chinese, lascars, moors, Japanese, Ethiopians, Kanarese, Gujaratis, Goan Christians, Brazilian Africans (free and slave), *mestiços*, African slaves and, intriguingly (1649), «the boys and blacks» employed in vessels sailing between India and Mascat.[14] Hence, quite typically, the three frigates and a galliot which left Goa in 1698 for the relief of Mombasa had on board 126 white and 376 non-white seamen and gunners.[15]

From the moment of their arrival in Asia the Portuguese made what use they could of local Christians, chiefly those of Malabar, soon reinforced from communities they themselves had converted, most notably Goa and its environs. Notwithstanding the many aspersions on the shortcomings of Goans as seamen and gunners, and despite a royal injunction of 1617 prohibiting their embarkation in major fighting ships, they continued, of necessity, to be recruited in large numbers. They were joined from time to time by Christians from Mylapore, so that it was nothing unusual to find Portuguese ships manned entirely by Indian Christians, like that 400-ton vessel from Cochin that Pyrard de Laval met in the Maldives on one occasion.[16]

Far more numerous, however, were Muslim seamen, reflecting the predominance of Islam in much of the early maritime economy of Asia, and so close did Portuguese dependence on their services become that by the seventeenth century the bulk of nominally Lusitanian vessels in the East were to all intents Muslim. Thus when in 1625 Father Jerónimo Lobo S. J. hoped to reach Ethiopia from India the voyage was to be undertaken in a Portuguese flotilla based in Bassein, largely manned by Muslims and destined, ironically enough, for a privateering foray into the Muslim-dominated waters of the mouth of the Red Sea. Six years later it was proposed to embark 150 gulf Arabs – shortly increased to 500 – at Mascat for the relief of Mombasa. In India itself there are countless references to sailors raised from what was generally termed the *terra dos Mouros*. The Zamorin of Calicut agreed (1631) to allow the recruitment of seamen in his realms «for the fleets of his Majesty», and it was subsequently accepted (1696) that the Portuguese could raise men there provided they paid the going rate. But not all potentates were so accommodating. The Captain of Ponda allegedly stopped potential recruits from reaching Goa from from the mainland in 1623, whilst there was a constant flow of complaints about the obstacles put in the way of Portuguese recruiting in the Goan hinterland – «without which», royal officials freely admitted, «we cannot live or sustain ourselves» – by the officers of the Adil Shahi.[17]

Yet notwithstanding such obstacles, and despite schemes, like that of the viceroy, the Conde de Linhares in 1632, to meet most of the requirements from the resources of Salcete, Bardez and Goa, the Portuguese continued, probably as much from convenience as necessity, to follow local usage. *Nakhudas* continued to raise crews for them and *sarangs* ran their ships, exercising such authority as to amaze Francesco Carletti when he sailed from Macao to Goa. The *sarang*, he recounts, had entire charge of the crew: «they make their understandings with him, recognize and obey him, so that even the Portuguese captain, the master and the pilot of the ship is (sic) commanded» by him. And to the further astonishment of this intrepid traveller the employment of a native crew also meant that, unlike in Europe, the men brought their families, or at least «their wives or concubines» with them. In western seas the presence of women on board entailed strict measures to cool male passions. But in Asia, fulminated Carletti – and he no prude – there were no such restrictions, resulting in spectacles «no less indecent than filthy and unseemly». Problems «impossible to make clear» arose, he cryptically complains. Passengers were upset and «no little scandal» was occasioned, especially, he revealingly adds, to recent converts to Christianity. Nor were these the only dangers and difficulties. In 1628 a Portuguese ship on passage from Cochin to Bengal got into trouble, whereupon an intrepid missionary caused a great stir by rushing, crucifix in hand, into «the quarters of the Moorish women, the wives of the sailors», to convert them whilst there was still time.[18]

For the rest crews were made up from slaves, mostly Africans, so that, as it was bluntly explained on one occasion, «our men will not die from overwork» – a view subsequently endorsed by the servants of other imperial powers. Black slaves had long been an integral part of the Iberian domestic economy, just as they quickly became a vital element in such maritime and military strength as the *Estado* could muster in Asia. Already in 1504 Albuquerque's homeward-bound fleet took some on board in the Cape Verdes to help it on its way, whilst others were picked up in Mozambique by his ships on passage to the East two years later. Before long African slaves were ubiquitous throughout Portuguese Asia, just as they were later employed, though never on so extensive a scale, by other European states. Thus when in 1622 the English intercepted a sizeable Portuguese ship off Jask only 70 of its total complement of 250 were white, and the rest slaves and Eurasians.[19] In 1636 it was the so-called Kaffirs of East Africa who, together with lascars, were said to provide most of the manpower for the royal galleons at Goa, and they came to be of increasing importance in supplying crews for the ships of the *Carreira*. The Viceroy of Portuguese India lamented the shortage of Mozambique Kaffirs in 1738, explaining that it was on them that «we usually rely for... deckhands». Not exclusively, however, for they were joined both by their fellows from West Africa, and by black slaves (and black freemen as well) from Brazil.[20]

When we turn to examine the trials and tribulations of seafaring we are, naturally enough, better informed about the lot of the literate and upper classes than that of the rank and file. In the early seventeenth century the Jesuit Father Lobo produced one of the most graphic accounts of a shipwreck ever written in any language. He was also remarkably perceptive and comforting on seasickness, whilst it is from his humane pen that we get some inklings of the misery of an African slave embarked (1635) in an Indiaman bound for Europe. When the first land was sighted this luckless individual believed the voyage, and his sufferings, were over. But as the ship held her course such was his despair that he refused to eat and «soon ended his life miserably aided by stout blows administered to him by his master to make him give up that diabolical obsession». Things were much the same on board native vessels. Some Jesuits sailed from Suakin to western India in 1634 in a local ship carrying pilgrims returning from Mecca. The fathers, believed by the faithful to be unclean were, to say the least, unwelcome. They had to sleep on the deck, quite literally under the feet of the seamen working the vessel, and there were further ructions when they tried to prepare their meals lest they should contaminate their fellow passengers' food. Equally intimidating was the passage undertaken by Father Lobo from Chaul to Goa in a Panjim *almadia* – a fast, oar-propelled, canoe-like craft, «whose only virtue», he sourly observes, «was its ability to flee», and in which he was, like the others on board, obliged to lie in the bilge, under the planking which supported the oarsmen.[21]

Hence the death rate at sea was appalling, commonly reaching 50% of those embarked in outward-bound Indiamen in the sixteenth and seventeenth centuries. The causes are well-known. Ships were grotesquely overcrowded, demoralizing and debilitating those travelling in them. Crews suffered from exposure, since for the majority there was no shelter from the elements. Apprentices in Indiamen slept on deck, as did those who had failed to buy or secure berths, and as did soldiers in the East, though they at least enjoyed the (inadequate) protection provided by palmleaf tents erected on board. Clothing was usually unsuitable. There was, as in Europe as a whole, a reluctance to wash and a willingness, particularly amongst Iberians – or so northeners alleged – to treat a ship as one vast cesspool. Medical care was minimal, and in any case generally useless, though things started to improve in Indiamen from the end of the seventeenth century with the appointment of two friars from the nursing order of St. John of God to each. Vessels of the *Carreira*, desperate for hands, commonly embarked sick and under-nourished men in Lisbon who, if they survived the rigours of the first stage of the voyage, like as not succumbed during a halt in the lethal climate of Mozambique, «that cemetery of the Portuguese».

As crews dwindled the survivors were left to shoulder more and more tasks. Nor was there much to sustain them. Before the mid-1700s seamen's food, especially in Indiamen, was of poor quality and little variety. Fresh fruits and vegetables were rarities. The staple items were bread, oil, water, wine, vinegar and onions, together with low grade salt cod and salt meat – as fine a recipe as any for wrecking digestive systems. Supplies were usually inadequate and deteriorated rapidly, whilst even ships that left Portugal relatively well-stocked soon ran short, generally, it was the common opinion, through that familiar combination of corruption and inefficiency. And of what little there was seamen could expect less, with the Crown ordering (1740) that they should have only one meal a day. The archaic, not to say anarchical manning system used in vessels of the *Carreira* meant that, unlike other European craft, they carried no cook. There could, therefore, be sailors by the score all endeavouring to prepare their individual meals on the galley fire at the same time. Not only did this ensure those disasters proverbially associated with a superabundance of cooks, but also meant that the sick, unable to compete, went unfed. Seamen, thought the Marquis of Távora in 1750, were not given to soft-heartedness and would be more exercised by the death of one of the hens they kept to supplement their diets than by the demise of half a dozen or so of their comrades. There was some prospect of more varied and attractive food when in Asia the Portuguese adopted, as they did in so many other matters, local practice. To the traditional staples there were added rice, lentils, mangoes, coconuts and the like. But old habits die hard. Cheap rice was soon in use and French deserters made clear to the Abbé Carré the inadequacies of an insipid tropical cuisine of salt fish and boiled rice.[22]

A formidable maritime death rate was not peculiar to Portugal, nor indeed to the early modern centuries. Nevertheless there was a widely held belief that until the eighteenth century Portuguese ships – Indiamen especially – were on the whole dirtier, unhealthier and unsafer than those of other European nations. Nor is there any shortage of gruesome anecdotes as to the horrifying conditions which might prevail on board – corpses left rotting below and only discovered by accident; rats gnawing the amputated leg of some wretch as he lay engulfed in squalor, filth and a stench that knocked men down. Not surprisingly burial at sea was an everyday occurence and conducted, moreover, in a way that appears to have been uniquely Portuguese.[23] According to Pyrard de Laval the unweighted corpse was lowered over the ship's side as the master called the assembled company to prayer. It was a simple, not to say austere, ceremony in comparison with what took place in other European vessels. Bodies, weighted so that they would sink, were sent on their way with a salute fired by the ship's guns and, in Spanish craft, with a final shout of farewell from all on board. Nor was Portuguese practice entirely satisfactory, since the unballasted remains of the deceased were all too likely to be washed or blown back to become the ship's eerie and unwelcome escort.[24]

Narratives such as Pyrard's also supply graphic detail on some of the less horrendous aspects of seafaring. They have much to say about navigation, whether by astronomical observation or deadreckoning – the calculation, that is, of a ship's approximate whereabouts from the distance sailed in a given direction at an estimated speed. Pilots, as is well known, could produce some desperate results, with the weaker brethren, of whom there was no shortage, sometimes unable to identify the continent, let alone the coast, they were approaching. Nor were things necessarily better when navigation was in local hands. Father Lobo recalls how in 1625 he found himself off Socotra *en route* for the Red Sea in a Muslim-manned Portuguese ship. He was alarmed – and rightly so since she narrowly missed being wrecked – at the insouciance with which the crew retired for the night, not caring, he complains, «to stand watch (but) sailing under their lucky star, as they say, which means trusting entirely to luck». This was deadreckoning with a vengeance. But in less cavalier fashion it was practiced for centuries by Arab, as indeed by other seamen. Readers of Joseph Conrad's classic, *Lord Jim*, will remember how, in the ill-fated steamer at the heart of the plot the Asian crew «slept through the night, and only the reliefs of quartermasters and lookout men being called». And Arab ships were still being sailed and navigated successfully in such fashion to within living memory – and like as not still are – with one professional observer describing a voyage in 1938 in which the master «never took bearings... never fixed his... position». But he performed all the proper Islamic rites, prayed to Allah and turned to Mecca five times a day.[25]

Equally valuable are the insights we are given into how vessels were worked – like the division of crews into watches or the responsibilities of particular officers – and the glimpses we get of the daring ingenuity of men labouring to save some foundering ship, with carpenters and caulkers put over the side onto rafts being flung about by the sea as they tried to stop leaks.[26] In peace or war, and in fair weather or foul, all such duties and functions were undertaken, especially in Indiamen, and as in the vessels of other European nations, within that framework of religious observation which endured, in some degree or other, both ashore and afloat, until this century. In the ships of the *Carreira* the *Te Deum* was usually sung on rounding the Cape of Good Hope. Prayers were said every evening and morning, and on Saturday night *Salve Regina* – performed daily in Spanish craft – was sung, followed by readings from some work of edification by the pilot. Dry mass – that is without consecration of the elements, forbidden at sea – was said daily, or at least on Sundays and Holy Days by the ship's chaplain who also performed all other regular ecclesiastical functions.[27]

Vessels sailing between Asian ports, or to and from the East, commonly carried members of the missionary orders *en route* to, or returning from, some station. These, and particularly the Jesuits in their heyday, greatly added to the vigour and intensity of shipboard spiritual life. They would confess crews and passengers when death and destruction threatened. They endeavoured, by preaching, teaching and suitable entertainments to reinforce the faith of seamen, or perhaps, more accurately, to introduce them to its rudiments. They tried, like pious officers elsewhere, both Catholic and Protestant, to restrain the uncouth behaviour and to moderate the foul language for which Christian sailors were notorious – unlike those lascars who, according to John Fryer in the late seventeenth century, «never let their Hands do any labour but they sing a Psalm». The efforts of the fathers were, however, tempered by an awareness of the likely unhappy consequences of too strict a regime. They likewise did their best to wean crews (and others) from such evil practices as eating meat in Lent and indulging in the inflammatory pleasures of card games, which usually ended in brawls. They similarly struggled, as did the commanders and chaplains of other European ships, to prevent their charges from reading chivalric and indecent books. The combination is an intriguing one and further suggests a higher level of literacy among Portuguese seamen than they are usually credited with and a better taste than might be anticipated, for among the works condemned are those of Boccaccio. A notable sixteenth century English commander, it is worth recalling, refused to put up with *Orlando Furioso*. The Jesuits in particular also acted as almoners, tended the sick and, by no means least, mediated in those incessant squabbles and disputes which flared up among men living in such close and unpleasant proximity.[28] More remarkably still we even find (1618) one versatile father piloting a vessel fleeing from the Dutch through the waters around Sulawesi, with which he was fortunately familiar.[29]

Seafaring was not, however, all hardship and disaster. Official records, in their very nature, are concerned with reports of, and investigations into, mishaps. Travellers tales inevitably pay particular attention to alarums and excursions. And of course the much quoted *Tragic History of the Sea*, which seemingly portrays Portuguese seamen as unsurpassed in the arts of foundering, was produced to encourage mariners to learn from the errors of their predecessors. Calm seas and prosperous voyages elicited, on the other hand, little comment, at least from passengers, other then complaints of boredom. How some seafarers held such gloomy prospects at bay is reflected in the conduct the Jesuits sought to restrain or moderate, and in the royal instructions, like those of 1672, for the ships of the *Carreira*, which listed among indictable offences blasphemy, sodomy, the reading of prohibited books and the use of loaded dice or false playing cards. Earlier versions, which can be paralleled from other parts of Europe, forbade gaming, swearing and brawling, all of which could lead to serious disorder.[30]

But neither Indiamen nor other vessels were merely mobile dens of iniquity and some members of their complements passed their time in useful, profitable and indeed pleasurable ways. Jesuits travelling to the East compiled, as we know from the labours of Father Wicki, detailed and invaluable accounts of their experiences – over 100 for the period 1541-1598 alone.[31] So, too, as in the craft of all nations, crews spent much time fishing, adding alike to the variety of their rations and breaking the tedium of a routine passsage. Pyrard de Laval recounts how off the Cape of Good Hope, the Portuguese, using lines up to 600 feet long, took creatures so big that four men were needed to handle them. Father Lobo describes the way in which albacores and bonitos were caught, and how those first taken were auctioned for charity. But he also gruesomely tells of sharks hauled on deck, blinded, and then used «as substitutes for bulls in mock bull fights», whilst others, with buoyancy attached to their tail fins, were thrown back over the side for the pleasure of watching them «struggle to swim without being able to sink».[32] And, such brutal pastimes apart, there are plenty of indications that crews and passengers, especially those with means and money, could, as on land, have a comfortable existence and indeed enjoy themselves. In vessels of any size and consequence grandees, *fidalgos*, ecclesiastical dignitaries and wealthy merchants had their own cabins and were attended by their own servants and slaves. Not for them old fish and rotting meat, but select cuts from livestock carried in the ship and slaughtered as required, as also were hens, of which, for example, Carletti embarked 100 at Goa in 1601 for his homeward journey. And such a diet was rounded off with candied fruits, preserves and other delicacies together with, as one who travelled in this noble style relates, «as much water as we wanted». The death rate in elevated social circles was consequently far less than among the lower orders, whilst this high living had the further benefit that such magnates, in the ancient tradition of «good lordship» also provided for «many persons besides their ordinary retainers».[33] So, if all went well, which was by no means unknown, a sea voyage could be idyllic. When a viceroy was taking passage in an Indiaman he and the *fidalgos* on board might gather of an evening in the ship's stern gallery to chat or gamble, whilst lesser mortals could walk and talk on the upper deck, «between the mainmast and the foremast». There might be festive occasions, as when, for example, after some naval victory, the valorous were knighted. There were entertainments, some of them of considerable cultural merit. In 1688, under a tropical night sky, an audience of over 500 assembled on the *Nossa Senhora da Conceição* to witness «a comedy... performed on the quarterdeck», with some of the spectators perched in the rigging. Earlier in the century Pyrard de Laval, on board an Indiaman which had just rounded the Cape of Good Hope, admired the staging of «a very pretty comedy», prepared during the ship's passage from Goa. In Africa the shipwrecked Father Lobo was impressed by «a comedy presented very beautifully by the sailors», preceded though it was by the somewhat incongruous spectacle of a bullfight against cows. Such dramatic performances and assorted literary endeavours – like the Jesuit-inspired competition on one occasion for the best poem in honour of St. Francisco Xavier – were not peculiar to Portuguese seafaring, and there are mentions of works by Lope de Vega being staged in Spanish vessels, and by Shakespeare in English East Indiamen. Nevertheless the impression is that such productions were more common among the Portuguese, casting further interesting and favourable light on the cultural standards of their seamen.[34]

Equally remarkable were the manifestations, from time to time, of popular culture. On Whit Saturday an Indiaman at sea would be decorated with whatever finery could be mustered. Then a boy «emperor» was chosen, enthroned and crowned to the accompaniment of suitable pageantry. The officers of his court were drawn from those of the highest social rank on board, and surrounded by them the emperor – shades of Sancho Panza – distributed «islands and lands». Mass was heard on Sunday, guns were fired and a great feast held at which the emperor was waited on by his high-born servants. Then came more junketings, music (fifes, drums, bells, reinforced on one occasion by bagpipers from a vessel in company) and the inevitable Portuguese fireworks. But in the evening all returned to normal and the reign of «the emperor for a day» was over. Such doings were yet another manifestation of that popular urge, widespread in the early modern centuries – as for example among Caribbean pirates – to reverse the existing social order, or, as was said, to turn the world upside down. The inspiration, other than the enduring injustices of human existence, stemmed from classical and biblical teaching on the transitory glories of this life and the coming of a time when the exalted would be humbled and the humble exalted.[35]

There were also less edifying entertainments and pleasures. At Kung, so the Abbé Carré relates, officers and crews came ashore when paid to the house of the Portuguese Augustinians where, Sundays included, «tables with dice and cards were arranged on every side... even in the main entrance». In much of the Asian country trade – as, for instance, between São Tomé and Goa in the early 1600s – vessels coasted from port to port, allowing crews to sleep ashore every night. Better still, they could sample whatever local produce and other delights were on offer, besides engaging in trade, legal and otherwise. So, too, in the *Carreira* there were halts in Mozambique (unbeatable for the illicit acquisition of gold and ivory), St. Helena («a veritable paradise») and Brazil, where Portuguese sailors, in addition to conducting their private commercial ventures, were so enthusiastic in their pursuit of women as to outrage the local populace and provoke pitched battles from time to time.[36] But clearly for many, whether seamen or passengers, who, for whatever reasons found themselves afloat, the supreme joy came when the voyage was over. In India the incoming ships of the *Carreira* were greeted by fleets of small boats bearing «much food» and providing cheering music before whisking the influential off to the delights of hot baths, proper clothes, opulent meals and freedom from seasickness. And what ordinary sailors felt can be gathered from a splendid Japanese screen painting, now in the City Museum at Kobe, of a great ship, newly arrived and unloading, on whose yards and rigging figures wearing those distinctive baggy Portuguese breeches can be seen performing various feats of acrobatic daring which must be expressions of pure joy.[37]

Such euphoric reactions are hardly surprising. The overriding impression from a great variety of sources, Portuguese and other, is that for those who ventured to sea in the early modern centuries, and particularly for those who undertook voyages of any length, survival demanded skills, or luck, of the highest order. Even the best navigational practice was inadequate. Knowledge and understanding of the behaviour of the weather were sketchy, which meant that ships were at the mercy of the elements to a degree now hard to appreciate. Vessels, and not just those of the Portuguese, regularly set sail in no condition to face, let alone survive, storms. Homecoming ships of the *Carreira* were as is well known, grossly overloaded, whilst Father Lobo sailed from Goa in one which had a huge leak, playing like a fountain. Such, however, was the general eagerness to quit India at the earliest opportunity that nobody was prepared to report it. Human helplessness and inadequacy in the face of the sea was, and indeed still is, echoed in the popular culture of all seafaring peoples. As the sixteenth-century Portuguese adage so succinctly puts it: «*Se queres saber a Deus rogar, entra em o mar.*»[38]

Craft of every sort were regularly overwhelmed by the elements, like that local *kora-kora* (or *proa*) in which in 1604 a Jesuit father was sailing from Ambon, and whose native rowers swam off to save themselves leaving him to his fate. [39] Navigational incompetence and the inherent deficiencies of ships meant that, as the saying went, land was all too often encountered before it was sought, or that vessels were swept helplessly ashore – a common fate for Indiamen on the south-eastern littoral of South Africa. In such desperate circumstances discipline might well go by the board. When, for example, in 1602 a ship was lost in the Maldives, her crew fell to fighting and swearing. They ignored their officers, ate all they could lay their hands on and plundered the vessel, urging that they had to make the best of what little time remained. True, such disasters could inspire men to ingenious and heroic efforts to save ships and those in them. But, equally true, racial and social frictions could be exacerbated. Soon after the carrack *Belém* foundered on the African coast her black slaves became restive at the sight of fellow blacks living quite freely, whereupon the Portuguese survivors, fearing that slaves and natives might make common cause against them, reacted with panic-stricken brutality. Often enough, too, and hardly surprisingly, morale collapsed in such moments and ships drove to destruction to the accompaniment not only of the roar of the sea and the howling of the wind but also to a chorus of «cries, tears... and pleas for God's mercy». Men promised, as is their wont, to renounce their evil ways if spared, or to undertake some extraordinary penance, like those who swore that could they only be brought to a Christian shore they would «make a procession barefoot and on (their) knees to the nearest church». More remarkably still, elements of a primeval popular culture came to light. Crews of Iberian ships tried to placate the elements by casting holy relics into the sea, and indeed Portuguese Indiamen carried banners depicting these which were displayed in times of peril. And Father Lobo records what he disapprovingly dismisses as the «superstitious piety» of those who worshipped St. Elmo's Fire as it awesomely flickered on the ship's yards, with the crew summoned to their devotions by the wail of the bosun's whistle.

Nor were these the only dangers the oceans could offer. Blown off course, vessels ran out of water, as happened with a privateering expedition to Sind in the 1620s, happily saved by the skills of one described as «a foreigner» who knew how to distil sea-water. Another ship, having lost her way on passage from Goa to Manila in 1627, was so short of food that her company debated throwing the native hands over the side to preserve what little they had «for the white men». There was the ever-present danger of capture by enemies, local or European, and the equally common peril of being drowned by falling from aloft, or from those «seats of convenience» slung over the side for use as lavatories. So frequent were such mishaps that as early as 1560 the Crown, with that astonishing attention to detail that characterized its heyday, ordered all Indiamen to carry lifebuoys for the rescue of those unfortunates lost overboard.[40]

To the blows inflicted by nature were added those devised by man. There were disputes or worse in individual vessels, particularly those of the *Carreira*, between, on the one hand, the socially privileged (captains, *fidalgos*, merchants) and on the other lesser mortals like common seamen whose indispensable skills meant that they were able, on many occasions, to get their own way.[41] There were conflicts in fleets and flotillas between aristocratic commanders, whose celebrated (or notorious) individualism in interpreting – or more likely ignoring – orders could lead to collisions and other debacles. Inefficiency was commonplace, with, for instance, a Portuguese galley in action off Ambon in 1591 so poorly ballasted that, as was complained, she rolled about «like a child's swing» and was accordingly unable to use her guns. And things got worse rather than better with the passage of time, so that in 1744 the Marquis of Castelo-Novo sourly observed of the fever-ridden Portuguese way station of Mozambique that although his compatriots had been there for over two hundred years it still possessed «neither a magazine, nor materials, nor an artificer, nor iron tools for the repair of shipping».[42]

Like those of other nations vessels were regularly set on fire by heedless cooks and smokers, notwithstanding the stringent rules intended to restrain their incendiary proclivities. Thieving, brawling and fighting were common amongst crews, despite the liklihood that the guilty would end up being ducked from the yardarm or imprisoned in the filth, stench and darkness of the bilges. More serious still were mutinies, some of a racial or religious origin. Thus in 1593 the Chinese slaves in a galley, foolishly written off as «soft and effeminate», rose up one night and murdered all the Europeans on board. Some years later Carletti was travelling from Japan to Macao in a vessel «built in the Japanese style», commanded by a Luso-Japanese and with Japanese crew. Trouble started when a Portuguese kicked a Japanese – «one of the greatest affronts that they can receive from an enemy» – and was considered to have insulted the entire Japanese nation. In next to no time, whilst the ship drifted out of control, open war threatened to break out between the Japanese and the rest, with the Japanese Christians siding with their unconverted compatriots against their non-Japanese co-religionaries. Carletti was rightly apprehensive as to the likely outcome of such a conflict, and it was only the diplomatic skills of some Jesuits on board that saved the day. The story has many points of interest. The Portuguese were sailing in what was to all intents a Japanese ship, and were accordingly beholden to the Japanese. Yet all this notwithstanding, and despite nearly a century's experience of dealing with this proud and bellicose people, they misunderstood and mishandled a delicate situation. And the whole episode reveals the barely-veiled hostility that underlay their multi-ethnic society.[43]

This brief survey of seafaring in the *Estado da Índia* gives some idea of the many and well-publicized harzards of such an existence, together with a hint of its less familiar pleasures. We get some momentary glimpses of human behaviour in times of gravest peril, together with occasional insights into those latent popular beliefs which then surfaced, just as we can fleetingly hear the authentic voice of the seamen of the age. Portuguese sailors, who have not on the whole enjoyed a good press, are shown to have had in their ranks not only some who were technically competent, but also those who were literate and indeed cultured. Another remarkable field of missionary endeavour is further illuminated. Our understanding of the extent to which Portugal, with increasingly inadequate resources in manpower, was dependent on that of indigenous Asia is enhanced. And perhaps most significantly we can appreciate the degree of mutual incomprehension between Europeans and non-Europeans in a multi-ethnic society, and the fragile foundations of, and frequent stresses within, such communities.

NOTES

[1] Alfredo Botelho de Sousa, *Subsídios para a História Militar Marítima da Índia* (4 Vols, Lisbon, 1930-56); A. da Silva Rego, «Viagens Portuguesas à Índia em meados do século XVI», *Anais*, II ser. 5 (1954), 81ff; C. R. Boxer, ed. and trans., *The Tragic History of the Sea, 1589-1622* (Hakluyt Society, Cambridge, 1959); *id, Further Selections from the Tragic History of the Sea, 1559-1565* (Hakluyt Society, Cambridge 1968); Josef Wicki, «As relações de viagens dos Jesuítas na Carreira das naus da Índia de 1541 a 1598», *II Seminário International de História Indo-Portuguesa* (Lisbon, 1980); A.J.R. Russell-Wood, «Seamen ashore and afloat: The social environment of the Carreira da Índia, 1550-1750», *The Mariner's Mirror*, 69, I (1983), 35-51; Anthony Disney, «The World of long-distance voyaging in the seventeenth century: The Lisbon-Goa fleet of 1629 as a case study», in K. S. Mathew, ed., *Studies in Maritime History* (Pondicherry, 1990), pp. 143-158; Geneviève Bouchon, *Albuquerque, Le lion des mers d'Asie* (Paris, 1992).

[2] *The Voyage of François Pyrard of Laval, to the East Indies, the Maldives, the Moluccas and Brazil*, trans. and ed. by Albert Gray assisted by H.C.P. Bell (2 vols, London,

1887-1890), II, Pt. 1, 186; G. V. Scammell, «The pillars of empire: Indigenous assistance and the survival of the *Estado da Índia* c. 1600-1700», *Modern Asian Studies*, 22, 3 (1988), 473-489 at 486.

[3] *Pyrard de Laval*, II, Pt. I, 195ff.

[4] Bouchon, *Albuquerque. Le lion des mers d'Asie*, p. 228.

[5] Francesco Carletti, *My Voyage Around the World*, ed. and trans. Herbert Weinstock (London, 1965), p. 228; *Pyrard de Laval*, II, Pt 1, 186ff.

[6] Disney, «The Lisbon-Goa Fleet», p. 148.

[7] *Pyrard de Laval*, II, Pt 1, 200; Botelho de Sousa, *Subsídios*, IV, 392; G. V. Scammell, «Manning the English Merchant Services in the Sixteenth Century», *The Mariner's Mirror*, 56, 2 (1970), 131ff.

[8] Bouchon, *Albuquerque*, p. 166.

[9] *Pyrard de Laval*, II, Pt. 1, p. 192; Bouchon, *Albuquerque*, p. 16.

[10] *Pyrard de Laval*, II, Pt. 1, 190ff; *As Gavetas da Torre do Tombo*, ed. Centro de Estudos Históricos Ultramarinos (11 vols, Lisbon, 1960-75), IV, n.º 3060, p. 135; Bouchon, *Albuquerque*, p. 118; G. V. Scammell, «European exiles, renegades and outlaws and the maritime economy of Asia, c. 1500-1750», *Modern Asian Studies*, 26, 4 (1992), pp. 641-661. at p. 644.

[11] *As Gavetas*, IV, no. 3346, p. 388; *Pyrard de Laval*, II, Pt. 1, p. 193; Russell-Wood, «Seamen ashore and afloat», p. 37; Scammell, «Manning the Merchant Service», 131ff.

[12] P.S.S. Pissurlencar, ed., *Assentos do Conselho do Estado, 1618-1750* (5 vols, Bastorá, Goa, 1953-57), IV, Appendix, p. 476.

[13] Pissurlencar, ed., *Regimentos das Fortalezas da Índia* (Bastorá, Goa, 1951), pp. 95, 118, 439 ff; G.V. Scammell, «European shipowning in the *Estado da Índia*, 1500-1700», *Indica*, 26, 1 & 2 (1989), p. 119f.

[14] Pissurlencar, *Assentos*, III, p. 513; Russell-Wood, *art. cit.*, p. 38; Scammell, «Pillars of Empire», p. 486.

[15] Boxer, «The *Carreira da Índia*, 1650-1750», *The Mariner's Mirror*, 46, 1 (1960), p. 35f.

[16] Pissurlencar, *Assentos*, II, pp. 120, 128; Scammell, «Pillars of Empire», pp. 486-8; A.B. Bragança Pereira, ed., *Arquivo Português Oriental*, New Edition (11 vols., Bastorá, Goa, 1936-40), IV, II (2), p. 8; *Pyrard de Laval*, I, p. 62.

[17] Scammell, «European shipowning», p. 132; *id*, «Pillars of Empire», p. 487.

[18] Carletti, *My Voyage*, pp. 185-6; Scammell, «Pillars of Empire», p. 487.

[19] G.V. Scammell, «Indigenous assistance in the establishment of Portuguese power in Asia in the sixteenth century», *Modern Asian Studies*, 14, 1 (1980), 1ff; Raymundo António de Bulhão Pato, ed., *Documentos Remittidos da Índia ou Livros das Monções* (5 vols., Lisbon, 1880-1935), IV, p. 162; Samuel Purchas, *Hakluyt Posthumus, or Purchas His Pilgrimes* (Glasgow, Maclehose eds. 20 vols., 1905-07), IV, pp. 232, 256; Bouchon, *Albuquerque*, pp. 70, 82.

[20] Pissurlencar, *Assentos*, II, n.º 44; Boxer, *Carreira da Índia*, pp. 40-1; Russell-Wood, «Seamen ashore and afloat», p. 37.

[21] M. G. da Costa and C.F. Beckingham, eds., *The Itinerário of Jerónimo Lobo* (Hakluyt Society, 1984), pp. 20, 286-7, 294, 306-7.

[22] *Pyrard de Laval*, II, Pt. 1, p. 126ff; Boxer, *Carreira da Índia*, p. 42; *id*, «Mozambique as a way-station for Portuguese East-Indiamen», *The Mariner's Mirror*, p. 48, 1 (1962), p. 3ff, especially pp. 11-12; Russell-Wood, «Seamen ashore and afloat», p. 43; Jean Aubin, «Un voyage de Goa a Ormuz en 1520», *Modern Asian Studies*, pp. 22-3 (1988), 417ff at pp. 427-30.

[23] Disney, «The Lisbon-Goa fleet», p. 151; Russell-Wood, «Seamen ashore and afloat», p. 43.

[24] *Pyrard de Laval*, II, Pt. 1, 196ff; Norman Newton, *Thomas Gage in Spanish America* (London, 1969), p. 43.

[25] Lobo, *Itinerário*, pp. 80, 306; Joseph Conrad, *Lord Jim* (Penguin ed., 1949), p. 77; Alan Villiers, «Sailing with the Arabs», *The Mariner's Mirror*, 47, n.º 4 (1961), p. 242ff.

[26] *Pyrad de Laval*, II, Pt. 1, p. 189ff; Lobo, *Itinerário*, pp. 303, 310.

[27] *Pyrard de Laval*, II, Pt. 1, p. 186ff; J. Wicki, ed., *Documenta Indica* (18 vols., Rome, 1948-88), VI, p. 295; Boxer, *Carreira da Índia*, p. 48.

[28] *Doc. Indica*, III, p. 390ff; V, p. 326; VI, p. 235, 772, 780; XVI, 805; *Purchas*, XVI, pp. 44-5; Disney, «The Lisbon-Goa fleet», p. 150.

[29] Hubert Jacobs S.J., ed. *Documenta Malucensia*, III, *1606-1682* (Rome, 1984), 367.

[30] *Doc. Indica*, V, p. 364; Boxer, *Carreira da Índia*, p. 45.

[31] Wicki, *As relações*, pp. 2-4.

[32] *Pyrard de Laval*, II,Pt.II,p.294; Lobo, *Itinerário*, pp. 8, 22-3.

[33] *Pyrard de Laval*, II, Pt. I, p. 86, 127; Carletti, *My Voyage*, p. 228; Boxer, «Mozambique Island», p. 12.

[34] Lobo, *Itinerário*, pp. 27, 35, 366; *Pyrard de Laval*, II, Pt. I, p. 190; II, Pt. II, p. 295; Boxer, *Carreira da Índia*», pp. 47-8.

[35] *Doc. Indica*, V, p. 366-7; XII, p. 881. The relevant biblical text is in Mark 9, 35.

[36] Russell-Wood, «Seamen ashore and afloat», p. 41.

[37] Lobo, *Itinerário*, pp. 44-6; Disney, «The Lisbon-Goa fleet», p. 154; Kobe City Museum (Japan), Namban Screens.

[38] Scammell, «European seamanship in the Great Age of Discovery», *The Mariner's Mirror*, 68, no. 4 (1982), 357ff; Lobo, *Itinerário*, p. 302; *Doc. Indica*, VI, p. 306.

[39] Hubert Jacobs, ed., *Documenta Malucensia*, II, 1577-1606, (Rome, 1980), p. 651.

[40] Lobo, *Itinerário*, pp. 12, 74, 326, 360-1, 377; *Doc. Indica*, IV, p. 623; Boxer, *Carreira da Índia*, p. 50.

[41] Russell-Wood, «Seamen ashore and afloat», pp. 46-7.

[42] *Doc. Malucensia*, II, p. 293; Boxer, «Mozambique Island», p. 17.

[43] *Doc. Malucensia*, II, pp. 388-9; Carletti, *My Voyage*, pp. 136-8.

XII

After Da Gama: Europe and Asia since 1498

The years 1997–1998 witnessed Britain's return of Hong Kong to China; the fiftieth anniversary of the independence of India and Pakistan; and the much less publicized 500th anniversary of the arrival of the Portuguese in Asia. So were marked the beginnings and end of European empire in the East, and so, too, a new global distribution of power was recognized. The appearance on 20 May 1498 of a Portuguese fleet commanded by Vasco da Gama at Calicut (Kerala, S. India), combined with the penetration of the Caribbean six years earlier by a Spanish flotilla under Christopher Columbus were, it has often and eloquently been urged, the prelude to a fearful saga. In next to no time Europe was enriched, non-European populations and ecologies destroyed, indigenous states and economies overthrown, a peculiarly European violence introduced into lands previously innocent of such ways, and the yoke of European colonial rule and hegemony eventually imposed.[1] In short, as India's Independence Day Pledge (1930) pithily put it, subjection to empire meant economic, political, cultural and spiritual ruin.[2]

Before turning to these vast and emotive themes, the pioneering Iberian voyages merit some comment. Both da Gama and Columbus sailed not from the vibrant heartland of western capitalism, but from relatively affluent pockets in regions otherwise amongst the continent's most backward. Both expeditions were inspired by expectations of great wealth tempered by strange dreams of freeing Jerusalem from the infidel and extending the bounds of Christendom.[3] Both commanders were destined for the Orient, long if imperfectly known in the West as the rumoured source of untold riches and the alleged site of assorted wonders and delights. Part of one immense landmass, Europe and Asia were joined by routes of great antiquity, travelled

[1] K. M. Panikkar, *Asia and Western Dominance* (London, 1953), is one of the classic statements.

[2] Jim Masselos, 'India's Republic Day: The Other 26 January', *South Asia*, XIX (1996), 183–203, at 188.

[3] Luís Filipe F. R. Thomaz, *De Ceuta a Timor* (Linda-a-Velha, 1994), pp. 189ff.

from time immemorial by migrating peoples, conquering armies and intrepid merchants and missionaries.[4]

But that there might be a direct and easier sea route to the East was increasingly appreciated in late medieval Europe. Hence it was that da Gama and Columbus came to accomplish voyages amongst the most remarkable ever made under sail. Here, however, the similarity ends. Columbus was a foreigner of obscure birth employed in a country obsessed with blood and status. His 1492 voyage was the outcome of his own initiative and persistence, made in what was little better than a scratch fleet. Da Gama, on the other hand, was a distinguished member of the Portuguese royal household; his expedition the culmination of a lengthy Portuguese search for a sea route to Asia round or through Africa. It was meticulously prepared under that close royal supervision which for a time ensured that limited Lusitanian resources were profitably directed to the pursuit of what were identified as the most desirable ends.[5] Columbus sailed westwards for Cathay across waters unknown to Europeans other than the Norse in the early Middle Ages and to encounter a world which again only they in Europe had briefly experienced. Da Gama eventually reached his goal in a voyage lasting roughly eleven times as long as that of Columbus, and of which the first leg alone (to the Cape of Good Hope) involved 93 days out of sight of land. But whereas in the Atlantic Columbus found his own way westwards, da Gama followed where his compatriots had led, and once he entered the Indian Ocean he was on the rim of a huge, ancient and thriving maritime economy whose sea links extended from East Africa to South China. Hence whilst Columbus vainly searched the Caribbean for traces of the Grand Khan, the Portuguese were able to sail in the wake of native seamen, making the passage from Malindi to western India under the direction of an Arab pilot. Hence, too, with China notoriously absent from the Caribbean, the Spaniards soon turned to conquest and colonization. In Asia, on the other hand, the Portuguese, like their European successors, initially fanned out, as the existing patterns of commerce dictated, skirting the centres of oriental military strength and political power, and generally establishing themselves by one means or another in bases already in exist-

[4] G. V. Scammell, *The World Encompassed. The First European Maritime Empires c. 800–1650* (London, 1981), pp. 103, 162.

[5] *Ibid.*, pp. 233, 302–3.

ence. The name of Columbus is consequently commemorated in scores of cities, states, districts and provinces in the Americas whilst that of Vasco da Gama is recalled in only one small port in western India.

That Asian sailors might have voyaged to Europe before, or at the time of the first Portuguese oceanic expeditions, though not improbable, is like as not fanciful. True, the Chinese had been on the coast of East Africa in the early 1400s and clearly had ships capable of undertaking lengthy passages. But these ventures were essentially extended coastwise voyages following established routes. Such experiences were little preparation for encounters with the formidable Atlantic, for which no pilots were available and of whose wind systems Asians had no knowledge. But in any case China, in 1500 probably the world's richest and most powerful state, had no need or inclination for such adventures. It could obtain all it needed from its own resources or through existing commercial channels. Mongol pressure on its northern frontiers was more than enough to occupy its energies, and the prevailing ethos was hostile to trade and other vulgar and unscholarly activities. The Portuguese, on the other hand, poor and unimpeded by any such inhibitions, launched themselves with relish into a world whose wealth was to strain their resources in metaphor and simile. Spreading with amazing speed along the arteries of maritime Asia they were established alike in the Persian Gulf, Malaysia and China within little more than a decade after reaching India.

Such achievements, compared with an almost century-long struggle to reach the southern tip of Africa, or the heavy going made by Iberian conquistadores in many parts of the Americas, convinced pious contemporaries of divine approval of Lusitanian endeavours. They likewise persuaded many subsequent commentators that the successes of so tiny a state stemmed from superior European morale and technology reinforced by violence of an order unfamiliar to the East. That in the early days the Portuguese were violent is true enough, even if not always so violent as was once thought.[6] But violence and brutality were nothing new to the East, which had already experienced, amongst other things, the doings of the Mongols. Unpleasantries such as death on a bed of arrows are depicted in

6 Anthony Disney, 'Vasco da Gama's Reputation for Violence: The Alleged Atrocities at Calicut in 1502', *Indica*, 32, 2 (1995), 12–28.

pre-European Hindu art, as are, from time to time, scenes of violence and warfare.[7] Sea fights figure in medieval sculptural fragments preserved in Old Goa,[8] whilst in the mid-fourteenth century Ibn Battuta was eloquent on the ravages of Indian and Indonesian pirates and other Asian villains addicted to 'warfare on the sea' and who, like Europeans after them, used seapower to tax trade.[9]

Nor, in any case, should the nature and scope of Portuguese—and subsequent European—success in Asia be overestimated. There were no substantial territorial conquests before those of Britain in India, starting nearly three hundred years after da Gama's arrival. Albuquerque might have talked wildly in the early 1500s of conquering the subcontinent, just as in the time of Philip II like-minded Spaniards thought that China, Japan and much else besides could be similarly disposed of. But ardour cooled with experience, with officials of the Dutch East India Company conceding, after defeat in Travancore (1741), that Europeans were powerless 'against the natives' and that wars were furthermore impossibly expensive.[10]

Europeans made a better showing at sea to begin with, and after some setbacks the Portuguese destroyed the fleet of the Egyptian Mamluks and their Indian allies (1509). Portuguese sailing ships carried substantial batteries of artillery, whereas the traditionally-built craft of the Indian Ocean and Arabian Sea, with their planking sewn together, and not nailed, as was western practice, were unable to mount comparable weaponry since they would have disintegrated on its discharge. But the imbalance was more apparent than real. The Chinese had large numbers of nailed vessels equipped with guns which were, admittedly, fewer and lighter than those in European ships. More significantly, as early as 1508, according to the Portuguese, craft equivalent to those from Europe were being built in the East. By the end of the sixteenth century such vessels were far from rare, whilst the Japanese and Koreans had developed formidable armed ships of their own. Moreover, the sheer size of the oceans of Asia meant that before the eighteenth century it was impossible for

[7] George Michell, *The Penguin Guide to the Monuments of India*, Vol. I: *Buddhist, Jain, Hindu* (London, 1989), pp. 52, 245, 431, 437, 460.

[8] *Ibid.*, pp. 384–5.

[9] *The Travels of Ibn Baṭṭūṭa A.D. 1325–1354*, Vol. IV, translated with annotations by H. A. R. Gibb and C. F. Beckingham (London, Hakluyt Society, 1994), pp. 800, 803, 808, 824, 865, 882.

[10] Scammell, *World Encompassed*, pp. 237, 320; K. M. Panikkar, *Malabar and the Dutch. Being the History of the Fall of Nayar Power in Malabar* (Bombay, 1931), p. 118.

Europeans to impose more than localized maritime hegemony. And in any case, even as late as the 1700s, oar-propelled indigenous craft could overwhelm heavily-gunned western sailing ships inopportunely becalmed. Not surprisingly, Europeans made extensive use of native vessels in both trade and war.[11] It is, of course, true that initially the Portuguese had better guns than most available in Asia. Such weapons had indeed long been known there. They were employed in Vijayanagara in the fourteenth century and in China much earlier, but, with the exception of a handful (probably of Turkish origin) there were few of any size when da Gama arrived. Technological advantage did (and does) not, however, guarantee military success. Rudimentary firearms could be rendered useless by tropical downpours. Slack discipline and a prodigiously leisurely rate of fire could find gunners caught unprepared by swift enemy attack. And such advantages as firearms might confer could be dissipated by Europeans who, like those sixteenth-century Portuguese, insisted on displaying chivalrous valour by doing battle armed only with sword and lance.[12] Moreover, Asian fighting men soon had European-style weapons. Some were manufactured locally, with, for example, Albuquerque referring (1513) to an Indian craftsman able to make guns as good as those of Bohemia. Far more were obtained by capture or by purchase from European renegades, and by the eighteenth century they were being bought in the West. Hence it was that from the late 1700s British armies in India faced indigenous forces whose equipment differed little from their own. Nor should it be forgotten that for long a lavish use of abundant manpower rather than the latest weaponry allowed Persian, Mughal and Chinese armies to give good account of themselves.[13]

The volume, weight and quality of European weaponry were not, however, originally at issue, since the Portuguese kept clear of the

[11] G. V. Scammell, 'Indigenous Assistance in the Establishment of Portuguese Power in Asia in the Sixteenth Century', *Modern Asian Studies*, 14, I (1980), 1–11 at 3. Reprinted in *Ships, Oceans and Empire. Studies in European Maritime and Colonial History 1400–1750* (London, 1995); *id.*, *The First Imperial Age. European Overseas Expansion c. 1400–1715* (London, 1989), p. 87; *id.*, 'European Shipowning in the Estado da India, 1500–1700', *Indica*, 26 (1989), 119–34, at 125. Reprinted in *Ships, Oceans and Empire*.

[12] M. Augusta Lima Cruz, 'A viagem de Gonçalo Pereira Marramaque do Minho às Molucas, ou os itinerários da fidalguia Portuguesa no Oriente', *Studia*, 49 (1989), 315–40, at 325.

[13] Scammell, 'Indigenous Assistance', 3; P. J. Marshall, 'Western Arms in Maritime Asia in the Early Phases of Expansion', *Modern Asian Studies*, 14, I (1980), 13–28.

major seats of Asian power and for a time encountered no substantial or sustained opposition. They originally faced an uncertain alliance of minor Indian Muslim powers and the Mamluks, who were soldiers rather than sailors and on the very point of being overthrown by Ottoman Turkey. This formidable empire, which certainly came to entertain Asian ambitions, fortunately then had other irons in the fire, notably in Iran and the adjoining lands and in eastern Europe. China was likewise engaged elsewhere when not sunk in xenophobic isolation. Thus neither in the Indian Ocean, nor in the seas east of Sri Lanka, was there any dominant power and least of all any dominant naval power at the crucial moment of European penetration. Vitally, too, westerners could usually find some indigenous ally. The Hindu ruler of Cochin welcomed the Portuguese rebuffed by his ancient rival the Samorin of Calicut, just as local connivance eased their establishment in Melaka (Malacca) and Macao. The Dutch and English East India companies subsequently received liberal concessions on the Coromandel coast from potentates or officials eager to ensure that the commercial and fiscal benefits likely to arise would flow into their own and not their neighbours' coffers.[14] And British expansion in India was notoriously underpinned by agreements with native princes.

Just as vitally, Europeans could cut costs, reinforce scarce military and naval resources, and redress an otherwise overwhelming numerical inferiority by employing Asian seamen and troops. In the early modern centuries the bulk of Portuguese armed strength in Asia comprised African slaves, together with Indian, Japanese, Ethiopian, Malay, Iranian, Arab and other fighting men. By the mid-1600s the forces of the Dutch East India Company included Ambonese, Sri Lankan, Bandanese and Indian troops, whilst the French, endeavouring to establish themselves in India in the late seventeenth century, employed Hindus trained in European styles of fighting and particularly well thought of. But all were eventually eclipsed by the British who, starting with a handful of Muslims and Rajputs in the seventeenth century, had some 60,000 Indian troops in their service by the late 1700s. And as the empire grew others were recruited, with Asians accounting for 60% of the ill-fated force in Malaya in 1941. But in better days India provided, and at no charge to the metropolitan exchequer before the 1930s, an army of a size the British would have otherwise been hard pressed to muster, allowing Bri-

[14] Scammell, *First Imperial Age*, p. 79.

tain to play a role in world affairs at a cost her tax-payers would have balked at meeting.[15]

So by an admixture of force, determination, luck and diplomacy, first Portugal and then other European states secured footholds in Asia. The arrival of da Gama was to mark the end—though this was hardly apparent at the time—of Europe's subjection to those incursions from the East which it had endured since Antiquity. It likewise heralded the beginnings of western hegemony in Asia. Where the Portuguese led, others followed. Rivalries brought conquests and the consequent creation of those territorial empires—the British in India and beyond, the Dutch in Indonesia, the French in Indo-China—which endured until their downfall was occasioned, directly or indirectly, by Japanese victories in the Second World War. Initially, however, the presence of the Portuguese changed very little. Some minor potentates (as at Melaka) were unseated and, more remarkably, Lusitanian intervention saved Ethiopia from the Ottomans. So, too, the Portuguese were the unwitting abettors of those formidable seafarers, the Omani Arabs, whose fleet was modelled on the ships captured when they took the Portuguese stronghold of Mascat (1650). But this hardly amounted to much in an Asia which witnessed the spread of Islam, the rise of the Mughal empire and the resurgence of China in the seventeenth and eighteenth centuries. Then, however, the East was sucked into European rivalries, became central to European grand strategies, and was often the victim of forces originally deployed by one western power against another. As part of their campaign against the united (1580–1640) Hispano-Portuguese empire the Dutch attacked Portugal's Asian possessions. France and England clashed in, or over, India in a global struggle lasting from the late 1600s to the defeat of Napoleon. To gain access to the subcontinent the French endeavoured to seize Egypt at the end of the eighteenth century. To counter a renewed threat the British subsequently occupied Java and Mauritius (1810–1811). French reverses in India hastened its conquest by Britain, in turn deflecting French ambitions into the Pacific and, later, Indo-China. For much of the nineteenth century Russia and Britain manoeuvred for advantage on the north-west frontier of India. By roughly 1900 Europeans had gobbled up most of South and South-East Asia

[15] *Ibid.*, pp. 81–3; Marshall, 'Western Arms', 26; Carl Bridge, 'The Malayan Campaign, 1941–2, in International Perspective', *South Asia*, XIX (1996), 169–82, at 173.

and repeatedly attacked and humiliated China. An emergent USA opened Japan by force and annexed the one-time Spanish Philippines. To protect India, Britain moved into Iran in 1906 and, alleging the same good cause, established its authority over great tracts of the Middle East after the First World War. But already the writing was on the wall for European empires. Japan, having mastered western technological and industrial skills, humbled Russia at the beginning of the twentieth century and America, Britain, Holland and France soon after.[16]

These shifts in power were accompanied, or occasioned, by far-reaching economic changes. The Portuguese, on their arrival in Asia, had encountered an ancient and complex commercial network reaching by land and sea from Europe itself to China. It was far larger, and probably handled traffic of far greater value than anything known in the West. Because of the constraints of distance and seasonal wind changes it was conducted through entrepots such as Aden, Hormuz and Melaka. It tapped alike the luxurious products of China, the gold and ivory of East Africa, the cotton textiles of India and the spices of Indonesia. What little that was needed from Europe could be received via the Middle East, whilst Arabia supplied horses and Iran silk and precious metals.

This economy was linked directly to that of Europe by the route pioneered by da Gama. True, the importance of the Cape passage was to falter from time to time as the ancient alternatives through the Red Sea and Persian Gulf revived in the later sixteenth century. Nevertheless, following the appearance of the Dutch and the English, deploying far greater maritime resources, its pre-eminence was assured till the opening of the Suez canal. One result was that European vessels now sailed, often non-stop, voyages of previously unequalled distance and difficulty. The Portuguese made the passage from Europe to western India, interspersed with some even longer runs, in the 1500s. The Dutch subsequently sailed to Indonesia, whilst from the eighteenth century ships were working from Europe to southern China, and in the 1800s directly to and from Australia. The flow of Asian goods to the West consequently increased. Some were familiar commodities, such as pepper. Some were former rarities, like the superb cotton and silk textiles of which the Portuguese alone were importing some eight million yards a year in the early 1600s. And some were new, notably tea, which began to flood into

[16] Bridge, 'Malayan Campaign', 171–2.

Europe around 1700. To these were subsequently added raw materials to meet the needs of western industries—Indian jute, for example, or Australian wool, whose carriage, incidentally, gave an added lease of life to the sailing ship in the nineteenth century.

The Asian economy had meanwhile also been linked to that created in the Atlantic by the Iberians. From the early 1500s American silver was being shipped to Europe, from whence some went on eastwards to help pay for western purchases there. So, too, from the mid-sixteenth century American bullion was sent across the Pacific to Manila, from where it reached China and beyond. In the opposite direction oriental luxuries were carried for sale in Spanish America, or for despatch, via the Atlantic, to Europe.[17] A commerce so lucrative, directed to consumers of legendary affluence inevitably spawned a whole nexus of clandestine routes. By the early 1600s returning Portuguese Indiamen illicitly disposed of part of their ladings in Angola or Rio de Janeiro from where they eventually found their way into the hands of the plutocrats of Spanish Peru, charged three times the prices prevailing in Lisbon. In the course of time such ties became more and varied. By the end of the seventeenth century Madagascar pirates were providing the West Indies and North America with bullion, precious stones, spices and textiles in exchange for guns and liquor. Not long after British ships were bringing Mexican silver to India from the Philippines, just as at the end of the eighteenth century American craft were carrying Canadian furs to China and New Englanders were busy whaling in the Pacific.[18]

The close and complex relationship of eastern and western economies in the present day thus has lengthy antecedents. A good part of the wealth of the Iberian Americas was spent on the purchase of oriental wares. The massive upsurge in European consumption of tea—one million lbs in 1700; 40 million in 1780—stimulated demand for Caribbean sugar to sweeten it. More sugar needed more slaves to produce it, and consequently more of those commodities used in their purchase. Amongst these were Indian textiles, which between 1699 and 1800 accounted for nearly a third (by value) of all goods exported to Africa by English slavers.[19] Then, of course,

[17] Scammell,*World Encompassed*, p. 328.

[18] G. V. Scammell, 'European Exiles, Renegades and Outlaws and the Maritime Economy of Asia c. 1500–1750', *Modern Asian Studies*, 26, 4 (1992), 641–61, at 655; *id.*, 'The Columbian Legacy', *Itinerario*, 17 (1993), 21–42, at 37. Both reprinted in *Ships, Oceans and Empire.*

[19] Paul Butel, *Européens et Espaces Maritimes, vers 1690–vers 1790* (Bordeaux, 1997), pp. 79, 156.

famously or notoriously according to taste, the troubles of the English East India Company with unsold tea helped precipitate the War of American Independence. And not least, Asian skills and Asian muscle have long found employment in the West.

In the East the arrival and subsequent behaviour of Europeans brought various shifts and changes in the pattern of trade. Portuguese attempts in the early 1500s to stop the flow of Indonesian spices to the Red Sea led local seamen to open a new direct route well clear of their bases. Meanwhile demands for suitable cargoes for homeward-bound Portuguese Indiamen brought an increase in the carriage of luxury goods, rather than traditional primary products, by Indian coastal shipping. Iberian presence and policies converted the hitherto obscure Manila to an entrepot whose commerce reached from the Pacific coast of America to Malaysia, China, Japan and India, whilst Dutch attempts to monopolize the spice trade ruined the pepper ports of Sumatra. The settlement of Australia eventually provided an unlikely outlet for Bengali cattle, just as the needs of the Indian army for mounts subsequently offered a market for New South Wales horses.[20]

More significant and sinister was European penetration of the Asian inter-port or so called 'country' trades. In some cases new routes were opened and new commodities carried, in others new directions or dimensions were introduced. Slaving, for example, was endemic in pre-European Asia as in much of the rest of the world. On their arrival the Portuguese gladly accepted and rapidly expanded what they found. They imported Africans by the thousand, bought slaves in India, Madagascar, China and Sri Lanka, enslaved prisoners of war, and from the early seventeenth century were heavily involved in slave raiding in Bengal. The Dutch followed suit, with the East India Company enslaving prisoners taken in its campaigns or opponents of its rule. Others were purchased in Madagascar, but eventually the majority came from Bali, Timor and the neighbouring islands. The English were slaving in the Indonesian archipelago in the early 1600s, and in Madagascar by the end of the century, from

[20] Scammell, *World Encompassed*, p. 272; *id.*, *First Imperial Age*, p. 204; Sanjay Subrahmanyam, *The Political Economy of Commerce; Southern India 1500–1650* (Cambridge, 1990), pp. 147–56; James C. Boyajian, *Portuguese Trade in Asia under the Habsburgs, 1580–1640* (Johns Hopkins University Press, 1993), p. 66; J. L. Anderson, 'Piracy in Eastern Seas, 1750–1850. Some Economic Implications', in David J. Starkey, E. S. van Eyck van Heslinga and J. A. de Moor (eds), *Pirates and Privateers* (Exeter, 1997), pp. 87–105, at p. 88.

where cargoes were carried to the West Indies and (eventually) to Virginia, Buenos Aires and Brazil, in which endeavour they were soon joined by the North Americans. Other slaves were later shipped from Africa, India, Madagascar and the Seychelles to the plantations of Mauritius.[21]

The Portuguese crown itself briefly engaged in the country trade, as did throughout its career, and on a much more substantial scale, the Dutch East India Company, whereas the involvement of the English company was comparatively modest. The commerce, legal or otherwise, of private individuals was another matter. In this the Portuguese were pre-eminent and seemingly ubiquitous till about 1650. Then they were eclipsed, as were all others, by the English, who before long were trading to China, shipping Muslim pilgrims from northern India to Mecca, despatching Indian textiles to the Persian Gulf, operating between Surat and Indonesia and between Madras and the Philippines, and sending Indian goods—not least opium—to the Indonesian archipelago.[22]

Such activities, often backed by indigenous capital or undertaken in partnership with indigenous merchants, by no means destroyed or even undermined those of local entrepreneurs, who might indeed profit from the new dispensation. A tight-knit group of Brahmins accounted for the best part of the taxes collected in and around Goa in the seventeenth century, whilst the bulk of the capital invested in the port's trade was non-Christian. Following the expulsion of the Portuguese from Japan in 1639, the Chinese (the only Asians allowed to trade there) easily held their own against the Dutch (the only Europeans permitted to do business there) in the import of silk. Asian merchants similarly dominated the export of Bengal silk well into the eighteenth century. Long after 1700 the trade of Myanmar (Burma), Thailand and Vietnam flourished free from European pressures. In the 1700s the Dutch failed to exclude Arab traders from Sumatra and Borneo, where even a century later they could still get the better of westerners. The open commercial world of Malaysia survived into the 1800s. Native-owned ships engaged in long hauls

[21] Public Record Office, Kew, HCA 13/85, fols 279–85; Scammell, *First Imperial Age*, p. 108; S. Arasaratnam, 'Slave Trade in the Indian Ocean in the Seventeenth Century', in K. S. Mathew (ed.), *Mariners, Merchants and Oceans. Studies in Maritime History* (New Delhi, 1995), pp. 195–208.

[22] Scammell, *First Imperial Age*, pp. 106–7; Om Prakash, 'Europeans, India and the Indian Ocean in the Early Modern Period', *South Asia*, XIX (1996), 15–25, at 21.

figure in the stories of Joseph Conrad, who himself served as an officer in a steamer belonging to a Singapore Arab.[23]

Nevertheless from the late 1700s the picture began to change rapidly and dramatically. Britain's conquest of Bengal brought her merchants decisive advantages over native competitors—de facto exemption from taxes; cheap opium vital for dealings with China. The ensuing subjugation of India and the abolition of the commercial monopoly of the East India Company converted the subcontinent into an ideal market for the products of a rapidly industrializing and eventually free-trade Britain. From the early 1800s there was a massive influx of machine-made Lancashire cotton textiles, already running at 56 million yards a year by 1832. Other markets were soon opened, like China, persuaded by force of the blessings of free trade. Other products—railways for example—soon followed, and by 1900 the East was taking 20% of British exports.[24]

Commerce with and within Asia enriched European states, companies and individuals. In the mid 1500s the monopoly of the import of spices, combined with the proceeds of dealings with Africa, accounted for half the revenues of the Portuguese crown.[25] At the end of the century there was wonder at the wealth of Iberian merchants trading to Asia—and, as none before had ever done, to America and Africa as well—and enjoying profits of 40%. Whatever the subsequent misfortunes of Portugal's eastern empire, even in 1721 an ex-viceroy could set off for home with a shipload of silks, diamonds and porcelain. A new breed of sea captain emerged with the commanders of English East Indiamen who were able to retire in affluence after a few voyages, enriched by the carriage of wealthy passengers, the profits of private commercial ventures and the sale of their office. English country traders, like their Portuguese predecessors, commonly made fortunes, with Elihu Yale already worth £200,000 (or twice the assets of a contemporary London plutocrat), by the

[23] Henriette Bugge, 'Silk to Japan. Sino-Dutch Competition in the Silk Trade to Japan, 1633–1685', *Itinerario*, XIII, 2 (1989), 25–41; Susil Chaudhury, 'International Trade in Bengal Silk and the Comparative Role of Asians and Europeans *c.* 1700–1757', *Modern Asian Studies*, 29, 2 (1995), 373–86; Jos Gommans, 'Trade and Civilization around the Bay of Bengal *c.* 1650–1800', *Itinerario*, XIX, 3 (1995), 82–108.

[24] Peter Mathias, *The First Industrial Nation. An Economic History of Britain 1700–1914* (2nd ed., London, 1983), pp. 270, 273, 382.

[25] Scammell, *World Encompassed*, p. 277.

late seventeenth century.[26] Such sums were soon eclipsed by the loot harvested by some of the servants of the eighteenth-century English East India Company, which itself was able to pay a cheering 10% dividend in 1766. And for a time the Dutch and English companies presented the remarkable and unprecedented spectacle of commercial organizations controlling territorial empires.

Nor were these the only rewards, quite apart from the resultant prestige, of holding the East in fee. The large-scale arrival of Indian cotton goods in Europe from the late 1600s revolutionized the continent's textile industry by revealing how it could make such fabrics itself. Dutch and English re-exports of oriental produce to Europe and North America in the same years helped in a fundamental reshaping of the pattern and scope of the West's overseas trade. Early dealings with Asia—the resources required; the lengthy delays in returns on capital; the non-commercial expenses in the East—created in the English and Dutch East India companies trading organizations of a size hitherto unknown, and eventually employing business techniques of unprecedented sophistication. England's determination in the early modern centuries to monopolize the provision of Asian (and other) goods to its Atlantic possessions was a major element in the country's emergence as the world's leading maritime and imperial power. Between 1831 and 1877, under the so-called 'culture system', Holland annually milked Java of a sum equivalent to a third of the current Dutch budget, and all spent for Holland's benefit. British India payed for the powerful and prestigious Indian army, raised and deployed solely as Britain required. Asia offered excellent markets for the products of British industry and consequently work for British mills and factories, with India, for example, taking nearly 20% of British textile exports in 1913. Besides which there was the substantial bonus that since by the early years of this century the United Kingdom's trade balance with India, China and Japan was favourable, the surplus could be used to clear deficits elsewhere. And if empire was not necessarily the fountain of wealth for private investors of Marxist legend, it could still do them proud, with British Malacca Rubber paying dividends ranging from 10% to 75% in 1912–19.[27]

[26] C. R. Boxer, 'The Count of Ericeira and the Pirates', *History Today*, XXIV (1974), 854ff.; Boyajian, *Portuguese Trade*, pp. 90, 132; Prakash, 'Europeans, India and the Indian Ocean', 21.

[27] Mathias, *First Industrial Nation*, p. 290.

Such pleasing returns accrued not only to Europeans, but also in some measure to those indigenous agents and associates who, as the saying goes, helped them shake the banyan tree. In the early modern centuries vanias and Parsee brokers in western India did well from dealings with the Portuguese Estado and its denizens. Bengal Parsee and princely entrepreneurs were, in the early nineteenth century, among the first to invest in new-style clipper sailing ships used in the lucrative Chinese opium trade. Some Indian landowners subsequently benefited from the rising prices of those crops whose production British policies encouraged.[28]

Inevitably, however, there was another side to the coin. The once extensive Indian shipping industry foundered in the face of western competition in the nineteenth century, just as mechanized English cotton production, using cheap American raw materials and favoured by the government's dedication to free trade, dealt grievous blows to its manually-powered Indian competitor. Nor was this by accident. Until the 1920s Britain, in its own interests, banned India from introducing those protective tariffs which would have helped it develop a similar industry. The subcontinent's economic evolution was consequently unbalanced, leaving it at independence (and after) an overwhelmingly peasant-based agrarian society. Together with China—once the world's two leading manufacturers—it joined the greater part of the East in the archetypal colonial role of providing raw or semi-processed materials. It supplied, as did China, tea, whilst Malaya provided tin and rubber, Indonesia sugar (to the detriment of traditional agriculture) and then oil, and Australia wool and coal.

Such a relationship germinated the seeds of its own destruction. European industrialists liberally sowed dragons' teeth by providing plant and equipment to those Asian entrepreneurs whose competition would overwhelm their compatriots. Imperial and colonial possessions, witnessing the behaviour of their masters, were decreasingly inclined to accept the status quo, and European states, occasionally troubled by doubts and increasingly by political and economic difficulties, were decreasingly willing and able to maintain it. Already by the 1630s the Portuguese Estado, reeling from the blows of European attack and competition, was unable to make ends meet.

[28] G. V. Scammell, 'The Pillars of Empire: Indigenous Assistance and the Survival of the Estado da India c. 1600–1700', *Modern Asian Studies*, 22, 3 (1988), 473–89. Reprinted in *Ships, Oceans and Empire*; Mathias, *First Industrial Nation*, pp. 290, 436; Bhaswatti Battacharya, 'A Note on Shipbuilding in Bengal in the late Eighteenth Century', *Itinerario*, XIX, 3 (1995), 167–74.

A century later magnates of the Dutch East India Company were bemoaning the costs of war against local powers. Subsequent British expansion in the subcontinent was in part inspired by hopes of new resources to meet existing commitments.[29] In the prelude to the Second World War, with the Indian market penetrated by Britain's major industrial competitors, the use of the Indian army overseas to be paid for, and a once favourable trade balance now adverse, the erstwhile jewel in the British crown had lost most of its allure. Worst of all, one-time colonies, or subjects of empire, formal or otherwise, showed, as America had long since done, that what Europe could do they could do as well and often better. Less than a century after the arrival of Commodore Perry in Japan the country had established itself as one of the world's most potent economies. The model was soon emulated in varying degrees by South Korea, Taiwan, Singapore and Malaysia, marking, together with the current economic resurgence of China and its reappearance on the international scene, a shift of the global centre of gravity from Europe and the Atlantic to the East and its oceans. Before the Second World War America's trade with Asia was a third of that with Europe. In 1993, however, the USA received between 1.4 and 2.3 times as much from the major Asian exporters as did Europe. And significantly, too, in 1988–89 American universities had over nine times as many Asian students as did their European equivalents.[30]

II

Europeans were known in Asia and Asians in Europe long before da Gama's voyage. But the new sea route and the assertion of western authority in the East brought travels and migrations as astonishing as those in the recently-opened Americas. In the sixteenth and seventeenth centuries Portuguese missionaries made their way to the court of the Mughal emperors, reached China, Japan, the islands of South-East Asia and even Tibet, whilst Iberian adventurers tried their luck in Thailand and Cambodia. With the prospects of settlement few before the colonization of Australia and the chances of survival no better, numbers were insignificant. There were at best

[29] Scammell, *World Encompassed*, p. 294; Panikkar, *Malabar and the Dutch*, p. 118; P. J. Cain and A. G. Hopkins, *British Imperialism* (2 vols, London, 1993), *passim*.

[30] Bridge, 'Malayan Campaign', 172; *The Economist*, 21 January 1995, p. 71; *id.*, 4 February 1995, p. 50.

perhaps 5,000 Europeans in what remained of Portugal's Asian empire in the mid-1600s. And after 500 years of war and trade there are no more than roughly two million European graves in present-day India.[31]

Even so, such figures recall migrations inspired by the whole gamut of human hopes and delusions: to do notable deeds; to save souls; to make a fortune. Catholic missions resumed their labours in the sixteenth century and were joined, after a considerable interval, by those of other denominations. There were optimists seeking the rumoured delights of the East, like those Englishmen who jumped ship in early seventeenth-century Japan, or the beachcombers of Polynesia later. There were adventurers, such as those Portuguese frontiersmen who in the sixteenth century became rulers of principalities, or their fellow Europeans who subsequently set up as mercenaries or ended as men of influence in the service of local potentates. There were those engaged in piracy and allied pursuits even in the heyday of British naval and imperial power, just as there were those melancholy figures, familiar to readers of Joseph Conrad, hiding from a dubious past in some backwater. There were merchants of every sort and, with the passage of time, increasing numbers of those destined to rule empires, together with the troops to defend or extend them. There were convicts, scattered about by the Portuguese and English in the early modern centuries, and later dumped in Australia by the British. Almost from the beginning there were occasional sightseers and, more remarkably, women. Some were the wives of officials, others the less fortunate shipped out to become the spouses of rank-and-file westerners. Their growing presence from *c.* 1800 damped down expatriate liasons with local females and probably intensified division from, and antipathies to, indigenous peoples. The feeling was mutual, with many eastern women disapproving of what they considered the immodest dress and behaviour of their European sisters.

Western settlement in Asia, with its massive populations and hostile climates was rare but not unknown. It was pioneered by the Portuguese whose *casados*, married to (Catholic) indigenous or Eurasian wives, often became shrewd businessmen, besides siring a tenacious colonial population which the mother country could never

[31] Jaap R. Bruijn and Femme S. Gaastra (eds), *Ships, Sailors and Spices. East India Companies and their Shipping in the 16th, 17th and 18th Centuries* (Amsterdam, 1993), p. 201; Philip Davies, *The Penguin Guide to the Monuments of India.* Volume II: *Islamic, Rajput, European* (London, 1989), p. 81.

have provided itself. Occasional English traders, having made their pile, remained in Asia in the seventeenth and eighteenth centuries, as later did some former servants of the British raj. In the Pacific it was a different pattern. Spain colonized the Philippines and Britain later settled Australia and New Zealand. Here, as earlier in America, there was seemingly land without people, as was notoriously not the case for most of the East, and here, too, there were climates in which Europeans could flourish. The outcome was the usual depressing saga. In Polynesia, Melanesia and Australia peoples who had previously lived in isolation succumbed to the impact of unfamiliar diseases and ways of life. As in America, the survivors became an aboriginal underclass, eventually struggling to reassert their right to land, with 40% of Australia currently subject to native claim. Meanwhile European outposts, like New Zealand and Australia, in an overwhelmingly non-European world, struggle to find some sense of identity.[32]

European presence and policies in the East intensified some existing human migratory patterns and created others. With the Spanish opening of the Pacific there began that flow of Filipinos, Indonesians, Chinese, Japanese and others to the west coast of America which has continued and intensified ever since. The long association with Africa was strengthened as Goans and Indians sought the opportunities of the continent's eastern littoral. Growing western demand in the nineteenth and early twentieth centuries for such Asian commodities as tea, sugar, tobacco, coffee, palm oil and rubber required more workers for their production. Hence the recruitment of indentured labourers (committed to serving for a given period of time in some specified place, in conditions which might be tantamount to slavery), from areas in which, commonly through sheer population pressure, unemployment or under-employment were endemic. Chinese and Javanese were used in Sumatra and Malaya; Indians in Assam, Mauritius, Myanmar, Sri Lanka, Fiji and Malaya. Following the abolition (1833) of African slavery, Asian indentured labour spread to the sugar plantations of the Caribbean and its fringes. Asians built railways in Canada, Africa and Peru or mined gold in South Africa. Their more fortunate compatriots did better. In the first half of the twentieth century rank-and-file police in Britain's eastern colonies were usually Indians, who were likewise becoming ubiquitous in service industries and trade. So new multi-racial societ-

[32] Scammell, *First Imperial Age*, p. 169; *The Economist*, 19 April 1997, pp. 71–2.

ies emerged—about 50% of Guyana's present-day population are, for example, of Indian descent. Islam and Hinduism took root in new settings and new ethnic and cultural frictions sprang up.[33] Indian seamen, skilled, plentiful and, like other Asian labour, cheap, were employed by the Portuguese in the East almost from the date of their arrival. By the early 1600s they regularly crop up in vessels working to and from Asia, and were subsequently much in demand for steamers (in stokeholds especially) with lascars (over 47,000) accounting for roughly 16% of all the hands (some 287,000) serving in British ships in 1912.[34] And, as needs no detailing here, recent decades have witnessed a huge flow of Asians to Europe, the Middle East and the USA, many escaping from political regimes not to their liking and more seeking better opportunities than their homelands can offer. But not all movement was on such a scale or governed by such crude imperatives. Japanese Christians visited Rome in the sixteenth century, and somewhat later a Chinese sage was ensconced in Oxford. In the days of European empire friendly local potentates came west, commonly to engage in the social round, and scions of the professional upper classes supporting the British raj arrived, as did Jawaharlal Nehru, to be educated as English gentlemen.

III

The achievements of Europeans in Asia, as indeed in the world at large, not surprisingly gave them a high opinion of themselves and a much less enthusiastic view of the rest of humanity. Asians were by and large lumped together as a poor lot, with the Indians dismissed by the Portuguese, on the briefest acquaintance, as 'dolts'. True, Japan and China early elicited admiration, chiefly based on ignorance. And clearly such polities, as indeed India, were not of that order of 'savages' so widely encountered elsewhere. The Chinese were included amongst those 'wise pagans' who had anticipated the truths of Christianity, and were idealized by some innocent French

[33] Jean-Dominique Giacometti, 'Les Communautés Indiennes d'Outre Mer entre les Deux Guerres Mondiales. Un Essai d'Historiographie Critique', *Itinerario*, XVII, 2 (1993), 37–52; and the contributions of Richard B. Allen, Marina Carter, P. C. Emmer, Madhavi Kale, Marieke van Klaveren and R. Shlomowitz to *Itinerario*, XXI, I (1997).

[34] C. Ernest Fayle, *A Short History of the World's Shipping Industry* (London, 1933), p. 289.

intellectuals of the Enlightenment. Voltaire enthused over the 'sublime ideas' of Brahminical religion, whilst ancient traditions of European Utopianism were reinforced by the discovery of islands such as Tahiti whose inhabitants led the idyllic existence of Noble Savages in equally idyllic settings. But if India, China and some other Asian societies were recognized in the late eighteenth century as having reached 'civilized', not to say 'commercial', status, there they had stuck, with their inhabitants degenerating into treachery, avarice, selfishness and worse. Indian religion, thought that eminent Victorian John Ruskin, was no better than 'a barbarous grotesque of mere savageness'. Others dismissed Indonesian medicine as little more than a mishmash of superstitions, and Max Weber attributed China's economic shortcomings to its adherence to the teachings of Confucius.[35]

So it was, as an Anglican bishop of Hong Kong deplored (1860) that westerners aired their 'contemptuous dislike' for their fellow men, whilst a few years later a Goan essayist remarked that the Portuguese considered themselves so superior to the local Indians that any one imagined himself capable of storming a whole township of them. In late imperial British India whites automatically assumed entitlement to native salutes. That some people were better than others, that some had inherent defects, and that those with dark skins were inferior were tenets of lengthy ancestry in Europe. They re-emerged and were reinforced in the triumphant Iberia of the early modern centuries. Casting an eye over the East, an eminent Jesuit wrote in the late 1500s 'all these dusky races are very stupid and vicious'. It was further agreed that Eurasians were likely to imbibe similar vices with the milk of their native mothers or nurses. Subsequent colonial and imperial powers were of much the same opinion. By the mid-nineteenth century British views of the peoples of Asia ranged from disenchantment to a patronizing paternalism that accepted that, weaned from their evil ways, they might, under proper direction, be set on the road to emulating European achievement. Tensions and antipathies between Europeans and Asians were a theme of western writers of the late nineteenth and early twentieth centuries, notably explored in E. M. Forster's *A Passage to India*

[35] J. S. A. Elisonas, 'An Itinerary to the Terrestrial Paradise. Early European Reports on Japan and a Contemporary Exegesis', *Itinerario*, XX, 3 (1996), 25–68; P. J. Marshall, 'Lord Macartney, India and China: The Two Faces of the Enlightenment', *South Asia*, XIX (1996), 121–31; and cf. the strictures of Edward W. Said, *Orientalism* (London, 1978).

(1924). Louis Couperus warned fellow Dutchmen (1900) of the perils of inter-racial contacts in Java, whilst the less salubrious Europeans of Joseph Conrad's novels freely vent their loathing for non-whites, savages and half-castes, Christians included.[36]

True, there were many important exceptions to this generally depressing chronicle. A pragmatic tolerance, if nothing more, developed in the course of business or politics, as when, for example, in the early centuries Europeans needed local money or aid. Moreover, since until the nineteenth century the western presence was predominantly male, Europeans of necessity took indigenous mistresses and some acquired indigenous wives. In the 1600s both the Dutch and English East India companies planned, or experimented with marriage of the lower orders to suitable local women, as had long been Portuguese policy. In India some affluent Europeans purchased and espoused converted (and white) Middle Eastern girls, whilst in the late eighteenth century Major Palmer married his elegant Muslim lady, the happy family group recorded in Zoffany's well-known painting. That such unions might have less felicitous outcome is equally well known from Conrad's novels.[37]

IV

Western penetration to the East was accompanied by the accumulation of a huge amount of assorted fact about the non-European world, much of which, admittedly, was to remain unpublished to our own time. Lands previously largely or wholly unknown were mapped and described in accounts often of the highest standard, with Portuguese pioneers insisting on their personal knowledge of what they reported and endeavouring to attain accuracy through the critical handling of evidence. The late eighteenth century witnessed charts and descriptions of the Pacific by James Cook and his French contemporaries, produced by expeditions whose members included artists and, as was never previously the case, learned (if cantankerous) observers. The study of oriental languages was pioneered by the Portuguese in the sixteenth century to facilitate the work of the Catholic missions. From the late 1700s societies were established in India

[36] Scammell, *World Encompassed*, pp. 237, 267, 288, 432; Jurrien van Goor, 'Dutch "Calvinists" on the Coromandel Coast and in Sri Lanka', *South Asia*, XIX (1996), 133–42.
[37] Scammell, *First Imperial Age*, p. 188.

and Indonesia to investigate the worlds in which Europeans found themselves. By the mid 1800s some Britons were endeavouring to preserve India's architectural heritage and in the following century were engaged in archaeological excavations in the subcontinent.[38]

As it was known or imagined, Asia made a profound, though never fundamental impact on western culture and society. From the early sixteenth century it attracted those seeking to escape the shackles of European convention, or to find opportunities denied them at home. Madagascar could still be imagined the setting for a Utopian pirate community in the early 1700s, just as the Pacific islands were later identified as primeval paradise.[39] The Victorian radical Annie Besant settled in India to pursue theosophical speculations. Other Europeans joined meditative ashrams or idealized Asian craft-based industries as the answer to the soulless factories of their own continent. That archetypal Englishman, Baden Powell, urged the merits of Japanese *bushido* on his Boy Scouts. In the early centuries some Europeans were converted to Islam—usually, but not always, at their own volition—and a few others, as among the Portuguese in Japan, became Buddhists. Our own times have witnessed a lively western enthusiasm for oriental or allegedly oriental religions, whilst the great Asian diaspora has brought the still wider dissemination of major faiths.

Since the days of da Gama eastern plants, drugs, artefacts, ceramics, books, animals, carpets, rugs, screens, furniture, archaeological fragments and even sartorial styles have reached Europe. Asian words abound in western languages: amuck (Malay); loot (Hindi); gingham (Malay); pyjamas (Persian); dinghy (Hindi) and many others in English alone. The Chinese stern gallery was early incorporated into western ship design for comfort and convenience and the Chinese chain pump likewise adopted for safety. The bungalow (deriving from an Indian village hut) is now a universally popular domestic dwelling. Oriental foods and styles of cooking enlivened European cuisine and today flourish the world over. Eastern models

[38] C. R. Boxer, 'When the Twain First Met: European Conceptions and Misconceptions of Japan, Sixteenth–Eighteenth Centuries', *Modern Asian Studies*, 18, 4 (1984), 531–40; Jeremy Franks, 'Eighteenth-Century Chinese Vessels at Canton: The Paintings at Skärva, Sweden', *The Mariner's Mirror*, 83, 1 (1997), 21–40.

[39] P. Labrousse, 'Les Indes Sauvages ou la chimère de la transgression amoureuse: l'Insulinde dans la fiction française (1712–1939)', in Denys Lombard (ed.), *Rêver l'Asie: Exotisme et Littérature coloniale aux Indes, en Indochine et en Insulinde* (Paris, 1993); Butel, *Européens et Espaces Maritimes*, pp. 206–7.

and motifs were emulated by western potters and textile makers, and from the mid-nineteenth century oriental and pseudo-oriental influences were much in evidence in British interior decoration.

European arts and sciences have incorporated an enormous amount of Asian material, detailed in Donald Lach's magisterial survey.[40] Yet in essence the dazzling achievements of western culture in the last five hundred years owe little to external influences, but were inspired and sustained by forces from within the continent itself. An impact the East certainly had, though significantly enough, western curiosity about, or receptiveness to, Asian cultures often stemmed from some purely European problem or debate. A conscious exoticism first appears in the *Peregrinaçam* (1614) of the Portuguese author Fernão Mendes Pinto, some of whose Golden Age compatriots treated the East, often with great felicity, in poetry and prose alike. India features in English drama from the sixteenth century, whilst later plays, melodramas and operettas deal with even remoter regions. Ultimately Asia, unlike the Atlantic world, was a stimulus to, and setting for, some of the finest writing in modern English (Joseph Conrad and E. M. Forster). It similarly inspired many others of more than mere competence, as well as producing a prolific middle-brow literature, of which Rudyard Kipling was probably the most accomplished practitioner.

Oriental dancing (first Indian, then Thai and Cambodian), known and admired in the West from the early nineteenth century, left its mark on Russian ballet of the great pre-revolutionary days. In music eastern influences were far stronger, particularly in the last one hundred and fifty years or so, and especially on composers struggling to escape from the shadow of Germanic tradition and excellence. Indian, Japanese, Chinese and Indonesian subjects and echoes occur in the works of many, though admittedly often minor, composers. The presence of the Orient is probably at its most dramatic, in every sense, in Puccini's *Madam Butterfly*, with its Japanese theme and ingenious use of some Japanese musical conventions. The subtler Debussy was fascinated by the Javanese gamelan and the potential of bells and chimes, subsequently explored by other musicians. In the visual arts the East made its most obvious impact in the various buildings reflecting, from the eighteenth century, the cult of the

[40] D. F. Lach and Edwin J. Van Kley, *Asia in the Making of Europe* (3 vols, Chicago, 1965–93).

supposedly Chinese (Chinoiserie), notably the Prince Regent's Pavilion at Brighton together with countless 'temples' elsewhere. But it was in painting that Asia made its greatest and most enduring mark, with Japanese styles and techniques influencing the work of artists as different as Beardsley, Van Gogh, Whistler and Manet.[41]

Whilst fashions came and went, statesmen and publicists wrestled with the abiding problems of trade and empire. In the early modern centuries the length and rigours of the Cape route, and the initial endeavours of Portugal to monopolize it, inspired English, French and Dutch searches for other possibilities, either via the North Pole, or round or through the Americas. The same period witnessed much experiment as to how the riches of the East were to be best exploited. The Portuguese tried a royal monopoly of certain Asian trades. The English and Dutch established joint-stock monopoly companies, whose operations brought impressive refinements in commercial technique. As wealth and possessions were accumulated there was speculation as to how parent societies were being affected. Sixteenth-century Portuguese men of letters inveighed against corruption and the decline of martial virtues arising from the unbridled pursuit of riches. Later pessimists saw Europe in danger of succumbing to oriental 'luxury, effeminacy, profligacy and debility'. In the seventeenth and eighteenth centuries investors in the Dutch and English East India companies regularly voiced their concern that dividends were in jeopardy from the adventurous policies of employees. There was heated controversy in England as to the wisdom of exporting bullion, and then on the role of India and the East India Company in the economy of Britain and its empire. Seventeenth-century Portuguese and Dutch publicists did their best to justify the monopolies their compatriots were endeavouring to enforce in Asia. The depressing fate of such tropical paradises as Mauritius perhaps inspired the first stirrings of environmentalism.[42] By the later 1800s the duties and responsibilities of colonial powers were much in the air, with India and its problems exercising some of Britain's most powerful minds. Debate ranged over appropriate architectural styles for the subcontinent, its proper form of government and the functions of the metro-

[41] A rich fund of information and ideas in John M. Mackenzie, *Orientalism: History, Theory and the Arts* (Manchester, 1995), which takes a wider view than Said's influential *Orientalism*.

[42] Richard H. Grove, *Green Imperialism. Tropical Island Edens and the Origins of Environmentalism 1600–1860* (Cambridge, 1995).

politan state. Now controversy has shifted to Euro-American exchanges on whether the East has discovered the elixir of economic growth.

V

The impact of the West in Asia was more profound, enduring and far-reaching in its consequences. European missions introduced to the East other forms of Christianity to join that of the Syrians long practised there. In simple terms of numbers converted, the achievement was hardly significant. Nor surprisingly. The early missions were up against Islam, more likely to make converts than provide them. They faced ancient and distinguished cultures, many of whose tenets were diametrically opposed to those they advocated. They similarly faced social conventions with which they were unfamiliar, and societies whose ruling classes—notoriously in China—held Europeans in low esteem, useful only as the suppliers of new technologies. They furthermore faced a galaxy of languages and scripts difficult to master. They were weakened by the paucity of their numbers, by quarrels within and between denominations, and by attitudes to race and colour which were not, to say the least, helpful. They were also tainted with the suspicion of being the forerunners of European conquest. And not without reason, for their greatest successes came in areas where, as in the Spanish Philippines or around Portuguese Goa, Europeans were the rulers.[43]

Nevertheless the early modern centuries witnessed, through the labours of the Iberian Catholic missions, the creation of pockets of Christianity over a huge area—in India, Malaysia, Indonesia, Myanmar (Burma), Sri Lanka, China, Japan, Indo-China and beyond. Some were to endure, as in the Philippines, Asia's only Catholic country, where in 1995 some four million of the faithful turned out to meet the pope. Others, as in Japan in the early seventeenth century, were quickly and brutally, if not entirely, suppressed.[44] Other missions joined the Iberian pioneers, like the French Jesuits who enjoyed a considerable success in their country's future colony of Vietnam. The renewal of European religious zeal in the nineteenth century, following the lull of the rationalism and tolerance of the

[43] Scammell, *First Imperial Age*, pp. 192–201.
[44] *The Economist*, 21 January 1995, p. 71; 11 January 1997, pp. 92–3.

Enlightenment, saw British Protestant missions active throughout India and as far afield as the Pacific, where by the 1820s the Polynesian and other archipelagoes had been converted. Meanwhile in Indonesia the Dutch were in process of creating some of the largest concentrations of native Protestants in the East. Particularly influential from the mid-1800s were evangelical and fundamentalist sects, many of them North American. Some were millenarian and some plain fantastic, but in lands like Korea, much oppressed by neighbours, they could enjoy astonishing success, with Protestantism now only slightly less popular than Buddhism in the southern half of the country.[45]

Of a different order and consequence was Asian acceptance of European science and technology, as when in the late seventeenth century the Chinese were persuaded of the merits of the West's mathematics and astronomy. It was, however, in war that, after a slow and lengthy process, some of the profoundest effects were eventually manifested. From an early date many Asian peoples had acquired, one way or another, European or European-style firearms, removing any potential inferiority to the West. The frequent European prohibition of the sale of guns and powder to unfriendly natives testifies to western belief that the possession of such armaments conferred some benefit. As indeed it might well do against opponents entirely without them. Hence the anxiety of nineteenth-century Polynesian chiefs to secure muskets and the white renegades needed for their use and repair. But where such weapons were generally available their impact was for long modest, notably in the wars between Asian powers from the sixteenth to the mid-eighteenth century. Firearms and artillery were of little moment in the campaigns of Shah Abbas of Iran; in those of the Mughals; or in those of the Chinese against Russia in the late 1600s. More relevant to success were the sheer volume of manpower deployed; the skills of commanders and the shortcomings of their opponents. So, also, in difficult terrain, of which there is no shortage in the East, European weapons could well be useless, as in Mughal operations against the Uzbeks (1646). Nor, on the other hand, did such arms save indigenous Indian states from the British in the eighteenth and nineteenth centuries. Only when from the late 1800s Japan assembled and employed on a large scale

[45] Williston Walker *et al.*, *A History of the Christian Church* (4th ed., Edinburgh, 1986); Kurt Aland, *A History of Christianity*, translated by James L. Schaaf (2 vols, Philadelphia, 1985–6); S. Neill, *A History of Christianity in India* (2 vols, Cambridge, 1984–85); *The Economist*, 10 December 1994, p. 85.

a great weight of the latest military and naval weaponry did the situation change dramatically.

Armaments were but one aspect of Asia's eventual acceptance and emulation of European technology. Western-style printing, introduced into India by the Portuguese in the sixteenth century, became widespread under the British later. Amongst other things it facilitated a substantial output of devotional literature (both Hindu and Muslim), leading to an intensification of cultural identities and religious divisions.[46] From the late 1800s Asia received or embraced—in some places more enthusiastically than others—the entire paraphernalia of western industrialization. Roads, railways, engineering works, textile mills proliferated. Mobility was radically increased first by the bicycle, then by assorted motorized vehicles. Irrigation works improved agriculture. Better transport and the speedier and easier movement of goods and peoples had massive social and economic consequences. Asian manufactures, mostly textiles to start with, flooded westwards in ever-increasing volume and variety, and the East now houses some of the world's major manufacturers.

Asian shipping and shipping industries have been revolutionized. Local peoples acquired western-built vessels, or, notwithstanding injunctions against sharing 'knowledge and techniques' with them, soon discovered how to build in western fashion. Indian Ocean shipwrights began to produce craft whose planking was nailed together European fashion, instead of sewn according to vernacular tradition. Vessels with full complements of western-type guns were known in Indonesia and Japan *c.* 1600. In China the highly efficient traditional build was modified to take artillery of the size and weight of that of the West, and the European stern rudder was adopted. Only government prohibition prevented—as also in Japan—further experiment. Even so, by about 1700, some of the humblest Chinese vessels showed marked European influence in their rig and general appearance. Portuguese and Dutch techniques were emulated in Indonesia, whilst the language of the Arabian Gulf, home of some of the world's finest seafarers, absorbed many western (often Portuguese) nautical terms. By the early eighteenth century the ships of the redoubtable Omani Arabs were of essentially western design, and many indeed

[46] Rupalee Verma, 'Western Medicine, Indigenous Doctors and Colonial Medical Education', *Itinerario*, XIX, 3 (1995), 130–41; Carmo da Silva, 'Evangelização e Imprensa nos Seculos XVI e XVII na India', *Boletim do Instituto Menezes Bragança*, 167 (1993), 71–101; P. J. Marshall, 'Assessing British India', *The Historian*, 45 (1995), 3–8.

of western origin. Big Indian craft from Surat were sheathed below water in the same way as their European counterparts, and in 1710 local builders were said to keep a sharp eye on western developments, measuring English ships that arrived and making replicas of any that took their fancy. Some nineteenth-century Asian owners were able to employ European sailing vessels of the latest design (like clippers), whilst others made do with craft pensioned off from more exacting trades, but still nevertheless intensifying the impact of western technology. Then Asia, having accepted metal hulls and mechanical propulsion, went on to become the home of some of the world's biggest shipowners (as in Japan and Hong Kong), just as Japan and Korea became builders of some of its biggest and most advanced vessels. Meanwhile traditional craft as different as the Arab dhow and the Chinese junk have embraced the internal combustion engine, and the tiniest fishing boats almost everywhere have begun to sport outboards.[47]

On land there was scattered across Asia in the course of the centuries a rich assortment of western buildings, civil, military and ecclesiastical. Europe is recalled by the red-tiled roofs and painted stucco houses of Goa, by its spectacular Counter Reformation and Baroque churches and monasteries, or by the remains of Dutch houses in Java. Vestiges of pre-revolutionary France survive in Pondicherry and of a more modern France in Indo-China. There are early Dutch tombs in cemeteries such as that of Ponneri (Pulicat, India) and British at Madras and elsewhere. Substantial parts of vast seventeenth-century Portuguese forts still stand at Goa and Diu. There are imposing remains of British fortifications of the 1700s in Calcutta, and throughout India there are churches ranging from the robust and fortress-like seventeenth-century Anglican St Mary's (Madras) to those raised by assorted denominations over the last one hundred and fifty years. Onetime British India likewise possesses a galaxy of grand houses, and an amazing collection of variegated Gothic buildings of the nineteenth and early twentieth centuries—law courts, government offices, railway stations—together with a handful of palaces in the French or Spanish style, built at the whim of Europeanized princes.[48] Few seafronts are more evocative in their different ways of Europe than those of Mumbai (Bombay) or the Shanghai Bund. Imperial pride has few more spectacular monuments

[47] See the remarks of Bao Leshi and R. J. Barendse in *Itinerario*, XIX, 3 (1995).
[48] Davies, *Monuments of India*, II, p. 149.

than the government buildings of New Delhi. And Asia's acceptance—in the material sense at least—of Euro-American values has no more visible testimony than the proliferating forests of skyscrapers.

But these are merely the most obvious manifestations of far profounder influences. Some parts of Asia adopted, or had wished on them, western-style forms of government. The onetime Portuguese possessions constituted, under a viceroy and a collection of councils, the Estado da India. Other governmental structures were introduced into Indonesia by the Dutch and into Indo-China by France. India supported for a time the full panoply of the autocratic British raj, but eventually became, like Japan, home of a European-inspired parliament. European place names were scattered across the map of the East. Through force, persuasion or convenience, European languages came into use, first Portuguese, or some variant thereof, which long served as the commercial lingua franca of much of South and South-East Asia; then Spanish in the Philippines and Dutch in Indonesia; and now the more or less universal English/American. A still expanding body of western-style cities has come into being, some developments of existing sites (Mumbai), others new creations (Macao, Singapore). Various approximations to European educational systems were introduced. Western initiatives brought in new crops, like those imported from Africa and America by the Portuguese, or the relocation of old ones, notably tea to India by the British. European dress has been widely adopted. Addiction to Euro/American mass culture is growing, and the latest fads and fancies can be encountered even in the outbacks of China and Indo-China. More intriguing, given the many and dramatic reverses suffered by western arms in and since the Second World War, is the common emulation of European military and naval tradition. Military bands from China, Japan and India, whatever music they may perform, are full of European instruments. Those of Cambodia and Vietnam play in an unmistakably French style, whilst Scottish-inspired pipe bands, used alike by Pakistan, India and the Gurkhas, give an additional and splendid edge to familiar British tunes of glory.

Significant elements of western culture have met with enthusiastic reception in the East. Vestiges of Portuguese folklore lingered on till our own day in Sri Lanka and Indonesia. The entrepreneurial spirit, over whose European origins so much scholarly ink has been spilled, is shared now even by those Australian aborigines prospering on the fruits of mining and tourism.[49] Western-style democracy, with its attendant apparatus and problems, has taken root in India and Japan, just as earlier European settlement had introduced it to Australia and New Zealand. John Ruskin's hostility to the course and impact of industrialization in Britain had a profound influence on Gandhi's thinking. The western literary forms of the novel and the short story currently have outstanding exponents in India and Japan. And perhaps most remarkably, western music, and especially that of the eighteenth and nineteenth centuries, has found some of its finest interpreters in Asia, Japan in particular.

But Asian reaction to the West went far beyond acceptance or emulation. The very existence of European colonial empires; the educational systems they introduced; and the ease of communication resulting from the employment of western languages fostered the growth of national sentiments. The dangers inherent in the success of Christianity and a dislike of western materialism fuelled Buddhist resurgence in late nineteenth-century Sri Lanka. The unpleasing repercussions of European industrialization inspired Gandhi to teach that India's response to this challenge must lie in policies deriving from the country's own essential beliefs, whilst the message of Marx and his disciples has been stood on its head by the leaders of modern China.[50] Japan's enthusiasm for Euro-American culture and technology has of late occasioned some soul searching over the country's loss of identity and jettisoning of attractive traditional values. So, too, the spectacular economic growth of many parts of the East in recent decades has sparked off debate on the nature and significance of 'Asian values', linked by some to Confucian roots and by others to the punning concept of an early Japanese 'Industrious Revolution'.[51]

By accident, design, but more often unavoidably, there were fusions of cultures. In the pioneering days of the Portuguese in India the missions complained that Christians were firing off guns at Muslim feasts and lending jewelry to participants in Hindu festivals. In the seventeenth century Catholic and Protestant religious ceremonies—weddings especially—in India were enlivened by performances by troops of Hindu dancing girls and the thunder of native drumming. Europeans in the subcontinent learned to eat rice, drink

[49] *The Economist*, 19 April 1997, pp. 71–2.

[50] Michael Roberts, 'Teaching Lessons, Removing Evil: Strands of Moral Puritanism in Sinhalese Nationalist Practice', *South Asia*, XIX (1996), 205–20.

[51] *The Economist*, 21 January 1995, pp. 72–3; 22 March 1997, pp. 105–6.

arak, bathe regularly and enjoy the pleasures of massage. The Christian message was itself orientalized. The Catholic missions of the early years endeavoured to persuade indigenous peoples, as in the Americas, that they were merely restoring ancient ways and continuing the earlier apostolate of St Thomas.[52] The Jesuits accepted various Indian and Chinese customs as compatible with Christianity, just as they and others condoned caste, with the Anglicans building a church in New Delhi for members of the lowest stratum as late as the 1930s.[53] In Indonesia it was complained at the end of the nineteenth century that Dutch Protestantism was being 'Javanised', and as almost everywhere in the mission field there were greater or lesser degrees of syncretism. St Michael is depicted with a Hindu demon at his feet in pious seventeenth-century Goa and Hindu Goddesses are assimilated to the Virgin Mary in Indo-Portuguese art. In Japan there still survives a form of Christianity kept alive following the suppression of Catholicism in 1638, and now barely recognizable as such. Pontius Pilate has become Ponsha and Piroto, enforcers of Herod's decrees, and though Mary gives birth in a stable the innkeeper, who had initially spurned her, repents, and in true Japanese style invites her to stay and take a hot bath.[54]

In similar fashion Asian languages absorbed European words—400 in modern Malay for example—for unfamiliar objects and ideas. There also developed various patois and creole tongues as the language of a dominant European people was modified by local usage and understanding, or where vernaculars were brought into new associations. Besides the well-known Pidgin English there was the admixture of Portuguese and local tongues used in Timor, together with the Javindo (Dutch and Javanese) and Petjo (Dutch/Malay/Javanese/Chinese) of the former Batavia.[55]

As well as such curiosities there were other and generally more pleasing cultural fusions. Influenced by western exemplars, initially supplied by the Christian missions, Chinese, Japanese and Mughal artists experimented with realism and perspective, and those of the imperial Mughal court took to working in a style unmistakably

[52] Jurrien van Goor, 'Dutch "Calvinists" '; Luís Filipe F. R. Thomaz, 'A História do glorioso San Tomé, de sua partida de Hierusalem té sua morte', *Boletim do Instituto Menezes Bragança*, 162 (1991), 33–56.

[53] Davies, *Monuments of India*, II, p. 144.

[54] Teotonio R. de Souza, 'O Património Artístico Cristão de Goa', *Boletim do Instituto Menezes Bragança*, 172 (1994), 57–65; *The Economist*, 11 January 1997, pp. 92–3.

[55] Thomaz, *De Ceuta a Timor*, pp. 613–35; 637–65.

Indian yet perceptibly western. From an early date European themes and patterns were incorporated alike into Japanese picture screens, Chinese porcelains and Indian carpets and textiles, usually to meet the tastes of western buyers. Local craftsmen might execute the European design of some building in their own idiom, as was famously the case with the now ruined Jesuit church in Macao. Local builders might likewise embellish their work with western features. India, for example, possesses—dating from the early 1800s—mosques showing European and indeed classical influences, and Hindu temples with church-like bell towers. Western and oriental views of town planning are felicitously blended in the elegant Jaipur (Rajasthan), whilst throughout large areas of colonial Asia European architects and their disciples were great devotees of the orientally-inspired bungalow. And, most remarkably, late imperial British India witnessed building in the amazing so-called Indo-Saracenic style, perhaps reaching a pinnacle (in every sense) with the Madras law courts which incorporate, amongst other things, Buddhist shapes, Mughal domes, and, to meet all contingencies, a minaret and a lighthouse.[56]

The political, economic and cultural conflict or co-operation outlined above stems ultimately from the pioneering voyage of Vasco da Gama. Maybe if the Portuguese had not so tenaciously pursued the search for a direct sea route to Asia, some other power would have. But it was the Portuguese who succeeded, and once they had done so there began a quickening flow of European goods, money, peoples, manufactures, ideas and armed strength eastwards. In return, the East initially provided luxuries, then people and primary products, a handsome measure of imperial loot, ideas more rarely and now the whole range of manufactures. The encounters of Europe and Asia left the West fundamentally unchanged, as, too, was the East until, in the last century, led by Japan, it began to emulate and in many instances—in the material sense at least—to outshine Europe, so giving a new twist to the venerable concept of Industrial Revolution and enhancing the acuteness of Adam Smith's celebrated dictum (1776): 'The discovery of America and that of a passage to the East Indies by the Cape of Good Hope are the two greatest and most important events recorded in the history of mankind'.

[56] Michell, *Monuments of India*, I, p. 318; Davies, *Monuments of India*, II, pp. 79, 88, 293, 371–2.

ADDENDA ET CORRIGENDA

Article I

p. 73 At title. See now the excellent discussion of the Anglo-Scottish wars of the early sixteenth century (and much else besides) in N.A.M. Rodger, *The Safeguard of the Sea. A Naval History of Britain*, Volume I, 660–1649 (London, 1997).

Article II

p. 105, lines 1–3. Some indication of work on shipping since this was written is given in my *Ships, Oceans and Empire. Studies in European maritime and colonial history, 1400–1750* (Variorum, 1995), amplified by Rodger, *Safeguard of the Sea*.

Article IV

p. 1, paragraph 1, last line. The social and economic context is established in detail by Barry Reay, *Popular Culture in England, 1550–1750* (Harlow, 1998) and Keith Wrightson, *Earthly Necessities: Economic Lives in Early Modern Britain* (Yale University Press, 2000).

Article V

p. 348, paragraph 2, line 1. For riots now see Reay, *Popular Culture*, chapter 6.

p. 353, paragraph 2, line 8. The authority of naval officers was enhanced as a result of events during Anson's circumnavigation of the world. An Act was passed in 1747 'for extending the discipline of the Navy to crews of His Majesty's ships, wrecked, lost or taken, and continuing to receive their wages … .', Glyndwr Williams, *The Great South Sea. English Voyages and Encounters, 1570–1750* (Yale University Press, 1997), p. 231.

Article VI

p. 158, paragraph 2, line 1. The trade was stimulated by a provision of the Anglo-Spanish agreement of 1667 that logwood carried on board English ships in the Caribbean was not to be regarded as contraband. See Philip Woodfine, *Britannia's Glories: The Walpole Ministry and the 1739 war with Spain* (London, 1998), p. 110.

p. 160, paragraph 2, last line. There is abundant detail on the scope and organization of smuggling, and of the role of Spanish colonial officials in Lance Grahn, *The Political Economy of Smuggling: Regional Informal Economies in Early Bourbon New Granada* (Boulder, Colorado, 1997).

p. 161, paragraph 1, last line. For Jamaica as an entrepot for Spanish bullion, see Woodfine, *Britannia's Glories*, pp. 91–2. T.G. Burnard, 'Prodigious riches: the wealth of Jamaica before the American Revolution', *The Economic History Review* LIV/3 (2001), pp. 506–524, gives additional detail on the value of Jamaican smuggling and on the decline of the island's trade with Spanish America in the later eighteenth century.

p. 168, paragraph 1, last line. New insights into clandestine trade are provided by E. Pijning and J.M. Pedreira in their contributions to *The Hispanic American Historical Review* 81/3–4 (2001).

Article VII

p. 1. At title. On trading companies and their role in Britain's maritime economy and commerce see now Nicholas Canny, ed., *The Oxford History of the British Empire*, I (Oxford, 1998) and P.J. Marshall, ed., *The Oxford History of the British Empire*, II (Oxford, 1998).

Article IX

p. 39, paragraph 1, line 1. There is a useful discussion of Whit revels in Barry Reay, *Popular Culture in England*, chapter 5.

Article X

p. 185, paragraph 2, last line. Intelligence and espionage during the Anglo-Spanish war have recently been examined by Geoffrey Parker, *The Grand Strategy of Philip II* (Yale University Press, 1998).

p. 190, paragraph 2, line 5. Country trade is the subject of the valuable if controversial work of James C. Boyajian *Portuguese Trade in Asia under the Habsburgs, 1580–1640* (Johns Hopkins University Press, 1993). New perspectives are opened by the seminal studies of Professor Luís Filipe F.R. Thomaz, such as his 'Portuguese Control over the Arabian Sea and the Bay of Bengal: A Comparative Study', in Om Prakash and Denys Lombard, eds, *Commerce and Culture in the Bay of Bengal, 1500–1800* (no place of publication given, 1999). Some of the fruits of Professor Thomaz's work are conveniently accessible in Sanjay Subrahmanyam, *The Portuguese Empire in Asia, 1500–1700; A Political and Economic History* (London, 1993).

p. 190, paragraph 3, line 4. For the Gulf route see now Anthony Disney, 'The Gulf route from India to Portugal in the Sixteenth and Seventeenth Centuries: Couriers, Traders and Image-Makers', in *A Carreira da Índia e as Rotas dos Estreitos* (Angra do Heroísmo, 1998), pp. 527–550.

Article XI

p. 440, column 1, paragraph 2, line 2. Whit festivities are usefully discussed in Barry Reay, *Popular Culture in England*, chapter 5.

Article XII

p. 514, paragraph 2, line 8. There is a splendid recent study of da Gama by Geneviève Bouchon, *Vasco da Gama* (Paris, 1997).

p. 526, paragraph 1, last line. See the illuminating account of the situation in Bengal as a result of the 'Permanent Settlement' in Philip D. Curtin, *The World & the West: The European Challenge and the Overseas Response in the Age of Empire* (Cambridge, 2000), pp. 96–9.

p. 529, paragraph 2, line 17. The use of eastern indentured labour in former West Indian slave colonies is examined by Herbert S. Klein, *The Atlantic Slave Trade* (Cambridge, 1999), chapter 8.

p. 533, paragraph 2, line 1. Early modern European 'Images of Asia' are briefly discussed by Walter Demel, Edwin J. Van Kley and Peter J.A.N. Rietbergen in *Itinerario* XXV/3–4 (2001), pp. 34–87.

p. 534, paragraph 2, line 3. The cultural impact of India in early modern Europe is interestingly, if not always persuasively argued by Joan-Pau Rubiés, *Travel and Ethnology in the Renaissance: South India through European Eyes, 1250–1625* (Cambridge, 2000).

INDEX